The Must-Have Mom Manual

The Must-Have Mom Manual

Two Mothers, Two Perspectives, One Book That Tells You Everything You Need to Know

Sara Ellington and Stephanie Triplett

BALLANTINE BOOKS NEW YORK

Ballantine Books Trade Paperback Original

Published in the United States by Ballantine Books, an imprint of The Random House Publishing Group, a division of Random House, Inc., New York.

Grateful acknowledgment is made to the following for permission to reprint previously published material:

Mothers in Action: Excerpt from Mothers in Action on page 305 courtesy of Sophia West.

The Parenting Group: All materials from Parenting.com, *Parenting,* and *Babytalk* on pages 51, 169, 226, 248, and 413 are reprinted with permission from The Parenting Group © 2009.

Library of Congress Cataloging-in-Publication Data

Ellington, Sara.
The must-have mom manual : two mothers, two perspectives, one book that tells you everything you need to know / Sara Ellington and Stephanie Triplett.
p. cm.
Includes index.
ISBN 978-0-345-49987-5 (pbk.)
1. Motherhood. 2. Parenting. 3. Mother and child. I. Triplett, Stephanie. II. Title.
HQ759.E435 2009
649'.1—dc22 2009000920

Printed in the United States of America

www.ballantinebooks.com

9 8 7 6 5 4 3 2 1

Book design by Liz Cosgrove

"What is REAL?" asked the Rabbit one day, when they were lying side by side near the nursery fender, before Nana came to tidy the room. "Does it mean having things that buzz inside you and a stick-out handle?"

"Real isn't how you are made," said the Skin Horse. "It's a thing that happens to you. When a child loves you for a long, long time, not just to play with, but REALLY loves you, then you become Real."

"Does it hurt?" asked the Rabbit.

"Sometimes," said the Skin Horse, for he was always truthful. "When you are Real you don't mind being hurt."

"Does it happen all at once, like being wound up," he asked, "or bit by bit?"

"It doesn't happen all at once," said the Skin Horse. "You become. It takes a long time. That's why it doesn't often happen to people who break easily, or have sharp edges, or who have to be carefully kept. Generally, by the time you are Real, most of your hair has been loved off, and your eyes drop out and you get loose in the joints and very shabby. But these things don't matter at all, because once you are Real you can't be ugly, except to people who don't understand."

—Excerpt from *The Velveteen Rabbit,*
by Margery Williams (a brilliant and very real mother of two)

*This book is dedicated to mothers everywhere—
for they know best what it feels like to be Real.*

Contents

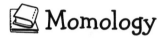

Work-Life Balance

Your Expanding Family

The Scoop on Schools

Mother to Mother

For Your Quick Reference

The "Characters" in This Book

Stephanie

(the messy, breast-feeding mom
who returned to her career)

Husband: Tim
First child: Sara
Second child: Timmy

Sara

(the superorganized, bottle-feeding mom
who left her job to stay at home)

Husband: David
First child: Anna
Second child: Cade

Momology

Introduction

Thanks so much for picking up *The Must-Have Mom Manual*! We're glad you found this book and hope you will be too. We're Sara Ellington and Stephanie Triplett, two moms just like you—moms who change diapers and drive carpool and get up for 3:00 A.M. feedings (at least when our children were babies—now the only reason we get up at 3:00 A.M. is if someone wet the bed). We may be authors and radio show hosts, but we live and breathe this mom stuff. We're not the moms you see on the magazines at the checkout aisle, with their round-the-clock nannies and fat bank accounts.

We've tried our best to compile the most useful information you need as a mom all in one convenient place. What you'll find on the pages ahead encompasses more than a year of research for our radio show and our book, input from the countless mothers we've met at book signings, conferences, and the bus stop, and, of course, our own experience as parents.

But before you plunge in, we thought it was important to tell you a little bit about the two of us. We're best friends who happened to find ourselves pregnant at the same time. Our first children, both daughters, were born just three weeks apart, which led us to write our first book together, *The Mommy Chronicles: Conversations Sharing the Comedy and Drama of Pregnancy and New Motherhood*. Although our timelines for becoming moms were the same, virtually everything else about our lives as mothers was completely different.

Because we took such divergent paths down the motherhood road, we're going to give you two completely different perspectives along the way. Well, at least most of the time. Every now and then we do agree. But oddly enough, it's our differences that have brought us closer. We've learned that we don't have to be the same kind of mom to be good ones. We've always respected each other's choices even when they were the complete opposite of our own. Too many friendships have ended due to mothers judging one another. The two of us are proof that a working mom and stay-at-home mom can be best friends. That a breast-feeding mom and bottle-feeding mom can be best friends. What has worked for one of us often just wouldn't have for the other because we're different people. That's the simple message we have always strived to share with other mothers: there's no one right way to be a good mom.

So the last thing we would ever want to do is to tell someone how to be a mom. That's not what this book is. (Besides, we've screwed up way too much stuff ourselves to preach to anyone else!) There is no one-size-fits-all formula for motherhood. This book is about making your life easier as a mom and paring down a lot of the information modern mothers have to weed through. If you're planning a trip to Disney World, we've got the best resources for you so you don't have to slog through a hundred websites at 10:00 P.M. when the kids are finally asleep in bed. Moms have more information thrown at them than ever and less time than ever to process it all. We've tried to combine all the important stuff you need in one handy resource. We figure we might as well keep sharing the knowledge we've gained as radio show hosts and moms. You can learn from our mistakes and our triumphs and, we hope, have more time to enjoy actually being a mom instead of spending it trying to find out where to order party favors. To do that, all you have to do is turn to page 172, for example.

How to Use This Book

So now you're probably wondering, "How the heck do I use this book?" Well, funny you should ask.

The Must-Have Mom Manual is divided into large sections, such as "Life with Your Baby" or "Marriage," which in turn are divided into chapters. Refer to the table of contents for chapters on the specific topics you're interested in. In some chapters you'll hear from both of us, while in other chapters you may hear from only one of us, depending on the subject matter and our individual experiences. At the end of each chapter, we've provided what we call "Clutter-Busting Resources" for you. These are the most useful resources we've used ourselves or found through research for our radio show and this book. We've done at least some of the legwork for you, which should save you hours searching online and at the bookstore.

Meet Stephanie and Sara

About Stephanie, from Sara

I know that after reading *The Must-Have Mom Manual* you're going to love Stephanie as much as I do. Okay, almost, because unfortunately we can't put a little sound card inside this book with a recording of her laugh. So you'll just have to take my word for it when I tell you she has the most wonderful, infectious laugh. And even though she's really the funny one of the two of us, she laughs at all my jokes and sounds as if she means it. That alone is enough to make me love her. There's nothing like a friend who laughs at all your jokes.

Stephanie and I met in Virginia Beach working together at an advertising agency. She was the gregarious, outspoken account executive who got things done and I was the introspective copywriter who overanalyzed everything. Stephanie loved the writing aspect of her job, and after she wrote a few things that her clients loved, she naturally shifted to the role of copywriter along with me. We soon learned that our working styles were wonderfully complementary. Stephanie's the big-picture girl who cranks out paragraph after paragraph with a lightning-fast typing speed of 106 words per minute. I'm the one who goes back and checks for grammar and makes sure the period is on the correct side of the parentheses. Yes, I'm a bit anal. I've got more than one book on home organization. I like things in their place. I salivate over photos of neatly stacked towels in a linen closet. I'm going on and on about this because the only thing I really have on Stephanie is that I'm organized and she's messy. One night after a book signing we went to a McDonald's drive-through to get Diet Cokes (our lives as authors are completely glamorous). When the cashier handed me the change, I immediately flipped down the coin holder in my minivan and started placing the coins in all their appropriate slots. Stephanie looked at me, dead serious, and said, "Okay, first of all, that's really annoying, and second of all, that's *my* damn change."

I'm also painfully understated. If I have on big earrings, I am probably not going to wear a necklace too. Stephanie, on the other hand, likes bright colors, hair accessories, nail decals, and anything that is sparkly (stuff that I don't have the *cojones* to wear). I used to tease her that she was like fish attracted to anything shiny. Don't get me wrong—she's a great dresser and her house is beautiful. Although she will occasionally display a tacky piece of holiday décor, and then she'll inevitably call me and say, "You should see what's on my wall right now. You would just vomit."

I am always envious of her ability to get so much done. I was on the phone with her the other day and she said, "I've gotta go. It's Dr. Seuss's birthday and I'm taking green eggs and ham to school." I'm lucky if I get to my daughter's school on time to read to the class, much less bring food, for crying out loud.

Stephanie's husband, Tim, is a stage hypnotist (how fun is *that* to tell people at cocktail parties?) and he has to travel a lot. In fact, he is usually home only one week a month, but Stephanie is still full speed ahead, taking food to school, working, and getting the kids to cheerleading and baseball day in and day out, with very few breaks. And I rarely hear her complain. (Although Tim would probably beg to differ.)

Tim and my husband, David, hit it off just like Stephanie and I did. They enjoy being in each other's company immensely. As a couple, Tim and Stephanie are like a comedy tag team. After an evening with them you go home with your sides aching from all the laughter. Now this relationship we have as friends and couples has grown into a friendship among families. Stephanie and Tim's kids, Sara and Timmy, are absolutely beloved by our children, Anna and Cade. Even though they don't get to see each other as often as they would like (i.e., every day), when they do see each other, it's like they were just together yesterday. In fact, my kids insist that Sara and Timmy are cousins, even though we aren't related. I know what they mean, though; it's a relationship that's too close to categorize as simply friendship.

I know you are going to enjoy Stephanie's hilarious yet practical take on "all things mommy" as you read this book. And you'll surely understand the sparkle she brings to my life and why I am blessed to share this journey with her.

About Sara, from Stephanie

I'm not sure that making colored meat for a school project is really all that impressive. But now it's my turn to gush a little about Sara.

Sara is the ultimate girlfriend's girlfriend. She has exquisite taste; owns the best purse and shoe collection of anyone I know; is a great cook, a great decorator, and a great mother; loves wine; and is just plain easy to be with. When you're around Sara you can relax. She's easily entertained and keeps her criticisms to herself. Now that I'm so close to her, I can see her holding her tongue when I've said something stupid—but it's hard to detect unless you know her really well (or you say a lot of stupid things and have lots of chances to notice the look). She's the smart, thought-out, careful one. I usually just spew out whatever comes to mind without thinking and hope people find the humor in it. But Sara is very polite and careful about people's feelings.

She loves dogs, particularly golden retrievers, and all of her dogs have undoubtedly had a more pampered childhood than I did. She and David have a beautiful house on a lake in Charlotte, North Carolina, and they love inviting people over for a day on the water or a relaxing dinner party. I love going to their house. If you get invited for dinner, you're in for a real treat because they have a talent for making dinner a fun yet relaxing event, with great ambience, a great meal, and a lot of laughs. I always plan to arrive at their house right at dinnertime.

The only frustrating part about Sara is that she's the ultimate organizer. She reads all those tedious organizing books from cover to cover, drooling over every page. She has a friggin' system for everything from grocery shopping to putting away toys. If the Container Store knew her name, they'd give her her own parking space. If there were a pageant for Miss Anti-Clutter USA, she'd hold the title year after year. She's a perfectionist when it comes to her writing—she's constantly telling me, "The period goes inside the quotes! How many times do I have to tell you?" or "Why can't you remember to indent?" (Like I care—don't they have editors for that?)

All I can tell you is that despite all our differences, we make a great team. We balance each other out perfectly. And now our children love each other too. It's so amazing to watch my Sara and her Anna playing together and realizing that these are the babies we wrote about in our first book, *The Mommy Chronicles.* And we've been through a lot together. Another chapter in our lives began last year when Sara told me she had been diagnosed with Hodgkin's disease (a cancer of the lymphatic system). I was devastated. How could someone so young and vibrant get something so awful? The good news is that she faced it head-on and after several months of chemotherapy is now cancer-free. It was torture for me to be so far away from her during such a trying time. I wanted to be there to bring her casseroles, clean her house, or take care of her kids. But instead, I had to wait patiently from Georgia and hope. She assured me she had plenty of casseroles, that taking care of our business was what she really needed from me. But I didn't get much done without her.

And I'm so proud of her for handling this illness with so much grace and strength. When I finally got to see her after her treatments were over, we spent a day together on the lake with our families. I was so relieved to see her still so energetic and happy. And we've decided that it was good that I wasn't so near her during her treatment because I've never seen what she truly went through—so nothing has changed our relationship. I still see her the way I've always seen her. And frankly, I'm glad I didn't too because it would have broken my heart to see her so sick.

The friendships that women have are one of the greatest, most valuable treasures of a lifetime. The secrets and support and dreams and challenges that we share are what make life more meaningful. We've learned a lot about motherhood from sharing our own ideas and methods and from listening to the countless other mothers we've talked to at book signings and through our radio show. And it is our dream that this book will help you, bring you some laughter, and remind you to treasure your own friendships, as opposed to judging those who choose to mother differently. Motherhood is different for each of us. We all approach it with different styles and methods, but in the end, we all have the same goal: to get them out of our house with as few scars as possible, a good education, a good understanding of right and wrong, and maybe a few manners, and then to hope that they'll love us as much as we love them and call us once in a while.

Choices of Other Mothers

From Sara

When did motherhood become a competitive sport? Talk to your own mother and you'll probably discover it wasn't that way in her day. But women have changed and motherhood has changed. Women are bigger players in the workforce than ever before, and it's about time! We're breadwinners and managers, doctors, business owners, and board members. And as a result, we've become more competitive than ever.

Those of us who do make the choice to stay at home with our children (and believe us, we know it is a privilege to have the choice) are often leaving significant careers and incomes behind. So it's natural that, being go-getters, we want to somehow equate motherhood to the career we left and, furthermore, to prove that we're really good at it. Better than you are, as a matter of fact. There are women who would never consider going back to work after having a child and there are those who can't fathom leaving their career. It can be hard for these two types of women to relate. Often they'll even criticize the other's choice. The same is true for the choice of whether to breast-feed or bottle-feed. Women feel so strongly about these issues that they become polarizing, often damaging or even ending friendships.

Stephanie and I are here to say it doesn't have to be that way. And it shouldn't be. I always say that no one holds the patent on "good mother." We really don't have the right to criticize each other. Not about these issues, at least. We're calling for some healthy mutual respect between moms. After the birth of our daughters, Stephanie went back to work and I left my career to be an at-home mom. Having Stephanie to talk with was a blessing for me because I was able to learn through her experiences that the grass wasn't always greener on the other side. Some days I really envied her. I went through a bad bout with postpartum depression and I missed my job more than I'd ever dreamed I would. Suddenly I had gone from being a self-sufficient woman to a mother financially dependent on her husband. Even though I wanted to be at home with my baby, that was a tough pill to swallow.

But Stephanie would e-mail me about dropping her daughter, Sara, off crying (both of them) at day care, about trying to pump breast milk in an office with no lock on the door, and about the stress of needing to leave early to pick up a sick child, and I would sigh with relief that I didn't have to do that. Then other days she would tell me about exciting business meetings and trips to places such as the Ritz-Carlton in Naples, Florida, and I would almost get sick with envy.

Then Stephanie would hear me say that I hadn't even gotten to take a shower that day or that I'd had a PB&J for lunch for the third day in a row. But when I'd e-mail that I had to run because my daughter, Anna, had woken up from her nap and I heard her crying, I know she'd wonder if someone was holding baby Sara when she cried at day care.

The reality is, those first months of motherhood were tough for both of us. And we saw it firsthand because we're so close, so we never considered criticizing each other. Stephanie relished every moment she could breast-feed and be close to her baby. But she completely understood why, suffering from depression, I chose to stop nursing. It's easy to criticize when we are looking in from the outside and don't know what a person is really going through. Stephanie and I knew.

No matter what choices you make as a mom, someone will eventually make a critical remark or judge you. It may come from a friend, a co-worker, even a grandparent. They may turn their nose up at the name you chose for your baby, recoil in horror when you say you're bottle-feeding, or recoil in more horror when you breast-feed in public. No one will agree with everything you do, and for some reason, once you become a mother people feel free to offer their unsolicited opinions to you on everything from cloth diapers to the Ferber method. And you know who's most guilty of this? We moms are.

So moms, let's all cut each other some slack and keep our unsolicited opinions to ourselves. Unless you witness something that warrants a call to social services, remember that we're all different and that the vast majority of us are doing the very best we can. They don't call it the toughest job in the world for nothing. Your respect, even when you don't agree, is the best gift you can give your fellow moms. And it's the best gift you can get in return.

Enjoying Motherhood

From Sara

I bet you had visions of motherhood similar to mine. During that dragging ninth month of pregnancy, I couldn't wait for the baby to arrive. I imagined a life just like in the diaper commercials—a happy, pudgy baby crawling around the house on freshly mopped floors. Or like in the photos in magazines of the adult working at a home office desk while the baby sat quietly on the floor playing with blocks. I figured blocks must entertain a baby for hours based on all the photos I saw of babies playing with them in magazines. If the blocks lost their luster, I had the baby swing, the vibration seat, the Johnny Jump Up . . . I was set. I couldn't wait to be at home, away from the eight-to-five grind. I would work on all those home projects I'd been putting off, hang pictures on the walls, enjoy leisurely mornings, cook delicious dinners.

As you and I both now know, I was delusional. I traded the eight-to-five grind, all right—for the twenty-four-hour grind. I couldn't believe how hard it was. After a few weeks with a newborn I realized it was going to be an eternity before my baby sat up, much less played with blocks. How in hell was I going to hang a beautiful arrangement of photos on the wall when I couldn't even find time to take a shower before 5:00 P.M.? I barely had time to sit down but got nothing accomplished. Laundry piled up, the house was a mess, and I greeted my husband every night with a very important question: "Want to go out to dinner?"

I didn't realize it then, but those first few months are actually an essential lesson on the reality of motherhood. It ain't like the pictures in the magazines, honey. But even if someone had told me that when I was pregnant, I wouldn't have heard it. I couldn't give up on the dream. Motherhood, like life, is messy and often chaotic, and those magazine moments I described are few and far between. Real motherhood is located somewhere on the far opposite end of the spectrum from Martha Stewart. It's taken me years to accept that. To let go of the dream of adorably dressed children with perpetually clean faces and neatly organized baskets of toys. But I have learned to pick my battles. It's okay if my daughter won't wear the cute pink linen pants embroidered with green whales because they're not coated in glitter. It's not worth the battle. If we don't relax a little, we can't give our kids the room to express themselves. We have to respect that they aren't little clones of us. My daughter loves glitter and is a complete pack rat. Need I say more?

The sooner we moms can drop the Martha Stewart expectations, the better. Believe me, I love her ideas for making handmade wrapping paper and felting your own wool as much as anybody. They're great . . . in theory. And if you have a staff of fifty people like Martha does. But c'mon, the vast majority of this stuff just isn't practical for moms unless their kids have left for college. And by that time your kids wouldn't be caught dead in one of those damn felted wool sweaters anyway. Real moms are doing all we can to get dinner on the table, homework done, baths given, and the dishwasher loaded before collapsing into bed. Not exactly magazine-worthy. The bottom line is that your child isn't going to love you more because you made her the perfect birthday cake or hand-sewn Halloween costume. What kids want most is your time and attention. That's what they'll remember.

If we get too obsessed over minutiae such as perfect party favors, we often miss the important moments, like seeing the pure joy on your child's face as she bounces in an inflatable moon walk with her friends. So quit sweating the small stuff and putting pressure on yourself to be the kind of mom that doesn't really exist or that leaves a kid needing a lot of therapy later on in life.

Guilt

From Stephanie

One week at ballet class, I was mortified because I forgot that my daughter, Sara, was supposed to wear her Halloween costume to class. She was the only little ballerina there dressed in the standard-issue pink tights and black leotard. Even the teacher donned an adorable purple fairy outfit with life-size wings. It had been a really busy week with the book promotions and the radio show and class parties at school, and the ballet thing just totally slipped my mind. As I sat in the studio lobby, I almost cried. I felt terrible. I couldn't stop thinking about how much fun it would have been to dance in her Jasmine or Wonder Woman costume—and how horrible it must be for her to be in there looking at all the other little princesses, fairies, and witches. When the class ended I gave her a big hug and explained how sorry I was. And amazingly enough, she was fine. She wasn't disappointed or upset at all. I had beaten myself up for no apparent reason.

The next week at preschool, she was supposed to wear her favorite hat. I don't know what the problem is with four-year-old girls and their clothes, but every morning at our house, the drama was surreal. She didn't like *anything* I chose for her to wear (even if she'd picked it out herself the night before). She always ran to her daddy to complain about panties that were too tight around her legs, sleeves that weren't long enough, something itchy, a strap that didn't feel right on her shoulder, etc., etc. These were all items of clothing that she'd worn previously without issue, but of course nothing would feel comfortable when you're comparing it to a nightgown or well-worn PJs that you just took off. So every day, by the time I left the house, I was sweating and yelling, and I started the day in a bad mood. My husband made a bad situation even worse because he catered to her every whim, helping her sneak back upstairs to choose something, anything else. The item she chose was usually inappropriate for the climate or didn't match. So then he and I ended up in a fight too, usually about how he was discrediting me and making her a brat. He couldn't see it. I could see very clearly that this had nothing to do with clothing or comfort. This was pure, unadulterated four-year-old manipulation, a power struggle pure and simple.

That morning's drama was yet another battle: mother against daughter, husband against wife. I was in such a state of frustration when I left the house, I forgot that it was "wear your favorite hat day" at school. As little Sara got out of the car, I noticed a few other students donning their Mickey Mouse ears or favorite baseball caps. My guilt from the previous week's ballet incident consumed me once again and I raced home as fast as I could to retrieve a hat in hopes that my little girl wouldn't be crushed upon the sharp rocks of preschool-age disappointment. I ran around the toy room, tripping over Barbie accessories and Legos, and managed to grab about five different choices so she could pick her favorite. I jumped back into the car and sped as fast as I could back to the school, only to get caught behind not one but *two* slow-moving dump trucks. I was really panicked by this time, knowing that the hats would surely be the very first thing the teacher would focus on and how terrible it was that I, the official room mom, had forgotten such a big event. As I approached the school at a painful twenty miles per hour, I heard myself screaming obscenities at the dump truck driver—in the privacy of my own car. I gripped the steering wheel tightly and tried to get a hold of myself. "Get some perspective," I told myself. "It's only preschool . . . she'll never remember this . . . you worked till midnight last night . . . give yourself a break." But my guilty-mother mind could only remember the previous week's forgotten costume at ballet class and the fact that I was the stinking room mom and I forgot! Oh, how could I?

Finally I reached the school, trying to keep it under fifty mph around the building and through the parking lot. My SUV came to a screeching halt in front of the door and I jumped out, looking like a cop in hot pursuit of a criminal. I hurried down the hallway with hats in hand, gathered myself as I reached the door of her classroom, and calmly stuck my head inside and asked to see Sara. The teacher gave me a sweet yet knowing smile. When my daughter reached the hallway, I calmly explained that we had forgotten her hat. She said, "I know, Mommy." I said, "Mommy ran home really fast and brought some hats for you. Which one would you like to wear today?" She quickly glanced through the collection, turned to me, and said, "I don't really want one—they make my head itch." There I was, standing in the Baptist church preschool hallway using every ounce of restraint I possessed to keep myself from cursing out loud. I could feel the blood vessels tightening in my head, the muscles in my neck beginning to pinch the bones of my spine, and my lips becoming magnetically attached to my teeth. I took a deep breath and in my best understanding mommy voice asked, "But doesn't it make you feel sad that you're the only kid without a hat today?" She replied very matter-of-factly, "No." *But honey,* I thought, *Mommy spent $7 in gas, lost three pounds, and knocked at least four months off my life span to bring you a #@!% hat.* "But honey," I said, "all the kids have one." "I don't care." "Okay, just pick one and wear it so your teacher won't be mad. Just pick one!" She begrudgingly chose Mickey Mouse ears with her brother's name embroidered on the back. I told her good-bye and pointed her back into the classroom.

Now, seeing as how this was a church preschool, it is my belief that it was divine intervention when Benjamin and his mom came rushing down the hall at that very moment, for it was clear she too had forgotten the all-important hat day. I greeted her and asked her if she had one. She was completely dismayed that it had slipped her mind, so I happily offered my collection in hopes that someone would benefit from my zealous efforts. Benjamin chose a dapper pirate hat and was quite happy about it. His mother thanked me gratefully and we quickly parted ways. After all, preschool only lasted for three hours, and that was hardly enough time to lick our wounds before we had to go back and pick the kids up.

From Sara

Stephanie and I always say that after women give birth there must be a guilt gene that gets turned on in our DNA. Because I don't care who you are—working mom, at-home mom, nursing mom, bottle-feeding mom, whatever—you're going to feel guilty for something. The working mom feels guilty for not being at home to play Candy Land with her child. The at-home mom feels guilty for wanting to stab herself in the eye if she has to play one more game of Candy Land with her child. Guilt is inevitable, so just accept it and try not to let it control your life. Sure, a healthy dose of guilt every now and then is good for us. It keeps what's important at the top of the list. But the problem is, most moms I know have such an overabundance of it that we beat ourselves up for everything. Dads don't do it. Men are blissfully uncomplicated about guilt. On the rare occasions they do feel guilty, they certainly don't dwell on it. And it's no wonder. They aren't in the bathroom flipping through magazine pages of perfectly spooky Halloween décor or the latest photos of Hollywood's "sexiest moms."

Guilt is just part of the deal when you decide to become a mom. I try to laugh about it with my mom friends. When I bring up something I feel guilty about, they always have their own self-berating stories to share, and we all walk away feeling much better. So the next time you start beating yourself up over some awful thing you did or more likely forgot to do, think about all the good things you did for your child that day. Count up every little and big thing from morning till night and I guarantee you'll look at your day differently. Besides, there is such a thing as doing too much for your child. A child who grows up without every path being perfectly paved for her will be much better equipped for real life as an adult.

Thirteen Things *Not* to Feel Guilty About

In the spirit of living with less mommy guilt, here's a little gift to you.

Venting to a Friend About a Bad Day or Your Kids Driving You Crazy

Getting things off your chest (when the kids are not in earshot) can really help you feel better. Venting to a friend lets you get your frustration out while on the phone instead of taking it out on your kids. I don't care how much you love being a mom, your kids are going to get on your nerves. Frequently. You need a place to release that frustration. So call a girlfriend and just get it out, honey.

Getting a Babysitter

It's important to get out sans kids with your husband or girlfriends for several reasons. Paying attention to your marriage is one of the best things that you can do for your children. Eventually it's going to be just the two of you again, and if you don't pay attention to your marital bond throughout the child-rearing years, you're not going to have much of a relationship left. Going out with the girls renews your energy and gives you some much-needed adult time. You'll be better at the job of mother for it!

Going Away for a Weekend with Your Husband or the Girls

Recharging your battery is essential for busy moms. We moms get little time for ourselves, which can leave us feeling drained and stressed. Taking some time to get physically away from your daily demands can do wonders, leaving you refreshed and renewed to be a better mom.

Not Having Your Child Enrolled in a Scheduled Activity

Just because your child isn't playing soccer, taking ballet, or going to summer camp doesn't mean she's going to be out of the loop or fall behind. Most experts agree that kids nowadays have too little time to simply play, explore, and use their imaginations. There's nothing wrong with sending them out in the backyard to entertain themselves for a little while. In fact, it's good for them.

Having a C-section

We've heard mothers say they felt like failures for having a C-section, and it always amazes us. Stephanie always says, "They don't hand out trophies in the delivery room." It doesn't matter how your child got into this world as long as he or she made it safe and sound. Plus, having a C-section is usually a tougher recovery than a vaginal birth anyway, so there's your badge of honor.

Not Breast-feeding

We realize the "lactivists" are going to get mad at us for this one, but too bad. No one else has walked in your shoes, and until they have, they shouldn't make judgments. If someone wants to take up a cause, how about deadbeat dads or abused children, instead of formula-feeding moms? Give us a break. The mother's health and well-being are critical to the baby's health and well-being, and if that means formula-feeding, then do it. Some women make every effort to breast-feed but can't because their milk doesn't come in or the baby doesn't get enough. No one should ever make these women feel guilty! Formula is of high quality these days. Sara's mom told us the formula she fed Sara's older sister was a concoction of Karo syrup and evaporated milk, and she grew up just fine. And Lord knows what's available to moms now is much, much better than that.

Discipline and Applying Consequences

Children used to be seen and not heard, but now the pendulum has swung completely in the other direction and children often rule the roost. Trust us, we know it's hard to make them sit in the time-out chair when tears are running down their sweet, chubby cheeks. But letting your kids off the hook does them no favors. Children who don't have boundaries and rules will have a difficult time adapting to school life and eventually to adult life. Even when that pitiful, remorseful child is telling you they love you and they're sorry, don't cut the time-out short. It's the truest sort of love to give them the tools they'll need throughout life. So don't feel guilty about it.

Not Looking Exactly the Way You Did Before You Had Children

Your spouse still finds you attractive and now appreciates your inner beauty more than ever, knowing all the challenges that you rise to as a mom. Sara's husband, David, says this should apply to dads too. However, David also says that all moms should feel guilty if they are not having enough sex with their husbands. We think we can all agree not to feel guilty about that one. David will have to write his own book.

Going Back to Work

It doesn't matter if you need to do it for yourself or for money. Either of those reasons will make your family more balanced and provide your children more benefits and opportunities for the long run.

Not Going Back to Work

If you are fortunate enough to have the choice to stay at home, you are doing something wonderful for your children, and since this is most likely a decision you and your husband made together, you shouldn't feel guilty about not contributing to the family income. Not to mention that your being home allows your spouse to concentrate more on his job. Your job has tremendous value, even if it doesn't come with a paycheck, and never forget it.

Your Kids Aren't Wearing Designer Clothes or the Latest Trend

Even if you are able to, it's not good to give your kids everything they want. You're helping teach your kids not to be defined by what they wear but who they are. If they want something special they can save their allowance or babysit or mow yards or do extra chores, and you'll be teaching them the value of working for something, saving for it, and of good old-fashioned hard work. Nothing makes you appreciate something like having to work for it.

Not Living in an Immaculate House

Sara's mom always says, "Your kids are never going to remember how clean the house was growing up." What they will remember is that you played Go Fish or went for a bike ride or played Barbies with them. Life with children is perpetually messy. And if you're playing with your kids or baking cupcakes for the school party instead of cleaning, that's okay in our book. Besides, as a very wise woman once told us, "Only dull women live in immaculate houses."

Asking Your Husband for Help if You're a Stay-at-Home Mom

Just because you don't earn a paycheck doesn't mean you don't work. That distinction doesn't belong only to the one who brings home the money. Being a mom is one of the toughest jobs there is. As one mom told us, "It's got to be right up there with coal mining." If your husband tends to forget just how tough your job is, it's time to go away with your girlfriends for a weekend and leave him with the kids. That'll refresh his memory.

Trusting Your Instincts

From Sara

Okay, let me just say that I didn't think I *had* instincts in the beginning. Those first few months were tough, to say the least. But after the middle-of-the-night feedings and the postpartum depression subsided, I started to make sense of things. And the instincts started to kick in. Or maybe I just got to know my baby and figured out what she needed. But it does take a little time, and as a new mom, I didn't trust myself at first. There must be millions of other moms like me, because I see a lot of parenting books out there. There are books on getting your baby to sleep, books on getting your baby to eat, even books from nannies who've never had children. There are a million so-called solutions waiting for you on the bookstore shelves, and if you don't want one of those, some relative is sure to offer you unsolicited advice.

The first thing you need to do is trust yourself. The reality is no one knows your baby better than you do. No one knows your family dynamics better than you do. Stephanie and I are living proof that what works for one mom won't necessarily work for the next. What works for one child won't necessarily work for the next. There is no one-size-fits-all solution to getting every baby on the planet to sleep, because babies are all different. I know this firsthand because it happened to me with my second child. Our first child, Anna, was an easy baby. She didn't have to be in her crib; she'd sleep anywhere—in the car, on the boat, in a restaurant. (My definition of the perfect child.) My husband and I took total credit for her easygoing nature too. We figured since we were relaxed and laid back, she picked up on our vibe. Then our son was born and we realized what complete idiots we were. He wouldn't sleep anywhere but his crib, made going out to a restaurant miserable . . . yet we were the same relaxed, laid-back parents we'd been with the first child. What happened? Apparently, our "vibe" didn't have a blasted thing to do with it. Apparently, children come into the world with their own personalities, high-maintenance or otherwise. Who knew?

Don't get me wrong—there were many books that helped me and books that helped Stephanie, and we'll tell you about them here. If you find one that works, great. But don't expect every method out there to be the perfect solution for you, because no one has all the answers for every family.

New mothers are constantly being fed the message that they are in serious need of help. They're being pressured on morning talk shows from experts who claim they have the answers to every problem a mom faces. Stephanie and I think moms are much more capable than that. We want to empower you to feel confident in the choices you make, even if they aren't the same choices your neighbor, your best friend, or your mom made. That's why there are two of us writing this book. We both have different perspectives and opinions on what worked for us. And our hope is that our experiences will help you in your unique life as a mom.

At the Hospital

1

Secrets to Improve Your Hospital Experience

What to Expect

From Stephanie

It's hard to tell you exactly what to expect because every woman experiences birth differently. I've always thought it was ironic that the biggest thing that will ever happen to you is the birth of your children, yet you have no control over the gender of your baby or when it will happen. During late pregnancy, I often pondered if it's God's sick way of proving to us that he is still in control. The one thing I can promise you is that it won't be anything like the way they portray it in movies. For one thing, there probably won't be any speeding to the hospital (sorry, guys). In fact, in my own experience, I was begging my husband to slow down over the speed bumps in the parking lot. And there probably won't be any yelling or shouting when you arrive. Don't be surprised if nobody is in a hurry to get you checked in. They've seen this plenty of times before, and they know you most likely have hours of labor ahead of you, so there's no need to rush. Once you get checked in, you'll go to triage to assess whether you know what you're talking about or if you're yet another crazy woman who has a little gas and thinks she's in labor. That's right, girls—you'll have to convince them to let you stay. Plenty of first-time moms get sent home. In fact, unless you are aware of some special situation with your pregnancy, it's really not a bad idea to spend some time laboring at home instead of rushing off to the hospital. Even if your water breaks, you are probably looking at several more hours of labor.

So let's talk a little about labor. That's what we're all most worried about, right? Again, it's hard to give you an answer. When Sara and I were pregnant, we used to watch the show *A Baby Story* on TLC every day. And we were both surprised over the differences in how women reacted to labor pain. Most women were very calm and quiet and acted as if there was nothing to it, while there occasionally was a screamer or two. We felt it had a lot to do with personality and age and maybe even the size of the baby.

My water broke early in the morning, but my contractions were not cooperating. I spent hours walking and walking and walking around the floor of the maternity ward, watching everybody else's babies be born and wondering when it was going to be my turn. I wasn't in much pain at all. I walked and talked and rested. When things weren't progressing, my doctor did some feeling around and decided that the baby needed to be turned slightly. My plan was to go as long as possible without the epidural (that's what everyone had programmed me to do). But when the decision was made to turn the baby, a nurse showed up and said, "Get the epidural, this is going to hurt." So, wham—I got the epidural. I pretty much breezed through the rest of the labor and birth with very little pain. In fact, it wasn't much worse than bad menstrual cramps. There are plenty of books that will explain the stages of labor, so we'll spare you the time of reading it again. The most important thing for you to know is to go with an open mind.

Birth Plans

Many books and birth classes urge you to create a birth plan. A birth plan is fine to help you prepare and think through the process in your own mind. But understand that once labor starts, you're in new territory and you have no control over what's going to happen next. The best thing you can do is to educate yourself about all the aspects of labor and delivery, remembering that childbirth doesn't follow a textbook and your plan may go out the window, especially when there are issues with the safety of you and/or your baby. My first delivery almost turned into a C-section. I was a little shocked when my doctor told me that we were going to have to do a C-section if things didn't improve in the next hour. But I wasn't scared because I had read about them, talked with my doctor about them, and pretty much knew what to expect. The doctors and nurses have done this many more times than you, and you have to trust them and follow their guidance, even if it contradicts your birth plan. Relax and go with it.

The Pain of Labor

Dilation, laboring positions, contractions, pushing, breathing, C-sections . . . learn as much as you can about the process of labor. Why? Because the more you understand, the less afraid you'll be, and the less fear you have, the less it will hurt. Being fearful will make it hard for you to relax, and the more tense you are, the more labor will hurt. Relaxing is the key to a better, less painful labor. My husband is a hypnotist, so I suppose I'm a little biased, but learning how to relax through hypnosis can help greatly. Most people just don't know how to completely relax, especially during an exciting event like childbirth. Learning a little self-hypnosis can really help your labor be much more enjoyable. Being too hungry or thirsty can make pain feel worse too. Be sure to eat something healthy and high in protein before you go to the hospital. The uterus is a muscle that needs energy and hydration to do its job. Some birthing centers are starting to allow laboring mothers to have light meals. And be sure to keep sipping water or juice during labor. Pushing a baby out is an intense athletic event and your body can become dehydrated.

When to Speak Up

From Stephanie

Now, we've told you to trust your doctors and nurses. But it is also important to know when to speak up. I'm from the old school of thought where you just respect the doctors and comply with whatever they want to do to you. (Girls are to be seen and not heard . . . can you believe our mothers taught us that?) But if you truly feel that something is wrong in the way you are being treated, then ask your nurse or doctor. Don't be afraid to ask questions—you're entitled to an explanation. Or have your birth partner or spouse ask for you. Things that seem scary to you are common procedures to those attending you. It's okay to speak up, but do it with grace and kindness. You don't want to piss these people off—you're going to need them later, trust me. I'll give you an example: When my daughter was born, she had some initial breathing issues that had to be handled right away. An hour had gone by while she was being monitored in a bassinet across the room. I heard the nurse mention that someone else was coming to bathe her or administer something, and I said, "Can that please wait? I haven't been able to hold her yet." Immediately they changed their plans and brought her to me. Perhaps they had gotten busy with her well-being and amidst all the medical protocols had forgotten about little ol' me, the new mother (it was a premonition of what motherhood brings).

Get Some Sleep

Once the baby is here, you'll be so excited to hold and feed your baby. These are some of the very best moments in your entire lifetime. But also get some sleep. Your body needs to heal, and the fastest way to do that is to sleep. The nurses will take good care of your baby. Please understand that you will not sleep through the night undisturbed again for months (yes, I said months, possibly even years). So take advantage of the most qualified baby sitters you'll ever have. Put a Do Not Disturb sign on your door in case of visitors, or let everyone know when you are going to rest. This may be your last chance for quite a while. The nurses will wake you when your baby needs you.

Managing Your Stay

Most of us spend hours thinking about what our birth experience is going to be like, even writing out a birth plan, but we typically don't give much thought to the two or three days we'll spend in the hospital after the baby is born. It's important to at least give a little consideration to that time. It's especially crucial to discuss your expectations with your spouse. Do you want him to spend nights with you in the hospital? Is there a place for him to sleep in the room? Do you want lots of visitors, or would you prefer to keep them at a minimum? If you'd prefer more quiet in the hospital, you can gently let friends and family know ahead of time. Do you plan on trying to breast-feed? Do you want help from a lactation consultant? Do you want to receive calls in the room, or would you rather your spouse share the good news with relatives and friends? Do you want everyone out of the room when you are nursing, or is it okay for certain people (say, your sister or your best friend) to stay? Talking about these details ahead of time will avoid stress and allow you to relax and enjoy your time with your new little one.

Have a Quiet Dinner

Ask your husband to bring takeout from one of your favorite restaurants, send the baby to the nursery, and enjoy a quiet dinner in your room at the hospital. Check to make sure your hospital allows this. Sara's childbirth educator actually recommended this idea. She said it was probably one of the last peaceful meals new parents would enjoy for a while, and boy, was she right!

The Aftermath No One Tells You About

From Stephanie

The only way I can begin this section is with "Oh my God!" This is the part of the birthing process that I was totally unprepared for. For me it was much worse than labor itself. I was totally unprepared and very upset that none of my classes or girlfriends told me about the recovery. I don't know why we mothers aren't more truthful with each other. Maybe it's because of that hormone that is supposed to make you forget everything so the species will continue to multiply. Or maybe it's that weird and stupid competition that we women engage in with each other. And of course you know that anytime you do get the truth out of a mother, including all the gory details, it's always followed with "But it's totally worth it because they're so cute and you just love them so much." And that's true; it is worth it.

But here's the part I wish someone had warned me about: once the epidural wears off, you're in pain. It wasn't just that, though. It was that I had to wear these disgusting panties made of what looked like fishnet material; that I had to wear the biggest maxipads I've ever seen; and that they make you take something called a sitz bath, which is supposed to make you feel better, but I hated them! I've only ever met one girlfriend who said she loved sitz baths, and I'm convinced she must be the only person who actually knows how to use one correctly. They'll also give you what is called a "peri bottle" (*peri* is short for *perineum*), which is a squeeze bottle that you squirt onto your private areas every time you use the toilet. Then you're supposed to pat yourself dry, apply a witch hazel pad, and replace your lovely fishnet panties and Volkswagen-size maxi pad. You're weak, exhausted, and very, very sore in places you didn't know could *be* sore in the first place. And then you have all these things you have to do to prevent infection and help with the healing process. I remember thinking that it was really hard to take care of myself during those first few days. I just wanted to sit and hold my baby; I didn't want to be bothered with sitz baths and peri bottles and weird underwear. The whole experience was disturbing and painful and completely unexpected. And to this day, I still don't understand what the damn fishnet panties are for. Maybe it was to help hold up the flabby skin of my stomach?

The other completely awful part of recovering during your hospital stay is when the nurse comes in and presses on your abdomen to help your uterus contract. This hurts a lot, and if you've been mean to your nurse this is her chance to get even, so you'd better be nice.

Nurses will check your stitches or incision and monitor your temperature regularly to help detect possible infections, and if you've had a C-section, you'll have to pass gas before they'll let you go home (that ensures that they put everything back correctly, since your entire intestinal tract was lying on an operating table just a few hours ago). The first time you have a bowel movement after giving birth is terrifying for most women. Just drink plenty of fluids and it won't be as bad as you envision.

So now you know, and I've included every gory detail. I hope, since you know what to expect, you won't be as miserable as I was. "But it's totally worth it because they're so cute and you just love them so much."

From Sara

I too was shocked at how much other moms conveniently left out of their birth stories. But do you really blame them? This stuff isn't exactly nice dinner conversation. That's why we're giving you the straight scoop right here.

Giving birth will no doubt be one of the most amazing, memorable experiences of your life. It will also be one of the most humiliating and messiest. You probably know that your baby will enter this world covered in a lot of disgusting stuff. But did you also know that after giving birth to your baby (and the placenta) a nurse will press on your abdomen to pass clots in your uterus? Yeah, me neither. You may also need stitches if you've torn or had an episiotomy. During all of this you will be mostly uncovered, lying there in all your postnatal glory. If you decide to bank cord blood, like I did with my second child (the stem cells from cord blood can be used to treat a number of potential diseases), expect to spend even more time in your exposed state. (You'll also want your gatekeeper to make sure no one pops into the delivery room uninvited at this time. See "Enlist a Gatekeeper" below.)

I felt great immediately after giving birth to both my children. I was flooded with relief that they had made it into the world unscathed and that I was no longer in pain. But Stephanie's right—when the epidural wears off, you will be very, very sore. Once you are in a regular hospital room, a nurse may bring you an ice pack to place inside those lovely underpants Stephanie mentioned. Yes, it's really, really cold and a little uncomfortable at first, but the ice will help with the soreness tremendously.

I also didn't realize how long I would need to wear supersize maxipads after giving birth. There's no other way to say it: you bleed a lot and for quite a while. That may also be another reason for the gigantic stretchy underpants.

As Stephanie said, the thought of going to the bathroom (and I don't mean urinating) for the first time can be a little scary. But don't worry, the nurse will give you stool softeners.

So there you have it: all the gory details no one else would tell you. Now you know why other moms give you that knowing look when you tell them you're pregnant.

Enlist a Gatekeeper

After exposing your most private parts during the birth process, you'll probably be ready for a little privacy. This can be difficult to manage when you have well-meaning friends and family who want to come to your room to visit and see your new bundle of joy. It's important to have someone watching out for you and managing the visitors so that you can rest, have the privacy you need to breast-feed, or get out of bed to go to the bathroom (which can be a bit of a process at first). Your husband or partner is an obvious choice for this role. Another option is a close friend or family member who will be spending a lot of time with you at the hospital.

There are several things your gatekeeper can do at the hospital to give you privacy and help you rest:

- Intercept visitors when you need privacy and ask them to come back a little later.
- Completely close the door to your hospital room when you need privacy. This will encourage visitors to knock before entering. (Believe it or not, some people will just walk right in!)
- Tape a piece of paper to the door that says, "Mommy resting. Please come back a little later."
- Ask visitors to step out if Mom needs to nurse or visit the restroom, or if a nurse comes in to check you.
- Notice if Mom is tired during a visit, and drop hints to visitors that it's time to go.

Let the Nurses Help You

From Sara

My advice to pregnant women is always "Take advantage of the hospital nursery." While you're in the hospital you have a staff of expertly trained and highly experienced neonatal nurses ready to help you. Let them! When my daughter was born, I felt guilty sending her to the hospital nursery, even though I was recovering from the rigors of childbirth and obviously needed some rest. Once after I'd asked the nurse to take her out of my room for a while I saw a card that said "Out on demand" attached to her bassinet in the nursery. I started crying! "Out on demand" sounds so harsh, like I was this horrible mother who demanded her child be removed from her room. I desperately wanted to be the best mommy on the planet, not one who kicked her kid out of her room a day after she was born!

I immediately brought her back to the room and kept her with me almost constantly. As a result, I was completely sleep-deprived and exhausted when I got home. I realized later I should have taken the opportunity to sleep when I had the luxury of these professionals to take care of my baby through the night. I would have come home at least a little rested. I have no idea why the nurses used that terminology—probably so they knew that the baby wasn't in the nursery for a certain test or shot, she was just there so Mommy could sleep. And it certainly wasn't any sort of judgment of me, even though that's how I interpreted it. Must have been the hormones. Although I do think the phrase "Out at mother's request" sounds much nicer.

When my second child was born, I was much wiser about the amount of sleep I was about to miss over the next three months. I sent him to the nursery and never had a moment's guilt over it. I knew I had the rest of my life to bond with him and that I would come home feeling much better if I got a couple of nights' sleep in the hospital. Besides, after a few weeks of taking care of my infant daughter I became well aware of how much better qualified those nurses were to take care of a newborn than I was. I took a class on infant CPR but wasn't sure I could actually perform it effectively if I needed to. And that was the extent of my medical knowledge. By the time I had my son I realized that the amount of time I kept him in the room with me wasn't a measure of what kind of mom I was. In the two and a half years since my daughter was born I'd gained the confidence to do what worked for me. And I came home a much happier and more well-rested mommy because of it.

From Stephanie

I have to totally disagree with Sara on this one. While I'm all for getting plenty of sleep (it's especially important when your body is trying to recover from delivering a baby), those first few days were magical moments and very important to me when it came to bonding with baby, and I didn't want to be apart. I was the only one who could breastfeed my baby, and if she needed comforting, I was certainly the best candidate. I used this time to rest with baby next to me in the hospital bed. My first child seemed so strange in that weird-looking cradle on the opposite side of the room, and she did a lot of crying until the nurse explained to me that babies like the warmth of their mother's body. As soon as I put her next to my skin, she became much calmer and we could both get some much-needed rest. My hormones made me worry that the baby would be left to cry in the nursery with so many other babies who needed attention, and I didn't want to take any chances that my baby's introduction to her new world would involve being upset or ignored. I wanted her right next to me. Newborns sleep a lot, and the key is to sleep whenever they sleep—especially after you get home. You should have no guilt about napping several times a day if you need to. You'll soon learn to turn off the phone, ignore the doorbell, and get some shut-eye.

My second child was born via C-section, and I can tell you that this is a totally different experience. Instead of suffering through labor, the suffering comes afterward. My incision was extremely sore for days, even weeks. It was draining to try to care for a newborn and allow my own body to heal at the same time. Dads and family members play a big role in the lives of new mothers who've delivered via C-section. It will be weeks before you're allowed to drive a car and months before you'll be permitted to go back to the gym or do anything too physical, and you won't exactly be excited about sex anytime soon either. I remember the first day I went back to the gym after the C-section—once I climbed up on the treadmill, I was so relieved that I actually was able to run again. I truthfully hadn't thought that I'd ever be able to. Your body does make a full recovery eventually, but I encourage you to get plenty of rest and give yourself time to heal. It's quite an ordeal for your body to recover from a C-section. Recovering from a vaginal birth takes only days, and I've never understood why some women elect to deliver their baby by C-section instead of a vaginal birth.

Sitz Baths

The authors of *Great Expectations* say, "We're almost positive no one actually knows how to use one. All we know is that a sitz bath is designed to rest under, or maybe over, the toilet ring, or maybe even on the floor, and is supposed to somehow facilitate soaking your privates in warm water. If, like us, you just don't get it, ask your care provider for advice about taking 'sitz baths' in the tub."

2

Tips for New Dads

First let's talk about what a dad can do in the delivery room to help Mom through the birth process *and* feel more involved himself. The great thing about the new role of dads in labor and delivery is the fact that they can actually participate, instead of sitting in the waiting room for hours and passing out cigars like they did in the old days. Now dads are actively part of the process right from the start. We wrote this chapter with dads in mind, so hand the book over to him or sit down and share this chapter together. It may be the last chance you get to sit quietly together for eighteen years.

During Labor

Dads, even though you are in the labor room, you should still expect a lot of waiting. Movies portray a huge rush to the hospital: throwing the suitcases in the car and speeding through streets in the family car (which is probably the only part most men look forward to—a reason to legally speed) while the mother is breathing hard, sweating, and cursing. Upon arriving at the hospital, nurses scurry the expectant mom into the delivery room and immediately people start screaming, "Push!"

Ah, that's not at all how it happens. And we'll never understand why the media seem to consistently portray it incorrectly. (Just like that whole thing about being pregnant for nine months. Nobody's pregnant for nine months. It's forty weeks, and that means ten months, people!) The reality is labor is typically a very, very long process that still involves a lot of waiting on the part of dads, even if they're doing it in the delivery room and not the waiting room.

Dads, here are a few things you can do to help your wife through the process:

- If there is a TV in your room, give her the remote, for cryin' out loud! Help her take her mind off labor, because the duration of it really wears you down.
- Treat her with the utmost kindness. Basically, act as if it's your first date again (even though this time there is no possible chance of having sex). Just pretend if you have to.
- Massage her feet. (No, we're not kidding.)
- Rub her back. (Ask the nurses to show you how to help ease labor pains this way.)
- Pay attention to her needs: she is excited, she is scared to death, the pain is going to go from mildly uncomfortable to very painful to even more painful, and there's no turning back.
- Bring her ice chips to suck on, get a cold cloth for her head, and fluff her pillow.
- Be her gatekeeper. She may be okay with visitors and phone calls in the beginning, but as her labor progresses and becomes more painful, she is going to want peace and quiet and to be alone—and she may be so focused on getting through the pain that she won't be able to tell people to go away. That's your job. (Stephanie's husband was down the hall doing impressions to entertain the nurses and wasting the battery on the camcorder filming himself. Don't do that.)
- Eat something before labor gets intense. When contractions are coming every two minutes, this is not the time to wander off to the snack bar to get a bite. Early on, when the time is right, go to the cafeteria and eat. You'll need strength to help her through the final stages of labor and for the birth. Some dads are shocked by the sight of all the blood, etc., and you'll be less likely to get queasy or pass out if you have something in your stomach. Even peanut butter crackers or nuts will do—something with some protein that sticks. (But don't eat in front of her! She will not be allowed to eat once she checks into the hospital, just in case she has to have a C-section. Anesthesia and a full stomach don't mix.)
- Be her intermediary. Women go into different states of consciousness during labor. It's her body's way of dealing with the pain, so don't be surprised if she gets a little distant or unresponsive to you. We know this is hard, but be her brain! If you see that she needs something, get it for her, or ask the nurse. Discuss ahead of time whom she wants in the delivery room and whom she doesn't. It's your job to make sure her wishes are carried out.

When the Baby Arrives

From Stephanie

When my daughter was born, special precautions had to be taken because my doctor found meconium in the amniotic fluid. Basically, that means that the baby had pooped during labor and there was poop in the fluid surrounding her. This can be dangerous if the baby inhales it into her lungs. Your doctor will know if this happens because he or she will notice it in the fluids that are being excreted during labor. I had labored for a very long time, and things started getting exciting and moving fast. I was the center of attention. People were gathered all around me, holding my hand, even cheering for me. I felt like I was an NFL star with all these fans and cheerleaders urging me on. But as I pushed my last push and the baby came out, in the very moment that I thought would be so triumphant, suddenly everyone just left my side and literally ran to the other side of the room to attend to the baby. Of course my doctor was there for the cleanup, but my cheering section, including my husband, dropped me like a hot potato. I kept asking, "What's happening? Is she okay? What's going on?" because I couldn't see her on the other side of the room.

It was almost an hour before I got to hold her—and even then I had to ask fiercely. The hospital gets caught up in their procedures sometimes and can forget the warm and fuzzy stuff. So be assertive—but respectful. Holding that baby is your wife's reward, and she needs to do it as soon as possible. It's really, really important, both for her and for the new baby. I had special circumstances because our baby needed medical attention, but even so, it was very hard to wait. And please take the time to thank her for what she has just done for you. This moment should be as romantic as your wedding—it's certainly as significant, if not more. She will remember your reaction at this moment for the rest of her life, and if you don't make it great, it *will* resurface at the hearing for your divorce.

So here are a few basic tips:

- Keep Mom apprised of what's happening with the baby.
- Try not to abandon her.
- Thank her profusely. She's just given you the greatest gift you will ever receive. No one can do for you what she just did. And the very first step you must take to become a good father is to recognize that.
- Bond with the baby! Bonding doesn't just mean mother-baby bonding, it means father-baby bonding. Lots of medical necessities will be taking place with Mom just after the baby is delivered, so take this opportunity to connect with the new member of your family.

The Postpartum Period

"Postpartum period" is the name for the time after the delivery of the baby, guys—and you need to be nicer to her than you've ever been to anyone in your entire life.

This is the part most new moms aren't prepared for. To some moms it's the toughest part of giving birth. The epidural, painkillers, and joy of the moment all come to a screeching halt—and suddenly they realize that they have to take care of this little need machine, but somehow have to take care of themselves too. She is beginning to absorb this monumental life change that has just occurred. This is a huge responsibility, and there's a lot to think about.

Remember that Mom is recovering from a major trauma—her body has just been through an ordeal, or even major surgery if she had a C-section. She's sore; she has bruises from all the IVs, epidurals, and injections; she's weak due to the effort of giving birth, the loss of blood, and the loss of sleep; she is still having contractions (that's right—they continue while the uterus returns to its normal size, and doctors and nurses will be coming in periodically to push on her abdomen to keep those contractions going, which hurts a lot); and she's going to have to work to keep her stitches clean by using this wonderful contraption called a sitz bath (I have to say I have yet to meet anyone who actually knows how to use one, but it has something to do with soaking your bottom in warm water, and it's just not much fun).

She's probably trying to breast-feed, which can be frustrating. Think back to those breast-feeding classes and offer help and support. One of the biggest challenges a brand-new mom faces is breast-feeding. Remember, if this is her first baby, she's never done this before, and trust me, it's really hard to figure it out because you can't tell how much milk the baby is getting. Give it time and don't make her more stressed than she already is. Her breast milk won't come in right away. At first, the baby will be getting a fluid from the breast called colostrum, which is clear and doesn't look like breast milk. Be patient. It might take as long as a month for Mom (and baby) to really get the hang of it.

Her body is doing crazy things. Hormones that had been raging in her body for forty weeks have just taken a nosedive. She may also experience a feeling of let-down after all the excitement is over. Consequently, she might be a little weepy or irritable, so be prepared for that. It's normal. Certainly don't make a big deal about it or make fun of her. (Otherwise you may get a flying remote control to the forehead. What can we say—it happens. And you've been warned. She's likely not going to be in the mood to be the butt of a joke right now.) Don't worry unless it doesn't pass in a week or so. If these mood changes persist, go with her to see her doctor because she may be suffering from postpartum depression. (See Chapter 6, "Postpartum Depression," for the signs and symptoms.)

Smart Dads Bring Gifts

The mother of your child has just been through forty weeks of sacrifice to bring this baby into the world. She's likely given up caffeine, alcohol, deli meat, canned tuna, soft cheese, sushi, hot tubs, Sudafed, cute clothes, and thin ankles for this baby. Then there are the hours of labor pains, the icky aftermath, the nursing bras and pads, engorged breasts, the toll on her body . . . enough said? For goodness' sake, the least you can do is pick out a special gift to honor her as a new mother. A ring or necklace with the baby's birthstone is a nice idea. A charm bracelet with the baby's name engraved on it is always a winner. And of course you can never go wrong with diamonds. Ask one of her girlfriends to go shopping with you or give you some ideas if you need help. Stephanie's husband gave her a ring with the baby's birthstone after the birth of each of their children and they have become cherished keepsakes. So don't be cheap! After you've seen her go through labor and delivery, you'll want to buy her the crown jewels.

Bring a Nice Meal to the Hospital

We're not talking a Quarter Pounder with cheese here, guys. If you can get it at a drive-through, that doesn't qualify as a "nice" meal to her, even if it does to you. Bring takeout from one of her favorite restaurants and enjoy a quiet dinner together, because you may not get a chance to again anytime soon.

Bringing Baby and Mom Home

Mom has most likely looked forward to this moment her whole life, so be sure you are prepared to capture it on film. Make sure to charge the camera and video recorder—and don't forget the film, memory stick, or tapes if your camera needs them! This is definitely your department because her mind will be on other things.

Remember She Is Recovering

Imagine having had surgery and then trying to recover while only getting a few hours of sleep a night and being expected to take care of someone else's every need. That's exactly what new moms go through after coming home from the hospital. Here's what you can do to help:

- Take off as much time from work as you can and help her through those first few days and weeks.
- Let her sleep!

- If you miss sleep, you will probably be tired and grumpy, but if she doesn't get sleep, the hormonal changes could spiral her into postpartum depression (and trust us, you don't want that).
- Hold down the fort at home with the baby if she needs to get out of the house for a few hours. (You can do it!)

She Is Going Through Major Hormonal Changes

Be the strong one, since you're not going through these hormonal changes. Your wife is not less interested in you, but her body is shifting from producing mating hormones to churning out nurturing hormones. Let her know that you still find her attractive, but *not* in a sexual way. We realize that her breasts just went from sex toy to baby food makers, but you have to try to remember that that's what they were really created for in the first place. We also realize that they may have just gone from a B cup to a D cup. As tempting as this may be, you'll need to restrain yourself. We're telling you this for your own safety.

Your wife doesn't love you any less. She's exhausted from the sleep deprivation. She's tired of being touched because she's had a baby attached to her all day long. And you just can't expect her to be exactly the same person she was before the baby came. The good news is, she will recover. This stage will only last a few weeks. Things will never be as centered on you as they once were, but you'll love your child so much that you won't mind the change. And a baby gives you so many more reasons to love each other (and to fight with each other too, for that matter).

Be the Gatekeeper at Home Too

Just like at the hospital, it's your job to be her intermediary at home. If she is resting or trying to nurse and doesn't want visitors, put a sign on the door that says, "Mother and baby bonding, please come back later." Friends will understand and appreciate knowing they didn't disturb the new parents. If visitors or family are already there and Mom wants privacy, gently get folks out of the room and give her some space.

She's Going to Want to Talk a Lot When You Get Home from Work

Just listen and don't try to *fix* anything. Try to remember that just because she's been home all day, that doesn't mean she's been relaxing. We've had this fight with our own husbands, and here's the only conclusion: she's working just as hard as you are, if not harder. It's the same amount of stress as you're dealing with at the office, but it's a different kind of stress. You may be able to reason with an upset co-worker and then leave the office for a break, but being at home with a crying baby is a different ball game. In fact, we've heard many seasoned dads say these exact words: "Going to work is easier." So

Dads and Babies

In the *Journal of Infancy,* Dr. Marissa Diener reports that babies who have a secure relationship with their father use more coping tactics to entertain themselves during times of separation from parents than other infants who were not securely attached to their father. Diener studied a hundred twelve-month-olds, testing their reactions to having the mother and father leave the child alone with a stranger for a brief time. During the separation, babies who had secure relationships with their fathers were easier to calm down, made fewer sad faces, and tended to use more coping tactics (like playing with objects) than those who did not.

don't expect to walk in the door to a hot meal like they did on *Leave It to Beaver.* That was television. Not reality.

When you get home from work you still have another job to fulfill before bedtime. I can tell you that after the baby comes, your wife has never been as happy to see you as when you walk in the door at the end of the day. She's lonely. She's been frustrated all day. If she once had a career, she's also frustrated that her workload now consists of diaper changes, laundry, cleaning floors, laundry, housework, and did we mention laundry? She doesn't get coffee breaks, a chance to chat on e-mail, or time to stand around the water cooler with her friends. And just as you wouldn't want to be at your job from 7:00 A.M. until 9:00 P.M., she doesn't want to be at her new job that long either. When you get home, all she can think about is that now she's going to have a little help (and every woman hopes for a clean but unrealistic fifty-fifty split), and she's really counting on that. So come home ready to start your second job. And really, that's not just being a good father, that's simply how it logistically has to work.

Parents don't get breaks or sick days. There's a lot of sacrifice involved. But the more involved you are as a parent, the more you'll get out of it. Your children will feel closer to you. You will have a greater influence on them. And these new relationships with your baby are the foundation for the kind of connection you'll have with your child when he or she is older. Don't be fooled by thinking that all this baby stuff is up to the mother and bonding with your kid can wait until later—it starts now.

Clutter-Busting Resources

WEBSITES

Ten tips for new dads
http://pregnancy.about.com/cs/forfathersonly/a/aadadtips.htm

Advice for dads
www.greatdad.com

Interactive Dad
www.interactivedadmagazine.com

All-Pro Dad
www.allprodad.com

Ten surprises of fatherhood
www.babycenter.com/advice-for-new-dads

Armin Brott, author of *The Expectant Father*
www.mrdad.com

Online community for new dads
www.brandnewdad.com

BOOKS

The Expectant Father: Facts, Tips, and Advice for Dads-to-Be
by Armin Brott

The New Father: A Dad's Guide to the First Year
by Armin Brott

After the Hospital

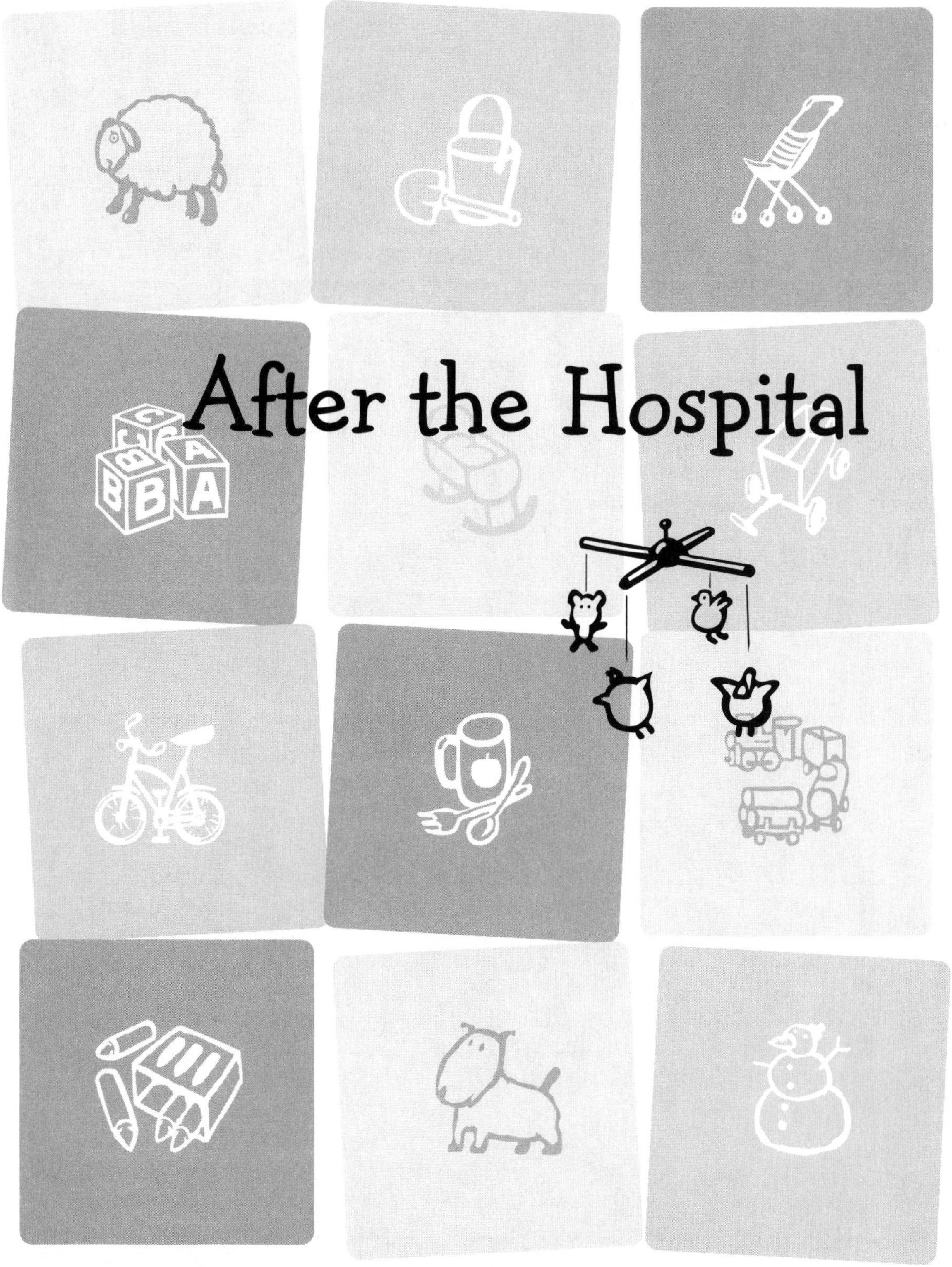

3

Breast-feeding vs. Bottle-feeding

The Bottom Line

Stephanie loved breast-feeding her babies and Sara hated it. Here are two different takes on how to feed your baby, and why you shouldn't feel guilty if breast-feeding doesn't work out for you.

Stephanie on Breast-feeding

The bottom line on breast-feeding is this:

1. Yes, it definitely is better for your baby for many reasons, but if it just doesn't work for you, it's better to feed formula and preserve your sanity.

2. Getting the hang of it doesn't come naturally, so you'd better make the time to take a class, and be very, very patient with yourself—it may take an entire month of sore nipples and pure determination before you get the knack (that's the part they don't tell you).

Breast-feeding is certainly a topic that the experts love to chew on. And there are very few topics that mothers and experts feel more passionate about than breast-feeding. There are breast-feeding leagues and lactation consultants that make new mothers crazy with guilt. For me, breast-feeding was fairly easy and I loved it, although I must warn you that it does take training and lots of patience. I often have new moms e-mail me and ask for my help on this topic. And I always insist that they take a course on breast-feeding before the baby is born. Now, I realize you're thinking, "Well, how did mothers do it before there were classes? Women have been breast-feeding for thousands of years!" But trust me, there are all kinds of tricks of the trade that will make it easier for you, make you less sore, and give you a better understanding of how your body works. I remember an episode of the sitcom *Murphy Brown* where Candice Bergen (Murphy) has just given birth and is sitting in her hospital bed talking about how suddenly her body is making milk. She says, "It's like you go through your whole life and suddenly bacon starts coming out of your elbow!" I couldn't have said it better myself. There are hundreds of books that give you great detailed information about the how-tos of breast-feeding, so I'm not going to get too medical. But following are a few of the things I learned about it that aren't in most of the books and which I think are really important for you to know.

Why Is Breast-feeding Better?

If you've taken the classes, you already know how vital it is to start breast-feeding your baby. Before milk, your body produces colostrum, which is a magical nutrient for your newborn baby. Also, breast-feeding releases chemicals in your own body that help your uterus contract.

First, it's interesting to note that there are all kinds of breast milk. Every mother's milk is different, and in fact your baby enjoys several kinds of milk during just one feeding, sort of like her own little two- or three-course dinner. At the start of a feeding, your baby gets an appetizer called *foremilk,* which is low in fat. The main course is called *hindmilk* and it is higher in fat and calories. This course is what makes your baby feel full and satisfied.

One of the most amazing things about breast milk is that it changes as your baby grows. If you compared the milk of a mother with a newborn and the milk of a mother with a six-month-old, you would find them to be very different, in appearance as well as in components. The nutrients change as your baby's needs change. Older babies need fewer fats and calories, so your milk content adjusts. How amazing is that? Isn't it great to be a woman? (That's one of the downsides to formula: it can't adjust with

More About the Amazing Components of Breast Milk

One of the best books about breast-feeding and breast milk is *The Baby Book* by Dr. William Sears and his wife, Martha Sears, who is a registered nurse. If you're interested in what breast milk is made of and how it works, this book is my favorite breast-feeding resource. *The Baby Book* talks a lot about the changing ingredients of breast milk, why it's sweeter than other milk, and all its components such as vitamins, brain-building fats, infection-fighting proteins, and more. This book will make you an expert on breast milk and answer all your questions about why it's so much better for your baby than formula. Much of the information in this section came from *The Baby Book.*

your baby's needs like your own breast milk can.)

It's also interesting that human milk contains more sugar than the milk of any other mammal. This sugar, called lactose, is great for developing brain tissue. Humans have bigger brains than most mammals, so we need more lactose. (And just to be clear, giving your kids SweeTarts is not going to improve their grades. Lactose and its components are a little more complicated.)

There are many, many reasons why breast-feeding is the healthiest choice for your baby. Breast milk is perfect for your baby at any given time. It contains enzymes that help your baby digest fats, so more of it is absorbed and less is wasted, which is good news for you because that means less smelly poop diapers. The nutrients in breast milk get absorbed better than the nutrients in formula because formula can't imitate the enzymes that help babies absorb vitamins and nutrients. Also, breast milk contains white blood cells and infection-fighting proteins called immunoglobulins. Colostrum, the first milk you produce, is loaded with these substances just when your baby needs them the most. Dr. William Sears explains it best: "The germs around you are continuously changing, but your body has a protective system that selectively recognizes friendly and harmful germs. This system is immature in babies. When a new germ enters a mother's body, she produces antibodies to that germ. These antibodies are then passed on to her baby via her milk." So breast milk is like immunizing your baby daily with updated germ-fighting antibodies.

What You Need to Know About Breast-feeding

- Preparation is key—take a class.
- Be patient. It often takes weeks to perfect and build your milk supply.
- The soreness is only temporary. Use Lansinoh ointment to relieve it.
- Avoid breast pumps for a few weeks, until your milk supply is plentiful. Breast pumps will not help increase your milk supply—only the baby sucking frequently can do that.
- Your milk is loaded with infection-fighting proteins and nutrients that boost baby's immunity and brain-building ability.
- It enables intense bonding between you and your baby.
- It's cheaper and more convenient than formula.
- It releases hormones that help your uterus return to normal.

Increasing the Milk Supply

To increase your milk supply, make baby drink more frequently. It's the *frequency* of feedings, not the *length* of feedings, that will increase your milk supply. Breast pumps cannot build your milk supply—only a baby's tongue on your nipple causes the release of hormones that increase the quantity of milk you can make.

Training and Patience

Breast-feeding isn't as easy and natural as you think. You have probably heard mothers talk about how sore their nipples became, and this is often because the baby wasn't latching on properly. There are all sorts of holding positions and tricks to get the baby to latch on properly, as well as ways to break the suction so it doesn't hurt when you have to remove baby before he's finished. Learning what works best is going to make it much easier to breast-feed.

The other thing that I talk to new mothers about frequently is that it takes lots of patience. It took about three or four weeks before my milk supply began to meet my baby's needs. In the meantime I had to supplement with formula. I had all kinds of lactation nurses scaring me about a thing called "nipple confusion," which means that if baby gets used to a bottle, he may not be able to switch back to the breast. Personally, I think there's no such thing as nipple confusion; I suspect it's just a ploy by those few hard-core, card-carrying La Leche League die-hard lactivists to scare you into breast-feeding. Nipple confusion (if there is such a thing) depends on the baby and the frequency with which the bottle and breast are exchanged. The concern is that it's much easier to get milk out of a bottle than out of a breast, so if your baby figures that out, he might get lazy about nursing. Also, if you do decide to supplement, you have to be careful not to get lazy as well. The only thing that stimulates more breast milk is your baby sucking. A breast pump will usually not stimulate milk production. There is a hormone that is released when your baby sucks, and only a baby's tongue can cause the release of these milk-producing hormones. A breast pump alone is not going to help your milk supply increase, and it's probably going to frustrate you because you'll pump for an hour and only get an inch of milk in the beginning. Remember, frequent nursing is more important than how long baby nurses when you're trying to build your milk supply. I have had a few mothers tell me that they were able to produce more milk by using a pump, but it's rare and much harder to do than just allowing baby to latch on and suckle.

There are actually many benefits to training your baby to take both the breast and the bottle from day one. First, it means that you can be more patient while your milk supply develops, and in the meantime your baby will be satisfied. When my first child was born, I tried so hard to follow the advice of a book that was popular at that time. It called for a stringent schedule of feeding based on the clock (not her desires) and warned against formula-feeding. Most babies lose a little weight at first, and should begin gaining

Nipple Preference vs. Nipple Confusion

An article in the February 2008 issue of *Babytalk* magazine calls nipple confusion "bunk." As one lactation consultant told Sara, there may be nipple *preference,* but not nipple confusion. Many mothers are able to feed their babies with both breast and bottle without issue. However, plenty of breast-feeding experts believe nipple confusion absolutely does exist and encourage breast-feeding moms not to introduce a bottle during the first few weeks of breast-feeding. We say the bottom line here is: do what works for you and your family!

in their first week at home. But I ended up taking my newborn back to the hospital only one week after her birth because she was losing weight. And as if that wasn't bad enough, my pediatrician scolded me for following the instructions of a book and not my own instincts. My baby was hungry. My milk was not mature enough to satisfy her, and she needed to eat. Once we began to supplement with formula, she became a much happier baby, and eventually my milk supply matured and I went back to strictly breast-feeding. Hungry babies cry a lot, so if your baby is doing a lot of crying in those first few days, consider whether he is getting enough to eat. Sometimes it's hard to tell how much he's getting from your breast. The amount of milk you can pump is a good clue to how much milk you are producing. Remember to pump after baby is finished eating if you are trying to store breast milk for other feedings.

Using both breast-feeding and bottle-feeding also makes it easier for moms who plan on returning to work, and for letting dads get in on the action. My husband loved being able to feed our baby. It gave them some one-on-one time to bond and it gave me a break. No matter how dedicated a mother you are, it's very hard to live your life around your baby's feeding schedule. It will give you a lot of peace of mind to know that if you're stuck in traffic coming back from the mall, your husband or babysitter will be able to feed your baby in your absence. It's great to get a break once in a while.

And for working moms, remember, once you go back to work, someone (other than you) is going to have to feed your baby. If your baby has had no experience other than your breast, you are going to have a fight on your hands. I made this mistake myself. Once my milk supply was going strong, I reverted back to strictly breast-feeding. It was quicker and easier and cheaper and I loved it. But an important industry trade show took place during my second month of maternity leave, and I told my boss that I would take a few days from my maternity leave and attend the show. Unfortunately, I didn't realize that my baby was going to refuse to drink from a bottle, and I didn't try giving her a bottle until the day before my trip. She absolutely refused it. She was crying. I was crying. The hormones were in full swing, and I'm sure I sounded like some kind of wigged-out maternal freak when I called my boss (whose wife was a nurse) and told him I couldn't make the trip because I couldn't get my baby to eat. Eventually, I did manage to get on the plane, and she did drink from a bottle. But the drama and stress that we all endured weren't worth it. And when I became pregnant with my second child, I made up my mind that the first lactation nurse who entered my recovery room and even whispered the words "nipple confusion" was going to find herself and her clipboard launched into the maternity ward hallway courtesy of my right foot, episiotomy or not.

Now, let's talk about patience. The first few weeks of breast-feeding can be really frustrating. Your nipples will probably be very sore; you won't be sure if your baby is even getting any milk; you'll be tired; and you'll start to wonder if it's really worth it. This is where patience and resolve come in. The first few days of breast-feeding, your breasts will be producing colostrum, and next you'll have something called transitional milk, which is a mixture of colostrum and milk. It may take a month before your milk (or any-

Take a Breast-feeding Class

Breast-feeding doesn't come naturally for most women. It will help tremendously to take a class before baby arrives. Proper techniques for latching on and holding baby during feeding will prevent nipple soreness, make your experience much more pleasant, and ensure your success.

thing that looks like milk) really starts flowing. During this time, your nipples are going to be sore. Every mother has her own story about what worked best for her: cabbage leaves, cold showers, compresses, you name it. The best thing I've found is a cream called Lansinoh. It's a pure, hypoallergenic, pesticide-free lanolin. Apply it immediately after every feeding, and you don't even have to wash it off before baby nurses the next time. It is truly a miracle and will prevent your nipples from becoming so sore. All the mothers I know swear by it. The other part of having sore nipples is that some women experience a terrible burning sensation as their letdown reflex kicks in at the beginning of each feeding. It hurts, and it's a sensation that I will never forget. I remember picking my feet up off the floor and cringing in pain each time my daughter began to suck. Even my husband would stand by and wince on my behalf. But just know that this will eventually reduce to a tingling feeling once your nipples are no longer sore. It usually takes a while for your nipples to become accustomed to the demands of a sucking baby. So hang in there and wait it out. The adjustment period is usually only a couple of weeks. It will be worth it because you'll have the convenience and closeness of breast-feeding your baby for months ahead. You can do it.

What's in It for You?

Every time you breast-feed your baby, hormones (prolactin and oxytocin) are released into your system. Dr. William Sears tells us that these "mothering hormones" are chemicals that help you form a bond with your baby and sharpen your mothering instincts. Don't you love science?

Another benefit is the bonding that takes place between mother and baby. I'm not saying that you can't bond with your baby if you're bottle-feeding, but there is a very unique closeness that you experience with your baby when you can feed him with your own body. I loved breast-feeding my children. I loved how still they were and how I could just hold them close for an hour or more, touching their little cheeks and rubbing their little bald heads. It won't be long until they'll be up running around and won't be able to sit still for more than a few minutes at a time. So be sure not to take this time for granted. When you sit down, don't get distracted. Focus on the job at hand and enjoy it. Dr. Sears recommends that you make a breast-feeding station. Put a little table by your favorite chair that has all the things you'll need so you won't have to be interrupted: the phone, a glass of water, tissues, a good book, snacks for a toddler or sibling, even some relaxing music.

Some women claim that breast-feeding helps you burn calories and lose weight, but that's not necessarily true. Yes, you do burn more calories. But you also have to take in more calories. Now you're really eating for two. Also, I found that my body actually held on to some of the "baby weight" while I was breast-feeding—an observation confirmed by experts, who note that your body will maintain its emergency stores of fat when you're breast-feeding. In case there's a famine or some natural disaster and there's no food for Mom. So don't be surprised if you actually don't lose the last of your baby weight until after you're done breast-feeding.

You should also know that studies show that women who breast-feed have a lower incidence of breast cancer. Breast-fed babies and breast-feeding mothers tend to be generally healthier as well.

Breast-feeding is much cheaper than formula, of course, and much more convenient than sterilizing bottles and nipples and running to the store at midnight because you didn't realize you were running low on supplies.

As we've noted, breast-feeding also stimulates production of the hormone oxytocin, which in addition to helping you bond with baby causes your uterus to contract back toward its normal size. And, contrary to popular belief, you can't blame breast-feeding for droopy breasts. It's pregnancy that causes changes in the shape of your breasts—that and gravity. There are plenty of mothers who did not breast-feed who complain about having droopy breasts.

Breast-feeding is very relaxing. Your milk contains proteins that help baby relax and sleep soundly. The hormones released due to sucking also relax the mother. You'll be able to sleep better when you finally do get to sleep. And you'll have a few minutes to just relax and enjoy being with your baby every few hours. It's a forced break in a hectic day.

Last but certainly not least, my favorite benefit of breast-feeding: gorgeous cleavage. Now, this does not hold true for everyone. If the good Lord already blessed you with a generous amount of cleavage, breast-feeding may be uncomfortable at times. But for those of us who somehow missed the cleavage line on the day the boobies were being handed out, it's time for a little justice. If you are small-breasted and have suffered insults about wearing a Band-Aid as a bra and all the other abuse, this is *your* time. Breast-feeding is likely going to be much easier for you than for those well-endowed women you've been envying since junior high. You won't have to worry about blocking the baby's nose while he's eating, and you won't feel as engorged. Plus they're beautiful! For the first time in my life, I felt very blessed by the mammary goddesses, and on several occasions, I spent an afternoon in Victoria's Secret trying on sexy bras that never fit in my pre-pregnancy days and admiring my newfound gifts. For those of you who haven't read our first book (*The Mommy Chronicles*), you'll find more about my adventures in Chapter 8, which is titled "Ruling the World with an Iron Underwire." I am not ashamed to admit that part of the incentive for nursing my babies for so long really had nothing to do with the superiority of breast milk—it was simply because I looked so good in a bikini and men suddenly became mysteriously more polite. Go figure. (No pun intended.)

Breast Pumps

Until your milk supply is strong, I would recommend not even trying to use a breast pump—it's just going to frustrate you because you'll pump for fifteen minutes and have about a quarter of an inch in the bottom of the bottle to show for it. Breast pumps shouldn't be that hard to use, and you'll have better luck by waiting until you have breast-feeding mastered before you take on the challenges of a breast pump. If you do need a breast pump, be sure to choose an electric pump. If time is an issue, choose a model with two collection units so you can pump both breasts at the same time (it's a little hard to get the hang of juggling both, but you can pump in half the time). Hand-operated pumps require a lot more effort and just aren't as effective. And don't rely on batteries. Make sure you have an AC adapter. If you have to pump in the car, stop by Radio Shack with your pump and pick up an adapter for your car cigarette lighter; you'll probably be able to use the same one required for your portable DVD player. (You'll find out how valuable a DVD player is as soon as you have to take a road trip with an impatient toddler.) Some hospitals provide breast pump rentals. This is an affordable way to get a great breat pump. Call your local birthing center and ask if this service is available.

Breast-feeding in Public

There are all sorts of controversies about women breast-feeding in public. You should know that it is legal to breast-feed in public in the United States. There are only a few states that have passed laws to explicitly put into words that it is legal, but it is legal in every state. That doesn't mean that you won't encounter people who may ask you to leave because they are bothered by you nursing. If that happens, you can remind them that it is legal and normal, but please be tactful and don't react with anger. If you are asked to leave by a business, you can report it to the National Alliance for Breastfeeding Advocacy (NABA).

But here's the thing all breast-feeding mothers need to realize: the fact that it's legal to breast-feed does not mean that it's legal to expose yourself in public. If you use discretion and keep yourself covered, you probably won't have any problems. I myself have breast-fed on airplanes, at malls, in restaurants, and even once on a tour bus. I used a little cape that fastened around my neck and gave my baby and me plenty of privacy. These are available at most baby stores. Even a blanket or towel tucked into your collar can work just as well (as long as baby doesn't get handy and pull it off).

No Nudity Required

The right to breast-feed in public does not give you the right to be nude in public. Be discreet, ladies!

The right to breast-feed does not give you

the right to make other people feel uncomfortable. I recently visited a picnic area at a lake with my husband and children. There was a mother there breast-feeding her child. She was wearing a bikini and made absolutely no effort at all to conceal her breast, even after her baby had stopped sucking. She took her sweet time putting her top back in place and even walked around a little before doing so. And even I, a breast-feeding advocate, was appalled and insulted that she felt no remorse in exposing herself in front of my family. Breast-feeding in public doesn't give you the right to whip your boobies around for everyone to see. If you feel the need to make a spectacle of yourself or feel strongly that your breasts are nice enough to share with the general public, they make strip clubs for that and they'll even pay you.

If you're going to breast-feed in public, *cover up*. The key to stopping the controversy is simply discretion. The goal is to feed your baby without people around you knowing what's going on. If you're breast-feeding in public to prove a point, then you're doing it for all the wrong reasons.

Weaning Your Baby

I liken weaning my baby to their first day of kindergarten. It's like an ending to a stage of their life that I never wanted to happen. I breast-fed my son until he was almost eighteen months old. My smart-alec sister used to tease me, pretending to be my son when he was a teenager: "Oh, sure, sure, I can go to the movies after football practice. I just need a few extra minutes so I can drive home and breast-feed first." (Very funny.) I loved breast-feeding both my children, and I knew he'd be my last, so it was very emotional for me to give up that remarkable closeness. It was the end of a warm and dreamy stage in our lives as mother and child, and I was in no hurry to lose it. Being able to feed my baby with my body was always a miraculous thing to me, and I never felt more womanly or motherly. Not all mothers share my "dream state." Some are relieved and feel a new sense of freedom when the time comes to wean their baby. And there's certainly nothing wrong with that viewpoint either. The experts try to reassure us that weaning is part of the process of bringing up a healthy child. It's supposed to be a celebration of moving into the next phase of independence. (Whatever.)

The amazing thing about your body is that it will make only as much milk as you need. It is truly an incredible system! And it will only take your body a few days to recalculate and react to a diminishing demand. After a few months back at work, I was able to cut my breast-feeding down to only nighttime feedings, which worked brilliantly because I didn't have to pump breast milk for the day care workers anymore. They gave her baby food and formula during the daytime hours, and she got breast milk during the evening, nighttime, and early morning hours. This is also a great stage in the weaning process, because you can serve baby food to your growing baby but still breast-feed her during the evening hours.

When to Wean

Most experts recommend weaning sometime around baby's first birthday. The inherent sucking need usually dissipates around nine months of age, so some may lose interest around that time. But if you can't hold out that long, please don't feel guilty. Sometimes babies have to be weaned earlier than that. I had to stop at seven months with my first baby: I injured my back while carrying her car seat, and because I had to take muscle relaxants and pain pills, I couldn't breast-feed her any longer. She was already used to taking a bottle by then, so it wasn't too hard a transition for her at all. I, on the other hand, was in a state of panic and guilt over the fact that my breast-feeding stint was over against my will. Just stay open-minded—sometimes things happen that are out of your control.

Weaning Step by Step

Never wean your baby by taking away the breast cold turkey. We're not talking cigarettes here, ladies! Weaning is a slow and gradual process. Weaning too fast can cause painful engorgement for you and can be very distressing for your baby. Remember that this whole breast-feeding thing isn't just about food—it's also about a close connection with Mom too. You can start by skipping one feeding per day; choose the feeding that is most inconvenient for you. Once baby starts eating baby food and then soft table foods, you

Clutter-Busting Resources

WEBSITES

La Leche League
www.lalecheleague.org

From the American Academy of Family Physicians
www.familydoctor.org

Mayo Clinic
www.mayoclinic.com/health/breast-feeding

Parenting* and *Babytalk
www.parenting.com
Great articles and FAQs about breast-feeding

Lansinoh
www.lansinoh.com
This is the product we recommend for preventing sore nipples

National Alliance for Breastfeeding Advocacy
www.naba-breastfeeding.org

BOOKS

***The Baby Book: Everything You Need to Know About Your Baby from Birth to Age Two* (Revised and updated edition)**
by Dr. William and Martha Sears

may find that weaning isn't some project that you have to pay attention to—it will just start to happen on its own as you and baby start to do more things together and get preoccupied with new toys or places to go. Replace breast milk with formula or baby food and continue to eliminate one feeding per day. Most moms save the bedtime feeding as the last one to give up.

Sara on Bottle-feeding

The bottom line of bottle-feeding:

> **1. You have the right to feed your baby formula without guilt.**
> **2. Breast-feeding isn't right for everyone.**

Nothing stirs up an argument between mothers faster than bringing up the subject of breast-feeding versus bottle-feeding. Friendships have dissolved over the choice of breast or bottle. It's an issue that goes to the core of how women see themselves as mothers. Activism for breast-feeding is at an all-time high, with some women so militant in their beliefs that they call themselves "lactivists." There's even a group called Militant Breastfeeding Cult. I wish I was kidding. (I have a suspicion that breast-feeding is not going to solve the other slew of problems these poor kids are going to have one day as a result of being raised by these women.)

Before I had children I never knew about these groups or the zeal with which some women feel the need, even the responsibility, to convert everyone around them to lactivists. Most new moms who do choose to bottle-feed are blindsided by the criticism piled on them by breast-feeding moms who feel it is their right to judge those who don't nurse. This kind of divisiveness is exactly what Stephanie and I want to try to change among mothers. That's why I am telling you my story of why I chose to bottle-feed and Stephanie's reaction to my choice.

When I was pregnant, I read several books on breast-feeding and took a breast-feeding class at the hospital (and forced my husband to go with me), so I thought I was as prepared as I could be. My older sister, who had tried breast-feeding her children years before me, warned me that it wasn't easy. I shrugged off her comments with a "that's not going to be me" attitude. It was going to work for me. Boy, was I wrong.

Trying to nurse in the hospital was a challenge, to say the least. Every time I would attempt to breast-feed Anna, someone would inevitably pop their head in the door or a nurse would come in to take my blood pressure or visitors would knock on the door and ask if they could come in. In spite of all my preparation, I was a complete breast-feeding novice, ill equipped to handle the social challenges it created. Looking back, it's clear to me that part of what ruined breast-feeding for me was the awkwardness of it all. But I wasn't ready to give up yet. I figured things would get better when I got home.

Another, more serious problem cropped up a week after I gave birth. Postpartum depression reared its ugly head and I became a complete mess. I was weepy, felt consumed by irrational worries about everyone around me dying, and couldn't shake the feeling that nothing really mattered. I even had to force myself to eat because I had completely lost my appetite. Not exactly the state of mind conducive to breast-feeding. I didn't have the patience or even the desire to try to master breast-feeding in public, so I felt confined to the house. And when someone came over, I felt I had to go shut myself in a room to nurse the baby. Breast-feeding only added to the feeling of isolation new motherhood had created in me.

Deep down I desperately wanted to quit. I hated it. My breasts became engorged and extremely painful. I hated the leaks and embarrassing wet spots on my shirt. I hated hooking myself up to a pump that made me feel like mooing. And I really, really hated nursing shirts. With a passion. I wanted to feel like my old self again, and that meant trying to get my body back to some resemblance of what it once had been—without a baby attached to it. Feeling this way racked me with guilt. Even though I was miserable, the thought of quitting made me feel worse because I beat myself up about it. After the books and classes, I felt that bottle-feeding was almost up there with child abuse. And that just cemented the idea in my mind that I was going to be a terrible mother.

Cabbage: It's Not Just for Cole Slaw

My breasts became engorged about a week after the birth of my daughter. If your breasts become engorged, they will feel extremely full, hot, and painful for a couple of days. Even rolling over in bed hurts. Buy a head of cabbage and keep it in the fridge. Placing the cool cabbage leaves over your breasts will ease the pain and discomfort.

Fortunately, I have an awesome husband and an awesome doctor. The doctor told me that if I wanted to quit, then to quit and stop feeling guilty, doctor's orders. He told me all three of his kids had been bottle-fed and they were fine. He said, "If you can change one thing and make everything else in your life so much better, why wouldn't you do it?" My husband agreed. He wanted the old me back too. Or at least a wife who wasn't constantly crying.

When I finally made the decision to quit I felt liberated. The feelings of guilt snuck in from time to time, but eventually they went away. Bottle-feeding allowed me the mobility that breast-feeding (and my own awkwardness) didn't. I began getting out of the house more. I started taking antidepressant medication and within a month I felt like myself again. Not that motherhood didn't have its challenges and trials, but now I felt I could handle them.

What I finally came to terms with is that I had a responsibility not only to my baby but to myself too. I was the person who was the most important to my baby's survival and well-being. And if breast-feeding made me feel like putting my head in the oven, was that really helping anyone? I decided that happily bottle-feeding my baby was better than miserably breast-feeding her. Better for me and better for her.

Like Stephanie, I believe that breast-feeding is the best way to feed your baby. But there are many other factors that have to be considered—the mother's mental health being one of the most important. That's my only beef with the breast-feeding activists: the mother tends to be left out of the equation. For many of these people, there is no excuse for not breast-feeding. You're a failure if you don't. Period. That's really an unfair stance to take. We are all different, with different needs. I'm thankful I have a friend who gets that. Breast-feeding was a wonderful experience for Stephanie, but she never tried to push it on me. She never once made me feel guilty for bottle-feeding. Not once did she act sanctimonious about the fact that she breast-fed and I didn't (well, except for the fact that she constantly talked about her cleavage). That's what we mothers need to do for each other: respect our differing choices. With all the information mothers are given about breast-feeding these days, you can bet any mother who is feeding her baby formula is dealing with guilt on some level. So be her friend and don't add to her guilt by looking down on her. We don't always know all the reasons a woman chooses not to nurse. And until you've walked a mile in someone else's shoes, you have no right to judge.

But the reality is, if you are a bottle-feeder, someone is probably going to make a comment to you at some point. Something along the lines of: "Oh, you just *have* to breast-feed!" "My children never got sick because they were breast-fed," "If you had just tried longer, it would have worked," or "Too bad you didn't give it a chance." Hearing these comments, it's impossible not to have visions of this person's prodigy child reading at age four—in Spanish—while your kid runs around with a bucket on his head banging into walls. And surely it's all because you didn't breast-feed him. You have *ruined* his life.

Relax. Formula now is a far cry from what it used to be. No, it's not breast milk, but it is wonderful, healthy nutrition for your baby. Some of the most intelligent people alive today were formula-fed. If your kid is running around with a bucket on his head, blame it on the genes from his father's side of the family, but don't blame it on formula. And remember, no one has the right to make you feel guilty about your choice to formula-feed. Know that you made the best choice for you and your family at the time. Let the lactivists have their combat boots. Because when it's all said and done, nobody's going to win a medal.

The Benefits of Bottle-feeding

No Iron Deficiency

Here's the little secret no breast-feeding advocate is going to tell you: breast-fed babies are often iron-deficient. When my daughter was a baby the pediatrician would ask me at every well check whether she was exclusively breast-fed. Finally I asked him why, and he said because they are usually deficient in iron, whereas formula-fed babies aren't because formula is fortified with iron.

Sharing the Nighttime Feedings

It was easy for my husband and me to share the middle-of-the-night feeding responsibilities because he could give the baby a bottle just like I could. This allowed me to get some much-needed sleep and get over my postpartum depression faster.

Eat All the Garlic You Want

In a lot of ways, breast-feeding is like still being pregnant. You have to watch what you eat in case the baby reacts to it with gas, an upset tummy, or even an allergy. Spicy or garlicky foods often don't go over well with an infant. You also have to be very careful about what medicines you take, how much caffeine you drink, and consuming alcohol.

You Can Get a Break

If you have to take a trip (or want to take a trip) or go away for the weekend with your hubby, Grandma or the babysitter can easily give your baby a bottle. Exclusively breast-fed babies may have a difficult time learning to take a bottle, making it hard for mom to get a break or get away.

Bottle-fed Babies Sleep Longer

Formula takes longer for a baby's tummy to digest than breast milk, so they stay full longer and as a result sleep longer.

Have Formula, Will Travel

Bottle-feeding is more convenient now than ever. Formula companies such as Similac and Enfamil now make individual-serving-size packets of powdered formula that you can just mix with room-temperature water when you are out and about—no warming required.

What You Need to Know About Bottle-feeding

- You have the right to bottle-feed without guilt.
- Formula is a perfectly acceptable and healthy food for your baby.
- Your happiness as a mother should be a factor in the choice of how to feed.
- Breast-feeding and bottle-feeding both have their pros and cons.

The Bottle-feeding Mom's Bill of Rights

Only a mom can know what's best for her baby—and for herself. So, instead of letting someone else guilt-trip you, know your rights, as presented by Parenting.com's Emily Hebert.

1. You have a right to bottle-feed without guilt or lengthy excuses. Sure, some moms aren't able to breast-feed for health reasons. "There are women determined to breast-feed who just aren't able to produce enough milk," explains Phillip Stubblefield, M.D., a professor of obstetrics and gynecology at the Boston University School of Medicine. But whether it's health-related, because of painful side effects, or for another reason entirely, don't feel that you have to explain yourself to avoid being publicly ostracized. "Women have the right to decide what's best for themselves and for their baby," says Diane Sanford, Ph.D., who specializes in women's health. If you feel good about yourself and your choices, those positive feelings will get passed on to your infant.

2. You have a right to supplement nursing with formula or breast milk. Don't feel like you have to choose one method or the other. Many women prefer a combination of breast and bottle. (Be aware that if you choose to supplement with formula, you'll have a decreased milk supply if you don't pump regularly.)

3. You have a right to bottle-feed without trying to breast-feed first. "Trust your instincts," says Sanford. "There's not a lot of encouraging literature out there about bottle-feeding. The worst situation is if a mom wants to bottle-feed but is persuaded by others to breast-feed."

While breast-feeding may be ideal, there's nothing wrong with using formula, says Mel Heyman, M.D., a member of the American Academy of Pediatrics committee on nutrition and a professor of pediatrics at the University of California, San Francisco. What's most important to your baby's development is love, affection, and a close emotional bond. Says Sanford: "Whether it's breast or bottle, you can still provide these things to a baby."

Clutter-Busting Resources

Breast-feeding vs. formula-feeding

www.kidshealth.org/parent/growth/feeding/breast_bottle_feeding.html

Bottle-feeding basics

www.babycenter.com/refcap/752.html

4

Accepting Help

From Stephanie

Why is it so hard for some of us to ask for help? Is it because we hate feeling indebted to someone? Does asking for help send a message that we can't accomplish motherhood on our own? These are all thoughts that you need to put out of your mind because once your baby is here everything changes. The demands on a new mother are extraordinary, and on top of those demands, you'll be sleep-deprived and recovering from a major bodily trauma. This is no time for the supermom syndrome. Instead, sit back, relax, and enjoy whatever help comes your way. Let your relatives hold your baby, let them bring you meals, and use the new-baby audience to give yourself time to heal and rest. All moms know how it feels once the excitement wears off, everybody else goes home, and you're left feeling alone and overwhelmed. Here are a few tips to help you help yourself:

- **Sleep when your baby sleeps.** You'll feel as if you have a million things to do. But one of the most important things you can do is take naps. Turn off the phone, put a note on the front door, and sleep. Your body needs it, and your baby needs you to be well and rested. The laundry can wait, or you can show your husband how easy it is to separate colors from whites when he gets home. Growing a baby in your body and giving birth takes a lot out of a girl, and you need rest to fully recover.
- **Accept help.** If your neighbors or relatives offer, say yes! And don't be afraid to *ask* for help. Trust me, all moms understand. If you need something from the

grocery store or just a little babysitting, please ask. When I brought my son home from the hospital, my neighbors all got together and brought me dinner every night for a whole week. It was wonderful! I didn't have to worry about groceries or cooking, and it was fun to get new recipes. Some of them even included a little gift for the baby and his big sister. It meant more to me than they will ever know. In fact, every time I tell that story I get tears in my eyes. And now whenever one of the moms I know comes home from the hospital, I always try to bring her family a meal. Moms need each other, and we're always happy to reach out and help a fellow mom. That's why you shouldn't be afraid to ask if you need help.

- **Eat good food.** Think about what you're eating and put some thought into your own diet. Your body is recovering, you're probably breast-feeding, and your body needs the right nutrients to stay healthy. Eat plenty of nutrient-dense foods (not sugary ones like desserts). Think meats for protein, fruits, veggies, and (yes, even though you're worried about all that baby weight) carbohydrates. Choose healthy carbs like whole grains and fruit. Iron is an important nutrient for a breast-feeding mother, and you can find it in chicken, fish, and iron-fortified cereals. Your doctor will probably recommend that you continue taking your prenatal vitamins while you are breast-feeding to help meet the demands of your healing body. And if you are breast-feeding, you'll need lots and lots of water. Try to drink at least eight glasses a day. I used to feel thirsty every time baby latched on, so I made sure I never sat down to breast-feed unless I had a glass of water at my side. Even my husband became accustomed to bringing me a glass of water if he saw me sit down to breast-feed (I only had to ask three hundred times, but they can eventually learn).
- **Don't be afraid to leave the house.** The first outing with baby can be a little overwhelming, but don't be afraid to give it a try. Even if it's just a quick trip to the grocery store or to a friend's house, it will do you some good to get out and enjoy a change of scenery. (See Chapter 10, "Your First Outing with Baby.")
- **Find a way to connect with other new moms.** Play groups, Gymboree, or your local coffee shop will become the hub of your social life now that you're a mom. And it's easier to make friends than ever before because now you're in the club. You'll soon realize that whatever you're struggling with is normal—and you'll find out that your fellow moms either have a simple solution or are facing the same challenge. Women need women—we're just wired that way—and connecting with a few girlfriends will help ward off depression and hormonal mood variations (which is a nice way of saying that if you have some good friends, you probably won't be such a bitch to your husband).

From Sara

Whether we admit it or not, deep down, women want to think we can do it all. It's against our nature to ask for help. Personally, I think we'd all be much happier if we embraced the fact that each of us is just one person and can't do everything. But our heads are filled with stories about the women before us who raised children without indoor plumbing or disposable diapers and we think, *Who are we to complain?* We tend to forget that those women often had help from family that lived close by or even in the same house. These days many of us moms live hundreds of miles away from our parents and siblings, so the assistance we can get from family is sporadic at best.

There's something in a woman's nature that makes it oh so difficult for us to accept an offer of help or kindness, or even a compliment from a friend! Unfortunately, this mind-set holds true even at a time when we need help the most: after having a baby.

Can you imagine going into the hospital for several days to have surgery and then coming home only to be awakened every few hours by someone who requires that you take care of their every need? That's exactly what happens when you have a baby. New moms are expected to recover from the trauma of childbirth while getting less sleep than a Marine in boot camp. Why do we feel guilty letting Dad or a grandparent take one of the middle-of-the-night shifts? They didn't just push something the size of a watermelon out of something the diameter of a lemon. They aren't sore, don't have stitches, aren't bleeding profusely . . . heck, they probably don't even *know* what a peri bottle is. Hello? You're the one who's recovering, remember?

I made the mistake of trying to do it all after my first baby, and I wound up completely sleep-deprived and depressed. When baby number two came along I had learned my lesson. In the hospital, I let the nurses take him to the nursery every night so I could get a full night's rest. At home, I let my mother help with the nighttime feedings and got to sleep for more than just a couple of hours at a time. And I was much happier for it.

I always chuckle to myself when I hear expectant parents say that they don't want any extended family as houseguests when they come home from the hospital. They want time to bond with the baby and be a family. I've seen many new parents quickly change their minds once the baby arrives. Of course it's natural to want some space; it's just that until you come home with a newborn, you don't realize how often the baby needs to be fed and how many diapers you have to change and how sore and tired you are and how many bottles there are to sterilize. After a few days of getting little to no sleep, not having time to shower, eating cold pizza, and watching the pile of dirty laundry grow at an alarming rate, you quickly realize it's time to call in reinforcements.

After I had my daughter, Anna, my mother stayed at our house for a week. She made wonderful dinners every night, did the laundry, went shopping for groceries, watched the baby so I could take a nap—I don't know how I could have done it without her. When she graciously said to David and me that she could stay as long as we needed her, he said, "How about till Anna goes to kindergarten?"

If a friend or a relative offers to look after the baby so you can get some sleep, just say yes and thank you. Before you instinctively answer with no, remember that your body needs to heal and you need to rest. So if someone volunteers to help, take them up on it. Give the baby to a nurse or to Grandma or Daddy and sleep. Trust me, you're not going to miss anything if someone else takes care of your little one for a few hours.

Clutter-Busting Resources

Yahoo! Health: Recovering from childbirth
http://health.yahoo.com/topic/pregnancy/afterdelivery/article/healthwise/tp22262

Recovering after childbirth
http://welcomeaddition.com/afterchildbirth.aspx

5

Sleeping Babies

Any bookseller will tell you that the most consistent best sellers are books on how to get babies to go to sleep. That's because parents are sleep-deprived, miserable, and desperate. The truth is, sleeping or not sleeping happens in stages. There are going to be periods when your baby sleeps "like a baby," and there are going to be periods when it seems like baby won't sleep at all. There are all kinds of strategies for all kinds of families, and you just have to find the one that works for you—every family is different and every child is different. The most important thing to remember is that it's all a stage. If your baby is sleeping through the night, you'd better not brag about it, because it will change. And if your baby screams through the night, take comfort because this too shall pass. We chose completely opposite paths for our babies and their sleep strategies, and we hope you can learn from one of us.

Stephanie on Sleeping with Your Baby

There are plenty of experts out there who preach that sleeping with your children is a bad thing. But for my family, it was a wonderful thing. It all started in the hospital the night my daughter was born. I was exhausted from a very long labor. My husband was sacked out in the chair next to me, snoring. And our new baby was in the little Plexiglas bassinet on the opposite side of the room . . . screaming her head off. I had tried everything: feeding her, rocking her, talking to her—nothing was working. Finally a nurse came to my aid and told me to put her in bed with me. She said the heat from the mother's body sometimes comforted babies who weren't used to lying alone in a cold, hard bassinet. It worked like a charm, and worked for years afterward. Not only did she stop crying, but that was the first moment I really bonded with her. She went from feeling like a little alien in a plastic box across the room to my precious baby. I loved snuggling with her, and she loved it too because she immediately calmed down and slept.

When we came home from the hospital, I learned that breast-feeding and co-sleeping go together. I was able to feed her through the night without leaving my bed. She would latch on and nurse while I dozed, and then we could continue cuddling as she fell asleep, drunk with breast milk and comforted by the warmth from my body. I always felt sorry for poor Sara, who got up in the middle of the night, dragged herself to the kitchen to mix and heat a bottle, and then sat in a chair and fed her baby night after night, when all I had to do was roll over and go back to sleep. If you are breast-feeding your baby, I highly recommend you try co-sleeping. You'll be the most well-rested mother on the block.

The other advantage for me was that once I returned to work, it was a way for me to reconnect with her after being away from her all day. I loved being able to be close to her during the nighttime hours, since I couldn't be with her during the day.

The problem was that I was ashamed to admit to anyone that I was sleeping with her. I knew it felt right. I knew it made her happy. I knew that my husband and I shared beautiful moments together lying in our bed with our little sleeping beauty between us, talking about how perfect she was and how in love we were with her. Even he enjoyed being so close to her. I knew it made breast-feeding easier during the night, and I loved it. But I had heard so many bad things associated with sleeping with your baby. I even lied to the day care workers (how they ever got her to sleep in a crib during the day, I'll never know). And then I found *The Baby Book* by William and Martha Sears. Suddenly I knew why it felt so right, and I was armed with the knowledge to plead my case if anyone questioned my decision to sleep with my baby. I learned that anyone who looked down on me for this choice had simply been made ignorant by our societal beliefs and simply didn't know all the benefits associated with co-sleeping. And I was just the mother to educate them. (Note: The Searses' books helped me more than any other baby books I found, and so you'll find that I refer to their works often. My parenting style matched with their theories, and I feel their books explain topics in more depth than most.)

I have to say I totally agree with Dr. Sears when he explains that it is "a natural, appropriate, and desirable part of development for a baby to be dependent. A baby needs to have needs." Babies aren't *supposed* to sleep through the night. Our culture has some sick and twisted contest going on in which everyone tries to be the first to get our babies to sleep through the night. If you start bragging to me about how your six-week-old is sleeping through the night, you'd better buckle up, because that is a ridiculous thing to say and I'm going to take you down. Babies are not programmed to sleep through the night. That's why they need parents. Babies sleep differently than we do—they have shorter sleep cycles and they don't sleep as deeply—so they wake up during the night. If

The Benefits of Sleeping with Baby

- Baby falls asleep easier and stays asleep longer.
- It makes nighttime breast-feeding much easier.
- Mother gets more rest.
- Don't be ashamed of co-sleeping; it's actually the norm except in the United States.
- Recent studies show that it may help prevent SIDS.
- It's a great way to reconnect and bond with baby.

you're forcing your newborn baby to sleep through the night by letting him cry it out, you're probably causing your baby to miss an important stage in his development, the stage where he learns to trust you. And by the way, the medical definition of "sleeping through the night" is five hours.

Sleeping with your baby is not unusual. In fact, ours is one of the only societies in the world where sleeping with your baby isn't mainstream. Babies have been sleeping with their mothers since the beginning of time. It's very natural. I'm not sure when the "experts" decided that it was suddenly a bad thing to do. But putting your baby in a crib or even in a separate room is definitely an American custom that seems strange to the rest of the world.

There's also a method called, among other things, the cry-it-out technique. I know that a lot of moms have had great success with this strategy. It just doesn't work for every baby. For me, the cry-it-out method just didn't feel right. That's partly because our baby was so stubborn that when we tried it, she cried so long and hard that she actually vomited. To us, it seemed cruel to cause her to become that upset. And partly it's because of my belief that young babies aren't supposed to go to sleep on their own, or stay asleep through the night. Crying it out totally contradicted my own parenting style. Breast-feeding and co-sleeping meant a peaceful, quiet bedtime from babyhood through childhood. Breast-feeding at bedtime turned into reading stories, talking about the day, and tickling and cuddling them to sleep. As of this writing, my children are six and seven years of age and we regularly let them cuddle and fall asleep in our bed before we move them to their own rooms. It has become a special time of day for our family. It feels really good and it works for us. They'll be locking us out of their rooms soon enough.

You Won't Suffocate Your Baby

Suffocation is very rare, and usually happens because the parent is under the influence of alcohol or some kind of drug or sleep aid. If your baby is in bed with you, you know it even when you're sound asleep. Even though you are sleeping deeply, you are physically and mentally aware. But there are definitely precautions that have to be taken if you choose to sleep with your baby, which is why the American Academy of Pediatrics does not recommend sleeping with children under age two. Just like assembling the crib, there is some setup involved with co-sleeping:

- Use a guardrail so baby can sleep between the mother and the guardrail (not between parents). Fathers don't have the same hormones and instincts, and it's safer to keep baby on the outside of the bed rather than between two people.
- The same mattress rules that apply for a crib also apply for your bed. Do not put your baby on a pillow or a mattress that is too soft. He could bury his face into it and suffocate. Pillow-top mattresses are a bad choice for co-sleeping. And absolutely no waterbeds.
- Be sure that your bedding is not too heavy, and don't use too many pillows that could land on baby's face. Keep blankets, sheets, and pets away from your baby's face.
- Check your bed and mattress for gaps, such as between the mattress and headboard, where baby could get stuck. Some co-sleeping parents choose to put their mattress directly on the floor until baby gets a little older.
- Don't overdress your baby. Sleeping with your baby means you'll be sharing body heat, and babies can get overheated.
- A bigger bed works best. If you have a bed smaller than a king or queen, things are going to get a little crowded. A crowded bed is not a safe space for a baby.
- *Never* sleep with your baby if you have been drinking or are using any kind of drug that induces sleep or drowsiness.
- Always keep your baby on her back when sleeping.

Co-sleeping and SIDS

Studies have proven that sleeping with your baby can actually help decrease the chance of SIDS. The warmth from mother's body helps stimulate the part of the baby's brain that regulates breathing.

Frequently Asked Questions About Co-sleeping

Is SIDS More Likely with Co-sleeping?

Does sleeping with your baby increase or decrease the risk of sudden infant death syndrome (SIDS)? There are many opinions and many studies about SIDS. The best way to explain SIDS is that some infants have a diminished ability to rouse themselves from sleep. So if their airway is blocked or they are having trouble breathing, they don't automatically wake up. A recent international survey found that babies are much less likely to die of SIDS if they co-sleep.

By six months of age, a baby's breathing system matures and he can restart his breathing himself if it stops for some reason. Between birth and six months of age is a vulnerable period when your baby is learning to sleep deeper and sleep through the night, but his regulating system is not yet mature—that's when the risk of SIDS reaches its peak. Sleeping with your baby can reduce this risk because mother and baby begin to develop what Dr. Sears calls a sleep harmony. The mother's breath helps stimulate the baby's breath. Your baby feels your presence and is more aware, and some studies claim that warmth from the mother's body actually stimulates the part of the baby's brain that regulates breathing. And studies show that in cultures where co-sleeping is common, babies have lower incidences of SIDS. Babies who breast-feed and co-sleep with their mother wake more frequently and sleep for shorter periods at a time.

Will It Ruin Our Sex Life?

Co-sleeping didn't ruin my sex life. Becoming a parent ruined my sex life. I'm exhausted at the end of the day. After you become a parent, you'll soon realize that nothing is as important as sleep. Having a baby in our bed never affected our sex life. Our children sleep so soundly, they don't even know we're in the same room. (I know they'll appreciate reading that last sentence when they're in their teens.) Or there are other rooms in the house. You can always transfer baby into another bedroom for a while. And timing is everything. You have to work around their schedules whether they're in your bed or not.

Will They Have Trouble Sleeping in Their Own Room?

Yes, I have to admit, this is the part that has given us the most trouble. My children stayed in our bed for years. I loved it; my husband eventually thought it was getting out of control. Some experts agree that a good time to transition them to their own crib is around eight months of age, when they are mature enough to sleep through the night. Dr. Sears recommends sometime around age two or three. It's a lot like weaning them from the breast. Do it gradually, perhaps starting with a futon at the foot of your bed and then working your way to baby's room. Our children would always start out in their own rooms and end up in our bed before daybreak. And that's perfectly natural. I have friends who used the cry-it-out approach with their babies, and at age five they were climbing into bed with their parents in the middle of the night too. Why not embrace it? Snuggle with them while you can. The time goes by so fast, and soon they won't even want to hold your hand anymore, let alone cuddle in your bed.

Sara on Crib Sleeping

I had it all planned out when I was pregnant. The baby would sleep in the room with me at the hospital, then when she came home she would sleep in a Pack 'n Play in our bedroom so we could be close to her and keep an eye on her. Well, we kept an eye on her all right. I'll never forget the first night David and I spent at home as parents, away from the safety and security of the hospital and the ever-present nurses. We were terrified. Every time the baby made the slightest noise, I sat up and looked into the Pack 'n Play, only to notice that David was sitting up and staring too. We were sure she was going to stop breathing at any moment and that we needed to check on every little sound she made, all of which we easily heard because she was sleeping right next to our bed.

After three nights of this we were walking zombies. We knew we had to get some sleep, and we weren't going to get it with the baby in our room. So we moved her to her crib in her room, which was a whopping three steps away from our bedroom. We plugged in the baby monitor and went to sleep. And sleep we did—at least for two or three hours at a time, until she needed to be fed.

I never even considered putting the baby in the bed with us, but I have heard so many breast-feeding moms say how much easier it is. So maybe if I had breast-fed for longer I would have put the baby in the bed. Then again, maybe not, because I don't have a king-size bed like Stephanie. Size matters when you're co-sleeping. Those little boogers can take up a lot of room!

Even though I had no desire for co-sleeping with my kids when they were babies, I understood why it was important to Stephanie, particularly after she went back to work. Co-sleeping was a way for her to reconnect and spend more time with her baby.

Since I was at home with my baby, day in and day out, the break I got at night when I could put her in her own crib was heavenly. I needed that time to decompress and unwind. And when David and I went away for a few days when Anna was four months old, my parents were able to easily put her to sleep in her own crib because she was used to it.

Tips for Sound Slumber

Letting Babies Cry

After the baby had been fed, burped, and changed, sometimes she still wouldn't settle back down to sleep right away. After she was a couple of months old, David and I decided to let her cry for a few minutes at a time. We'd check on her but not pick her up, and she would soon go to sleep. It never took more than five or ten minutes, although that seems like a painfully long time when a baby is crying in the room next to you. We used to watch the clock until we could go back in and check on her. I didn't let her cry it out all the time, but sometimes after an hour of trying to get her back to sleep, it seemed like the best option. And my daughter quickly became a good sleeper and is to this day.

Twelve Is the Magic Number

A pediatrician told me once that twelve is the magic number when it comes to sleeping through the night. That's twelve weeks old and twelve pounds. That doesn't mean that your baby will automatically sleep through the night the moment he turns twelve weeks and hits twelve pounds on the scale. Rather, this is the threshold they must cross before sleeping through the night is realistically possible. For those sleep-deprived mothers out there desperate for relief, you'll be happy to know that both my babies slept through the night shortly after the twelve-week, twelve-pound mark. Hang in there.

Let Them Be Little

And let them sleep in the middle. Like the country song, that's what I believe. Now that my kids are older, I am a fan of co-sleeping . . . at least for a little while. Our kids love to fall asleep in the bed with Mommy and Daddy, and although we always move them into their own beds, they often end up back in ours. That's fine with me. Before I know it they won't even want to be seen in public with me, so I am enjoying this while I can. I just wish I had a bigger bed!

Pacifiers

The following sentence is the only thing you really need to know about pacifiers: *if it allows you to get some sleep and makes your baby happy, then use one.*

From Stephanie

Oh, sure, you're going to hear and read all kinds of horrors relating to the use of pacifiers. But it's all pretty much over-the-top nonsense. The bottom line is that babies are born with an intense need to suck. It's an instinct. They were sucking their thumbs in your womb. Pacifiers are a wonderful way to comfort a baby; however, not all babies like pacifiers. My daughter was one of those babies who really needed a pacifier for survival (both hers and mine). She was restless and found great satisfaction holding one in her mouth. My son, on the other hand, had absolutely no interest in a pacifier at all. He would spit it out as soon as it touched his lips. Fortunately, he was such an easy and happy baby, he didn't need one. But some babies do need to "learn" to hold the pacifier in their mouths. They'll spit it out and start to cry, so you have to keep putting it back in until they get the hang of it.

So what's all the fuss about pacifiers? Much like every other parenting standard we stress about, the pacifier taboo is simply a societal thing. Pacifiers bother adults way more than they bother children. Apparently there was a time when pacifiers were considered unacceptable. That's why you'll eventually hear Grandma or some senior citizen comment negatively about your baby's pacifier. Just ignore them—remember, these people come from a time when baby formula was a concoction of evaporated milk and Karo syrup and medical research believed that breast-feeding was bad for babies (you can remind them of that if you find it useful). There is nothing about using a pacifier that is bad for your baby, and you need the peace and quiet for your own sanity.

Some of the Arguments You'll Hear Against Pacifiers

1. "Pacifiers cause nipple confusion." There's that phrase again. Honestly, when did the word *nipple* become so confusing? Some experts believe that baby will get confused and have trouble breast-feeding if you're introducing too many nipples in the beginning. I've personally never heard of that actually happening. I'm sure there are a few cases of it out there, but I think it's rarer than the experts would have you believe. As a lactation consultant once said, "There may be nipple preference, but not nipple confusion." No baby is going to stop breast-feeding because he prefers his pacifier to his mother's breast. Puh-leeze.

2. "A pacifier will deform your baby's teeth." Here's what I've always wondered: how can it harm your baby's front teeth when they're all going to fall out before the child is five anyway? Granted, if your child is using a pacifier past age two, you could see some malformations in your child's bite. Pacifiers are for babies only, not toddlers. If your toddler is running around with a pacifier in her mouth, you probably *are* abusing the privilege. It is best to get rid of the pacifier around the time baby starts walking.

3. "It's too hard to get rid of them." Here's the funny thing about pacifiers. It's not the kids who are afraid to try to get rid of them—it's always the parents. We dreaded trying to take our daughter's "passie" away. We thought it was going to mean days of sleep deprivation, crying, and gnashing of teeth. But in fact, it took less than two days to break her of the habit. There was no crying involved. She asked a few times and we told her it was "all gone," and that was that. I can't tell you how many mothers have told us the same story. "It wasn't as bad as we thought." This is probably the *only* time as a mother you'll ever be able to mutter that phrase. And when you do decide the time is right, quit cold turkey and stick to your guns *no matter what*, or the second time you quit could be as bad as you were anticipating. Consider that getting rid of a pacifier is a lot easier than trying to break the habit of thumb sucking—you can't leave their thumb at home—and since thumb sucking usually goes on longer, it definitely can cause bite malformations.

One Final Note About Pacifiers

Please be careful not to replace your own hugs and mommy comforts with a pacifier. Babies need to be held and comforted by their parents. So don't let yourself get into the habit of shoving a pacifier in your baby's mouth every time he cries. Don't forget, they cry for many reasons.

AAP Recommendations on Pacifiers

The American Academy of Pediatrics approves of the use of pacifiers in baby's first year. The AAP also says giving babies pacifiers at naptime and bedtime may reduce the risk of sudden infant death syndrome.

Clutter-Busting Resources

Dr. Sears on co-sleeping
www.askdrsears.com/html/10/t102200.asp

Safe co-sleeping from Club Mom
www.clubmom.com/display/268366

All about pacifiers
http://parenting.aol.com/parenting/onlyonaol/search/1,20391,,00.html?invocationType=parents&search_string=pacifiers&submit=Search

Pacifiers may reduce SIDS
http://abcnews.go.com/GMA/OnCall/story?id=1199058&page=1

Great pacifiers to purchase
www.sassybaby.com

6

Postpartum Depression

From Sara

I never in a million years expected postpartum depression (PPD) to happen to me. I thought it was some kind of fringe thing that happened to just a few women who probably weren't cut out to be mothers in the first place. So what did I have to worry about? I wasn't going to be one of *those* women. I was sure of it. (I don't know where these beliefs came from or if I even realized I held them—I certainly never said anything like that out loud.) Though clearly way off the mark, these ideas were certainly in my subconscious.

The reality is, postpartum depression isn't a fringe thing at all. Roughly one out of every ten women will go through depression after giving birth. And many experts say that number is a very conservative one. Postpartum depression is incredibly common, although you wouldn't know it because few women talk about it openly. I was one of those women. Postpartum depression snuck up and pulled the rug out from under me. It rocked my foundation and made me question nearly everything I thought I knew about myself.

When I found out I was pregnant, I was thrilled. I couldn't wait to be a mother. My pregnancy was planned after five years of marriage during which David and I had traveled and bonded. We loved the city where we lived, and we were building our dream home. The timing was perfect. Everything I always wanted was coming to fruition. I planned to leave my career and become a stay-at-home mom. I counted down the days with anticipation, painstakingly decorating the nursery, reveling in picking out colors and patterns. One night after a baby shower, I sat on the floor of the nursery and assembled our new stroller, then put stuffed animals in it and pushed it around the house as David laughed at my goofiness. I pored over *What to Expect When You're Expecting* and *Your Pregnancy Week by Week*. I bored my friends talking about how big my developing baby was. "This week the baby is the size of a banana!" I'd announce as their eyes glazed over.

No one was more ready and more excited to become a mom than I was. Postpartum depression? I didn't give it a second thought. What I didn't understand is that just because you *want* your baby doesn't exempt you from PPD. Women who go through depression aren't less capable of being mothers; they don't want their babies less or become depressed because their baby wasn't planned. But I had to go through it myself to truly understand that.

Everything was fine until about a week after I gave birth to my daughter. I'd had lots of help from David and my mom and mother-in-law. I felt fine, just as I'd expected. Then the time came for David to go back to work and for the grandmothers to return to their homes a state away. The first day alone it hit me full force. A week of very little sleep, nose-diving hormones, and two huge life changes (motherhood and leaving my job) all came crashing down on me. I felt as if my life was over. I was now responsible for another human being, and the weight of that felt like too much to bear. I was jealous that David was able to get in his car and leave to go to work with other adults. I went stir-crazy and counted the hours until he came home in the evening. And I cried a lot. I was committed to breast-feeding, but it seemed that's what I spent every minute of the day doing. I was confined to the house because I didn't feel comfortable nursing in public or in the car. I felt as if the walls were closing in on me.

PPD Signs and Symptoms

- Changes in appetite and sleep patterns
- Exhaustion
- Feeling hopeless, sad, or depressed
- Frequent crying
- Loss of interest in activities you used to enjoy
- Withdrawal from friends and family
- Feelings of guilt or worthlessness
- Lack of interest in the baby
- Trouble doing normal daily tasks
- Lack of motivation
- Thoughts of harming baby or self

The baby began to feel like a burden, not a joy. With each passing day, I lost interest in her. Though I never neglected her, I was just going through the motions. Neighbors and friends came to visit and I forced smiles and acted as if everything was fine. I tried to pass off my lack of joy as just being overly tired. Gifts arrived in the mail and the boxes sat on the kitchen counter unopened. I couldn't imagine ever feeling like a normal mother. I wondered what was wrong with me and feared that I'd made a terrible mistake deciding to have a baby.

"Postpartum depression is not a character flaw but a chemical imbalance."

—Paul A. Gluck, M.D., American College of Obstetrics and Gynecology

At first I thought it was the "baby blues" everyone talks about, even though it felt a lot worse than the blues. All the books said the baby blues usually passed within a week or two. So I waited. Every morning I'd wake up and take my mental temperature to see if I felt any better, but I didn't.

I'd always been an avid reader, but suddenly I had no interest in books. I love interior decorating and home design magazines and television shows, but at that point I couldn't have cared less. Everything felt pointless. I felt hopeless. And I couldn't shake it.

Two weeks (which seemed more like two years) passed with me in this dismal state and I still wasn't improving. I was overcome with despair, and the truth is, life didn't feel worth living. Yet I still wasn't able to talk to anyone about it other than my mom, David, Stephanie, and one or two other friends. Even then, I couldn't admit to anyone the depth of what I was really feeling. It was too awful and I felt too ashamed. It still pains me to write about it all this time later. No mother wants to think of herself as having a lack of interest in or desire for her child, even if it is the result of a collision of hormones, sleep deprivation, and emotional upheaval.

Is It the Baby Blues or Postpartum Depression?

The baby blues can be characterized by mood swings, sadness, crying, irritability, and trouble sleeping. The symptoms are not severe and tend to go away within a few days or a week after giving birth. With postpartum depression, however, these symptoms don't go away, don't improve, and can interfere with a woman's well-being and her ability to function on a daily basis.

David and I decided that it was time for me to see my doctor. My regular obstetrician was on vacation, so I met with one of the other doctors in the group. I was nervous about admitting what I was going through to a doctor, but I was so miserable that I figured if he could help me, it was worth it. Dr. Craig Gourley put me instantly at ease. By the reassuring expression on his face, I could see that what I was saying was all very familiar to him, and I knew I was in a safe place to be open and honest. "I'm trying really hard to breast-feed," I said, fighting back tears, "but I just don't like it." Tears started rolling down my face.

Dr. Gourley said, "My wife breast-fed for about fifteen seconds and she said that was enough for her." I looked up, and he was grinning. I felt a tiny smile break out on my face. "Sara, if you want to quit, quit," he said earnestly.

"But, but . . . ," I sputtered, "breast-feeding is so much better for the baby."

"Yes, but it has to be working for *you*. You have to take into consideration your well-being. If you can change this one thing and make everything else in your life better, then that's what you should do. And whatever you do, don't beat yourself up about it."

"But . . . I feel guilty," I said.

At that point Dr. Gourley turned to his credenza, picked up a photo of his three kids, and handed it to me. They looked like normal, healthy teenagers. "Listen, I'm a doctor and my kids were all bottle-fed. Look at them; they're *fine*."

Dr. Gourley went on to say that thousands of women had suffered from PPD and had gotten through it. We talked about all the major changes going on in my life at that

Sleeping in the Hospital

I checked into the hospital at 3:00 A.M. My daughter wasn't born until the next night at 8:00 P.M. Then I decided to keep her in the room with me through the night so that I could nurse her. As a result, I got very little sleep in the hospital. I came home seriously sleep-deprived. With my son, I took advantage of the wonderful, highly trained baby nurses and let them feed him through the night. I got two solid nights of sleep in the hospital before coming home, and it made a big difference.

moment: I'd just given birth, I was exhausted from the rigors of taking care of a new baby, I'd left my career to become a stay-at-home mom, and I was no longer financially independent. He explained that hormones can actually create a chemical imbalance in the brain in some women. Hormones result in drastic changes in the body during and after pregnancy, and some women are much more sensitive to those changes than others because of receptors in their brains. Then there's the sleep deprivation new moms endure. Even if you're getting six or seven hours a night, you're rarely sleeping straight through, which doesn't give the brain and body enough time to go through all the sleep cycles and get the rest they need. And if you happen to go into labor in the middle of the night, like I did, plus keep the baby in the room with you through the nights in the hospital, you're already significantly lacking sleep by the time you arrive home. Sleep deprivation alone has been known to cause depression. So you can see how these factors can collide and lead to a big problem.

Dr. Gourley advised me to get out of the house every day and to try to get some exercise (which is really hard to do when you feel that the world is about to end), since exercise is a known mood elevator and releases endorphins that can help with the depression. He also suggested that David take on the middle-of-the-night feedings so I could get a few nights of uninterrupted sleep. Then he gave me a prescription for an antidepressant that I could fill if I wanted to. And most important, he said words to me that I will never forget: "This *will* get better."

That conversation was a turning point for me. Leaving Dr. Gourley's office that day, I felt something I hadn't felt in weeks: hope. Until that point, I hadn't believed that things would get better. I'm sure it's difficult for anyone who hasn't gone through postpartum depression to understand how a woman can be on an absolute high after the birth of her healthy baby only to fall into an incredibly dark place just a few weeks later. That's the cruelty of PPD. You have so much to be happy about—how could anyone feel hopeless? Well, I am here to tell you it happens. It happens to women who have no history of depression and to those who do. It happens to those who feel incredibly prepared and those who don't. It doesn't mean that anything is wrong with you as a mother or a person. Postpartum depression is a physiological issue. It isn't a character flaw.

Treating PPD

Medication

The good news is there's help. There are lots of ways to treat PPD, but what most people talk about is antidepressants. Not everyone needs medication, but many women do. When the doctor wrote me a prescription for an antidepressant, the stigma that still surrounds mental illness slapped me right in the face. In my mind, taking medication meant admitting failure. It meant something was wrong with me that I couldn't fix on my own. And shouldn't we be able to fix our mental problems on our own? Pull yourself up by your bootstraps and all that? For me, the reality was that unless I knew how to stop the reuptake of serotonin in my brain (that's the chemical process through which my antidepressant worked), I wasn't going to be able to fix my problem. I don't know about you, but I missed that class in college.

Yet I still couldn't bring myself to fill the prescription. Two more weeks passed and I still felt utterly miserable. I was sinking deeper into depression and had made myself a wreck fretting over whether or not to take the medication. Finally I said, "Enough!" and filled the prescription. When you get low enough, you don't care about social stigma anymore. I just wanted to feel better; I didn't care how.

Now my only regret is that I didn't take the medicine sooner. After a week of taking it, I could feel a difference. After the second week I felt much better. And after three or four weeks I felt like myself again. Medication gave me my life back. At last I could enjoy my baby. I could smile and laugh again. Life was worth living, and I began to love motherhood the way I always knew in my heart I would.

There are a lot of misconceptions about antidepressants. They don't make you feel happy all the time or make you numb to your emotions and the events going on around you. They just make a depressed person feel normal again. (I was fortunate that the first medication I tried worked and I experienced no side effects. Some women may have to try several medications before finding one that works with the fewest side effects. Of course, discuss this with your doctor.)

The fact that the medicine helped me had an added benefit of making me realize that my depression was also a physiological problem and something that happened to me, not something I brought on myself. Medicine doesn't fix character flaws. It corrects chemical imbalances. That's an important realization for a new mother affected by PPD.

Common Misconceptions About PPD

- You brought it on yourself.
- It's a character flaw.
- It means you're a bad mom.
- It's something to be ashamed of.
- You're the only mom who's ever felt this way.
- This is all in your head.
- Mothering is natural—you should instantly know how to do it.
- No one can help you.
- You won't be able to breast-feed if you take medicine. (Talk to your doctor first, but many antidepressants are safe for nursing moms.)
- Taking medicine is a crutch; you should be able to pull yourself out of this on your own.

Postpartum depression doesn't just make you feel miserable; it makes you question everything you thought you knew about yourself. It turns your life upside down. I was so sure I would love motherhood and be great at it—if I was wrong about that, what else was I wrong about? But I wasn't wrong. Something was chemically unbalanced in my brain and was making me feel this way. Once my mind was balanced again, I was the mother I wanted to be.

Help for PPD

- Getting out of the house every day
- Exercise
- Sunshine
- Uninterrupted sleep
- Accepting help from friends and neighbors
- Talking about your feelings to friends
- Professional counseling
- Talking to your doctor
- Antidepressant medication
- Joining a support group for moms with PPD

Getting Help

Postpartum depression affects women differently and at varying levels of intensity. What worked for me may not work for others. But one thing is sure: if you feel that you are suffering from PPD, you should go see your doctor immediately. PPD is not a condition to be taken lightly, and it is easier to alleviate if you tackle it early. Too many women smile and pretend everything is okay because they don't want to admit that anything is wrong. That's what I did. I hid my feelings from everyone but a few close friends because I was ashamed. If only I had known how many other women could relate to what I was going through or had been through it themselves.

On the other hand, you are certainly not obligated to tell everyone and their brother about your situation. As long as you talk to your spouse and your doctor and get help, it's up to you if and when you tell others. There may be certain people with whom you don't feel comfortable sharing your postpartum depression, and that's okay. It's no one else's business. Only confide in those with whom you feel completely safe and comfortable. The last thing you need during this time is to be subjected to the judgment and criticism of people who are ignorant about postpartum depression.

Please, get help if you are suffering. It's the best thing you can do for yourself and your family. Life is too short to spend it feeling miserable. Especially when you have a new life to bond with and cherish.

From Stephanie

I didn't have postpartum depression. I had the occasional blues; commercials for dog food and long-distance phone service could make me cry; and I definitely had days where I would just sit down and weep out of the frustration of not being able to get anything done other than hold and feed the baby. Other than that, I spent the first few months reveling in being a mom. I loved holding my baby all day long, and I just wanted to be with her and kiss her tiny cheek every minute of the day. That's also because I knew my time as a stay-at-home mom had an expiration date on it—three months, after which my maternity leave would be over and I would have to go back to my old life. I had terrible angst about going back. Just thinking about it would make me cry (I too did a lot of crying). But for the most part, I was joyous about having a new baby.

So I was probably the worst possible person Sara could talk to during this time. When she would start to complain about how bad she felt, I would try to relate by telling her about how I cried over a commercial I saw on television, and she would assure me, "No, you don't understand what I'm feeling. This is much worse than that." When I wasn't trying to console her, I was talking about how wonderful it felt to be a mom, how I was dreading going back to work, and what new things my baby had learned to do that day—all of which probably just made her have even more guilt about what she was feeling. I had no idea what she was going through, and consequently she did a pretty good job of hiding it from me. Days and weeks would go by before she'd answer one of my e-mails or phone calls. Basically, I was a terrible friend. I just didn't get it. But I've learned my lesson. Now, when one of my girlfriends starts showing any signs of sadness after birth, I am like the PPD-NYPD—calling her, visiting her, badgering her to make sure she's not suffering from this overload of hormones.

And here's another thing that ticks me off about PPD. Why is it that we all struggle with taking medicine to make ourselves feel better? It's not your fault—your hormones are poisoning you and it's totally out of your control. Women feel so bad and deal with so much disappointment and guilt when they need a little medicinal help. That's crazy! Just think about how many overweight people take blood pressure medicine—they're not embarrassed about it. Many overweight people could correct their problem through diet and exercise, but instead have no problem popping a pill and even talking about it openly. Just think of the number of pills out there that people take to make their lives easier. Postpartum depression is a *real* illness. It doesn't mean that you're messed up, that you're a bad parent, or that there's something wrong with you. It simply means that your body either has too much or too little of some hormone or hormones that affect your mood. Women suffering from PPD should not be ashamed about taking medicine to feel better.

Moms and Antidepressants

From Stephanie

Women are victims of their hormones throughout their entire life. When we become pregnant, our bodies go through horrendous hormonal changes throughout the entire forty-week process. Then after the baby is

Hormones and Depression

Hormones produced by your thyroid gland drop sharply after childbirth. The decrease can leave you feeling sluggish, tired, and depressed. It can take several months for hormones to return to pre-pregnancy levels.

Sleep Deprivation and Depression

Few people are more sleep-deprived than a new mother, and research shows that there is a clear connection between lack of sleep and depression. The kind of sleep we get is important too. Intermittent sleep (the kind new parents are lucky to get) doesn't provide the same benefits to the brain as longer periods of consistent sleep do.

born, again our bodies are overcome with more colossal changes in our hormones. As we age, our hormones change, and the amount of stress that is suddenly piled on you as a mom can be more overwhelming than you ever imagined. As your kids get a little older, you'll discover that you're in need of a command center just to keep up with all the school assignments, birthday parties, swim meets, play dates, PTA meetings, dentist appointments . . . the list goes on and on. At some point in your life as a mom, you may discover that you are just not feeling like yourself. You're agitated easily, you're snapping at family members and friends, you can't find anything to be happy about, etc. These things could all be signs that you need a little help to get back on track. Sara and I know plenty of moms who take Zoloft, Lexapro, and other popular antidepressants—and they are all better moms because they've faced the issue and done something to fix it. I personally have had periods where I took an antidepressant, and when things calmed down, I weaned myself back off it again, with my doctor's help. Sara is still on an antidepressant and, now that she's realized how much better her life is with a little help from a pill, has no problem with it.

Clutter-Busting Resources

WEBSITES

Women's health from Department of Health and Human Services
www.4woman.gov

Postpartum Support International
www.postpartum.net

Moms Supporting Moms
www.momssupportingmoms.net

Postpartum Dads
https://home.comcast.net/~ddklinker/mysite2/Welcome_page.htm

BOOKS

This Isn't What I Expected: Overcoming Postpartum Depression
by Karen Kleiman and Valerie Raskin

Beyond the Blues: A Guide to Understanding and Treating Prenatal and Postpartum Depression
by Shoshana S. Bennett, Ph.D.

Down Came the Rain: My Journey Through Postpartum Depression
by Brooke Shields

The Mommy Chronicles: Conversations Sharing the Comedy and Drama of Pregnancy and New Motherhood
by Sara Ellington and Stephanie Triplett

7

Leaving Your Career

From Sara

I always knew I wanted to be a stay-at-home mom . . . that is, until I actually became one. Not to say that I have ever regretted the decision. I haven't. But the change has affected me in ways I never expected. And it's been a harder job than I ever imagined.

Work and Identity

Before having my first child I'd worked for ten years in sales and advertising. None of the positions had felt like a dream job—I always believed there was something more fulfilling for me down the road—so the idea of giving up my career wasn't hard for me to embrace. It was really doing it that was tough.

My identity is shaped by work much more than I ever realized before becoming a stay-at-home mom. Since graduating from college I'd always been able to support myself and live comfortably. Not once did I ever have to ask my parents for financial help. I was proud of my independence. I worked hard and my paychecks steadily grew. I won sales awards and earned recognition from my superiors.

When I left my job a few weeks before my daughter was born, it was hard to face the fact that I was now financially dependent on someone else. As the weeks and months passed, I started to feel awkward about making financial decisions. Even though quitting my job was a decision my husband and I had made together, I couldn't help feeling like the money belonged to him. I was working long, hard days taking care of our baby daughter, running the household, and occasionally doing some freelance writing. But deep down, I hated the fact that I couldn't pay the bills. Yet there was no easy solution. Going back to work meant putting my baby in day care, and I knew I personally couldn't face that.

I'd never worked harder in my life than I did in those first few months of motherhood, yet I'd never felt more devalued. American society still places a higher value on paid work than on the work of mothering. I didn't know how motherhood would define me.

But then I started thinking about my situation differently. Suddenly, instead of feeling trapped at home, I saw opportunity. Lots of opportunity. I was free of the pressure to earn a living, and I wasn't tied down to an eight-to-five job. If I could work around my kids, I could try something new. It was a very exciting thought.

That's when Stephanie and I decided to pitch our first book, *The Mommy Chronicles*, to agents. For years we'd talked about turning our saved e-mails into a book, and we finally decided to go for it. We spent hours upon hours crafting a book proposal and researching literary agents. I didn't know if we had a shot in hell, but it really didn't matter. It was something I was doing for me, and it was thrilling. Working on *The Mommy Chronicles* reconnected me to the working world even though I was still at home being a mom to my kids all day. I'd learned that I need that connection. At times it was stressful, and there were many nights I wished I could go to bed or sit on the couch and watch television instead of parking myself in front of the computer. But the job the book created for me gave my life balance. It didn't require being away from my children, and it gave me a goal, something to strive toward to satisfy my sense of accomplishment and myself.

Striking the right balance is key for moms. More than ever before, women establish careers before starting families. It's understandable for us to feel as if we have given up a part of ourselves when we leave work to be at home with our children. Many of the at-home moms I know volunteer or are active in politics. They've formed book clubs and bunko groups to stay connected and enjoy some non-mommy time.

I am a mother, but that is not all that I am. I am also a wife, a daughter, a sister, a friend, and an author. I want my children, particularly my daughter, to see me in that multidimensional way. I hope that my example will help her strike the balance she will need if she becomes a mother someday.

For some women, leaving work to be at home full-time with the children is the right choice. For others, it's simply not. And some women have no choice but to work. But one thing is for sure: stay-at-home moms work hard and deserve respect, and that means respecting yourself. Don't play small or diminish your role when someone asks what you do. It's a stressful, demanding, exhausting job. As one of my mom friends once said, "It's got to be right up there with coal mining." Motherhood is the most im-

Facts and Figures

- According to the U.S. Census Bureau, there were 5.6 million stay-at-home moms in 2005.
- Census Bureau statistics show a 15 percent increase in the number of stay-at-home moms in less than ten years.
- Forty-eight percent of children under the age of two are cared for solely by a parent.

portant job there is. You're not just changing diapers and singing lullabies. You're raising the next generation. So hold your head high and say it loud and proud: "I'm a stay-at-home mom!" ("I'm rocking the cradle and ruling the world, baby!" is also a good option.)

Pros and Cons of Staying at Home

Here are a few things to consider in deciding whether or not staying at home is right for you.

Pro: Flexibility

The flexibility of a stay-at-home mom is hard to beat. If your preschooler needs to come home early, you don't have to rearrange your schedule or talk to your boss first. You can get up in the morning when your kids do, and nap when they do.

Pro: Guilt-Free Time for Yourself

This has to be one of the best benefits of at-home mothering. When you go out with the girls or get a date night with your husband, you don't feel guilty about being away from your children. You've been with them all day!

Pro: It's No Longer an All-or-Nothing Decision

The possibilities aren't limited to working full-time or staying at home anymore. Many moms choose to stay at home with their children for a few years or until the kids start kindergarten. More and more mothers are launching businesses from home or working part-time from home. Telecommuting is more popular than ever. Organizations such as Mom Corps and Women for Hire (see "Clutter-Busting Resources") are cropping up to help moms get back into the workforce with the flexible schedules we crave. These organizations help match your skills with companies' needs. They also provide help with crafting your résumé, networking, and training.

Two or More

An employed mother's level of frustration tends to rise dramatically with the birth of the second or third child.

Often the decision to stop working is made after the birth of the second child, when the demands of motherhood and the costs of child care become even greater. The decision to leave your career or return to work is one that can change and adapt as your family does. As a new mom, I didn't grasp that. Not working felt like such a long-term choice to me, even though it wasn't. So, remember that the decision you make today doesn't have to be the last decision you make regarding work, and probably won't be.

Con: Isolation

Being a stay-at-home mom can feel quite isolating when you've been used to spending weekdays in an office full of adults. Babies don't give you much interaction in the early months, but as they grow you'll enjoy more smiles and coos. You'll also be able to get out and meet other moms at play groups, Kindermusik, and other activities for mom and baby. But it takes effort.

Con: Financial Stress

Can you afford to quit working? Are you and your spouse able to stick to a budget? How will your new situation affect your husband or partner? How will you feel about not making money? Do you and your mate have healthy attitudes toward money? Does he respect the job of an at-home mom?

Con: Loss of Sense of Self

How much of your identity comes from your work? How do you feel about the stay-at-home moms you know now? Will being a stay-at-home mom be satisfying for you?

Con: Problems with Division of Labor

How will you and your husband share the household duties? Will he do his share, or will he expect you to take care of all the household chores and errands since you are not working for pay?

Sara's Advice for Leaving Your Career

Make the Decision That's Right for You

I know it's hard, but try to take the societal influences out of your decision. Staying at home may be great for your best friend, but you are a different person. This is the time to toss out the expert opinions (because you can find an opinion in favor of or against nearly every choice) and evaluate what will work best for you and your family. Then you can make the decision you'll be happiest with in the long run.

Change Takes Time

Remember, regardless of whether you return to work or stay at home, there will be an adjustment period. Leaving a baby in day care is rarely easy for a new mom, but then those first few weeks and months at home tending to the unending needs of a newborn aren't exactly a walk in the park either. Your life has changed drastically now that you're a mother. Be patient with yourself and give yourself time to get comfortable with your choice (whether it is to work or to leave) before you change your mind.

Prepare, Prepare, Prepare

Preparation is key for making the transition to at-home mom work. Prepare financially by paying off all debts you can while you are still working. It's much easier to leave your job knowing you're not saddled with credit card debt or monthly car payments. This might also be the time to sock away some disposable cash for yourself and set up a household budget.

If you're interested in exploring work-from-home options, talk to your employer about possibilities while you're still on the job and on your manager's mind. Research at-home business opportunities, take a class, and network with other moms.

It's not too early to pick other moms' brains about good babysitters. Find out who the good ones are and let them know that you are interested in interviewing them. Any stay-at-home mom should have a few sitters at her disposal for doctor's appointments, errands, and just being able to get an occasional break.

Talk to another mom you trust about swapping child care responsibilities on a regular basis so you get a little personal time once or twice a week. It's free and it's a win-win for you both!

Stay Connected

Being a stay-at-home mom doesn't mean you have to stay at home all the time. Get out of the house, girlfriend! Mother-baby activities like Little Gym, Gymboree, Kindermusik, and play groups are great ways to meet and socialize with other parents (see Chapter 12, "Activities for Mom and Baby"). Some movie theaters offer special morning screenings that are baby-friendly. Stay in touch with your non-mom friends and hire a sitter so you can have lunch or dinner together. Join an online community for moms (they're in nearly every city) or a support group for new moms.

More Choice for Everyone

Recent surveys show that more and more mothers are making the choice to stay at home with their children, and it's not just a choice reserved for the most financially stable anymore. Many families are willing to pinch pennies so that one parent can be home with the children.

Clutter-Busting Resources

WEBSITES

The Mommies Network (find a group in your town)
www.themommiesnetwork.org

Mommysavers
www.mommysavers.com/stay-at-home-moms/becoming-sahm-right-decision.shtml

ClubMom.com
www.clubmom.com/display/206603

iVillage
www.ivillage.com

Ladies Who Launch
www.ladieswholaunch.com

Mom Corps
www.momcorps.com

Women for Hire
www.womenforhire.com

Mom Pack
www.mompack.com

BOOKS

Staying Home: From Full-time Professional to Full-time Parent
by Darci Sanders and Martha M. Bullen

The Stay-at-Home Mom's Guide to Making Money from Home, Choosing the Business That's Right for You Using the Skills and Interests You Already Have
by Liz Folger

8

Going Back to Work

From Stephanie

All I can say is, "You have my whole-hearted sympathy." There are few things in life that are harder than that first month after your maternity leave is over. I cried every morning. I cried for three weeks before my maternity leave was even over. I cried every time I had to take baby Sara back to day care at the end of a holiday weekend or vacation. And I know I could sit here at my keyboard and write until my fingers bled, and nothing I say will make you feel any better. But you can do it. Lots of mothers have. And there are many benefits to being a working mom, even though you'll have a few battles to fight along the way.

Co-workers

This is the sticky part. You have absolutely no idea what went down in the few months you've been away from the office—the gossip, the new protocols, the new clients, the current issues, you name it. Going back to work is going to feel a little bit like your first day at work. And that's exactly how you should approach it. Don't come charging back on a mission to make up for lost time and prove your worth. Take it slowly. You shouldn't feel as if you have to make up for three months of missed work. Work is work—there was plenty to do when you left, and there will be plenty to do for the next twenty years. Ask lots of questions. Talk to the people who were covering for you. Be open-minded. You may learn that they found a way to do something more efficiently than you did—and that's great. Remember, you're going to have to be more efficient than ever before. You have an important little someone waiting to be picked up at six o'clock *sharp*.

When I returned to my job after maternity leave, I soon realized that my co-workers had convinced themselves that I would be overtaken with maternal bliss and would never actually return. Sure, they welcomed me with flowers and cards and photo frames and took me to lunch my first day back. They really sucked me in. I was thrilled with how nice my co-workers were. But when the real cards were all dealt, I realized that at least two colleagues who had covered my territory and taken over my responsibilities apparently liked my job, because they began to fantasize about actually *having* my job. And for months afterward, I found myself playing the "I can do my job better than you can" game. I really had to make sure that I dotted every *i* and crossed every *t*, because the vultures were circling right outside my office door. (Or at least that's how they made me feel.) And I'm convinced the humming of the breast pump and the shrine of baby photos was making the taste of a fresh kill seem very possible.

It also didn't help that there was only one other mother in the office besides me. So it was as if I had survived some kind of alien abduction and returned to earth in a slightly altered form. They couldn't understand why my wardrobe went from perfectly polished and updated to wrinkled and stained with partially digested breast milk. The hairdo changed from long, silky blond to disheveled with dark roots. The dedicated professional who'd worked well past quitting time was now the first one out the door at precisely 4:59 P.M. every day. The fun girl who'd always wanted to go out for lunch now spent her lunch hour breast-feeding at the day care facility. And the little alien who'd done all this to me was now my first priority in life, and my job suddenly just didn't seem quite so all-important anymore. That's one of the great things about becoming a mother—it gives you perspective. It teaches you what really matters in life.

You'll be a better employee because of this new perspective. You'll see things from a higher perch. You'll know that even the toughest businessman is somebody's son or father. You'll begin to understand people better. You'll know what the photos in people's offices really mean. You'll finally understand why family is so much more important than career. And you'll get more respect. The title of mother is one that comes with enormous sacrifice, focus, and effort, and it does demand respect.

Secrets for Returning to Work After Maternity Leave

Management books will tell you that almost everyone can do their job well. The problems associated with performance usually have more to do with negotiating the multiple personalities that commingle in a place of business. Everyone knows how to do their job—it's all the psychological expectations that are going through people's minds that make things difficult. By contrast, for the last few months you've been spending every waking moment with someone who is pretty clear about what he or she wants. Basically, he cries and you know he either wants to eat, is tired, or needs a diaper change. Pretty simple. But now you're going to have to deal with adults with their own perceptions, needs, and expectations and they are anything but clear. So here are a few pointers:

- Be respectful and grateful to anyone who filled in for you while you were gone. Compliment this person and let her know what a wonderful thing she's done for you; ask her questions and ask her opinion (and just pray that she'll tell you the truth). She may be very proud of what she's accomplished in your absence and may be a little guarded about giving it back. Remind her how nice it will be to get back to her normal workload.
- Understand that there will be some co-workers who feel very resentful about the fact that they had to cover for you. The extra workload may have been stressful or even overwhelming for them. Be courteous, but ignore their resentment. That's their own, personal hang-up. You were doing an important job and you had every right to spend a few months nurturing the new life you created and allowing your body to recover. There's nothing more taxing to the human body than creating a life and giving birth. If they resent you, they're making a big mistake, and you should pour some sour breast milk on their carpet as soon as nobody's looking.
- Try to talk about something other than your baby. It's going to be hard because that's all you think about now. But they can't relate, especially if they're not mothers. And you'll bore them to death. There is just nothing interesting about your epidural, what kind of formula you're using, whether or not you should be using a pacifier, or how your breast pump now comes in an adorable pouch that matches your diaper bag. Try to speak the native language, and gush about baby only when asked.
- Don't make people uncomfortable. Let's face it: once you've been through pregnancy, labor, and delivery, your "filter" may be a little altered. You've gotten used to words like *breast, vaginal birth, nipple, circumcision,* etc. These are words that can make people feel uncomfortable around an office. If you are using a breast pump at work, do everything in your power to keep it a mystery. Nothing freaks out non-parents like a breast pump. It sounds weird, it looks weird, and it hooks on to your boobies—that's weird! Use every precaution when it comes to your privacy. Always lock your door. My office door didn't have a lock, so I made a sign to alert possible visitors. It had a cow print in the background and it simply said, "Making baby food—please come back later." (Humor is good at defusing an uncomfortable situation.) I was also careful about putting my freshly pumped liquid gold into a cooler to carry it to the refrigerator, and it was well concealed inside yet another cooler once inside the refrigerator. I just felt it would be odd for people to store their tuna sandwich next to my breast milk in the community fridge. And I didn't want to get caught in the hallway holding the little see-through plastic bag of freshly pumped milk. For crying out loud, it was just in my breast moments ago—it felt like walking down the hall holding my panties! Try to be considerate of your co-workers and don't do or say anything that will make them feel uncomfortable.

- Some people will actually be jealous. It's hard to believe, but very true. I actually had a co-worker make a comment in front of me about how she got in trouble for being late to work because she wasn't a parent. Of course, her excuse was because she had been out late drinking the night before and was nursing a hangover and overslept. I, on the other hand, had been nursing a sick infant through the night and had slept a total of two very restless hours, without the comfort of a cocktail. I've even had co-workers say things like, "I have too much work to do to leave on time every day." These are people who are still too self-absorbed to understand the tremendous demands of the job of parent. They think they're tired because they only got six hours of sleep last night. They don't yet know what life is really about. They don't know what being tired really feels like. They have no idea how much work it is to care for a tiny, new, defenseless life that counts on you for everything. They haven't had to sacrifice, stay up all night consoling a sick baby, or change outfits twice in one morning because they got spit up on. They have no perspective. All you can do is ignore their ignorance and pray that when they do one day have a child of their own, it will develop a severe, long-lasting case of colic.
- Plan for your first day back to be a Wednesday or Thursday so you can get a break sooner. A shorter first week will make it easier for you and baby because you can regroup.
- When you finally get home, turn off the phone, the TV, and the outside world and just concentrate on being with your baby. It's time to reconnect, and you'll be such a great parent because you will be more focused on your baby when you're together. Use that time wisely.
- Although there are challenges involved with continuing to breast-feed after returning to work, it will make you feel closer to your baby. Pumping during the day always felt as if I was doing something for her, even though I couldn't be with her. And your milk supply will change as you need it to. Plenty of working mothers breast-feed only in the mornings, evenings, and through the night and bottle-feed during the day. It's another amazing thing about breast-feeding—you'll only make as much as you need.

Getting Through the First Day

You're going to cry, a lot. That's okay. Keep in mind that your body has been releasing all kinds of hormones that cause you to bond with your baby. It's completely unnatural to have to be away from your baby so soon. But sometimes you just don't have a choice, and believe it or not, everything is going to work out just fine. It does get easier as time goes on. And keep in mind that your baby will never prefer a day care provider to you—it just doesn't happen.

The first few days are the hardest. When you leave your baby at day care, you must use what I call the "drop and run" method. The longer you linger, the harder it's going to be to say good-bye. You'll use this method again when your baby gets a little older and starts experiencing separation anxiety. Any mother, teacher, or day care worker will tell you to give them a kiss and get out as fast as you can. Your baby can feel it if you are nervous or upset, and you don't want to pass those feelings on. You want your baby to feel good things in her new environment. Ask the day care workers the best way (and time) to communicate with them once or twice during the course of the day, just for the first few days. Leave them your digital camera and ask them to snap a few photos so you can see what your baby's day was like and don't feel that you missed anything. Ask if you can stop by during your lunch hour. They will understand what you're going through, and if you communicate with them, they just may help get you through it. My daughter's day care workers were like my pediatricians. They were amazing resources for a new mom. But respect their schedule. A good day care is a well-oiled machine, and you don't want to arrive during baby's naptime.

Now, what about you? Drop baby off and touch up your makeup. It's time to find your old self again. Remember the girl who loved her career and her hobbies and her friends? The one who loved a good conversation that had nothing to do with breast milk, burping, or diaper rash? This is your chance to be you. It's sort of like you have two selves now: your mommy-self and your self-self. You have to learn to turn the mommy-self off while you're at the office. You can turn her back on again at quitting time. It's like flipping a switch on and off, and you'll get better at it with practice. Some women love this part of going back to work. It's a chance to reclaim their pre-mommy identity. Know that your child is being well cared for, and concentrate on being good at something besides being mommy. Just flip your switch and enjoy doing your job. You'll be a better mother because the time you do have together will be very special to you.

There's a lot of fulfillment in knowing that you are contributing to your family's financial well-being. It's a sense of accomplishment, and you should be proud of yourself because it's very challenging to be a working mom. It's a good feeling to spend money that you know you've earned. Most stay-at-home moms really struggle with spending money that their husbands made. Even though you're supposed to be a team, it's still a lot easier to explain to your husband why you spent that extra sixty bucks on that pair of shoes when you're contributing to the ol' bank account. And you're setting a great example for your children. They will one day be proud of you and your accomplishments. Your family's future will be much more financially secure, and you'll be able to give your children more vacations and spoil them with new toys and such. So feel good about what you are doing.

Enlisting Help

You Cannot Do It Alone

Juggling housework, career, and a new baby is one of the toughest things you'll ever do. It is impossible to do it alone, so get your husband involved. He should have daily responsibilities to help with the house and the baby just like you do. Get as much rest as you possibly can, and be sure to make time for yourself. It's important to keep your batteries charged when you have so much to accomplish. Learn to say no when it comes to volunteering for special projects or extracurricular assignments. Baby comes first now, and you'll regret taking on that extra workload when you can't spend that precious time with your baby.

Try to establish a backup plan on those days that the baby is too sick for day care and you have that big meeting at work. Babies are unpredictable—nothing is ever definite now that you have a baby in your life. So talk with family, neighbors, friends, or drop-in centers that can fill in at the last minute. The day will come when you will have to use your backup plan, so make sure you have one.

Housework

About one month into my stint as a working mom, I really thought I had it all together. I was bragging about having the laundry up to date and about how I was managing to put a hot, home-cooked meal on the table every night, and still spend quality time with my baby girl. But just a few months later, it all came crashing down on me. I just couldn't keep up with it all. My husband traveled almost constantly, I had no family in town, and I had a demanding, full-time job. I began to visit the drive-throughs more frequently, I was struggling to keep up with the laundry, and I nearly had a nervous breakdown over the housework. That's when, against my husband's wishes, I decided to hire a house cleaner. I spent so little time with my baby that when I was at home, I didn't want to put in hours cleaning the house. I figured as long as I was contributing to the bank account and as long as my husband refused to pick up a mop or a toilet brush, I was going to hire somebody who would. I told my husband that if he wanted to start cleaning the house once a week, I would fire the maid, but until then it was a necessary expense, and much cheaper than checking me into an asylum or paying for a marriage counselor. It was the best decision I ever made. It's okay if he doesn't like it. Better for him to be a little peeved than for you to be constantly exhausted and overwhelmed. That won't make you a good mother or wife.

Keeping Your Distance

I've heard about some mothers who know they have to return to work, so they try not to become too attached to their baby. Please don't do this. It doesn't work. It's not good for you or your baby, and you'll be missing out on so much. The first weeks you have with a brand-new life are one of the most special times you'll ever encounter. There is something so amazing about a new baby. It's like a hundred Christmas mornings rolled up into one fleeting moment. It's that brief period when your baby doesn't belong to anyone else but you. And it's over in a blink. So don't waste a minute of your time worrying about returning to work. You'll be able to make the separation, and you'll know that you've done everything you can to give your baby the very best start in life because you love him or her with everything you've got.

Guilt

Nobody has as much guilt as a working mother. I drove myself insane with guilt, especially on those days when my baby was feeling sick and I had to get to work for an important meeting. There are some days when little babies just need their mommies, and sometimes Mommy just can't be there. You can't win. If you take your baby to day care knowing that she doesn't feel well, you'll feel guilty. And if you call in sick and stay at home with your baby, you'll feel guilty that you're missing work. Frankly, I don't have any words of wisdom for you. It is never an easy choice to make. But I can tell you this: if you are in a work situation that pressures you or berates you when you have to stay home with a sick child, find a new place of employment. I'm not saying it's okay to abuse the privilege, but you shouldn't be reprimanded for having a sick child if you are within your allotted number of sick/vacation days. And there's a good chance you will have to use some vacation days to care for a sick child. (Remember, day care centers expose your baby to a lot of germs.) So use your vacation days sparingly. Keeping everything in perspective will tone down your feelings of guilt. Your family is always much more important than any job.

Clutter-Busting Resources

Returning to work from maternity leave
www.mayoclinic.com/health/working-life/WL00034

Easing the transition
http://att.iparenting.com/babies/worktransition.htm

9

Day Care

How to Choose

Stephanie's Day Care Drama

If you're struggling with the decision of choosing the right day care, then please read this story. After you read the disaster that I experienced, you should be prepared for just about anything.

First, you should know that, just like every mother, I was distraught at the thought of putting my baby in day care and going to work for eight hours a day. I haven't yet met a mother who was happy about the end of her maternity leave. So we did our homework, took the tours, and talked to as many mothers as we could find (having just moved to a new city), and we chose a day care facility about five minutes from our home. It was one of the most expensive in Atlanta at the time—at least $100 a week more than some of the others. But hey, this was our precious little baby, so we were motivated to spare no expense.

The lesson we learned is that when it comes to day care, *expensive* is not synonymous with *best*. You see, this particular day care had very stringent schedules and very firm ideas about child development. I now refer to this particular facility as "baby boot camp." But at the time, I found no humor in their uncaring regimen. You see, they simply refused to give a three-month-old baby a pacifier. They told me it was "bad for her development." She was a breast-fed baby who was somewhat restless and very comforted by her pacifier. Also, since she was primarily breast-fed, she struggled with drinking from a bottle. My husband figured a way to get her to accept one: start with a pacifier, and then slide the bottle in. This was the only thing we found that would work.

On her first day of day care, they called me around noon to tell me that she had not eaten at all. Breast-fed babies at that young age can eat as often as every two hours. I had to leave work early and rush to the day care, only to find my three-month-old infant completely worn out from crying and hunger. She had a rash from crying so hard. I was furious!

Even though we begged them to use a pacifier just to feed her, they refused, and the second day of day care went much the same as the first. By the third day, I was looking for a new day care. But it's not that easy to find a slot in overcrowded Atlanta. There are waiting lists for day cares that parents sign up for early in their pregnancies. I was really upset, and my boss very wisely told me to go home and take a few days off and get it all worked out. Thank God for him. He is a great dad and a great boss, and he was right—I wasn't doing any good at the office in that condition.

That afternoon, I was sitting on my couch holding my baby girl, with a phone to my ear, researching day care centers, when something terrible happened. There was a noise that sounded as if we were being bombed. It was an extraordinarily loud and long crashing sound. The entire house shook! I jumped up with the baby in my arms and began to run out the front door, not knowing whether to stay in the house or head outside. My mind was searching for an answer—was it an earthquake or a tornado? Then I heard the car alarm going off, and as I hurried outside, I saw the source of the commotion. Two huge trees from the neighbor's yard had fallen. They crushed and obliterated *both* of our cars and landed on the roof of the house, taking out the garage door and a good portion of the bedroom wall. Nice. Just what I needed. The baby was screaming, I was crying, there was a power line flailing around in the street, and I was desperately trying to dial my husband at work and call the fire department. I just thank God that we weren't sitting in the car at the time because we would have been crushed. There had been a lot of

Tips for Choosing the Right Day Care

- Choose the day care that makes you feel the best and matches your parenting style.
- It's better to choose a day care close to your office rather than your home. You can get there faster in an emergency and don't have to worry about traffic conditions.
- Look for cleanliness and strict protocols. Food sinks should be far away from diaper-changing areas. Proper labeling of food and bottles is a must. Ask about their protocol for sanitizing baby's environment.
- Visit more than once and spend some time there. Be aware of how the staff responds to you.
- Your new caregivers are going to become members of your family and can prove to be a valuable resource for a new parent, so treat them as such.
- I chose a day care center over a private in-home nanny because I liked having witnesses to the caregivers' interactions with my child.
- Day care babies get less one-on-one attention, but they get to socialize and interact with other children, which is very beneficial, not to mention adorable.

rain in Atlanta in the past few months and it was a windy day. Apparently these two old trees had unhealthy root systems, and the combination of wet weather and wind weakened the roots enough that they couldn't support the weight of the trees, so they simply toppled over. The neighbors who owned the trees happened to be on their honeymoon, so there was no way to contact them. It took days to cut and remove the fallen trees and weeks to fix the damage. I can't understand why my boss didn't fire me. Between the emotions surrounding the day care issue, an additional week of maternity leave, and the photos I e-mailed him of our crushed cars, surely he must have thought I was a walking disaster waiting to happen.

Eventually I did find a wonderful day care, and I did manage to find my place in the office again. Maybe hearing my story will make any problems you encounter with your new day care seem a little easier. You will survive, I promise.

Location

The day care that I found was at a church. It was only two blocks from my office, so I could visit every day during my lunch hour. That worked out great when I was breastfeeding because I could nurse her every day at noon. Even when I was finished breastfeeding, I still visited her daily. We would walk around the church grounds, look at the pretty flowers, sit on the bench, and sing songs and play baby games. It was the perfect situation. I recommend choosing a day care that is close to your office, rather than close to your home. It's nice not to have to worry about getting stuck in traffic on the way to pick your baby up. And it's nice to get her into your possession sooner, even if it's by only a few minutes. If she got sick or there was a problem, I was only a short distance away. I could look out my office window and see the church where she was being cared for, and it gave me some peace to be so close.

Similar Parenting Style

The new day care we chose matched our parenting style. There were two wonderful ladies in the baby room who had worked there for many years. They rocked the babies in big rocking chairs, cuddled with them, and just loved them. There were no rigid standards and no focus on development (at least not for three-month-olds). They were there to help keep your baby safe, happy, and comfortable. In my opinion, tiny babies don't need developmental standards. They need to be loved and nurtured in the absence of their parents. They had little parades at Easter and July 4, where they decorated their strollers or cribs and wheeled them through the hallway as all the parents lined the walls and practically blinded each other with flashbulbs.

Whether it is a home-based caregiver, a nanny, a day care facility, or even a relative, my advice is to look for care that matches *your* style and avoid those who try to force their standards upon you. Ask a lot of questions about how they do things, and ask specific questions about something you might be struggling with. Being able to communicate well with caregivers is essential. They are going to be very important in the lives of you and your baby. They're practically a part of your family. So make sure they do it your way, and don't try to shove their own agenda down your throat.

Facility Standards

Check out as many day care centers as you can. Ask about the ratio of caregivers to babies. It shouldn't be more than four babies to each worker. Look for signs of cleanliness. Are the toys appropriate? Are they clean? Is the diaper-changing station far enough away from where food is prepared? Is the equipment safe and well maintained? Ask about their protocols for sanitizing toys, cribs, and carpet areas. If it makes you feel better, ask if you can bring your own bedding (I always told them that my baby was allergic to some detergents, so I had to supply my own bedding). Find out if any of the staff is licensed in CPR and ask to see their certificates. Do they wash hands after changing diapers? Do you see lots of antibacterial hand gels around the room? Don't rush—spend some time with them. See how it feels just to be there and how the staff responds to you. Visit several times: once by yourself just to ask questions, and once with your child so you can see how he or she feels about being there. And try to plan your visits during different hours of the day so you can see how they handle various time periods, like morning drop-off, afternoon pickup, and feeding time. But the most important thing is how it makes you feel to be there. Trust your instincts on this one and you'll probably be okay.

Remember too that there will be bumps in the road that you may have to work through. Treat these people like family. Don't walk out every time there's a problem or disagreement. No one is going to be perfect, and it's hard on you and your child to get acclimated to a new day care environment. In my situation, my husband and I had two meetings with the owner and caregivers at the first day care to let them know how we felt. They were unwilling to give even an inch, and after discussing it with our pediatrician (who didn't agree with their standards), we chose to move our baby.

Day Care or Nanny?

Call me paranoid if you want to, but my theory is that there are no witnesses in your home. I always felt safer having my baby at a day care facility where there was plenty of supervision and witnesses. Of course, there are drawbacks to day care. Your baby will be exposed to more germs. And there's the ordeal of transporting baby and all baby's belongings and supplies to another locale every morning. The good news is that it's usually cheaper than having in-home care. Generally, the employees are certified professionals who have had background checks by the facility. And like I said, never underestimate the power of witnesses.

They Get to Socialize

This is one of the most important perks of day care. They love to play with each other, even at a very early age. I'll never forget how our day care workers used to put all the babies in their bouncy seats and arrange them in a circle. They loved looking at each other and making sounds. It is very important to get your child used to other children at an early age.

Less One-on-One Attention

Babies at day care usually don't get as much one-on-one attention as babies who have their own private nanny. Baby is going to be a part of a group, not the center of the universe. But that isn't always a bad thing. It teaches them to be patient.

Do Your Research

Asking your friends, your pediatrician, and other mothers is still the very best way to find the right child care provider. Granted, it isn't foolproof. Different people have different opinions. My next-door neighbor gushed about the "baby boot camp" center that we ended up hating. But talking with other mothers is still a good place to start. When I've heard several mothers recommend the same thing, it's almost always a sure bet that it's going to be a good thing.

Friends and Relatives as Caregivers

As your child grows and changes, you may decide to move her to a different day care situation. You may have a friend who begins to care for children in her home, or maybe a relative becomes available for babysitting services. When it comes to young babies, it's my opinion that using a friend or relative is great. Be aware that you will need to set some boundaries with friends and relatives, and it's best to put everything in writing. When it's in black and white, you don't have to worry about any confusion. You'll want to include what your expectations are, what rules you have, when paychecks will be handed out, and what the plans are in case of sickness or cancellation. And even after all that, you'll have to be flexible. People are not perfect. There may be some things you'll have to accept in return for knowing that your child is spending her day with someone who loves her more than a day care worker might.

Remember too that even Grandma deserves a paycheck. Child care is hard work, no matter how much you love them. The greatest benefit of paying your babysitter-relative is that it gives you more control over the situation. If you're paying, they're a little more obliged to do things your way. A paycheck also keeps them dedicated. Now, I'm not talking about Grandma watching your baby while you take in a movie or do some shopping—free babysitting for a couple of hours is perfectly acceptable. But if your relative is caring for your baby on a daily basis, regular compensation is generally a must.

Using friends as sitters can be a true test of the friendship. You will have to discuss things up front to prevent confusion that can lead to disappointment. Set up protocols for what to do when the caregiver can't watch your children on a scheduled morning, for instance: what time would you like her to call so you have time to make other arrangements? You'll need to work out who is supplying snacks, lunch, and juice—will it be part of her compensation to provide supplies, or will you bring these items each week? You may want to discuss how you want your children disciplined, what television programs you don't allow, and what foods are acceptable and unacceptable. The more businesslike you make it, the more your friend will probably try to accommodate your wishes. If you drop your kids off and bolt, don't get upset when you find out that they had Oreo cookies for lunch and spent the afternoon watching HBO.

There are definitely advantages to having friends and family as caregivers if you can avoid the pitfalls and keep everything rational and out in the open. You won't be happy 100 percent of the time, and you'll have to remember that you probably wouldn't be happy with a day care facility 100 percent of the time either. It's going to be a lesson in holding your tongue and choosing your battles wisely. In my opinion, once baby starts to sit up and crawl, he'll be very happy in a situation where he can be around other babies his own age. Sure, you're going to have to deal with more colds and other illnesses, but the social skills he'll learn are very beneficial. Plus, he'll just have more fun.

For toddlers and children through age four, preschool can be a great option. You'll be amazed at how fast your child can learn when they're exposed to a curriculum at this age. Now, I'm not talking about having them doing calculus—I'm just encouraging you to find a situation that gives them plenty of time to play but includes instructional time as well. Kindergarten is serious business these days; some kids are even reading by the time they *enter* kindergarten. So any boost that you can give them is a good thing. The only downside is that most preschools are only part-day, so they are not going to be an option if you are working full-time. (See Chapter 46 for more about preschools.)

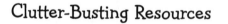

Clutter-Busting Resources

Day care: choosing a good center
www.familydoctor.org

The New Parents Guide
www.thenewparentsguide.com/choosing-a-daycare-center.htm

Drop-in day care checklist
www.parenting.com/article/Toddler/Daycare--Education/Drop-in-Daycare-Checklist

Twelve questions to ask before you hire a nanny
www.expectantmothersguide.com/library/EUSnanny.htm

"Who's Watching Your Child?"
www.parenting.com/article/Toddler/Daycare--Education/Who's-Watching-Your-Child-21334607

College nannies
www.collegenannies.com

Au pairs
www.aupairusa.org

Life with Your Baby

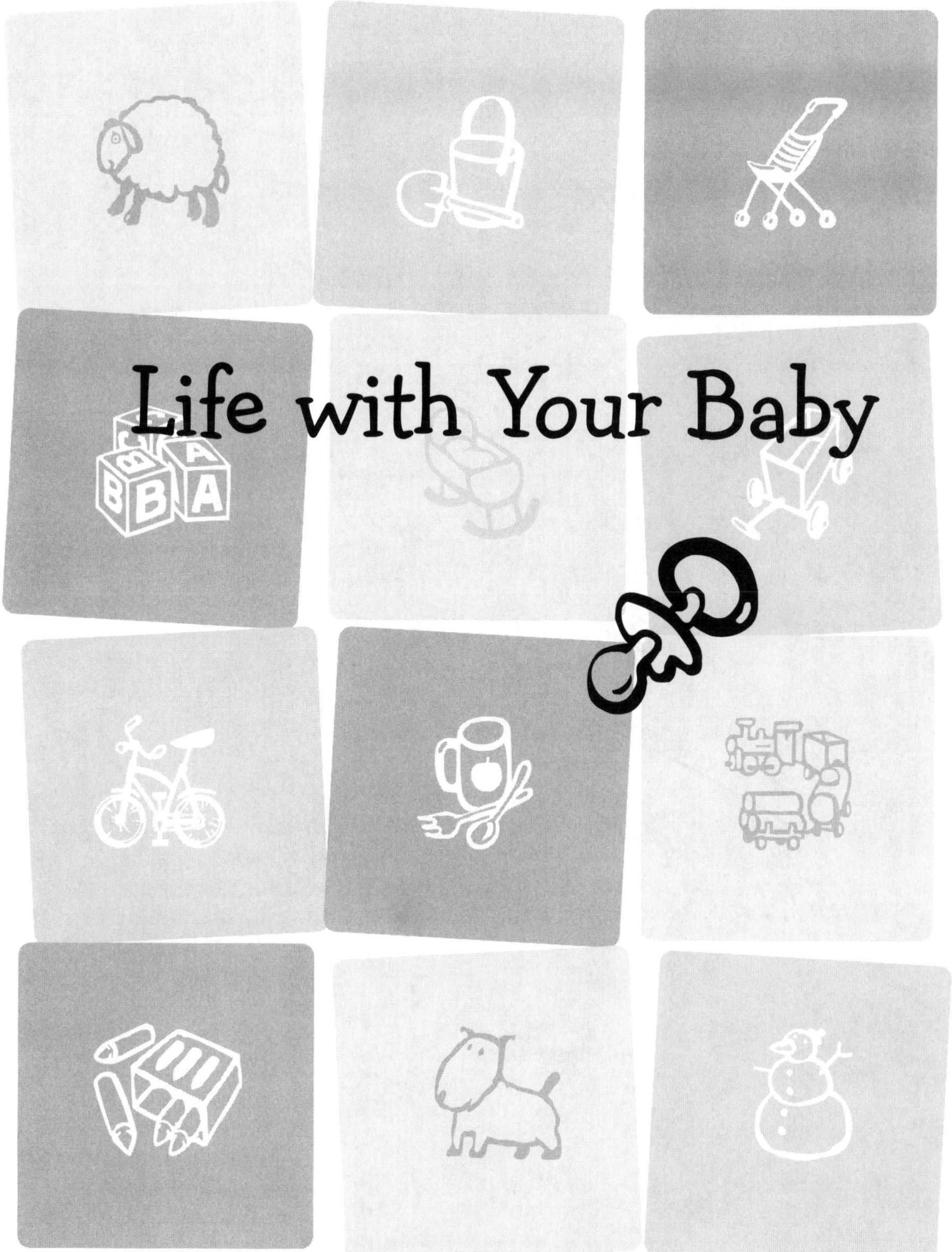

10

Your First Outing with Baby

No doubt about it—it's a little unnerving. You're probably worried that your baby is going to cry in public and embarrass you. You might be worried that she is going to catch some terrible virus. What if she soils her diaper and there's nowhere to change it? It's hard to know what to bring, how far from home you can safely venture and for how long, and exactly how you're supposed to set up and collapse that fancy new stroller. No one ever said this mommy thing was going to be easy, and leaving the house with a new baby is one of the first obstacles you must overcome. It's not that difficult—it just involves a little more work and a lot more planning. Here are some pointers to help you on your first trip into the real world.

Practice Collapsing Your Stroller

From Sara

I know this sounds like the most idiotic piece of advice you have ever heard, but let me explain why I am advising that you practice with your stroller before venturing out in public. I've often joked that you practically need an engineering degree to become a parent, what with all the gear that goes along with motherhood these days. So I should have known better, but I didn't do a couple of trial runs with the stroller prior to my first outing . . . and I paid for it. Like me, you'll probably discover that it's relatively easy to pop the stroller out of the back of your car and set it up in the parking lot. Heck, they practically set themselves up. However, collapsing one is an entirely different matter. There are buttons and levers you have to find and push simultaneously; some of this may even have to be done with your hands *and* feet. And you'll have to do it while contending with shopping bags, your purse, and a baby who is cranky and tired from her trip to the mall.

The first time I attempted this, my mom was with me. She put the baby in her car seat and loaded our items in the car, leaving me free to handle the stroller. And I *still* couldn't get the damn thing to fold down. As shoppers passed by my car, the stroller and I were practically in a wrestling match. I tried over and over to get it to fold down, using every ounce of my strength, until I was dripping with sweat. During the ordeal, I'd occasionally glimpse another mom cruise by with her baby happily perched in her "travel system," and I'd swear I could hear her snicker to herself. I felt like an idiot and I looked like an idiot. Finally I gave up and heaved the stroller, fully upright and very large, into the back of my minivan and slammed the rear door shut before it could fall out. When I got into the driver's seat, still sweating and breathing hard, my mother, who's known for being understated, looked at me and said, "That didn't sound like it went well." Stephanie has a friend with the same story except her stroller wouldn't fit in her car so she gave up and just left the stroller sitting in the parking lot at the mall. She figured it was better just to buy another stroller than waste another minute sweating and swearing in the parking lot.

The moral of the story is that unless you want to risk looking like a complete imbecile (who should have never been allowed to procreate) in front of all the more experienced moms, practice setting up and collapsing your stroller a few times before you head out.

When to Take That First Outing

From Stephanie

It's easy for a new mom to get cabin fever. You're going to hear all kinds of scary advice on this one. Some doctors recommend keeping baby at home until six weeks of age because a baby's immunity is stronger by then. Some recommend two weeks. Some will tell you that it depends on the time of year. And I've seen two-day-old babies at the grocery store who somehow, remarkably, survived (I can pretty much guarantee they weren't firstborns). So our advice is to use your own instincts. Remember that it is perfectly okay to take your baby outside. It's crowds that you need to be concerned about. Brand-new babies do need some time to strengthen their immune systems. But don't drive yourself insane trying to keep baby in a bubble. If you want to go to the store, then go to the store. I always kept my baby in her infant car carrier and draped a blanket over the top of it to keep her in her own little germ-free environment. I'm not sure how germ-free it actually was, but it made me feel better.

Just do your best. Making people wash their hands when they visit is a good idea.

Not letting sick people into your house for the first few weeks is perfectly acceptable. Eating canned spaghetti for three days in a row because you don't want to expose your baby to the grocery store is just plain nutty.

And don't beat yourself up when baby does catch a cold. All babies get sick in their first year of life; I think the average is about eight times. This really does build their immune system and will allow them to fight off germs when they start going to school.

What to Bring

This may seem like common sense, but actually, having a well-equipped diaper bag is a learned skill. Here's a list of the things you'll need to keep with you at all times:

- Diapers. Always bring extras. A good rule of thumb is one diaper for every two hours you'll be out, plus one or two extras.
- Wipes. These are now as necessary to you as oxygen—don't ever get caught without them.
- Blankets. These are useful both for covering baby and for covering a diapering surface that might be cold or dirty. (Or bring a changing pad for the latter.) And please remember that babies can get too hot sometimes, so don't overdo it.
- Formula. Bring extra in case you get delayed. It's also great to have some bottled water with you in case you need to make a bottle and can't get to a clean water source.
- Bottles and nipples. Ditto.
- Pacifier. If your baby needs one, always keep a secret replacement in your bag.
- Change of clothes for baby. Some accidents are too much for even the most absorbent of diapers.
- Infant Tylenol or Motrin. You never know when baby is going to get a fever or become grumpy from teething pain. Always keep some on hand for emergencies—you'll be glad you did.
- Hand sanitizer. This is for you. You might need to tidy up after a bad diaper change or before feeding baby.
- Ointment.
- Burp cloths or cloth diapers.
- Toys. To keep baby occupied.
- Zip-top or disposable diaper bags. One of these can be a real lifesaver because it's a place to contain the smell until you can locate the nearest trash can.
- Diaper Duck. A dispenser of plastic bags to dispose of dirty diapers or contain soiled clothing.
- Warm gear. Toss in a sweater, socks, or hat, depending on the weather.

- Ice packs. Useful if you are breast-feeding and need to keep the milk cool.
- Bibs.
- Snacks.
- Baby food. If your baby is in this stage, also keep a few extra baby spoons with you (restaurant spoons are too big).
- Sunscreen. Some lists recommend sunscreen, but be careful not to use it on very young babies (just too many chemicals for their small bodies). Shade is recommended until baby is at least six months old.

Other things to consider:

- Your diaper bag is a great place to keep an extra set of keys (moms lock their keys in their cars all the time because it's easy to get frazzled dealing with strollers and kids and all their belongings).
- If your child has allergies or needs a special medication, be sure to keep some in your bag.
- Disposable cameras—you never know when that "Kodak moment" is going to present itself.
- An antihistamine such as Benadryl, in case baby has an allergic reaction to a bee sting or bug bite.
- Snacks for you are nice too. Mommies often have to skip a meal.
- Always keep the name and phone number of your pediatrician with you.

Now that we've said all this, you're probably scrambling to find the phone number for the nearest U-Haul location so you can actually take the bag with you. Don't worry, we all walk around with all those things in our diaper bags. You'll learn that zip-top bags (in every size) and travel-size containers will allow you to haul everything you need without breaking your back. And now you understand why strollers have built-in storage.

The Backup Bag

Make a second backup bag for your car and just keep it in your trunk. Even the most organized mother has run out the door and forgotten to restock the diaper bag. Stocking your car with diapers, a change of clothes, blankets, extra bottles and formula, and even infant Tylenol can be a huge help in a pinch. Or it might give you a chance to help out another mom in need.

Tips for Unexpected Snafus

Stock the Car

Always keep extras in the car. Sooner or later, every mother runs out the door having forgotten to refill the diaper bag. I can't tell you how many times I've been at the mall and had another mother ask me for an extra diaper. It happens. So stocking your car is an essential backup plan. I was able to tuck some diaper necessities away in a pocket on the back of my seats, but some moms keep a small diaper bag in the car at all times. Of course, keep some extra diapers and wipes tucked away. It's great to have a towel—this works well in case you need to change baby in the car and want to protect your interior, and also if baby vomits in the car. Keep a spare change of clothing (top to bottom), and keep this habit going until at least age four. (There are potty accidents, mealtime accidents, playground accidents . . . the list goes on and on.) And if you're bottle-feeding, add a couple of bottles filled with powdered formula—you never know when you're going to get stranded, and baby formula isn't always readily available. Another thing I kept in the car that came in handy a few times was infant Tylenol or Motrin. Babies and toddlers get fevers at the worst possible times, and it's imperative to have these on hand. As baby ages, your in-car inventory will change to bandages, bug spray, sunscreen, snacks, and a well-stocked DVD library. When you're a mom, your car is like your second home. If you're well equipped, you'll save yourself lots of time and frustration.

Always Be Prepared for Bodily Fluids

From Sara

You'll notice that we keep recommending that you bring things like towels and extra clothing, and you'd better heed our warnings. We're not telling you this to scare you. We're telling you this because it's a fact of motherhood and if we prepare you, you won't be quite so freaked out when it actually happens to you (because it will). Kids vomit at the most inopportune moments and usually without warning. Even when kids are old enough to warn you, it usually happens something like this: kid walks into the living room and announces, "I feel sick," then immediately vomits on the rug.

Stephanie loves to tell the story about her son, Timmy, throwing up in the dance store. She had just picked him up from preschool and her daughter needed new ballet shoes, so they stopped in the dance store. It is this beautiful little store filled with pink tulle and ribbons and sparkly rhinestones. Timmy showed no signs of sickness at all. But just five minutes after walking through the door, he suddenly vomited violently all over the floor. Stephanie knew the owner but couldn't help being mortified that her kid upchucked in the middle of this woman's charming store among all the cute little pink slippers and tutus. The owner sold copies of our book in her store, and all Stephanie could say was, "Well, this is exactly why I wrote a book!"

Most of my bodily fluid stories seem to happen at the post office. Once when I was standing at the counter waiting to find out the difference in price between first class and parcel post, Anna vomited right into my open purse. She was perched on my hip, and my purse was slung over my shoulder and evidently must have looked like the perfect receptacle. I don't have to tell you how much fun it was to clean *that* up. Of course I didn't have an extra purse stashed in my car, but the container of wipes sure came in handy. A few years later Cade wet his pants right in the middle of the post office. Fortunately, the nice folks who work at my neighborhood post office are very understanding, even if my credibility as a mom-author has been totally destroyed as far as they're concerned.

Crying Babies

From Stephanie

I know you don't believe this, but if your baby cries in public, it will be okay. Babies cry, and everybody knows it. They cry in public all the time. It really doesn't bother anybody as long as *their* baby isn't the one doing the crying. Most people will have sympathy for you and try to help you. Sure, there are a few grumpy, crotchety, inhuman scrooges out there whom you'll encounter once in a while. Just ignore them; they were babies once too, and guess what, they cried in public. You can feel free to remind them of that fact if they give you a hard time.

Now, I'm not giving you permission to totally ignore other people's feelings. There are definitely places where you should avoid taking a new baby. Like a nice restaurant. If there isn't a kid's menu and balloons or crayons, then you're probably asking for trouble. People who are paying $50 a plate are usually after a different kind of ambiance than crying and poop smells. But if you are in a restaurant that is kid-friendly, then you have every right to be there. All you can do is *try* to keep baby quiet and happy. If it's not working, then just try to relax and eat your food. That's why you chose the kid-friendly destination, so you could relax along with the other parent patrons who understand your plight better than anyone.

What about going to a movie? There are plenty of theaters that offer daytime shows to give moms an opportunity to get out of the house and enjoy a movie surrounded by other empathetic mothers. You may not know it, but there's a mother code that states it's perfectly acceptable to bring a baby to a daytime movie. You gotta get out of the house once in a while, and other mothers understand that. You can absolutely feel relaxed during a daytime movie. We actually took our baby to a lot of movies when she was very young (at night as well as during the day). The sound didn't seem to bother her. We carried her in her infant car seat and rocked her with our feet, and if she did whimper, the movie was too loud for anyone to hear her anyway. That was a frequent night out for us when she was an infant. Plus, newborns usually don't cry as loudly as older babies, so try it while you can.

Diaper Changes in Public

From Stephanie

There is nothing enjoyable about changing your baby in public places. Today's SUVs and some minivans are a perfect height for changing your baby in the parking lot, and usually that was the surface I chose. Compared to the germ-ridden, unequipped changing areas offered by stores and restaurants, I felt much better about laying baby's backside on the carpet of my own car. I usually brought an extra cloth diaper or blanket along to use as a barrier between the surface and my baby's back. If I got caught without a blanket, I'd tear off a few paper towels and put them down. In your travels, you will find that many places—stores, offices, airplanes—do not offer diaper-changing areas. And you'll be tempted to lay your smelly, poop-smeared kid right on top of the nearest table, no matter who's watching. Try to use consideration and good judgment when faced with this dilemma. There is pretty much nothing you can do on an airplane except sit on the toilet and balance baby on your thighs to change him. Do *not* change a poopy diaper while in your seat, or you are going to earn a cabinful of enemies.

I must confess that I have changed my child's diaper on a table at a KFC restaurant. I was on a trip with two young children and I was struggling. When I realized that my baby needed relief from a poopy diaper, I wrestled both children into the bathroom only to find out that there was no changing table in the bathroom, and that was the last straw. I snapped, I admit it. I marched right out to the dining room, unzipped my diaper bag, unsnapped my baby's pants, and did the deed right there in the middle of everything and everyone. I'm sorry that the other patrons were victims of my tantrum, but it is absolutely unacceptable for a kid-friendly restaurant *not* to have installed a changing table. Over four million babies are born in the United States every year, and if kids wear diapers for two or three years, that means there's more than ten million kids in diapers each year. And you can't change them standing up, people! It is imperative that they be horizontal. So if you are considering opening a restaurant franchise and you don't spring for a changing table, don't be surprised when some stressed-out mother on the edge of sanity plunks her baby down on your serving counter and begins unsnapping his pants. Next, you'll notice a pungently unpleasant smell, but by that time it will be too late. You've been warned.

Clutter-Busting Resources

Checklist: packing your diaper bag
www.parents.com

Diaper Duck Travel Buddy Dispenser
www.munchkin.com

The Mobile Baby Care Kit
www.fatherhood.about.com

11

Car Seats

From Stephanie

I beseech you to make car seat safety a priority because I have been in a car crash with my children in the car. I was following a friend and was in unfamiliar surroundings when my cell phone rang. Just those two things combined proved to be too much of a distraction because as I reached for my phone, I realized that the left-turn signal had changed from a right-of-way arrow to a plain green (yield) and a car came barreling through the intersection and crashed directly into the rear passenger-side door—exactly in the spot where my four-year-old daughter was seated. The sound alone was terrifying. The intensity of the impact was unbelievable! The other car was totaled and my SUV's rear fender was smashed significantly.

Thankfully, everyone was okay. Both children were scared and crying. My daughter worried me the most because she got the greatest impact from the crash and was crying and saying that her chest hurt (which scared me to death). But the reason her chest hurt was because of the seat belt, which held her in place. She had a bruise over her breast bone, which proved to me just how well seat belts actually work. They do, without question, save lives. I am very grateful that both children were secured correctly in their car seats and that I was driving a big SUV. The mechanic at the body shop told me that if we had been sitting in a vehicle that was any lower to the ground, my daughter would have been crushed. From that day on, I never complained about how much gas my SUV used or how expensive the tires were.

Accidents happen when and where you least expect it, so never get complacent when it comes to your kids and car seats. No matter how much time it requires or how much they complain, take your time and stick to your guns—it could save their life.

From Sara

Your child's car seat is the most important piece of baby gear you own. Automobile accidents are the number one killer of children in this country. According to the American Academy of Pediatrics, car seats are 71 percent effective in reducing deaths for infants and 54–59 percent effective for reducing injury and death in older children. Although the vast majority of parents understand the importance of putting their children in child safety seats, as many as 70 percent of kids—*that's seven out of every ten*—are not properly buckled in, according to SeatCheck.org.

We moms live in our cars. We're driving carpool, taking the kids to tee-ball practice or dance. And we're usually multitasking—making a quick phone call to RSVP for a birthday party or confirm a sitter for Saturday night. Often the kids are loud or fighting, asking you to pick up something they dropped or put in a DVD for them (and in my car that means reaching under my seat, counting down three buttons, and pushing play). The point is, driving with kids is chaotic and can be dangerous. My son just transitioned to a booster seat and my husband and I were making a big deal about him being able to buckle himself until we realized that when he did buckle himself, the seat belt ended up in a twisted, loose mess that certainly was not going to keep him safe in a crash. We realized he still needs our help; in fact, he needs it more than he did buckling into a regular car seat! Take a minute to stop and check that your kids are properly fastened in their car seats. Accidents happen more often than any of us want to admit, so make sure your child is protected just in case it happens to you.

Car Seat Guidelines

Like most baby product categories, there is a myriad of choices available to parents when it comes to car seats (we'll use the terms *car seat* and *child safety seat* interchangeably here). To make matters even more confusing, car seat laws vary from state to state. And many of these laws are way out of date in terms of safety. Although there is no national car seat law, the National Highway Traffic Safety Administration has set the following guidelines for car seat use (as of this writing):

- Infants should ride in rear-facing child safety seats in the backseat until at least age one and twenty pounds. (If under age one but over twenty pounds, the child should still ride in a rear-facing seat but one that has been approved for heavier babies.)
- Never place a rear-facing seat in front of a passenger air bag.
- Once children reach age one and are heavier than twenty pounds, they should ride in a forward-facing child safety seat until they weigh forty pounds.

- When a child outgrows the forward-facing seat, he should ride in the backseat in a booster seat until he is at least eight years old, unless he is four feet nine inches tall, at which point he can properly fit into a seat belt.
- After outgrowing a booster seat, children under age thirteen should always use a seat belt and ride in the backseat. Kids of all ages are safest when properly restrained in the backseat.
- Secondhand child safety seats should not be used unless you are certain they have never been in an accident and you have all the parts, including instructions. Seats that are six years old or older should be discarded and never used.
- Always read both the vehicle owner's manual and the instructions that come with the child safety seat.
- It is important to remember that the best child safety seat is the one that correctly fits the child and the vehicle and is used correctly every time.
- Get your child's safety seat checked by a professional. Local law enforcement officers and/or the highway patrol will gladly check a car seat. Just call and ask them the best way to do so in your area.

Important Installation Tips

- Always read the instructions that come with your child's safety seat and then keep them in the glove box. If you are ever in a car accident, most insurance companies will replace your car seat, but they will want the owner's manual that came with that seat.
- Be sure to check what type of seat belts your vehicle has. Some seat belts need locking clips to be used with child safety seats. Most newer cars do not need these clips, but check your vehicle's owner's manual to be sure. If your seat does not require a locking clip, be sure that you've locked the seat belt correctly (usually you have to pull it all the way out and then let it retract to where the seat is tight and won't slip around or move).
- If your car was manufactured after 2002, it may have the LATCH system for securing child safety seats. LATCH is an acronym for "lower anchors and tethers for

One Great Tip for Securing a Car Seat

In some vehicles, especially large SUVs and vans, you can recline the back of the seat. Do this, and then install your car seat. When you have it as tight as you can get it, move the seat back upright again. This trick will get it supertight, especially for a forward-facing car seat. Make sure you check your seat each time you use it, in case someone else moves the seat or reclines it.

children." With LATCH, you do not need to use the seat belt to install your child's safety seat. Your vehicle *and* your car seat must come with LATCH in order to use this system for installation; otherwise you will need to use your car's seat belts.

General Car Safety Tips

- Be a good role model. Always wear your seat belt.
- Never leave your child alone in or around cars. Temperatures can reach dangerous levels extremely quickly. Sunroofs and power windows can be hazardous. Children can even become locked in the trunk. And tragically, every year children are seriously injured or killed when they are run over by a car in their own driveway. Make your children go inside the house when you need to move the car.
- If you buy a secondhand seat, make sure that it hasn't been cracked or damaged and that all the parts are present and in working condition. You should also call the manufacturer to make sure that no recalls or repairs have been announced for the seat.
- The CDC reports that over 9,100 children are treated in hospital emergency rooms each year due to non-traffic/non-crash car-related incidents. These include power window strangulation, vehicles set in motion by a young child, being run over in the driveway, hyperthermia, and others.
- All children should ride in the backseat at all times—no excuses!
- If there is no backseat in the vehicle or the backseat is full of other children, never put an infant in front of an active air bag.
- If there is only one child in the car, put her in the center rear—that's the safest place.
- If you must use your cell phone in the car, pull over to a safe spot and park first. A hands-free device is helpful, but no matter how good a multitasker you are, cell phones are a dangerous distraction.

Booster Seats

When a child has outgrown a traditional car seat, he is ready to move into a booster seat. How do you know when he is ready?

- He has reached or exceeded the maximum weight listed on the seat.
- His shoulders are above the shoulder harness slots.
- His ears have reached the top of the seat.

Remember, car seat belts are made for adults. Booster seats help adult-size seat belts fit children properly. When using a booster seat, make sure the shoulder belt goes across the shoulder and not the neck. (Booster seats with backs help position the shoulder belt correctly—put your child in a backless booster only when she is tall enough that the shoulder belt fits properly.) Check that the lap belt is snug across the top of the thighs, not the stomach. Also make sure the belt is not twisted or loose. And instruct kids not to put the shoulder belt under their arm. Children who are just transitioning to a booster often have trouble buckling up properly on their own. They may not be able to reach back and grab the seat belt, or it may become locked in place and you'll need to release it for them to buckle up. Unlike a five-point car seat, a seat belt has lots of play and kids can really get them in a mangled mess before they buckle. Don't assume your child has buckled up correctly in a booster seat just because she's "a big girl now." She still needs your help and watchful eye.

The Most Common Car Seat Mistakes

SeatCheck offers the following list of the most common child safety seat mistakes:

- Not using the right seat for a child's size and age
- Not placing the car seat facing in the correct direction
- Incorrect installation of the car seat in relation to the vehicle's air bags
- Incorrect installation and tightness of the child safety seat to the vehicle seat
- Not securing/tightening the car seat's harness and crotch straps
- Improper use of locking clips
- Not making sure the seat belt fits snugly across the child when using a booster seat
- Using a defective or broken car seat

And never use a car seat that has any of these problems:

- Has been recalled
- Has been involved in an accident
- Is more than six years old
- Doesn't have a label with the date it was manufactured and the seat name or model number
- Doesn't have instructions
- Is missing parts or has cracks in the frame

Frequently Asked Questions

Why can't I use a car seat that has been in an accident?

For years, parents were told they could not use a child safety seat that had been involved in a crash, no matter what. But in 2004 the National Highway Traffic Safety Administration changed its recommendations on replacing a car seat after a crash. If a crash is minor and meets *all* of the following criteria, the car seat is still safe to use:

- The vehicle was able to be driven away from the crash site.
- The vehicle door nearest the safety seat was undamaged.
- There were no injuries to any of the vehicle occupants.
- The air bags (if present) did not deploy.
- There is no visible damage to the safety seat.

If your accident was a moderate or severe crash, if any of the criteria in the list have not been met, or if for any reason you aren't sure if your child's car seat is still safe, you should replace it. Even if there appears to be no damage on the surface, internal structural damage could have occurred during the accident.

How can I find out if my car seat has been recalled?

There is a very good recall list found at www.carseat.org/recalls/recall.shtml. Or you can do an Internet search for "NHTSA Recall List," call the NHTSA at 1-800-424-9393, or call SeatCheck at 1-866-SEATCHECK.

What if my car only has lap belts?

Some older cars may only have lap belts in the backseat. You cannot use a booster seat with only a lap belt. However, you can use an infant-only seat, a convertible seat, or a forward-facing seat.

What if my child slouches or slumps in the car seat?

You can place rolled-up blankets or diapers around your child, but never behind or under him.

Should my child ride in a child safety seat on an airplane?

Most infant, convertible, and forward-facing seats can be used on an airplane. Booster seats, however, cannot. The Federal Aviation Administration and the American Academy of Pediatrics recommend that children be securely fastened in a certified child restraint while flying until four years of age. After age four, children can be secured with the plane's seat belts.

What if I can't afford a car seat?

There are many organizations that can either give you a seat or help you pay for one. Call your local police station or hospital first. If they have nothing available, contact the National Highway Traffic Safety Administration, the National Safe Kids Campaign, or SafetyBeltSafe USA. (See "Clutter-Busting Resources" on page 112.)

School Buses

Ever wondered why school buses don't have seat belts? If seat belts are so great and they save lives, why don't our school buses come equipped with them? Actually, there's been a very heated debate going on for some time about whether school buses are safer with or without seat belts. In 2007, seventeen states introduced seat belt bills, but none of them passed. Why? Some people believe that seat belts not only are unnecessary but also could be hazardous. They are worried that seat belts could be used as weapons or that unused belts could actually injure nearby students if an unfastened metal buckle flies around during an impact.

First, let's remember that school bus transportation is one of the safest forms of travel in the country, and much safer than riding in a car. Since 1984, an average of eleven passengers have died in school bus crashes each year, compared to the more than forty-one thousand people who die in motor vehicle accidents overall.

Here are the basic arguments against seat belts in buses, according to the National Highway Traffic Safety Administration:

- Seat belts are of no value in the majority of fatal accidents involving school buses.
- More children are killed around school buses (walking to and from the bus stop) than inside school buses.
- School buses are specifically designed with safety in mind. They are heavier and experience less crash force than smaller cars and trucks. School buses also have high padded seats specifically designed to absorb impact.
- There is no guarantee that students will use their seat belts. Studies have shown that improper use of seat belts can increase the risk of injuries.
- There is concern that seat belts could be used as weapons to strike or choke other passengers.
- Money proposed for seat belt installation could be better spent on other safety measures.

- If a bus has to be evacuated in an emergency, such as a fire, panicked or disoriented students might be trapped by their seat belts.
- Most believe that drivers would not be able to enforce or ensure the use of seat belts.

The NHTSA says that school buses are required to meet safety requirements over and above those applying to other passenger vehicles. The NHTSA feels that the best way to provide crash protection to passengers is through compartmentalization, in which children ride in a protective "envelope" consisting of strong, closely spaced seats that have energy-absorbing seat backs. The theory is that in a collision, these high seat backs prevent kids from being thrown great distances, and their impact-absorbing materials soften the blow. This concept is highly controversial since these high seat backs don't help much when a bus is hit from the side or rear, or rolls over. Over two hundred school districts across the country have adopted seat belts as an added safety feature and report usage rates from 80 percent to 100 percent.

Another argument suggests that since shoulder belts cannot be installed, lap-only belts could cause more head and abdominal injuries because the wearer is jerked forward from the waist in an impact.

Making drivers responsible for children fastening their seat belts is challenging. Unlike teachers, bus drivers must care for up to seventy students at a time while maneuvering a large vehicle and contending with traffic, weather, road conditions, and bus stops. Many people feel this is just too much to ask. One solution is to appoint a seat belt monitor on every bus.

Then there's the cost-benefit analysis. Installing seat belts in school buses would cost about $1,800 per bus, so outfitting the 440,000 school buses in the United States would cost nearly $800 million, and with an annual death toll of only eleven, how much lower can you go? Given that three times as many fatalities occur when students exit or enter their bus, some think the money might be better spent on educating the general public that when the school bus's stop sign swings out, it means you.

Seat belts on school buses have been endorsed by the American Medical Association, the American Academy of Pediatrics, the American Academy of Orthopedic Surgeons, the American College of Preventive Medicine, Physicians for Automotive Safety, and the Center for Auto Safety. If you agree that school buses should have seat belts, then write your local and state legislators. You can find sample letters on the National Coalition for School Bus Safety's website, www.ncsbs.org/legislature.

Clutter-Busting Resources

American Academy of Pediatrics car seat guide
www.aap.org/FAMILY/carseatguide.htm

Car seat laws state by state
http://babyproducts.about.com/od/statecarseatlaws

National Highway Traffic Safety Administration
Ease of use ratings for government-approved car seats
www.nhtsa.gov
888-327-4236

SEATCHECK

Check to see if your child's car seat is properly installed and check to see if your child's seat has been recalled
www.seatcheck.org
866-SEATCHECK (866-732-8243)

Consumer Product Safety Commission: Car seat recalls
www.cpsc.gov

SafetyBeltSafe
www.carseat.org

National Safe Kids Campaign
www.safekids.org

For safety in and around cars
www.kidsandcars.org

Federal Aviation Administration
www.faa.gov

12

Activities for Mom and Baby

From Sara

When I became a stay-at-home mom, the last thing I wanted to do was stay at home. I found some great mom-and-baby activities that were terrific for my children, got me out of the house, and helped me meet other moms. Isolation can be an issue for many new at-home moms, so it's important to find fun things to do with your baby. Although some of the activities can seem a little pricey, I've found that when you pay for twelve sessions of something up front you're a lot more likely to get there every week than if you attempt to go to the free children's story time at the public library (but then again, that could just be me). And, being easily distracted by household chores, I found that getting out of the house allowed me to give my baby my complete attention for an entire hour. No dryer buzzing, phone ringing, dog barking . . . just my baby and me. In my opinion, that was worth the $200 for Kindermusik (and the whining from David).

What to Expect

First of all, these activities are no longer just mother-and-child experiences. Many dads attend with their children, either with mom or solo. Of course you'll meet at-home moms, but you'll also meet working moms and dads who've stepped out of the office to spend some special time with their child. Sometimes there are nannies who bring children, sometimes grandparents.

With all these different folks, you'll encounter lots of different parenting styles and personalities. Everyone is there to connect with their child and give their child an opportunity to explore, learn, or play, so most of the time things go smoothly. Occasionally there will be a parent who lets their child fuss or cry when they should take them out of the room. In one of our Kindermusik classes, I watched a mom allow her toddler to run around and investigate all the electrical outlets on the other side of the room while the rest of us were sitting in a circle singing "Bright Red Cardinal." This kind of behavior can become distracting for the other kids, who then decide it might be fun to stick their fingers in the sockets too. Most instructors know how to handle these situations and can gently let Mom know she should take her unhappy baby outside or get her toddler back into the circle. If you experience a problem with another parent or child, discuss it in private with the instructor before or after the class. It's the instructor's responsibility to make sure everyone is comfortable and getting the most out of the program.

However, if another child is endangering your little one, of course jump in and stop the behavior right away. Some very young kids simply haven't yet learned how to play appropriately, so try not to get angry. Personally, I feel it's best to talk to the child's parent and let them handle the situation rather than talking to the child yourself. I was once in a jewelry store with Anna and the sales clerk told her to stop touching a necklace when I was standing right there (and for the record, I knew what she was doing and was okay with it). Anna was devastated. I wished the clerk had asked me to tell her not to touch the item instead of taking matters into her own hands. I always try to remember that when I have the urge to lecture other people's kids.

On the other hand, if the parent isn't present, sometimes you have to deal with the situation yourself and talk to the parent later. And please, when you take your child to Little Gym or anywhere else she is in contact with other children, *pay attention*! Nothing irks other moms more than a little kid who gets away with murder because his mother is constantly talking on her cell phone instead of watching him. Even the best instructor in the world simply cannot see everything that is going on all the time. Toddlers and young kids are constantly learning, constantly exploring boundaries, so even if you think your little angel could never do anything wrong, things happen. Be there to guide your little one; don't hand off that responsibility to someone else.

Programs

Kindermusik

I took both of my children to Kindermusik classes and we all absolutely loved it. My kids started when they were about a year old, but there are classes available for newborns and for children through age seven. Kindermusik classes are led by an instructor but parents participate with their children, exploring movement and music. The classes are pretty simple, especially for younger children, and parents are very involved, which can make you wonder, *What the heck am I spending $200 for?* The cost of the class includes take-home materials such as CDs, books, and specially designed instruments for children. Often these classes are available through a nearby preschool. You can find out more by calling 800-628-5687 or visiting www.kindermusik.com.

Gymboree

You may be familiar with the Gymboree children's clothing stores, but did you know about Gymboree Play and Music? They offer classes from ages newborn to five years. Age-appropriate activities are designed to stimulate development and your baby's interest in the world around her. There's a yoga-based mom and baby fitness class, a baby sign language class, music classes, and more. Many classes offer an opportunity for parent discussion at the end, which fosters connections between moms. For more information, call 877-449-6932 or visit www.gymboreeclasses.com.

The Little Gym

The Little Gym's tagline is "Motor Skills Made Fun." It's all about activity here, from gymnastics to cheerleading, karate to dance. Programs are available for kids ages four months to twelve years. If you're desperate for a night out, check out their Parents' Survival Night—on select weekend nights, kids can enjoy an evening of fun while parents get to enjoy a night for themselves. There are about a hundred Little Gym locations around the United States. To find a location near you, call 888-228-2878 or visit www.littlegym.com.

Stroller Strides

Founded by mom and fitness expert Lisa Druxman, Stroller Strides is a great way to get fit without leaving your baby. Stroller Strides offers many fitness programs moms can do with their babies. All you need to bring are your baby and your stroller—almost any safe stroller will do. Classes are held outside and may be canceled in severe weather. Stroller Strides recommends that your baby be at least six weeks old before starting classes, which generally last one hour. Call 866-FIT-4MOM or visit www.strollerstrides.com for information.

Mommy and Me

This great online resource offers a national directory of play groups, classes, and clubs so you can find the ones that are most convenient and appropriate for you. Visit www.mommyandme.com.

Story Time at the Public Library

Check the local branch of your public library for activities for kids. Many have story times, crafts, and other activities for toddlers. And best of all, they're free!

From Stephanie

I didn't do any of those hokey classes with my babies. Sara really enjoyed doing those things with her kids, and many other moms do too. Personally, I just didn't see the point in spending the money to do something that they'd never remember. All those baby music and gym classes seemed like a royal pain in the patootie, and frankly, when I quit my job with the arrival of our second child, we just didn't have room in the budget for classes to entertain our baby. We made our own fun using books like *The Toddler's Busy Book* to think of creative ways to entertain our young kids around the house and yard. If you don't have the time and resources to take your kids to these trendy baby outings, don't feel bad about it. They'll turn out just fine even if they can't play the cymbals by age two. One of the best, inexpensive ways to give baby some entertainment and a chance to socialize is play groups (see the next chapter).

Clutter-Busting Resources

WEBSITES

Kindermusik
www.kindermusik.com
800-628-5687

Gymboree Play and Music
www.gymboreeclasses.com
877-449-6932

The Little Gym
www.littlegym.com
888-228-2878

Stroller Strides
www.strollerstrides.com
866-FIT-4MOM

Mommy and Me online directory
www.mommyandme.com

BOOKS

The Toddler's Busy Book
by Trish Kuffner

13

Play Group Perks

From Stephanie

Play groups are a wonderful resource for moms. I joined a neighborhood play group when my children were babies, and the moms and our kids stayed friends until long after the kids were five years old. We went to each other's birthday parties and saw each other at the pool and at school. It was a great bonding experience and I'll never forget those mommies I shared so much time with those first years. By the time kids turn five, it's hard to keep play groups together. Families begin to have different interests and kids begin to have schedules, and it gets too hard to find a day when everyone can get together.

What to Expect

Let's be honest here: play groups are for you just as much as for your child. It's a chance to get out of the house, make some new friends, and, most of all, have adult conversation, which can be priceless to a mom who's had conversations about nothing but the Wiggles for two days. It can be very informative and reassuring to talk to other moms who are having the same challenges as you are. You're going to realize that your child is normal after all, and you'll get some great tips on handling the challenges. You can become part of a play group while your baby is still only seven or eight months old. Let them all sit around in their bouncy seats and smile and coo at each other while you visit with the other moms.

There are benefits for your child as well. You're giving him the opportunity to learn to share and interact with other kids. Play groups help your child develop language skills, and they're a great chance to play with new, more interesting toys and make some new friends. It's a change of scenery for baby and very stimulating.

It's also a chance to let children of various ages interact together. Younger children learn from older ones, and older kids learn how to interact with those who are younger. Close supervision is often necessary so things don't get out of control, but it's important for children to learn to understand and respect kids who aren't the same age.

Keep play groups simple. These meetings should not be stressful. Your house doesn't have to be spotless and you don't need to prepare fancy foods. These are moms just like you, remember? They understand. When I organized our weekly play group, I got a calendar and assigned a mom to each week. It was up to that mom to decide what the group would do that week and to get the word out. The hosting mom would provide a snack for the kids and for the moms, and everyone was in charge of bringing their own drinks (kid drinks are complicated—some moms cut juice with water, some prefer milk, and everyone needs their own brand of sippy cup to protect the living room rug). Sometimes we planned outings to the petting zoo or a local kid gym, but most times we met at the host's home and enjoyed their playroom in a relaxed, kid-friendly setting. As the children got older, we planned more sophisticated offerings, but never underestimate how much fun a kiddie pool and some water balloons can be.

There are two cons of play groups. One is that scuffles will occur. Kids hit, bite, cry, and make each other angry sometimes. Know this going in and be prepared to handle the situation gracefully. Scuffles in our group normally happened when we moms were having too much fun in our own conversation and weren't watching closely enough. And there's always going to be that one mother who "never watches her kid." Disagreements between kids aren't such a bad thing. It gives them a chance to learn how to work through their problems. It's a chance for you to teach them how to act and how not to act. Be respectful to your fellow moms. If you know that there is one "problem child" in the group, then be attentive during the meetings so you can prevent offenses or at least see what actually happened. And if you notice that your child is the one causing the problems, then it's time to hover over your child to prevent scuffles until she's better at interacting with her friends. When scuffles do occur, be polite. When the group is still new, don't correct someone else's child—moms can be weird about that. Kindly explain to the other mom what happened and let her discipline her own child. Once the group is more comfortable with one another, you'll all become okay with other people in the group correcting your child—in fact, it's a big help. But tread lightly in the beginning until you get to know the parenting styles and personalities of the other moms.

The other problem with play groups is sickness. Kids can be sick and not show signs for hours or days. Make a rule in your play

Sara's Play Group Tip

My local mom friends and I would schedule play group gatherings for late in the afternoon so we could enjoy a much-needed glass of wine together.

group that kids with fevers and runny noses are not allowed. Make sure to have them wash their hands before snack time and when they leave. And if you're the host, a good coating of Lysol spray does a great job of killing the germs left behind. Spray it on your toys, doorknobs, furniture, bathrooms, etc. Young children are experts at spreading bodily fluids (it's just what they do). And if your child has been sick, please give the same courtesy to your guests and disinfect your house and toys before they arrive.

How to Start a Play Group

The following helpful suggestions for organizing a play group are from www.toddlers today.com.

1. Start by deciding how structured your play group will be. Our group was just free-play time (that meant more mom time). Some play groups are more structured and divide the hour up into segments, like snack time, free-play time, circle time, craft time, etc. The only problem with all free play is that scuffles will probably occur more frequently.

2. Get the word out. If you have a large neighborhood, place a notice in the community newsletter. Local family magazines are a great place to find play group pals—most provide a free calendar listing. Make flyers or posters and place them in your local grocery store, church, pediatrician's office, or baby store (like Babies R Us). Think about posting flyers in places where you'll find moms with similar interests—for example, if you like working out, place one in your gym. (After all, this is for you too.)

You can also find other moms with common interests online at sites like www.themommiesnetwork.org. This network is located in twenty-five states and has twenty-three thousand members who form play groups (as well as other types of gatherings) based on neighborhoods, etc. Other sites to find play groups (or start one) in your area are International Moms Club (www.momsclub.org), Because I'm Mom (www.becauseimmom.com), and Mothers of Preschoolers (www.mops.org).

3. Be on the lookout for moms with kids the same ages as yours. It's perfectly okay to approach another mom in the grocery store or at the nail salon.

4. Keep the fun going. Planning is important to keep play groups interesting and keep members involved. Use the holidays to create fun theme parties for the kids with crafts and special games. Research and visit local venues that are age-appropriate.

5. Start with a small group. Six to eight children is a good number to manage. More than that makes it harder to have outings.

Parenting.com says to meet the moms first: "Once you've found some candidates, arrange a get-together—without the kids—to see whether you hit it off. You should also discuss how you'll handle sensitive issues. Is someone's child allergic to pets or certain foods? How will you deal with sharing, biting, and temper tantrums? Agreeing on a plan of action in advance will make sessions much more carefree."

Here are some other guidelines to consider:

- Will there be a membership fee to help with the costs of snacks? Will the host provide snacks, or will each child bring his or her own snack?
- How often will the group meet? How long will each get-together last?
- Is everyone expected to host, and if so, how often? Or will your group meet in the same location every week?
- Can older or younger siblings join the fun? Or should the group be limited to only a designated age?

Once the planning is done, remember to bring your camera. Play groups are an important milestone in your child's life. Some friendships will last for years. Your child's social calendar will emerge from your play group, bringing you birthday parties, holiday parties, and opportunities for other sports and outings. And play groups always provide memorable moments.

Clutter-Busting Resources

The Mommies Network
www.themommiesnetwork.org

International Moms Club
www.momsclub.org

Because I'm Mom
www.becauseimmom.com

Mothers of Preschoolers
www.mops.org

14

Dining Out with Your Baby or Child

From Sara

I've always loved going out for dinner, but as a mom, I enjoy it more than ever. Someone else prepares the food, serves it, takes the plates away, and cleans up the mess—what's not to love about that? Getting out of the house for a meal at a restaurant saved my sanity after my first child was born. I was suffering from a severe case of cabin fever (not to mention postpartum depression) and getting out was like therapy for me. Fortunately, Anna was a good baby and slept in her car carrier through most of our meals. I'm kind of ashamed to write it, but I remember actually putting her (in her seat, of course) under a table in a restaurant. I know, it sounds awful, but it was clean (I checked), it was nice and dark and quiet under there, she was out of the way of the servers, and she *was* sleeping.

Our habit of eating out continued even after I was back to normal mentally. We took Anna to restaurants all the time and she got very used to it. Even at eighteen months old, when toddlers easily get bored sitting at a table, she was a pleasure to eat out with. Then again, she also has an easygoing nature and that may account for most of her good restaurant behavior. Our son, Cade, was completely on the other end of the spectrum. I've spent many a meal standing outside the restaurant holding a screaming little boy while my food got cold and my wine got warm.

No matter what your child's disposition, it is a lot to expect that they'll sit still and be quiet through a long meal in a nice restaurant. On the other hand, it is *not* too much to expect them to behave appropriately in a kid-friendly atmosphere. My point is, life doesn't stop when you have a baby. If going out to dinner is something you enjoy, there is no reason to stop once you become a parent. Eating out is a great way to teach table manners to your children as they grow, and it can be a nice time for family bonding, away from the distractions and duties of home. It can also turn into a total nightmare. Here are some ideas for making dinner out with the family a happy, not humiliating, affair.

Infants

New moms are usually very apprehensive about taking a baby to a restaurant, but the truth is that when your children are babies, you should go out to eat as much as you can! Babies often sleep right through your meal at a restaurant. You usually enjoy a peaceful meal with uninterrupted adult conversation. However, when your baby becomes a busy toddler, that will all change. You'll be picking Cheerios, crayons, toys, and sippy cups off the floor. Spoons will be banged loudly on the table after knives and forks have been whisked out of reach. If your little one has just learned to crawl or walk, he'll be content confined to a high chair for about thirty seconds. You might get to enjoy a sip or two of your iced tea before the mayhem begins. So go ahead and take your baby out and don't stress. If baby does become fussy, you can always retreat to the bathroom or step outside for a few minutes. (By the way, later in this chapter we also have some tips on taking a toddler out to a restaurant, since we've probably scared you about that now.)

Shoot for Naptime

Try to plan your meal for a time when baby typically takes a nap. Lots of infants will fall asleep during a short car ride and (fingers crossed) continue sleeping through your meal.

Make Reservations

Timing is everything when you are eating out with a baby. Make a reservation so that you can be seated at a table as soon as possible after arriving. You don't want to spend half an hour of your precious night-out time waiting in a lobby or, worse, in a smoky, loud bar area.

Go Nice but Not Too Nice

The nice thing about going out to dinner with an infant is that you don't have to eat at Chuck E. Cheese . . . yet. You can eat at nice restaurants with other adults. But that doesn't mean a place with a five-diamond rating. Choose a happy medium—family-friendly but not overly loud. Dull background noise can be good for keeping baby asleep during the meal, but if the noise is too loud, you may have an awake, fussy, or screaming baby on your hands.

Don't Be Afraid to Ask Questions

It's perfectly fine to call ahead and ask if the restaurant has high chairs available or even if you can bring in your stroller. Sometimes it's easier to leave baby in a stroller that you can wheel right up to the table. You can ask when the restaurant is less busy so you know the best time to plan your meal out.

Bring Food

Okay, this is obvious, but we still have to say it. Don't ever leave the house without a food source for baby—breast, bottle, expressed breast milk—especially if you are trying to have a nice meal out. The one time you think you won't need it will surely be the time you will.

You Can Use a High Chair

You know those brown wooden high chairs you see at restaurants? Well, did you know that you can flip them over—yes, turn them upside down—and your baby's infant carrier seat will rest right on the two wood crossbars just perfectly? We have no idea if they were actually designed for this purpose, but most servers know this (although we have had to show a few) and will flip the chair over for you. Then you don't have to put baby on the floor under the table, like me. The only downside is that the bottoms of those high chairs can be really disgusting, so bring along antibacterial wipes to clean them off.

From Stephanie

Watch out—even though turning those wooden high chairs upside down seems like a brilliant idea, there are many restaurants that will ask you not to do that because they view it as a safety hazard. So don't be surprised if your server asks you to remove your infant car seat and use the high chair as it was intended. Some restaurants have wooden frames designed for holding an infant car seat, and you can ask for one of those. Otherwise, just ask for a booth or a couple of extra chairs.

Always Take Wipes

Now that you are a mom, antibacterial wipes should be in your possession whenever you leave the house—not for the baby, but for you! You may need wipes to wash your hands after changing a diaper, wipe off an icky changing station in a public bathroom, or clean off the bottom of a flipped-over high chair. I never thought about carrying wipes before I was a mom, but now I keep them in my purse and car at all times. Even though my children are older now, I still need wipes all the time. I think it's a habit that becomes ingrained in mothers and stays with you for the rest of your life. It's why our grandmothers always had Wet Ones (and tissues and Juicy Fruit) in their purses.

Dine at Off-Peak Times

Saturday night at seven is not when you want to head out to dinner with a baby in tow. Weeknights are less busy (particularly earlier in the week) in most restaurants, and you'll have a better chance of getting a more private table—so if your baby does get fussy, you don't have to worry about diners right next to you. You'll also get faster service, which means your meal won't take as long and your baby will probably sleep right through it. You may even get time for dessert! If you choose to eat out on the weekends, go early in the evening, before six o'clock if possible.

From Stephanie

On this I have to agree with Sara—it *is* all about the timing. We lived in Atlanta when our first baby was born, and we loved indulging ourselves at the nice restaurants Atlanta has to offer. Once we had a handle on her sleep schedule, we had no problem bringing her into five-star restaurants with us. We asked for a booth so we had plenty of room for the infant car seat, and she usually slept through the entire meal. The owner of one of our regular hangouts always greeted us in a heavy Italian accent and referred to her as "the baby that never makes a sound." We usually timed it just right for a late dinner (around 8:30 P.M.) to ensure that baby had just eaten and had settled in for bedtime. When we got home, we could move her from her car seat into her bed and she never woke up. I encourage you to do this as much as possible while your baby is young because starting when your child is about one year, you won't enjoy peace in a restaurant again until they're in their twenties.

Ask for a Table Near an Exit

It will eventually happen: your baby will fuss and cry in a restaurant, or he will have an explosion of diarrhea in his diaper that goes up his back and out the sides of his pants. The best thing to do in these situations is make a hasty exit to the bathroom or outside. And believe me, you want the shortest route there. It's no fun to weave your way through forty tables of wide-eyed diners with a poop-stained, screaming, red-faced baby in your arms (not that I've made that mistake—I'm speaking purely hypothetically here). So ask for a spot close to an exit (and not one with a fire alarm attached).

Older Babies and Toddlers

We have now entered serious territory. Dining out with little ones in this age group is not for the faint of heart. You will need every ounce of creativity, resourcefulness, planning ability, and patience that you can muster. I've found that a good stiff drink also helps.

The Noisier the Better

Now that your baby is older (and louder), noise is your friend. Your child's noise will be drowned out or at least muffled by the restaurant's din.

Order Your Child's Food First

Toddlers get really cranky really fast when they are hungry. Order your child's meal at the same time as you order drinks. Ask the server to bring out the food as soon as it's ready. It will be easier to entertain your child with toys, crayons, or books if her tummy is full.

From Stephanie

I have to disagree here. We found that having our children's food delivered before ours was a surefire way to ruin a perfectly good meal. As soon as our kids were done eating, they were ready to move, and instead of enjoying our food we had to constantly interrupt our meal to entertain or correct them, take them to the bathroom, or chase them around the table. I recommend always having something in your purse to keep the kids busy until the food is served—a few plastic army men, Pretty Ponies, or even lollipops (I'm convinced that lollipops don't spoil appetites). Then you can all eat at the same time, which will keep them busy and quiet while you enjoy your meal. The next time you're in a checkout line or at the dollar store, look for things you can keep in your purse that will keep your children busy.

Bring a Snack

Pack a little snack (that won't spoil your child's appetite) to keep her entertained while you are eating or before her food comes. Cheerios in a Snack Trap cup (see "Clutter-Busting Resources") are a great idea. If your baby is not eating table food yet, it's perfectly okay to bring her jarred (or homemade) foods and feed her at the table.

Bring a Sippy Cup

Most restaurants give children drinks that are too much and too big for them to handle, and often your choices are limited to sugary sodas. Bring a sippy cup with your beverage of choice, or you can order something at the restaurant and pour it into the sippy cup at the table. This is especially a good idea if you have two children because one drink is usually enough for both of them to share. And don't forget that bars offer all kinds of juice (you may have to remind your server that orange juice and cranberry juice can be obtained from the bar).

Bring Entertainment

Most chain restaurants that cater to families offer crayons and colorable kids' menus, but it's a good idea to throw a pack of crayons and a small coloring book in your diaper bag or purse before you leave. If your child is too young for crayons, don't bring a bunch of loose toys and teething rings because you will just end up spending your entire meal picking them up off the questionably clean floor. Instead bring a toy that suctions to the table (and preferably doesn't play music—you may not mind hearing "Twinkle Twinkle Little Star" forty-three times during your meal, but the couple next to you may feel differently). Sassy makes lots of these suction-type toys. They are great for high chairs and strollers too.

Request a Booth

If your child is old enough to sit in a restaurant booster seat, sitting in a booth, with your child on the inside and you on the outside, makes it easier to contain a busy toddler than sitting at a table.

If All Else Fails, Leave a Hefty Tip

If, in spite of your best efforts, your child screamed through dinner and most of his dinner is smeared all over the table and floor, then leave your server a generous tip and wait a few weeks before returning to that particular restaurant.

Stephanie's Purse

Since becoming a mom, I've always fantasized about being on that old game show (I think it was *Let's Make a Deal*) where the host would ask the audience for some crazy, obscure item and if you happened to have that item in your purse, you'd win cash. There's no way I could lose that game now! I could change a tire, disinfect a surgical suite, entertain a group of up to eleven preschoolers, and successfully stage a Broadway show with the contents of my purse.

Kids

From Sara

Bring Hand Sanitizer

How often have you gotten everyone seated at the restaurant table only to realize the kids' hands haven't been washed . . . and you just came from tee-ball practice? Or you're in the bathroom with the kids and the soap dispenser is empty? A thousand thank-yous to the person who invented hand sanitizer or, as some kids call it, "magic soap." What did moms *do* before this wonderful invention? Imagine the spread of infectious disease that could have been stopped if only it had been around two hundred years ago! Hand sanitizer should be in your possession at all times. I keep a small bottle in my purse and a huge pump bottle of it in the car.

Split a Meal

Even at restaurants that cater to kids, portions are usually way too large for one child to consume. Consider splitting a meal between two children—if you can get them to agree on a selection. We have plenty of sibling rivalry between our two, but David and I can usually get them to agree on one meal. Sometimes allowing one child to pick the meal and the other to pick the side will work. Most restaurants don't mind splitting the meal onto two plates or at least bringing you an extra plate so you can divide the food when it arrives. That way both kids get enough to eat without having leftovers. In my experience day-old chicken nuggets and french fries just don't reheat well, so they typically end up in the trash can.

Look at the Adult Menu

Unfortunately, most restaurant kid fare is the same no matter where you go: chicken nuggets, hamburger, hot dog, macaroni and cheese. Not exactly the healthiest choices. Before giving in to the chicken nuggets, take a look at the appetizer and entrees on the adult menu. Is there a healthier choice there that your child may like? Some restaurants will serve half portions of entrees as well, so don't hesitate to ask.

Lay Down the Ground Rules Before You Go

Clearly tell your children what is expected of them before going to the restaurant. "Use an inside voice in the restaurant. No yelling. No burping (that goes for you too, Dad). No kicking your little brother under the table. . . ." You get the idea. Don't wait until you are halfway through a miserable meal to try to regain control.

Basic Table Manners for Kids

From Sara

When children use some basic table manners, eating out is a more enjoyable experience for everyone. It helps to introduce table manners at home first. Waiting until you are out at a restaurant to teach manners is a lesson in futility. I try to teach manners at every meal—simple things like putting the napkin in your lap and waiting to begin eating until all food has been served and the blessing has been said. Complimenting the good ("Wow, that's great how you put your napkin in your lap") instead of nagging ("I've told you three times now to take your elbows off the table!") will motivate kids to remember their manners and keep dinner from becoming an unpleasant experience for them.

- Wait until everyone has been served before you begin eating.
- Put your napkin in your lap before eating.
- Wipe your mouth with your napkin, not your sleeve or bare hand.
- Eat with a fork unless the food is meant to be eaten with fingers.
- Don't talk with food in your mouth.

Great Products for Eating Out with Kids

PAMPERS BIBSTERS

Disposable bibs are great for restaurants because you don't have to pack up a dirty bib and take it home. These are handy to keep in your diaper bag.

TABLE TOPPER

You don't want to put a plate in front of a baby or toddler because it will end up on the floor. Take a Table Topper instead. These disposable plastic mats provide a sanitary surface for your child at the table. You can place finger foods right on the mat without worrying about germs. See www.tabletopper.com.

POTTY TOPPER

What a brilliant idea! Also made by the folks at Table Topper, Potty Topper is a disposable plastic cover you can place right over a public toilet seat to protect your child from germs. We sure know what a challenge it can be to keep little hands off the toilet when you're in a public bathroom. The Potty Topper has an adhesive backing so it stays in place, and wet spots from the toilet seat won't leak through. Check out www.tabletopper.com.

TOYS FOR EATING OUT

Rocking Horse Suction Cup by Sassy
www.sassybaby.com

Ocean Wonders Suction Spinner Fish by Fisher-Price
www.fisher-price.com

- Chew with your mouth closed.
- Don't put your elbows on the table while eating.
- Say please and thank you when asking for something or being served something.
- No gross talk at the table (bodily fluids, bathroom talk, or anything else gross).
- Don't say "Yuck," "I don't like this," or other negative comments when you are served food, especially when you are at someone else's home.
- Burping is not appropriate at the table. If a burp does slip out unintentionally, quickly say, "Excuse me."
- Boys should always wear a shirt to the table and should take off hats before sitting down to a meal.

Clutter-Busting Resources

WEBSITES

Advice with Dr. Dave and Dr. Dee
www.drdaveanddee.com

Family Education
www.familyeducation.com

Dining out with kids
www.foodfit.com

Seven mistakes not to make when eating out with kids
www.fodors.com/news/story_2628.html

BOOKS

Dear Miss Perfect: A Beast's Guide to Proper Behavior
by Sandra Dutton

Emily Post's Guide to Good Manners for Kids
by Cindy Post Senning, Peggy Post, and Steve Bjorkman

15

Traveling with Baby

Stephanie's Tips for Making Travel Easier with Baby on Board

Merely by coincidence, it seemed as if every major family event possible occurred the same year our daughter was born. From Great-Grandma's ninetieth birthday party to family weddings and vacations, our little baby accumulated more frequent-flyer miles in her first year of life than most seasoned business travelers. It was frustrating at first, but we soon learned the ins and outs of traveling with an infant. Having learned the hard way, I offer here some of my favorite tips to help make your next excursion better for you, your baby, and those poor souls sentenced to traveling with or near you.

Tip 1: Bring Extra

Extra diapers, extra wipes, extra clothing, and above all, extra formula. No matter their advances in passenger convenience, airports still don't sell baby formula, baby food, or diapers. We've experienced flight delays that have lasted for four hours or more. And in many cases, airlines prefer to keep you on board the plane. Don't put yourself, your baby, or your fellow passengers in a situation with a hungry, unhappy baby and no way to appease him. Bring at least two extra bottles. Store dry formula in a zip-top bag to make it lighter and easier to transport. I even save the measuring scoop from an old can of formula and keep it in the bag for measuring on the go. Flight attendants are always happy to fill baby's bottle with warm water. A drinking glass or coffee cup filled half full of hot water is great for warming jars of baby food. Never board a plane without stopping to buy a bottle of water for yourself and for cooling the coffee-hot water you'll be given once on board.

Tip 2: Sucking Prevents Painful Ear Pressure Changes

Try to adjust baby's schedule so he can be sucking (breast, bottle, or pacifier) during takeoff and landing. This will prevent any pain or discomfort in baby's ears due to pressure changes. The best flights we had were those in which I altered our baby's schedule so that she was eating during takeoff, which was followed by the usual nap. By the time we landed, she awoke happy and ready to entertain everyone around us.

Tip 3: Bring Some New Toys

Stash your diaper bag with a few new toys that baby has never seen. It will keep baby happy and busy for hours. Old toys just don't have the same appeal. Whenever we traveled, my diaper bag was always 20 percent diapers and food and 80 percent toys. You don't have to spend a fortune—just visit your local dollar store for a few new baubles. It is unrealistic to expect a child to sit still and quiet for several hours on a plane. They can't be still and quiet at home for more than a few seconds, and airplanes are no different.

Tip 4: Trade Your Diaper Bag for a Backpack

Trade in your trusty diaper bag for a convenient backpack to free up your hands. Stash all your baby's toys and supplies and your own wallet and necessities in it. This frees up your hands and fits neatly under the seat or stroller. Plus your husband won't mind carrying it as much as the cute pink and white one embroidered with the little bunnies.

Tip 5: The Stroller Rules

The airlines have it all figured out—and it couldn't be more convenient for you. Most airlines will allow you to check your stroller just outside the door of the airplane. That's right—you can practically wheel baby, stroller and all, right to your seat! Just check in with the gate attendant to get a special tag and claim check, which you place on the stroller handle. Just before you board the plane, collapse your stroller (take all your belongings with you) and leave it at the door of the airplane. Miraculously, it will be there waiting for you in exactly the same place when you land. (Sometimes you may have to wait a minute or two.)

There are just a few setbacks to warn you about. Getting through security can be a little challenging, as most airports will require you to remove baby and all your belongings and collapse the stroller so it will fit onto the X-ray belt. This isn't easy, especially if you're traveling as a single parent. Do yourself a favor and *ask for help*! There is always a security attendant available to lend a helping hand, and if not, just ask. Be sure to look for the family or handicapped lane, which most major airports offer. Remember to take your time so you don't get flustered. It's a big job and the people around you will be more understanding than you think.

Anything that is in or attached to your stroller when you check it may not be there when it's returned to you. So remove any plastic flaps, shopping bag nets, or cup holders that you've grown fond of. I suspect strollers get tossed around pretty well under the airplane.

Also, if you have the kind of stroller that allows your infant car seat to snap on, that too can be brought along. Just ask the gate attendant for two claim check tags and leave the seat next to your collapsed stroller when you board (unless you purchased a seat for baby and want to use your car seat to strap her into her seat on the plane). If you're a germ freak like me and want to protect your precious little baby's backside, or just want to preserve the condition of your car seat, tuck a large trash bag into your stroller and use it to cover the seat. Use the claim tag to close the opening of the bag. It will keep it clean and stain-free.

Tip 6: What Flight Attendants Say About Infant Passengers

Most flight attendants love their little passengers. They remind them of their own little ones waiting at home. Just be courteous, and plan ahead if you know you will need something. Attendants can't always operate within baby's immediate time frame.

Tip 7: Leave Extra, Extra Early!

It's impossible to sprint through a crowded airport terminal with a baby, diaper bag, and stroller in tow. Everything from parking to check-in takes longer with baby. You'll have to take detours from your normal route to find elevators. And just going through security takes three times as long. You will more than likely be required to unload and collapse your stroller and send it on the belt through the X-ray machines, along with your shoes and baby's shoes too. So make sure you're an expert at collapsing and opening your stroller with one hand. If you're not, then practice at home to become a "stroller master"—it will prevent frustration in the security line.

Tip 8: Ask for Help

Parking attendants, flight attendants, security guards, and even strangers—whoever happens to be in your path is a potential assistant when you're traveling with a little need machine. I've had total strangers carry my stroller down several flights of stairs. It's usually another dad whose kids are at home with Mommy and understands your pain. Take advantage of anyone willing to help you. And don't be afraid to ask.

Tip 9: Baby Must Be Accounted For

If you haven't purchased a seat for your baby, you are required to register your child's name with the airline at the gate. They will usually ask for this information when you check in your stroller.

Tip 10: Bring Extra Layers

The cabins of airplanes, going from too hot to too cold in minutes, are one of the most unpredictable environments you'll ever encounter. So come prepared to keep your little one comfy. Remember that babies can get too hot too. So dress baby lightly, and bring a sweater and/or extra blanket so you can add or take away as needed. A comfortable baby is a quiet baby.

Tip 11: Be Courteous and Relax

Don't stress yourself out by being overly concerned about disturbing everyone else on the plane. Most people either have been in your shoes or will be eventually. Most of the time, people will enjoy watching your baby play and interact with the other passengers. If you encounter a few who seem to have no compassion for your situation, don't fret. If they can't find joy looking into the face of a little baby, they were probably miserable before they were ever exposed to your little noisemaker. Just do your part: be apologetic and courteous, bring quiet toys, and try your best to keep baby happy and comfortable. In many instances, all you can do is apologize. And that's enough for most emotionally well-balanced passengers.

Tip 12: Bring a Backup Outfit

Be sure to bring an extra change of clothes for baby. Many airplanes don't provide a changing table. So you'll be forced to balance baby on your lap in the plane's restroom if a diaper change is required. I also recommend bringing a changing pad to protect your lap from baby's messes, and a zip-top bag for containing stinky diaper odors. Please don't subject your fellow passengers to a dirty diaper. Remember, you're in a confined space, so take care of any messes as soon as you safely can.

Tip 13: Take Your Time

Don't worry about being the first on board the airplane. The first time I traveled with my baby, I was insulted that people with children were not permitted to board first. Turns out that's a good thing. Keep baby in the terminal as long as possible. Take a nice, long stroll. With all the sights and sounds, the airport offers plenty of entertainment value. Baby will be trapped in the same seat with the same surroundings long enough during the flight.

Tip 14: Overnight Shipping Is a Friend Indeed

If you plan to be at your destination longer than a couple of days, ship as much as you can to your hotel instead of lugging it through the airport. Some of baby's familiar toys and belongings will make her much more calm and comfortable in this temporary environment, not to mention keep her entertained. Just use lots of bubble wrap and don't forget to turn the musical toys to the off position, or even remove the batteries. I was once called to the front desk to collect a box I had shipped. Judging by the glances I received, the front desk staff seemed to have lost their appreciation for "Twinkle Twinkle Little Star," having heard it incessantly for the last four hours. (I had put new batteries in all the toys for our trip.)

Tip 15: Beware of Hotel Cribs

We've all heard the reports: hotel cribs are sorely neglected. So watch out for loose parts, especially screws or other small parts that could be a choking hazard. Crib sheets must fit tightly so baby can't suffocate or get tangled. And mattresses should be extremely firm. If you are a proponent of co-sleeping (sleeping with your baby), then just request a king-size bed when you make your reservations.

Tip 16: Coffeemakers Are Key

Choose a hotel that offers an in-room coffeemaker. This is a fabulous way to heat baby food or water for bottles. Just remove the filter portion, let the heated water run directly into the pot, and immerse the baby food jar in the water (that's how they used to heat baby food before microwaves). But beware! We found that little jars of baby food get extremely hot on the bottom, so be sure to stir baby's food thoroughly to prevent burns.

Tip 17: Babies and Bars

Of course you have to avoid the smoke, but people who criticize parents for taking a baby to a bar don't know the whole truth. Outdoor pool bars or uncrowded bars (usually during the daytime) are a great place to get warm water for bottles or to warm baby food. It's a great place for baby to make a mess and have a good meal. And they even have juice!

Tip 18: Bathing Baby

I admit it, I'm one of those people who have never and will never feel comfortable using a hotel bathtub. So of course I wouldn't think of placing my precious baby's bottom in one either. For this predicament, I highly recommend one of those inflatable toddler tubs. They are safe and sanitary, and they deflate and roll up conveniently for storing within your already overstuffed suitcase. It's an inexpensive and easy solution for making baby's baths pleasant, familiar, and sanitary.

Having a baby doesn't mean that you have to avoid the trip—it just means that you have to plan ahead and be very well prepared. Relax, stay calm, and enjoy your adventure with your baby. Pick up souvenirs for baby's scrapbook. Try to look through your baby's eyes at this great adventure into her big new world. Traveling with your baby really can be a pleasant and memorable experience.

Clutter-Busting Resources

Traveling with Children from the Transportation Security Administration
www.tsa.gov/travelers/airtravel/children/index.shtm

Top 10 Safety Tips for Traveling with Children
www.airsafe.com/kidsafe/kid_tips.htm

Family Travel Tips
www.kidscantravel.com/familytraveltips/index.html

Life with Kids

16

Teaching Kids Values

From Sara

Every day with your children provides an opportunity to teach values. But it's important to remember not to expect too much of them at a young age. For example, children really only start understanding the difference between truth and dishonesty around age three or four, so you won't have much success trying to teach a two-year-old about honesty.

Even with four- and five-year-olds it's important to remember to keep it simple and to have realistic expectations. Building strong values doesn't happen overnight. It's a long, gradual process of teaching your child as he grows. Think baby steps.

I'll give you an example. Just the other night I was admonishing my seven-year-old daughter, Anna, for deliberately pushing her five-year-old brother, Cade, off the bed. I gave her this long speech explaining that I'd scolded her because I want her to grow up to be a strong, successful adult who makes good choices and does the right thing. Cade, who was listening intently, said, "Mommy, when I grow up I just want to be a grown-up." I thought, *Wow, he really has big aspirations for himself.* But then I remembered he's five.

Setting a Good Example

Children learn most about values from the example we set. If your child sees you picking up litter or holding the door for someone and asks why you did that, you can explain that it's important to take care of the world and to help others.

Children also see what's important to us in the way we spend our time and the goals we set for ourselves. If you make a point of devoting time to family every day, then your child will see that family is a priority in your life.

Sometimes the values we want to pass on to our kids may be relatively new to us as well. Maybe you're making an effort to take better care of the environment by recycling and using less electricity around the house. Even when we're the ones making baby steps, our children pick up on our intentions.

It's relatively easy for us parents to reinforce good values around our children, but we can't control what other people do when our kids are exposed to the outside world. Inevitably, our kids will witness something we wish they hadn't. We may not be able to control the outside world, but we can talk to our kids about what happened and give them our perspective.

Everyday Ways to Reinforce Good Values

Make Family Time a Priority

Reinforce the value of family by setting aside time together. Schedule a family game night or pizza-making night. Look for activities that allow you to talk and reconnect as a family.

Use Responsibility Charts or Chore Lists

It's important for kids to know that being part of a family means helping out and doing your share. One family member (ah . . . that would be Mom) shouldn't have to carry everyone else's load. Assign tasks appropriate for your child's age and keep track of the completion of their chores on a responsibility chart. (See "Clutter-Busting Resources.")

Don't Criticize Your Child's Efforts

Sure, it gets aggravating when every time your child takes her plate to the kitchen the dirty fork crashes to the floor. But resist the urge to criticize. Nothing discourages them faster. Kids usually want to help, so remember to make them feel good about their efforts, even if they're less than perfect.

What Does Your Family Value Most?

Think about how you spend your time and money and ask yourself, "In my child's eyes, what does this say about what our family values most?"

Give

From Sara

Share your abundance with others, whether it's tomatoes from your garden or money for a charity. Let your child pick flowers from your yard to take to a teacher or friend. These little acts of kindness go a long way in teaching generosity.

As your child gets older (around age five is a good time to start), sponsoring a child in an impoverished country is a wonderful way to teach them about those less fortunate. Most of us have children who play with an abundance of toys in their own beautifully decorated rooms, and they think everyone lives this way. There are many websites (see "Clutter-Busting Resources") that enable you to sponsor a child in another country (or even in our own country) for a small amount each month. Our family sponsors a child in Ethiopia, and I have been amazed that $24 a month has allowed this little girl to go to school, the family to buy a stove and food, and more. We receive letters from the family telling us how the little girl is doing, and always, always thanking us profusely for our generosity for this little bit of money that we don't even miss, which is transforming their lives. Anna and Cade even write letters to the little girl. It's been the most real way (besides putting them on a plane to Africa) for me to show them how fortunate they are and that from those to whom much is given, much is expected.

Don't get me wrong—we still have a long, long way to go with our kids. They haven't had an epiphany and decided to donate all their toys to charity. In fact, the other night we were reminding them of how fortunate they are and Anna said, "Oh, I know that. Whenever I have two wishes, I first wish for a turtle, then I wish that all the kids in the world have good food to eat and lots of toys." So there you go—once Anna gets her turtle, we can have an end to world hunger. But I keep reminding myself, baby steps. Someday I hope the turtle will be the second wish.

Appreciate Other Races and Cultures

Show your children by example that people are to be judged by the content of their character, not the color of their skin. Never, ever use derogatory terms or talk about another race or culture in a disrespectful way. Don't make fun of names that are different from your own culture. The Golden Rule is a good guideline: do unto others as you would have them do to you. We live in a multicultural world, which will only be more diverse by the time our children are adults. Choose books about other cultures to read with your child. If you don't teach your child to have respect for those who are different, your child is going to encounter many difficulties as she goes to college, seeks employment, and beyond. But the bigger reason is that it's just the right thing to do. Mutual respect makes for better neighborhoods, better workplaces, and a better society.

Respect the Elderly

Let's face it: as a country, we are not so good at showing our elderly citizens the respect they deserve. Youth is celebrated in our country, while the elderly are often dismissed as irrelevant. Nothing could be further from the truth. Chances are, whatever you are experiencing, your parents and grandparents have been through it before you. Children can learn so much from their elders. Fostering a relationship between your child and his grandparents is a great place to start. If the grandparents aren't close by, encourage your child (and your parents) to strike up a conversation via letters or e-mail. Ask your child to interview her grandparents. Prompt the grandparents to tell stories of their youth when you're all gathered at the dinner table. Share memories of your own grandparents and what they meant to you with your children. We owe these folks our freedom and our prosperity. These little lessons now will help your child fully appreciate that as an adult.

Respect the Opposite Sex

We all see our first models for how to treat the opposite sex at home, watching our parents interact. Boys form their opinions of women by watching how their father treats their mother. Does Dad talk down to Mom? Does he make jokes about women or tell his son he hits the baseball "like a girl"? Does Mom say, "Your father is such an idiot, he can't even find his keys"? We've probably all made comments about our spouse in front of our kids that we shouldn't have (yours truly are guilty as charged—we coined the phrase "Stupid Husband Stories," after all), and it's certainly not the end of the world to have the occasional slip. But if children are constantly hearing derogatory comments about the opposite sex, it's very likely to add up to a negative opinion in their young minds. Keep your jokes and sarcasm about the other gender reserved for adults-only conversations. It's pretty simple to teach your kids respect for the opposite sex. Show your child's father respect. Show both your parents respect. Teach by example.

"Studies have shown that one of the most powerful influences on how children grow up to treat the opposite gender is the way they perceive the relationship between their parents."

—Dr. William Sears

It's also important to monitor your child's friendships. If you hear inappropriate talk from your child and you know he's not learning it at home, pay close attention to those with whom your child associates. Steer your child toward friendships that reinforce your own positive values for the other gender.

Do the Right Thing

If a store clerk gives you too much change, don't keep it. Give it back, even if it mea
getting out of the car and going back into the store.

Be a Good Neighbor

Take food to the couple who just had a new baby. Mow the yard of the elderly man who's been sick. When your children see you caring about those around you, they learn the power of helping others and the power of (as Eleanor Roosevelt said) "doing what you can, with what you have, where you are."

Teach Respect for the Earth

Show your consideration for the environment and the world around us by taking the time and making the effort to recycle. Never litter, and if you see trash on the ground, pick it up and put it in a trash can.

Compliment Good Behavior

If your child does something good, tell him. There's nothing like the power of positive reinforcement!

Set Goals and Complete Difficult Tasks

When your children watch you stick with a tough task all the way to the finish line, they'll learn about perseverance, determination, and dependability.

Empower Your Kids (Especially Daughters)

From Stephanie

This is a very important element of raising a daughter. It's important to give your kids the chance to make some decisions—like what vegetable we're having for dinner tonight, or what she wants to wear that day. Let your kids teach you something (or at least let them think they're teaching you something). Let your kids show *you* how to play a board game. Often they'll come up with a much more fun way to play than what the instruc-

ds help you cook—let them choose what spoon or spatula to n use *your* favorite utensil. Assign them chores and give them ke they are accomplishing something. All these little things d a stronger sense of self-worth, which is invaluable, espe-

...ng Resources

...ES

...sponsibility charts
www.leapsandbounds.com

Character education
www.valuesparenting.com
www.teachingvalues.com
www.charactercounts.org

SPONSOR A CHILD IN NEED

World Vision
www.worldvision.org

Christian Children's Fund
www.christianchildrensfund.org

Save the Children
www.savethechildren.org

Pearl S. Buck International: Health and Education for Children
www.psbi.org

BOOKS

Becoming the Parent You Want to Be: A Sourcebook of Strategies for the First Five Years
by Laura Davis and Janis Keyser
www.becomingtheparent.com

Teaching Your Children Values
by Linda and Richard Eyre

Kids' Random Acts of Kindness
by Conari Press

17

Discipline

From Sara

Remember what an expert you were on disciplining kids *before* you became a parent? I sure was. I'd see kids out somewhere and say to myself or those I was with, "No child of mine will ever be allowed to act like that! That kid needs a spanking!"

David and I were talking the other night about how things have changed since we were in elementary school. Our daughter is in second grade and we have been appalled at the behavior of some of the students in her school. We both remember our own elementary school principals having a paddle in their offices. And there were rumors running through both our schools about a special paddle with holes drilled into it, to make the school-sanctioned butt-whuppin' even more painful. Looking back, it seems so barbaric now. Yet there are a couple of students I've encountered that I've fantasized about using the special paddle on. I am not a proponent of spanking, and I fully believe that the way many parents and schools disciplined in the past needed to change. But unfortunately, I think the pendulum has swung too far the other way. Although I don't spank, I don't let my kids get away with murder either. Brace yourself—I'm stepping up on my soapbox.

Every day I see children of good parents, people who I know want only the best for their children, acting like little tyrants, talking back to teachers, lifeguards, and other adults. I would have rather died than talked back to a teacher or other adult when I was that age. Why don't these kids respect authority? How did they get so incredibly big for their britches?

Parents love to blame that wonderful catchall: society. Oooooh. The big bad influence, society. At the top of the list is television. As I heard comedian Chris Rock's mother say the other day, "Every TV I've ever seen has an off button on it." I'm the first to admit that I have used the electronic babysitter. I still do sometimes. But I don't just let my children watch whatever they choose and I don't let them have a television in their bedroom, where I might not see what they are watching at night. As my children have outgrown *Blue's Clues* and *Barney,* I've been horrified to see what passes for kids' entertainment on children's channels. My kids know they can watch the Disney Channel (and thank you, Disney Channel, for always putting on programming I can trust), but when it comes to Nickelodeon or Cartoon Network, they have to get permission first. My son knows if it's not *Scooby-Doo* or *Tom and Jerry,* he's not watching Cartoon Network. Gone are the days when cartoons were a Saturday morning treat. And gone are the days when if parents saw a cartoon on the screen, they could safely assume it was children's programming. Now with shows like *South Park* and *The Family Guy* (which you certainly wouldn't want a child watching), the word *cartoon* is not synonymous with *child-appropriate.*

As parents, we must be vigilant about what our children see on television. If you don't, they will inevitably pick up things (habits, words, actions) you don't want them to. Many of the characters on these shows are crass, back-talking little punks. You wouldn't want your child hanging out with another child who acted this way, so why let him watch it (and laugh at it) on television?

The truth is, parents are the problem. There, I said it. The "society" your child has to deal with is other parents and their children. When parents get lazy or disinterested, others pay the price. The problem the parent ignores becomes the teacher's problem, the principal's problem, the lifeguard's problem, the coach's problem, the bus driver's problem, the neighbor's problem. And none of those people has the ability to fix the problem the way a parent does.

Parents now are busier than ever, with many parents both working full-time and doing all they can just to get dinner on the table, clothes washed, and kids bathed and in bed. It's so tempting to just let some of this discipline stuff slide. But as someone told me once, either you pay your dues now or you will pay them later. I agree with that. What you neglect now will come back to haunt you later, most likely in the teenage years when the stakes are much higher. When kids are young (and still think their parents hung the moon) is the time to lay the groundwork. We parents have more influence over our children than anyone else on the planet. Kids might never admit it, but what we do and say has the most impact on their lives.

Discipline is often confused with punishment. Discipline is really teaching your child and giving them boundaries, letting them know what behavior is acceptable and what isn't. Punishment is simply applying consequences. It's the penalty a child has to pay for breaking the rules. (This is the area where many of us, myself included, could use some improvement.) Discipline is often thought of as something negative—a "disciplinarian" is thought of as this stern, cold person who never cracks a smile. But the truth is, discipline is a gift you give your children. Without it, they become difficult people to be with, and they will struggle to relate to and get along with others their entire lives. I'm not saying to make your kids fall in line like the von Trapp children. We can let them be kids while teaching them along the way. When we guide our children with loving discipline, we show them that they are important, that we want to keep them safe, that their actions matter to us, and that they are worthy enough for us to expect the very best of them.

Setting Boundaries

The phrase "setting boundaries" sounds a little bit like psychobabble, but it simply means setting limits—teaching a child what is appropriate and what is not. Boundaries help children feel safe as they grow and realize the world is a big and sometimes overwhelming place. Boundaries help teach children self-control.

Boundaries must be reasonable and age-appropriate. You can begin setting boundaries when your children are toddlers, but you will obviously set different boundaries for a two-year-old than for an eight-year-old or a sixteen-year-old. In fact, boundaries should gradually shift as your children grow older so they can develop more responsibility.

In the beginning, boundaries will mostly have to do with safety—not touching electrical outlets, not throwing toys, and so on. As your child grows, boundaries continue to be safety-focused: wear your helmet when you ride your scooter, stay in the backyard, look both ways before you cross the street. But you will also include boundaries for proper behavior: sharing, waiting your turn, saying please and thank you, using an inside voice, putting away toys, and so forth.

From Stephanie

Keep in mind that boundaries should be different for different children. I know it sounds crazy, but my son behaves much better when I give him a little more space. My daughter was fine with stringent rules, but the same rules applied to my son just made him (and us) miserable. He just couldn't tolerate as many boundaries, and we learned that giving just a little made us all happier. He needed a little more independence. He needed to be able to say silly words (like *butt* or *poop*). He couldn't sit still as long as our daughter could. I don't know if this difference was due to gender, the fact that he was the younger one, or simply a personality style. Just keep in mind that the boundaries that work for some children may not be universal, and you should never judge another family if their boundaries are different from yours. (And feel free to remind your family members of that fact too.)

Applying Consequences

From Sara

It's my firm belief that consequences, if applied correctly, are the key to teaching your children good behavior. The problem is, sometimes we aren't consistent and sometimes we don't follow through. Like me, you've probably realized that yelling "Stop it!" over and over does nothing to put an end to undesired behavior. But if you tell your child, "If you throw Thomas the Tank Engine again, you will not be allowed to play with it for the rest of the day," and she knows you mean it, that has impact. But to get to this point, you have to have taken Thomas (or something) away before. Your child has to know you will follow through on what you say. It's not pleasant to take a beloved toy away from children. They cry, whine, complain, and sulk, and it's hard not to feel like you are a horrible parent. Really, the exact opposite is true. Behavior has consequences and you are teaching your child this valuable lesson, which will serve him throughout his life. Steel yourself against the drama and stick to your guns. If you say one more offense will lead to a consequence, then you'd better follow through. This is not the time to be wishy-washy. If you give in to whining, arguing, or crying, your child will quickly learn to repeat this behavior because it gets him what he wants. Don't give in! It's tough at first, but it will pay off, I promise.

Applying consequences eliminates the need for spanking (and yelling, for that matter). Every kid has a favorite toy or activity—Dr. Phil McGraw calls it their "currency." When you take away a toy or a privilege, it must be something that matters. If you take away something your child really isn't interested in anyway, the negative consequence of his behavior will be too small. Having to give up a play date with a friend, a trip to the pool, or watching television—these are things that will make an impact. The only exceptions I make are my children's loveys (the "security blanket" toys)—they each have one. Otherwise, any other toy can be taken away for bad behavior. (Of course, never take away something your child truly needs, such as a meal.)

With younger children, it's best to withhold the toy or privilege right away. Don't wait until later in the day or the next day because the child won't connect the behavior to the consequence. Sometimes there are natural consequences to bad behavior. If a child dumps out all the paints, she can't paint anymore. If she throws the cookies on the floor, there are no cookies left to eat. When situations like this occur, be sure not to reward the bad behavior by making more cookies or getting out more paints.

From Stephanie

Taking toys away from my kids never worked for me. They would just go play with something else. My children were never as attached to their toys as Sara's were. For example,

Sara's daughter had a stuffed bunny that was her special toy for years. My daughter's favorite stuffed toy changed from week to week or day to day. What worked well for my children was counting. If I got to the number three, they were in big trouble. I only had to apply the punishment a few times and after that the number three became a dreaded enemy. In fact, it worked so well that I could enforce my requests from across the room by simply holding up my hand and silently holding up fingers one at a time as if counting.

They could also go back to one or zero by doing something good or kind to another family member, or helping around the house. This counting system also worked well because the teachers at school used a similar system. Our preschool teacher used green, yellow, and red to enforce discipline. I encourage you to find out what system your child's teachers use and then adopt it at home. It will make it easier on you because your child will already be "trained" in that system. And it will make it easier on your child and his teacher too because of the consistency. This will also help in communicating with your child. For example, when I picked Timmy up from preschool, I'd ask him, "Did you stay on green today?" We both understood the question and its consequences.

I was convinced that this little counting ritual really made me look like I knew what I was doing in the parenting department. However, I'm the first to admit that I have no idea what I'm doing. In fact, I'm not totally convinced that anything we do (right or wrong) is going to make that much difference in our kids' behavior because personality traits are so strong. I know parents who do everything they can and their kids are still little monsters. My own kids have gone through stages where they've been referred to as "angels," but there have been other stages when . . . well, let's just say we weren't invited back. That's why you probably won't hear much out of me in this chapter. To be quite honest, I'm clueless. I've read a lot of stuff on discipline and I've done the best that I can. The only consistency I've noticed is that kids who feel loved and who have parents who spend a lot of time interacting and playing with them on the kids' level seem to be the easiest, most well-behaved kids to be around. And to quote one famous expert (Forrest Gump), "That's all I have to say about that."

Use Rewards and Praise

From Sara

Rewards are great ways to support good behavior. Rewards are different from bribes in that they are given *after* the desired behavior, not before. Responsibility charts are a great way to boost positive actions. I use magnetic charts from Leaps and Bounds. I put them low on the refrigerator and each week or two I reassess their responsibilities. Some items are mainstays, like "Do my homework" or "Make my bed." Others change depending on the season or what behavior we are trying to improve. "Try not to whine" used to be on my daughter's chart a lot, but fortunately we are finally getting past that.

Positive reinforcement goes a long way in encouraging the good behavior you want in your child. When you do need to correct a behavior, it will be much easier for you and your child if she has heard praise for what she's done right. You can make your praise really meaningful with comments such as "Wow, that was great how you shared with Susie. How did that feel to share your toy? I bet she will share with you next time you play together too."

Time-outs

The American Academy of Pediatrics says that time-outs should be a last resort after you have tried other methods such as withholding privileges. However, I've found time-outs to be pretty effective in certain situations in my house. My son is prone to temper tantrums and has a difficult time calming himself down. (A time-out also gives me a few minutes to calm down!) I put him in the time-out chair in our kitchen and he sits there until he gets control. Sometimes I use the microwave timer so he knows when the time-out is up and doesn't have to keep asking. My rule is no talking and no fussing in time-out. If you fuss, I add time to the timer. The general rule of thumb for time-outs is one minute per year of age. And the AAP says you can start using time-outs with children at age one.

Take care in choosing your time-out spot. Sending a child to her room for bad behavior can be counterproductive if she turns the time-out into playtime. Also make sure your child is safe and somewhere you can clearly see him. I use a small stool in my kitchen for time-outs. If your child refuses to go to the time-out chair himself, take him there and put him in the chair yourself. If he tries to get up or won't stay in the chair, hold him from behind at the shoulders. If you have to, you can hold the child in your lap for the allotted time. Whatever you do, don't let him escape from time-out and not "do his time."

Even though time-outs can be effective, they are certainly not appropriate punishment for every type of bad behavior. If your six-year-old throws rocks at his sister, he's getting off way too easy with just a time-out. Time-outs work best for less serious offenses and are more appropriate for younger children.

Now if only we moms could get someone to send *us* to time-out! Wouldn't that be nice?

Managing Kids' Behavior (and Controlling Your Own Reactions)

Give Effective Instructions

In researching this chapter I've learned why I struggle to get the kids to pick up their shoes or hang up their backpacks or set the table. I've been yelling my requests all over the house. And just as the experts said and I can personally attest, it's not very effective. The wise folks at FamilyFun.com say that if you want your child to perform a task, go to your child, touch her gently on the shoulder, even crouch down to her level, and say, "I'd like you to set the table," then walk with her to the silverware drawer. Wow, I'm going to try that!

Remain Calm

Count to ten, take deep breaths, walk away for a moment—whatever you need to do to stay calm and not lose your temper. We know, easier said than done when your child is wailing or has just bitten his little sister. But reacting to a temper tantrum with one of your own does nothing to help the situation. On the other hand, if you do let your emotions get the best of you and raise your voice or slam a door, it's not the end of the world. Hey, who hasn't at one time or another? That said, try to model the behavior you want in your children.

Think Before You Speak

I've gotten in the bad habit of being an automatic no-sayer. I just spew out no without really taking any time to think about the request. Often I am saying no to something that is really okay, so then I end up conceding and saying yes. If I had just stopped for a second to think, I would have said yes in the first place instead of sending my kids the message, "Mom is going to say no to almost everything. If you keep asking, she will eventually say yes."

You Don't Have to React

It's very hard not to react when your child is crying or throwing a tantrum. When our children are infants we moms have hormones that make sure we are responding to their cries, to ensure survival of the species. But as your child gets older, his outbursts have less to do with survival and more to do with his will. You don't have to react. Don't let your child's crying or yelling get to you. Kids are allowed to cry. Let them have time to react and get their emotions out. You can even leave the room and tell them that "Mommy is going to take a time-out until the crying is over." (Of course I'm talking about temper tantrums here, and not crying that has to do with an actual need.)

Realize That Different Children Have Different Needs

If you have more than one child, no doubt you know that they come into this world with different temperaments and personalities. One child may be a natural rule follower, while another may challenge every boundary. Children also learn and develop at different rates. The discipline methods that worked for your first child may not work for your second or third.

"Next to love, a sense of discipline is a parent's second most important gift to a child."

—T. Berry Brazelton, M.D.

Mix Things Up with a Little Humor

Don't be afraid to use a little humor when dealing with minor behavior issues. Sometimes on long car trips when our children are whining and nagging at each other—those oh-so-annoying exchanges such as "Stop copying me!" "Don't sing that song!" "Don't put your foot on my seat!" that are all said in a nasal whine—my husband and I will start talking that way to each other. Our kids immediately get quiet and start listening to us. "See how you sound?" we say to them. They laugh and it breaks the pattern of brother-and-sister squabbling. The only problem is that they keep saying, "Mom and Dad, do it again!"

Condemn the Behavior, Not the Child

Years ago, before I was a mother, I heard a famous therapist say that you should never tell your child, "You're a bad girl" or "You're a bad boy." She said it was important to distinguish that the behavior is what's bad or wrong, not the child. That thought stuck with me, and I have tried to be conscious of that in my parenting and in the way I talk with my children when disciplining them. Who knows, they may still need a lot of therapy later on, but the idea makes sense to me.

Make Discipline a Learning Experience

It's important that your child knows exactly what she is being disciplined for. If you just say, "Go sit in time-out!" without saying why, your child may not fully understand what she has done wrong. A simple explanation will suffice: "Since you wouldn't let your brother have a turn on the video game, you have to sit in time-out for five minutes." When the time-out is over, remind the child again what the punishment was for and make sure she understands.

Listen to Your Child

Often kids act out or misbehave simply to get attention. Negative attention is better than no attention at all. Children subconsciously know that if they throw a temper tantrum, Mom or Dad will be forced to stop what they are doing and pay attention. Take a moment to listen to your child. Pay attention to nonverbal cues that your child may need to talk to you or just need some attention. Turn off the television, pause in what you are doing, and listen. Encourage your child's talking with comments such as "Tell me more," or "Then what happened?" Respond to your child in a way that lets her know you understand—for example, "You seem really happy about that!"

What Kids Want Most from Their Parents

Time. That's what kids want most from their parents. When they can't get your attention by doing good things, they will get it by misbehaving. Pay attention to your kids and spend time with them. Play a game together, go fishing, take a walk, ride bikes together, make cookies—whatever you and your child enjoy doing. Turn off the cell phone and the television and give your child your attention.

Set Realistic Expectations

Let your kids be kids. Don't set behavior standards that are unreasonable for any kid to live up to. Children are clumsy and messy. Accept that milk will get spilled and that furniture, clothes, and carpet will get stained. Kids need opportunities to be loud, to run, and to be messy. Expecting them to behave like little adults all the time is ridiculous. Enjoy their goofiness while it lasts. Channel your own inner child and be silly with them. Before you know it, they'll be too cool to be seen in public with you anymore.

Sara's Conversation with Her Son

Sara: "Cade, be good for Miss Veronica while you are playing at Jenna's house today."

Cade: "Mommy, I am always good for other people."

Kids Save Their Worst for Their Parents

Remember that kids will save their worst behavior for the safe environment of home. When my daughter started kindergarten, she was an absolute pill when she came home every day. She'd been on her absolute best behavior for nearly seven hours, and she let all the tension, negativity, and frustration fly when she got home. I reminded myself that it was a good sign that she felt safe letting all that out when she got home. And as the year went on, it got better. Her little brother and I learned to give her a little space to decompress each day when she got home.

Spanking: The Pros and Cons

Americans are currently split fifty-fifty on the issue of spanking, as this discussion from DrPhil.com shows.

The Pros

- Spanking can be effective on a short-term basis in getting children to change any negative behaviors that prompted the spanking.
- Spanking has been shown to be most effective in two- to six-year-olds when used in conjunction with milder disciplinary methods, such as reasoning and time-outs.
- In a study, mothers who combined reasoning with negative consequences (such as spanking) had the most success in changing negative behaviors.

The Cons

- Long-term consequences of spanking can include increased aggressiveness, antisocial behavior, and delinquency.
- Weaker associations with spanking, such as a failure to learn right from wrong, subsequent criminal behavior, mental illness, and child or spouse abuse as adults, have also been suggested.
- Physical punishment can send mixed messages to a child and reinforce aggressive behavior. When parents model aggressive behaviors by spanking, they reinforce the idea that physical aggression is the way to get what you want.
- Spanking is associated with a poorer relationship between the parent and child. Children who were spanked feel less attached to their parents and less trusting of them. The more the child was spanked, the less close the parent/child relationship.

From Stephanie

I spanked my kids in the beginning. I always joke that I wasn't sure if it helped them, but it sure made me feel better. And truthfully, that is spanking in a nutshell. Most parents who spank their kids are doing it out of anger and frustration, not because they're trying to teach them something. I did find that it worked better when they were young (around three or four) because you just can't reason with children at that age. As my kids got older, I stopped spanking them. At first, spanking became the last resort. When all the other correcting, coaching, pleading, and threats didn't work, I had to resort to what I call DEFCON 1 level, which meant a good spanking. Spanking is great for stopping younger children in their tracks and breaking a pattern of unwanted behavior. But I soon realized that it was making my kids hit each other and other kids. Spanking was sending the message that it was okay to hit. When I began using other consequences, the frequency of their hitting and aggression became less.

It is super-important that you never lose your cool in front of your kids. They will model your frustration and reactions with amazing accuracy. Standing them in a corner while you go outside to cool off is one of the most important tactics you'll have to learn as a parent. Otherwise, the attitude that you displayed will come back, aimed directly at you. Remember too that anger puts a barrier between you and your child, and it's a barrier that is very hard to break down. It may take weeks or months to repair the damage done by just one of your adult temper tantrums. There is nothing—I repeat, nothing—that a young child can do that should cause rage or extreme anger in you. If you are having those feelings, then seek out help from a professional because those are not normal feelings. Hitting a child out of rage is unacceptable behavior, and you need to face the problem and make changes to prevent it.

The Discipline Hall of Shame

Here are seven surefire ways to annoy or lose friends (both yours and your kids') and raise an annoying brat.

1. **Not disciplining your kids at someone else's house.** When you're at a friend's house, be sure to let your child behave in ways he is never allowed to at home. Hey, the other mom will discipline him if needed, right? She won't mind.
2. **Not believing a report from a third party that your child misbehaved.** That teacher is so uptight. She just has it out for your little angel. There's no way he threw rocks at the other kids on the playground.
3. **Ignoring or glossing over a problem.** So what if little Johnny is six and still bites his little sister occasionally? He'll grow out of it.
4. **Blaming someone else (or society) for your child's problem.** He's using those words because he heard them on television, not from us.
5. **Not requiring your child to respect authority.** I know he talked back to the lifeguard at the pool yesterday, but that's just his personality. All the boys do it.
6. **Allowing inappropriate behavior.** Okay, so he was being loud in the library, but we were just there for a few minutes.
7. **Setting a bad example.** Sure, the kids are supposed to be quiet while the clown is performing, but it's okay if I chat with the other moms.

From Stephanie

Item #2 in this list is possibly the most frustrating for me and all parents. It's very hard to know when your child is lying for the sake of self-preservation. Kids are cunning, and sometimes they just plain get mixed up because they're kids. When another kid tells you something that your child did, I think it's important to remember that there are always two sides to every story. But when another adult tells you that your child has done something, you're an idiot to question it. I once told a friend that I heard her son call my daughter a swear word. I was standing three feet from him when he said it (I was in my garage and he didn't know I was there). When I confronted her, she told me flat out that she didn't believe me. I assured her that I had not misunderstood him, but she still didn't buy it.

Another mother showed up at my doorstep to confront me when I called the sheriff out to handle her teenager (the second time). This was after I watched him tear down the sidewalk in front of my house on a motorized scooter and almost take out my four-year-old, who was innocently riding his tricycle on our sidewalk. The first time we called the authorities to complain about her son was because we were driving down our street at 11:00 P.M. and were startled by several teenage boys standing in the middle of the street, bent over with their rear ends in the air like they were going to moon us. This boy cursed at me (I've since heard him using the very worst of profanities around the tennis courts and pool), talked back to me, and showed absolutely no respect for me or the deputy. Is it surprising that his mother showed up at my door to chew me out? No. She assured me what a sweet-natured boy he was and how he had trouble dealing with adults because he was so introverted. He certainly wasn't suffering from shyness when he told me I ought to be more worried about the cars speeding up and down the street instead of him, or when he was disrespectful to the uniformed officer. She also suggested that perhaps I was confusing him with other boys in the neighborhood. Whatever the case, she was not going to believe that her little angel had done anything wrong. I understand why parents react this way, but it's not healthy. It's called denial.

If you've had a similar experience with a parent in denial, the only thing you can do is realize that it's their problem, not yours. It is out of your control, and your only recourse is to keep your child away from that child if unacceptable behaviors become frequent.

I think it's important for us to remember that our kids' bad behavior is not a reflection on us. Kids make mistakes, and it doesn't mean that we're bad parents. Not believing or choosing to ignore another adult bringing up a problem, however, *does* make you a bad parent. So be careful how you react when a fellow parent brings something to your attention. Consider wisely how your reaction affects your child's future, as well as the other children he will come in contact with. Often other people can see things that you can't see because you are too in love.

Clutter-Busting Resources

WEBSITES

The American Academy of Pediatrics
www.aap.org

Keep Kids Healthy
KeepKidsHealthy.com

FamilyFun.com
www.familyfun.go.com/parenting

Dr. Phil McGraw
www.drphil.com

BOOKS

Parenting for Dummies
by Sandra Hardin Gookin and Dan Gookin

Touchpoints
by T. Berry Brazelton, M.D.

18

Sticky Parenting Decisions

From Stephanie

Every day of our lives as moms involves an endless series of parenting choices, from what they will wear that day to what you're feeding them to how to discipline them. And not all of those choices are so cut-and-dried.

Now, for those of you out there who know me personally, you've seen how my kids behave. And you know that I, of all people, have absolutely *no* business giving parenting advice. In fact, our books are about the fact that we really have no idea what the hell we're doing—and neither does any other mother. We're all just absorbing the facts and trying to figure it out as we go. So we brought in some backup for this chapter. Sara found a great article in *Real Simple* written by Sarah Humphreys, the magazine's special projects director. We thought the information was so useful to moms that we invited Sarah to be on our show (and in our book). Sarah's article discusses some of the common decisions parents make each day and helps us realize if our choices are realistic. Are our choices really about what's best for our kids, she asks, or more about our own egos?

Is it better to eat Pop-Tarts for breakfast or nothing at all?

Having Pop-Tarts is like eating cookies for breakfast. But they're so fast and easy and portable. And there do seem to be some vitamins and minerals claims on the side of the box. So how bad are they?

The experts say: Go with the Pop-Tarts. Getting something into their stomach is more important than "good" or "bad" food. Just add a serving of milk to balance out the sugar (milk provides protein, fat, and carbs), and the combination will help give Junior enough energy to make it till lunchtime. That said, kids should have at least one-third of their daily nutritional requirements at breakfast. The best breakfast is a high-fiber, low-sugar cereal, fruit or juice, and a glass of milk.

Should you enforce coordinated outfits or let them dress themselves?

From Stephanie

What mom doesn't struggle with this one? And let's face it, this one really is about our own egos. I've always said I wanted to write a note to the teacher explaining that I wasn't a bad mother if my five-year-old came to school with her hair hanging in her face. She hated wearing a barrette or headband and didn't like me messing with her hair in the morning. It was either have a big, ugly fight or let her go to school in a good mood and with her hair in her face.

The experts say: Children should be dressed appropriately for the weather, and parents can add structure to the choice (as in school vs. party), but otherwise, let your child experiment. It's just not worth the struggle.

Should you cater to your kids' demands at the dinner table or let them go hungry?

From Stephanie

I am always taking up for moms—I'm their biggest advocate—but this is one pickle that moms get themselves into that makes me crazy. Your kids will learn to eat what you give them. Period. If you give them too much sugar, candy, soda, and fast food, they are not going to eat anything healthy. Healthy stuff doesn't taste as good as sugar and fast food, so once they discover how good that stuff is, you've changed their taste in food. Don't get caught in the trap of "My kid won't eat that" and "My kid won't eat anything except chicken nuggets." It's your job as a mom to make sure your kids are eating healthy, and the less sugar and fast food you give them, the more healthy stuff they are going to be willing to eat and the easier your job will be. Ask any nutritionist; she'll tell you the same thing. If you want your kids to eat healthy, cut the sugar and fast foods out of their diet until they start to like healthy foods again. Then you can add a cookie or treat once in a while.

Shortly after college, I worked at a veterinary hospital. One of our favorite calls was when pet owners would phone frantically to tell us that their dog hadn't eaten in about three or four days. We always knew what was behind this. Question: "What was the last thing you gave him to eat?" Caller: "Table scraps." Question: "And what did you have for dinner that night?" Caller: "Steak and gravy." Question: "Well, if I gave you steak and gravy and then tried to feed you dry kibble, would you eat the dry, crunchy stuff or hold out for the steak?" The dogs would eat eventually, when they got hungry enough and realized that there was no steak around the corner. It's just the way the world works. Your kids will not starve themselves, I promise.

So, do my kids eat fast food and cookies? Yes. But I didn't give them that stuff until they were a little older, and only for special occasions. My kids are six and seven, and they *ask* for broccoli, asparagus, shrimp, berries, and salad. They love any kind of ethnic food (especially Japanese and Chinese). We've always tried to offer them whatever we were eating, and they learned to like it. We try to limit fast food to once a week (when we're rushing to practices), we don't chew gum at all (I ask them if they want to have the dentist drill holes in their teeth to fill cavities, and if so, they can chew gum . . . that usually works), and we only have soda when we go out to dinner or for a special occasion. They've had doughnuts fewer than twelve times in their entire lives. Not because I didn't *want* doughnuts more often than that, but because I like the fact that my kids like healthy stuff and I don't want to screw that up. Now that you totally hate me, let me reassure you that this is the one single parenting thing I've actually done well. My son swears sometimes, both my kids are slobs, I've let them watch too many PG movies, and they're both terrified to go anywhere in the house by themselves because they're convinced that Doc Ock (the villain from *Spider-Man*) lives in their bedrooms . . . but their diet is great. I'm not telling you this stuff to brag—I'm just giving you the cold, hard facts in an effort to make your life easier and your kids' diets a little healthier. Childhood obesity is out of control, and you have to realize that if you let your kids eat junk, they will become overweight and have health problems—if not now, then later. We all need to get serious about what we are feeding our kids.

The experts say: Don't cater. It's a child's job to learn to eat what the adults are eating. Try to offer a variety of foods at mealtime—the meat or main course; rice, pasta, or bread; a fruit or veggie; and milk. So even if your child eats only two of the above, at least they're getting dietary requirements. Don't worry about getting a balanced meal into your kid at one sitting. What he or she is eating over the course of a day or week is more important.

After a hard day at work, is it okay to rest or do you have to play with your kids?

The experts say: You need downtime. Depriving yourself of food, rest, and fun for the sake of your kids is not going to make you a good parent. It's probably going to make you a grumpy parent. People feel guilty when they work a lot, so they often want to give all their free time to their kids. But that may not be realistic. If you don't take care of yourself, you risk getting burned out and exhausted. It's okay to say, "Give me a half hour to take a bath and then we'll play." (However, I'm not sure that is realistic for the spouse who's been home with the kids all day.) If you're a stay-at-home mom, finding time for yourself is tricky. You have to make some arrangements with your working spouse that you both agree on. For example, you get to go out and run errands on Tuesday nights and have time to shop or be with friends on Thursday night. That way both of you know what to expect, and nobody gets disappointed.

Should you choose their books for them or let them read the ones they ask for (the ones that you *hate* reading)?

The experts say: Let them read anything they want. You and your kids don't experience a book in the same way. They see things in it that you don't. As long as they're reading and you're reading to them, that's what's important. And remember too that just because something is a classic doesn't mean it's good for your kids. Be sure to pay attention to recommended age ranges. Also, it's important to listen—if your five-year-old says something is scary, then it *is*.

I let my daughter watch a movie that was made for kids, one with Wallace and Gromit, and she became convinced that her daddy was the were-rabbit from the movie (a big, not-so-scary, oversize rabbit that devoured vegetable gardens at night). When it started to get dark at night, she would suddenly get nervous and refuse to sit in his lap or get anywhere near him. It was both sad and hilarious. We tried everything—we showed her figurines of the were-rabbit in the toy store, we laughed about it, and we talked about it—but for at least three months Daddy *was* the were-rabbit, and there was no convincing her otherwise. Now she laughs about it, but at the time she was genuinely scared. To me, there was nothing scary at all about the were-rabbit, but she perceived it completely differently. And perception is reality, especially to a five-year-old.

How old should your kids be before you stop letting them see you naked? And at what age should siblings of the opposite sex stop taking baths together?

First of all, we ask you, is it even possible to take a shower without your kids coming into the bathroom? Stephanie says it's a rare occurrence that she gets an entire shower without someone coming in to plead his or her case. Sara's kids love to press their faces up against the glass. (Thank goodness for the steam!)

The experts say: Nudity with the parent or sibling of the opposite sex probably should be phased out when a child is between ages four and five for these reasons:

- Your child will soon be entering school and nudity is not accepted at school.
- Most families in our society practice modesty, so a child who is interested in looking at other people's bodies can get into trouble.
- It is more comfortable for children to learn genital anatomy from siblings and friends of the same age than from seeing their parents nude.

The bottom line is that every family is different. When it starts feeling weird, then start closing the door. Remember that whatever you choose to do, you are setting examples for privacy and modesty that will affect your kids' attitudes and behaviors about nudity for a long time.

As for shared baths, you should set some boundaries—like no touching private parts. Your kids will probably let you know when they don't feel comfortable bathing together anymore.

Should you decide whom your child can be friends with?

The experts say: You and your child have very different perceptions, so the kid that you can't stand could turn out to be your son's hero. It's easy to control your child's playmates when they are young. As they get older, controlling whom they choose as friends gets more complicated. You will eventually have to trust your child to make a good decision and surrender to the fact that it's out of your hands. That's why it's so important to teach your child manners and values like kindness and honesty. Friends can have a lot of influence on a child's behavior, but be reassured that the core values they learn at home usually become ingrained. In most cases, children will choose friends who have similar values and personalities to their own.

If you notice a friend being rude, talk to your child about how this behavior makes you feel and why it's bad. And if the friend habitually treats your child badly, you can help her realize that maybe she doesn't have a real friend in this person after all. If the friend's behavior is extremely irritating and you're convinced that he is a bad influence, chances are your child is aware of it too. Your child may just need a little help in saying no. Tell your child that he's no longer allowed to play with his friend and explain why.

Remember too that kids can be labeled pretty quickly, so if you haven't seen the child who has the "bully" label, invite him over and decide for yourself. Kids will have to deal with bad kids sooner or later, and by doing this, you're teaching your kid a valuable lesson about giving people a second chance. Make sure to tell your child up front that you will step in if there is a problem.

Is it okay to tell a little white lie to protect your child?

From Stephanie

Are you kidding? I lie to my children constantly. Sometimes it's our only defense as parents. Most of us lie to our children . . . think Santa Claus and the Tooth Fairy, and let's not forget some of our favorites, including "Your face is going to get stuck like that" and "Don't swallow that gum, your stomach will stick together!"

Sometimes their questions are just too difficult to explain in a way they would understand, so we have to invent things. For example, how do we answer the "where do babies come from" question? Well, it's the stork, of course! (By the way, how can they be satisfied with that answer? We suggest answering that question truthfully—Robie Harris's book *It's Not the Stork* is a good place to start. What in the world does a stork have to do with the birth of a baby, and who invented *that* tall tale? And how can such a ridiculous thing have endured for so many generations?)

We don't go to church very often (okay, never), but when I can't answer one of their questions, I defer to the ever-popular "Because that's the way God made it." Who can argue with that? It makes more sense than a stork leaving a baby on your front porch. Telling a little white lie now and then won't hurt them, and sometimes it even protects them from an ugly truth. We are not teaching them to lie; we're just letting them be kids.

From Sara

I get a lot of difficult questions from my son, Cade. If I tell Anna the sky is blue, she accepts that as fact and moves on. But if I tell Cade the sky is blue, it spurs a litany of questions: "Why is the sky blue? What makes it blue? Why are the clouds white? Why isn't the sky blue at night?" and on and on until I practically need to call in a meteorologist for help. This is the same kid who one day, on our way home from his church-based preschool, said to me, "If God was Jesus's father, was Joseph his stepdad?" He was four! I could just imagine what it was going to be like when he turned eight or nine.

How Did Storks Start Delivering Babies?

Research states that this legend goes back as far as pagan times, when civilizations were eager to have high birthrates. Some credit the Europeans for this legend because the European white stork spends wintertime in Africa but returns every spring to nest, often on the roofs and chimneys of houses. Since many babies are born in spring, people began to associate storks with fertility and good luck. Lithuanians, Poles, and Ukrainians believe that storks bring harmony to a family on whose property they nest.

For the really tricky questions, I usually start by responding with the (admittedly lame) question, "What do *you* think?" This tactic rarely works (especially with Cade), but it does buy me some time to consider how I want to answer when the question inevitably gets repeated.

I think the questions about spirituality and death are the most difficult. My husband and I got a lot of those kinds of questions last year after I was diagnosed with cancer and both of our dogs passed away. Fortunately, my cancer was an extremely curable type and I had an excellent prognosis, so I didn't feel the need to tell the children that my illness was life-threatening unless things took an unexpected turn. I was fully open and honest about all other aspects of the disease, but I didn't feel that there was a need to scare them with the possibility of something so awful when it was only a remote possibility. I don't think that's lying; it's just a purposeful omission of some of the facts. Parenting isn't a court of law, and you don't always have to give kids "the whole truth and nothing but the truth." They are kids, after all, and there is no reason to level realities on them that they are not emotionally ready to handle.

Last year both of our dogs died within a period of two months, which was really hard on the entire family. We got lots of questions from the kids about heaven, and I tried to give them positive answers because it helped them cope to think of their four-legged buddies being in a happy place, having fun all day and eating all the dog bones they want. Is there a heaven for dogs? I don't know. But when my kids ask me, yes, there absolutely is.

The experts say: Yes, a little white lie is appropriate sometimes. One of the experts gives the example of the Easter Bunny. At three, children can't differentiate truth from fantasy very well, so letting her believe in something that's not real isn't a big deal. (Personally, we think the Easter Bunny is a really bad white lie. Sara always says the Easter Bunny ruins it for Santa Claus. After kids get past three years old, it's pretty hard to buy into the notion of a big, human-size bunny hopping into the house with a basket full of treats. Once they start to doubt that, then it raises questions about Santa Claus. The point is, choose your white lies carefully.)

What Happens When You Tell a Little White Lie and Get Caught?

According to Stanley Greenspan, author of *Great Kids: Helping Your Baby and Child Develop the 10 Essential Qualities for a Healthy, Happy Life,* it's not the end of the world. Greenspan suggests you say to your child, "I had a good reason for not telling you, but I should have told you the truth." If you have a good relationship, it will be no different from what happens when a good friend tells you a little white lie. You're going to forgive him because the context of the relationship matters more.

Children are contextual beings. Is the relationship one of trust and warmth? Or is it one of constantly shifting sands? The relationship is what the child takes with him, not the one event.

There are times, however, when a little white lie simply isn't appropriate. For example, if Grandpa is suffering from Alzheimer's, you should offer a simple explanation like "Grandpa has a problem that sometimes goes with getting older." Not discussing it only causes more anxiety in the child's mind and he has to create his own explanation about what's happening.

If a pet dies, don't tell your child Rover went to live on a farm. Dealing with death is a normal part of life, and the death of a pet should be handled with as much truthfulness and openness as you feel your child is ready to handle.

Should you correct their homework or let them turn in wrong answers?

The experts say: Reviewing homework with your kids is a great idea. The more help a child gets in understanding his schoolwork, the better. It gives parent and child time together and shows that the parent is concerned about how well he is doing in school and that school is important.

If you see a wrong answer, point it out and give your child the chance to do it again and get it right. Don't just correct the work and give it back. The teacher can tell when you do that. Plus it doesn't help your child understand what she did wrong, so she'll have the same problems again in class when you're not around to help.

When is it okay to leave your child in the car? What if you are just running in to get coffee at the coffee shop and you can see the car the whole time?

Although we don't want to hear it, the answer is . . . *never*!

The experts say: The North Carolina Department of Health and Human Services points out that on a normal summer day with a 93-degree temperature, the temperature inside a car can get as high as 125 degrees in just twenty minutes. In just forty minutes it can get up to 140 degrees. Heat exhaustion can occur at temperatures above 90 degrees and heat stroke can occur when temperatures rise above 105 degrees. Some parents think it's okay to leave kids in the car with it running and the air-conditioning on. That also can be a fatal mistake. Kids can get trapped in power windows or shift the car into gear, endangering themselves and others. And sometimes kids get trapped in a trunk. Don't let your kids play around unlocked vehicles either. In some states, it's illegal to leave a child in a car, and the states that don't have legislation on this are starting to put laws in place.

People leave children unattended in or around vehicles more frequently than you may think. KidsInCars.com has documented more than 3,580 incidents involving children left alone in or around motor vehicles since 2000. There are all kinds of dangers involved when leaving kids inside a car, so just don't do it. If they're sleeping, either wake them up or come back later. It's not worth the risk.

TEN THINGS TO DO EVERY DAY FOR YOUR CHILD

So now that we've covered some of the things *not* to do, here's a great reminder of the things we should be doing for our children. This list came from the book *Parenting for Dummies* (IDG Books Worldwide, Inc.), and we think it is a perfect summation (and reminder) of what we should be focusing on every day.

1. **Give them lots of hugs and kisses.** Your whole family needs to feel your love every day. Not just your kids, but your parenting partner too.

2. **Tell your family that you love them.** Even though you show your love in everything you do, they still need to hear the words.

3. **Tell your family that they're special,** and tell them specifically why you think so (it's great for their self-esteem). And do things to make them feel loved, like putting little notes in their lunch boxes or having a special date with just one of your children at a time.

4. **Feed your family nutritious food.** It's important that you *and* your kids eat the right foods. Not only are you setting a good example, you're also teaching your children about making good food decisions. And you're keeping them healthy.

5. **Read to your kids.** Reading to your kids gives you a great excuse to have quiet one-on-one time with them. It also starts them on a good habit. Kids who are read to every day develop higher IQs, have better vocabularies, and end up with increased language skills. If you want your kids to be successful adults, this is crucial.

6. **Talk to your kids.** I have a sign on my refrigerator that is a quote from Dr. Phil: "Talk to your kids now about the things that don't matter—or they'll never talk to you about the things that do." Make time to talk to them so you know what they're doing, where they've been, and what they're thinking. Talking to your kids also starts a habit of open communication between you and your family.

7. **Have special time with your kids.** Spending individual time with your kids is essential if you have more than one child. Each child should be made to feel special and important. By spending time alone with your kids, you'll help them not to feel lost in a large group. They'll feel more like an important and special member of the family. Go on a special "date night" with one child at a time. This little event means so much to them and it will give you a chance to really focus on each one individually.

8. Practice good manners at every opportunity. The best way to teach good manners is to use good manners. Make a habit of please and thank you.

9. Be patient even when you don't want to be. That's a hard one, but you've got to learn how to stop, take a breath, and react appropriately.

From Stephanie

Sometimes when I feel my temper beginning to build, I stop myself and whisper to myself, "Respond with love," before I actually respond to them. It helps me keep my heart in the game even when the situation is stressful.

10. Be approachable at all times. Be a true friend to your children. You want them to be able to talk to you about anything, or ask you questions that are bothering them. Never send the message that you're too busy to talk to them.

19

Birthday Parties

From Stephanie

I don't know about your neighborhood, but in my world, kids' birthday parties have gone completely over the top. When I was a kid, I remember five or six friends spending a couple of hours in our burnt-orange-and-avocado-colored kitchen with pointy party hats and Pin the Tail on the Donkey. We thought that was a good time. Nowadays parties consist of pony rides, a theme, a clown, a moonwalk, goodie bags, custom invitations, and thirty of your child's closest friends. What's going on?

I have to admit, I don't really mind it. I was an event planner in my pre-mom career, and I love the whole ordeal. I've done it all, from pirates (complete with homemade treasure maps and a mast and sail erected in the backyard) to princesses and cowboys. But if it's not something you enjoy and you're stressing out about your child's party, then please, don't do it. If you're doing it to keep up with the Joneses and you don't truly enjoy it, then you honestly shouldn't be doing it. Don't compare yourself to other mothers—everybody has different talents. Your kid might not have party napkins that match the theme of the cake, but he might be the first one in his class to read because you're a great teacher. We all have different strengths, so don't beat yourself up if you feel like you can't pull off the perfect party.

What Age to Start

Around four or five years of age is a good time to start birthday parties. By this age, your child has some definitive friends, has developed a taste for toys, and knows how to handle cake and ice cream.

From Sara

Four or five years old for the first party? Personally, I started throwing parties for my kids at age one. Yes, it was a party for the adults, not the kids, but it was still so much fun . . . especially for me, but for the kids too. Even if you invite only the grandparents, parties at this age are adorable. I just loved all the babyish themes, from bubbles to rubber duckies, and I loved getting to choose! Okay, I know it sounds selfish, but there are only a few years (at best) that you will get the joy of being able to choose your child's birthday theme. Before you know it you will be buying Transformer plates and napkins or a cake with a Barbie stuck in the middle of it wearing nothing but frosting for a top that the boys at the party will decide to wipe off with their fingers to make her naked! (Then again, maybe we just have a bunch of little pervs in our neighborhood.) My son wants a Pokémon party this year. Pokémon? Have you *seen* the color scheme? Ick. But I'll always have the memories (and the photos) of his first-birthday "puppy dog" party or his second birthday "let's go fishing" themed cake and invitations, and of getting to dress him in cute little outfits that coordinated with the party colors. This year it's Pokémon and a T-shirt and jean shorts.

Throwing a Party for Your Child

There are plenty of ways to make your child's birthday memorable without all the hullabaloo. For example, pick three or four of your child's favorite friends and take them to a ball game or the zoo and buy them each a souvenir. Spend your budget on a few special friends instead of feeding and entertaining the whole neighborhood. We checked with our friends at Parenting.com, and here are a few other guidelines (with a little of our own advice thrown in) to help you make some sense out of the birthday party debacle.

How Many Kids to Invite

The general rule for the number of children to invite, which is usually ignored, is your child's age plus one. For toddlers, it's best to invite at least one friend she sees a lot and is comfortable around. If your child goes to day care and is used to dealing with crowds, she can probably handle a few more guests.

Invitations

From Stephanie

Don't underestimate the importance of invitations. Personally, I *love* invitations. They are one of my favorite parts of planning a party. But invitations are more than just a fun theme. Be sure to put a lot of thought into your invitation so you can effectively and efficiently communicate your plans. This is your chance to tell parents:

- Whether they should plan to stay or drop off
- If the child needs to wear or bring any particular type of clothing (like a themed costume or a bathing suit and towel for a pool party)
- Specific pickup instructions and times
- Directions, phone numbers, and a website for the destination, to prevent guests from getting lost
- Your child's age, to help your guests choose an age-appropriate gift
- Your phone number and/or e-mail address, even if you're not requesting an RSVP, in case your guests have questions
- Any special circumstances (for example, you are requesting guests to bring books as gifts, or donate to a certain charity in lieu of a gift)
- If you are planning an outdoor event, instructions for inclement weather, like an alternate rain date or location

Anything that your guests may have a question about should be included in your invitation—it will reduce the number of phone calls you'll have to return.

Some moms enjoy using e-mailed invitations to get the word out. Websites like eVite.com and Sendomatic.com have kid-related templates and make it easy to send invitations and account for your guests. The only sticky part is making sure you have everyone's e-mail addresses.

What About the Food?

From Stephanie

When it comes to food for a child's birthday party, use the KISS method (keep it simple, stupid). I once spent a lot of time preparing spinach and artichoke dip and some other fancy snacks (I had the parents in mind) for a birthday party. Nothing got touched except the Cheetos and pretzels. Chips, fruit, Chex mix, and juice boxes really are the best way to go. They're just too busy to spend time eating.

If you are asking parents to stay for the party, please be sure to provide water and sodas for the adults. I once went to an indoor pool party where the hostess had forgotten "grown-up drinks" and I nearly passed out from the heat and dehydration. And as far as I'm concerned, it's okay to serve beer and wine to the adults during a child's party. As long as it's done responsibly, why can't the parents have some fun too?

And here's a tip for serving ice cream. In the heat of distributing cake and ice cream, things can get a little backed up if you're trying to hand-dip ice cream onto the plates. So opt for the single-serving containers, or put cupcake papers onto a cookie sheet and dip the ice cream into them the night before. You can even add sprinkles and a cherry. It makes passing out the ice cream go much faster, and it's pretty and thoughtful. I've done that at two birthday parties because I thought it was such a good idea. The only problem is that in the frenzy of serving the cake, I totally forgot about the ice cream in the freezer . . . twice. There goes my Mother of the Year Award yet again.

Just a couple more things, the most forgotten yet essential supplies at a birthday party: a lighter for the candles, and film and new batteries for your camera (that'll getcha every time).

Opening Presents at the Party

Whether your child opens presents at the party is strictly your decision based on your child. Personally, we like to see the birthday child open our present. And it's also a great opportunity to teach your child to show gratitude. Be sure that you have a talk with your child before the party and explain that their friends have spent time and money to pick out a special gift for them. Try telling your child to look the person in the face when they say thank you. Be sure to teach your child how to handle special situations before the party, like what to do when they get a duplicate gift. You can even make a little game out of it, like, "What would you say if Benjamin gave you an iron for your birthday?" "Thank you very much, I really like it." If your child reacts badly to a gift during the party, immediately correct her gently and ask her to apologize. Birthday parties can be a great time for children to learn how to give and receive gracefully, and to learn that it's not always about them.

Those in the "open after the party" camp believe that opening gifts can send already excited kids over the edge. Opening presents after the party means that you get to avoid the frenzy of torn paper, lost cards, and hurt feelings, and it extends the celebration for the birthday child and allows him to wind down a little.

One dilemma we've seen happen time and time again at parties happens when the birthday child begins opening gifts and is absolutely mobbed by party guests. Plan ahead and provide a special chair or table for the birthday child, and ask all other guests to sit down on the floor in front of them so everyone can see the presents. If your child gets swamped by ten other kids, he or she can get overwhelmed and/or overstimulated, plus it just destroys any chance of getting good photos.

Goodie Bags

Are goodie bags really a must? Most party planners and moms agree that providing your guests with a goodie bag is important. It's a great way to show that you appreciate the time they've taken to shop for a gift and attend your party. And like it or not, most kids expect a goodie bag these days. But it doesn't have to be extravagant. Anything more than $5 per goodie bag is ridiculous.

Parenting magazine advises to get creative with your parting gifts, like sending everyone home with a packet of seeds to plant in their garden, or modeling clay. One mom simply handed out a small box of sidewalk chalk to each guest. Another great idea is to provide a picture frame and take a photo of each guest at the party and include it in your thank-you notes. The frames can even match the party theme, and can often be a craft project, which helps keep the kids busy during the party. We recommend a great company called Oriental Trading (www.orientaltrading.com). They have everything under the sun for any theme and will help you stick to your budget.

Thank-You Notes

From Stephanie

Yes, you have to send thank-you notes, but the truth is that sometimes it just doesn't happen. I have thank-you notes sitting on my to-do stack right now—it's April and my daughter's party was in December (probably *not* going to happen). Sometimes I send an e-mail to the group and tell them how much it meant to have them help celebrate with us; Emily Post wouldn't agree, but I say it's better than nothing. If you just can't get it done, then make phone calls and explain that you got busy and thank them via phone call. Another solution that's becoming more popular is having the birthday child write one thank-you note to the group and then sending out copies. It's cute, it's easy, and it gets the job done.

Be sure to get kids involved in the thank-you note process. Young children can draw a picture of the present and then you can write the note and maybe sign their name. You can even find thank-you notes with fill-in-the-blank sentences your child can complete by writing a word or two. By age six, your child should be able to write his own note (don't worry about spelling). If you've lost track of who gave what, don't mention the gifts specifically—just thank your guest for coming and being a part of your child's special day.

Sara's Thank-You Note Tip

A really cute idea for thank-you notes is to upload a picture of all the party guests (or the guest of honor) to Shutterfly.com and have note cards made with the picture on the front. This is relatively inexpensive and it's a nice way for guests to get a photo from the party (girls especially love these). The note cards are available in color or black and white.

When Your Child Is a Guest

RSVPs

From Stephanie

When your child gets a party invitation, you absolutely have to RSVP! This is a big pet peeve of mine. It's a simple thing to do and it's very important to the person planning the party. It's also a great opportunity to talk about details like a gift preference, if you can drop off or stay, what time to pick up, etc. Many party destinations require (and charge) according to a pre-party head count, so be sure to call and make your plans known. Pick up the phone as soon as you receive the invitation—it only takes a few seconds.

RSVP Tip from Sara

Instead of asking all party invitees to RSVP, I like to put "Regrets Only" with my phone number and e-mail on the invitation. That way only the folks who *can't* make it have to call. I also appreciate this on invitations I receive.

Dropping Kids Off at Parties

At what age can you drop your child off at a party? The general rule is age five, but this really depends upon the parent who is throwing the party and on your child.

From Stephanie

I was always one of those parents who hung around as long as the host didn't mind, especially in the case of pool parties. Usually by age seven, it's understood that the kids don't need their parents to accompany them. When in doubt, ask your host when you RSVP.

How Much to Spend on a Birthday Gift

The average gift cost is between $5 and $15. Remember that the most expensive gifts don't always turn out to be the favorites. And it's perfectly acceptable to spend a little more on the friends who are closest to your child. It's a good idea to call the mother planning the party and ask what her child is interested in so you can make a good gift choice—children's interests change quickly.

For a really great perspective on birthday parties, check out this website: www.mommarama.com, written by fellow mom Susan Kawa. We think she does a great job in summing up what birthday parties are truly for:

> The birthday kid is supposed to figure out:
>
> 1. How to function as the center of attention without being a complete ass
>
> 2. How to host all her friends at once and pretend to care about their comfort and inclusion

3. How to smile and thank folks for giving her a gift she hates, or that she already has nine of

4. How to write a thank-you note, or at least sign a thank-you note (or, at the absolute bare minimum, not shoot paper footballs at Mom while she writes them)

The partygoers can learn:

1. How to function at a party without crying, wetting their pants, or trying to ride the dog

2. How *not* to be the center of attention for a change

3. How to *give* gifts to someone else and not get them back . . . ever

4. How to leave a party without crying, wetting their pants, or trying to ride the dog

Clutter-Busting Resources

www.parenting.com
www.orientaltrading.com
www.amazingmoms.com
www.familyfun.com
www.shindigs.com
www.birthdayexpress.com
www.birthdaypartyideas.com
www.mommarama.com

PRINTED PARTY INVITATIONS

www.sweetumsstationery.com
www.finestationery.com
www.thestationerystudio.com
www.polkadotdesign.com
www.stacyclaireboyd.com
www.paperstyle.com

E-MAIL PARTY INVITATIONS

www.evite.com
www.sendomatic.com
www.mypunchbowl.com
www.pingg.com

FILL-IN-THE-BLANK THANK-YOU NOTES

www.activitiesforkids.com/birthday/thankyou.htm
www.myexpression.com

PHOTO THANK-YOU NOTES

www.shutterfly.com

20

Talking to Your Kids About Sex

"Where do babies come from?" It's the question we all dread. So exactly how do you talk to your kids about, ahem, the birds and bees? What is the appropriate age? Just how much do they really need to know? These are questions all parents will eventually face. And since this book's span is from birth to age six, you might be wondering why we chose to include this chapter. You will be shocked to learn that you need to start having these talks with your children well before kindergarten. (Yeah, that freaked us out a little at first too.)

When to Have the Talk

You may be surprised that today's experts recommend you begin talking to your children about sex as early as age four or five! That doesn't mean you tell them *everything* at that age; it just means that you start talking to them about their bodies and the opposite sex. Here's why:

- By learning the facts from you first, they get accurate information (unlike what they'll learn on the playground), and you'll be opening an important line of communication, making *you* the go-to person for such discussions and questions. You send the message that it's perfectly okay to talk about such matters with you. If they find out from someone else, they may think they have to keep it a secret from you.

- You'll be able to present the facts in a comfortable, accurate, and loving way. Children don't have the perception of sex being "dirty." So they're just listening to someone they love giving them the facts. Be sure not to drag your own baggage and perceptions into the conversation.
- You'll be protecting them from sexual predators. Statistics say that *seven out of ten girls and three out of seven boys are approached by sexual predators by the time they are eighteen years old.* The book *It's Not the Stork* by Robie Harris does a great job of explaining to young children what is appropriate and what is not appropriate when it comes to touching. And it teaches them to have a voice—that it's okay to say "no" or "don't" when an adult makes them feel uncomfortable. This should definitely be a part of your sex education discussion. This book was designed specifically for five-year-olds.

From Stephanie

I read Robie Harris's book to my daughter when she was seven. She started asking lots of questions, and we felt it was time to give her some definitive answers. I have to admit, it wasn't as bad as I thought it was going to be. *It's Not the Stork!* covered so much information about body parts and their names and how a woman's body works that by the time we came to the part about the penis entering the vagina, it wasn't a big deal at all—it was just more information. She asked a few questions, and I told her that if she thought of any more questions, she should come back to me to ask. I also talked to her about the fact that her friends' mommies wanted to be the one to tell their own daughters about this special information and that she shouldn't discuss it with her friends. I kept reminding her of that for a few weeks after our discussion and it worked well—she kept it between us. I was surprised to realize that this really was a great age to discuss it, because now she's gotten used to it and it doesn't seem like such a big deal. She's not interested in boys yet, she isn't dealing with puberty or hormones, and there are no outside influences affecting the way she views sex—it's simply something that people do that her mom told her about, period. I'm hoping that it will continue to not be a big deal when her friends begin talking about it more frequently. But I can assure you that this is a great age and we're certainly off to a good start.

What Parents Need to Know

Studies show that kids who feel they can talk with their parents about sex—because their moms and dads speak about it openly and listen carefully to them—are less likely to engage in high-risk behavior as teens than kids who do not feel they can talk with their parents about the subject. Encourage questions to keep the lines of communication open.

Up to Age Three

This is a good time to teach your child about correct names for body parts and good touch vs. bad touch. It's normal for your child to explore his or her own body. Teach your child that her body is her own and that she has the right to privacy. No one should touch her in areas that are private (areas that are covered by her bathing suit).

Allow your child the pleasure of exploring his own body. Toddlers like to touch themselves as they bathe and get their diaper changed. We all know how much they love to be naked. Let your little one know that you understand it feels good to touch himself, but this is something for him to do in private. Young children are especially good at reading our body language and facial expressions. Be careful that you aren't saying one thing while your body language and facial expressions are saying another. You really don't have to worry about masturbation unless it becomes more important than playing—and if this is the case, you should talk to your family doctor.

Children Three to Six Years of Age

This age group sometimes likes to play doctor. Many parents overreact when they discover or hear of such behavior. It's hard not to. But remember that it is not sexual—at this age it is merely curiosity. Freaking out is not the right way to react. Direct your child's attention to another activity and have a talk with him later. Explain that our bodies are private and that we must keep our bodies covered in public. Set limits without making your child feel guilty. This is a great opportunity to talk about the differences between girls and boys.

We would also warn you not to let your little boy urinate outside. We've met parents who think this is cute, but it tends to send the wrong message and it will eventually get him into trouble, like when he decides to unzip and pee in front of your neighbor's daughter. Not only is peeing outside unsanitary, it's important that your son learn when it's okay to unzip and when it's not. Teaching modesty to boys is a good idea because they seem to come out of the womb with a natural love for getting naked.

Around Age Five or Six

Depending on the maturity level of the child, at about five or six you can say that the baby grows from an egg in the mommy's womb (a special place in a woman's stomach that grows babies) and comes out of a special place, called the vagina. There is no need to explain the act of lovemaking because very young children will not understand the concept. It's okay to say that when a man and a woman love each other, they like to be close to one another. Tell them that the daddy's seed joins the mommy's egg and then the baby begins to grow. Most children under the age of six will accept this answer. Answer your child's questions in a straightforward manner, and you will probably find that she is satisfied with a little information at a time.

By Age Eight

By this age girls (and boys) should have information about menstruation, some of which may be provided in school. Instructional books are helpful, but mothers should also share their own personal experiences with their daughters, including when their periods first started and what it felt like, and how, like many things, it wasn't such a big deal after a while.

The "Birds and Bees"?

When should parents sit children down for that all-important "birds and bees" discussion? Never! Learning about sex should not occur in one all-or-nothing session. It should be more of an unfolding process, one in which the child learns, over time, what she needs to know. Questions should be answered as they arise so that the child's natural curiosity is satisfied as she matures and this keeps the lines of communication open.

If your child doesn't ask questions about sex, don't just ignore the subject. At about age five, you can begin to introduce books that approach sexuality on a developmentally appropriate level.

Nudity in the Home

Every family sets their own standards for nudity, modesty, and privacy. Some families shut the bathroom door; others leave it wide open. Every family's opinions and values are different, but children must be taught about privacy. Parents should explain limits regarding privacy the same way that other house rules are explained—matter-of-factly—so that children don't come to associate privacy with guilt or secrecy.

A Note on Slang from Sara

Experts say it's important to teach our children the correct terms for parts of their body, instead of using cute words like *winky.* Sometimes kids end up coming up with a term of their own. My four-year-old son still calls his rear his "butt-hind." I'm sorry, but that's just too darn cute to correct. There are real reasons to use the proper terminology, though. Sexual predators tend to use slang or cutesy names for private parts to try to lure children. So teach kids the appropriate terms. But beware—they will (we can promise you) shout out a word like *vagina* or *penis* at the worst possible time. Just ask Stephanie. She can tell you a great story about her daughter proudly announcing that her brother had a penis and she had a vagina while they were standing in the checkout line at the grocery store.

When I told my son about the word *penis,* he didn't seem the least bit interested. He waited until we were at my in-laws' to start yelling at the top of his lungs (for no apparent reason), "My peeeenis! My peeeenis!" Thanks, buddy.

Movie Reviews for Informed Parents

Once you become a parent, you begin to look at movies in a whole new light. Movies that you thought were safe according to their rating or that you remember to be mild can surprise you, revealing too much too soon in front of young children. There's a great Website, www.kids-in-mind.com, that gives scene-by-scene descriptions and rates movies based on violence and gore, sexual content and nudity, profanity, substance abuse, and more. The movie reviews are so detailed, you'll know exactly what to expect when you get to the theater. There have been several movies that I've chosen to avoid based on the information I received from this website. It reviews new releases as well as thousands of older movies. And did I mention it's free?

Our Favorite Books

One of the best resources we've found to help parents talk to their young children about sex is a book called *It's Not the Stork! A Book About Girls, Boys, Babies, Bodies, Families, and Friends* by Robie Harris. This book has adorable illustrations and helps guide you through talking with your child about these topics. Be sure to read the book on your own first, and use paper clips to hold pages together if your child isn't ready for a certain page yet. You probably won't find many of those pages in this book.

Robie Harris has books for every age group that are an amazing resource for parents. They give you a road map to help you know what to say, how much to say, and how to say it in a warm and loving spirit. Look for *It's So Amazing! A Book About Eggs, Sperm, Birth, Babies, and Families* for children age seven and up. And *It's Perfectly Normal: Changing Bodies, Growing Up, Sex, and Sexual Health* for children age ten and up.

Clutter-Busting Resources

WEBSITES

American Academy of Child and Adolescent Psychiatry
www.aacap.org/cs/root/facts_for_families/talking_to_your_kids_about_sex

Talk with kids
www.talkingwithkids.org

Parenting
www.parenting.com

Detailed movie reviews
www.kids-in-mind.com

BOOKS

It's Not the Stork! A Book About Girls, Boys, Babies, Bodies, Families, and Friends
by Robie Harris

It's So Amazing! A Book About Eggs, Sperm, Birth, Babies, and Families
by Robie Harris

It's Perfectly Normal: Changing Bodies, Growing Up, Sex, and Sexual Health
by Robie Harris

21

Sleeping Kids

From Stephanie

Every living creature on this planet needs sleep. Some animals (and my husband) spend as many as twenty hours a day sleeping! Sleep helps us pay attention and concentrate. It helps us retain what we've learned, and it keeps our bodies healthy and helps us grow. Amazingly, there are still a lot of mysteries surrounding sleep. Scientists are not exactly sure what the brain does while we sleep; some suggest that the brain sorts and stores information, restores the supply of important neurochemicals, and solves problems.

There are plenty of books written on how to get your baby to sleep, and they're usually best sellers. That's because parents are desperate for a good night's sleep! Sara and I took very different approaches to sleeping when it came to our babies. (Please see Chapter 5, "Sleeping Babies.") I loved sleeping with my babies in my bed, while Sara took the disciplined approach of teaching her children to go to sleep in their own beds. Different approaches worked for us because we had two very different perspectives. I was a working mom, so sleeping with my baby at night was a way to reconnect with her and make up for lost time. Sara was a stay-at-home mom, so after being with her baby all day, she looked forward to having some time to rest without a baby in her bed. There's nothing wrong with either choice. I know Sara agrees with me when I advise you to do whatever you have to do to get some sleep (for the sake of you and your baby). If they go to sleep easier with you beside them, then do that. If you are exhausted and need your own space at night, then teach your children how to sleep in their own beds.

The funny thing is, no matter how disciplined you are about putting baby in her own bed, there's a very strong chance that at some point, your children are going to end up in your bed. It's a normal part of development. Children are terrible sleepers and they have active imaginations, so nighttime can be frightening and they will need the security of your company. As of this writing, my kids are five and seven and we often lie down with them until they fall asleep, and then transfer them to their own beds. And sometimes, especially after my husband gets back from a long business trip, all four of us end up sleeping in the same bed together. We love snuggling with them (on most nights) and we realize that now is the time to just enjoy it because much too soon, the time will come when they won't even want us in their bedroom, let alone in their bed.

From Sara

David and I are both serious sleepers. We could sleep in until at least nine every morning if finances and the kids would allow it. Fortunately, our kids are pretty good sleepers too. Although I do believe a certain amount of training is involved with that. As I've said, we put our babies to sleep in their own cribs instead of co-sleeping. But I always laugh because even when our kids made the transition to "big-kid beds," they still seemed to end up in the bed with us all the time. I didn't mind it much, although my husband definitely got tired of being kicked in the head. When they show up at my side of the bed (it's always been my side for some reason), it's just easier to pull them into our bed than to try to get them back to theirs. For a while Cade slept in one of those Little Tikes race car beds, and those just aren't too comfortable when you're a full-grown adult, especially a sleepy one who's been awakened at 3:00 A.M. I prefer my own bed, even if I have to put up with little feet in my face.

Our son still joins us in the middle of the night fairly often, but our daughter is older and generally sleeps through the night in her own bed. Which, in my scientific opinion, means that wanting to sleep with Mom and Dad is something they outgrow. And I am in the same camp as Steph on this one. Like the country song says, "Let 'em be little, let 'em sleep in the middle." Before you know it they won't want to be seen with you in public anymore. So enjoy being their safe haven and snuggling with them while you can.

Letting your kids share your bed occasionally does have its advantages. For one thing, it allows you to *really* see how they sleep. Cade had problems with his adenoids, which affected his breathing during sleep, and I became much more aware of the problem when he would come and get in our bed early in the morning. He also developed pneumonia once and I suspected it because when I lay down with him so he would take a nap, I noticed he was breathing really rapidly in his sleep. I immediately called the doctor, and sure enough, pneumonia.

David and I have done just about everything to get our kids to go to bed. We've lain down with them in their own beds, let them fall asleep in our bed and then transferred them to their beds, played soft music in their rooms, used a nightlight, not used a nightlight . . . there's been a lot of trial and error. However, I do think it's important to establish a bedtime routine. In our house, after pajamas are on, it's time to brush teeth and go to the potty. Then we generally read for a little while, either all of us together or with each child individually before turning out the lights and tucking them in.

Both Anna and Cade sleep with a lovey every night. "Lovey" is Dr. T. Berry Brazelton's word for blankets or stuffed animals children become attached to. In Dr. Brazelton's book *Touchpoints*, he says he is happy to see children with loveys because that means they are able to self-comfort. (Whew!) Anna has had New Bunny since she was about two years old, and as Stephanie often jokes, "there is nothing *new* about New Bunny." He's threadbare, floppy, and faded, with stuffing coming out of him. And that's exactly what makes him so wonderful. Of all the toys and gadgets Anna has, she would be most devastated if she lost New Bunny. He is the shabbiest thing she owns, but she loves him the most.

Cade's lovey is a small blue crocheted blanket he calls Blank Blank. He loves to curl his toes through the holes in it as he is falling asleep at night, which is why he refuses to wear socks to bed, even on the coldest nights. He used to drag Blank Blank behind him all the time like Linus. He'll wrap it around his neck, use it as a pillow, and sometimes pretend it's a cape.

I didn't encourage my children to get attached to these items; it just happened. But they have been wonderful "security blankets" for the kids when they went to the grandparents or stayed with a sitter. On the other hand, loveys do get lost (hence New Bunny, who replaced Old Bunny) as well as smelly and gross from being peed on, vomited on, dragged through the dirt, and who knows what else. I have had to go back to stores to find them, had them mailed from Grandma's house, and torn the house apart trying to find one of them at bedtime or when it was time to get in the car. I once found Blank Blank wadded up and stuffed into the bowl of the toilet with the lid neatly closed over it. Swear to God.

Having these objects to sleep with has really helped my children. When we first moved them into their own rooms (they used to share a room), their loveys helped them feel safe sleeping in a room alone. Their loveys are less crucial now. They can sleep without them if they have to, and I've noticed recently that New Bunny is at times forgotten when Anna falls asleep at night. Which is kind of bittersweet. She's growing up and gaining more and more confidence, but my little baby girl is not a baby anymore.

We never, ever said that she was too old to be sleeping with New Bunny or that she

"Parents often feel uncertain about loveys, especially when they are ratty and pathetic. They think that a child with a lovey looks neglected. Actually, the opposite is true in my experience. . . . This child has already demonstrated her inner strength. She shows us that she has been nurtured at home. The ability to self-comfort is enhanced by parents who nurture."

—T. Berry Brazelton, M.D.

ought to get rid of him because he is so ratty and worn. Like the Velveteen Rabbit, he is shabby only to people who don't understand. I've assured Anna that even after she has no interest in New Bunny, Mommy is going to place him in a special memory box and keep him forever. For me, New Bunny will always symbolize my daughter's childhood. The same goes for Blank Blank. Okay, I have to go blow my nose now.

Now that you've heard our opinions on sleep, here are a few things that are helpful to know when it comes to kids and sleep.

Sleep Facts

Sleep is an individual thing, and some will need more than others. Sleep has to be taken seriously because your kids need it for proper brain function and many researchers believe that too little sleep can affect growth. Too little sleep definitely has negative effects on your child's immune system. And any mother will tell you that sleep (too little or too much) can influence your child's mood.

It's good for you to be aware of the different stages of the sleep cycle because it will help you understand how your child sleeps. When we sleep, we repeat all these stages about every ninety minutes.

Stage 1: During this stage, your brain tells your muscles to relax. Heart rate begins to slow down and body temperature drops slightly.

Stage 2: This is the stage known as light sleep, and your child is easily awakened during this stage. If you are going to move a sleeping baby or child, make sure you wait until they are past this stage.

Stage 3: This stage is a deeper state of sleep. Your blood pressure gets lower, brain waves slow down, and your body is less sensitive to temperature and sounds. It's much harder to be awakened now. This is also the stage when people sleepwalk or talk in their sleep.

Stage 4: This is the deepest stage of sleep. It is very hard to wake up from this stage, and if you do, you'll likely be disoriented.

REM (rapid eye movement) sleep: We've all watched our children sleeping and noticed their eyes moving around beneath their eyelids. During REM sleep, your heart beats faster and breathing is irregular. This is the stage when people most often dream. Even though your eyes are moving rapidly, the rest of your muscles are relaxed and resting.

Sleep and Growth Hormone

The highest amounts of growth hormone are secreted in the body during deep sleep. Inadequate sleep results in lower levels of growth hormone being released, which can lead to height and growth problems.

Can you see why it's important to understand sleep cycles when it comes to your children? Adults can go directly from being awake into a state of deeper sleep quite quickly. Babies and children can't. Babies enter sleep through REM sleep first. They need more help going to sleep. Sleep cycles are shorter in babies and children, with more periods of light sleep than deep sleep. As children get older, their ability to sleep will become more mature and they will get better at it.

Here are some facts, according to age, from the National Sleep Foundation.

Infants

Infants typically sleep nine to twelve hours during the night and take thirty-minute to two-hour naps one to four times a day—fewer as they reach age one.

It's best to stick to a regular schedule for daytime naps and bedtime. Create a consistent and enjoyable bedtime routine.

Toddlers

Toddlers need about twelve to fourteen hours of sleep in a twenty-four-hour period. When they reach about eighteen months of age their naps will likely decrease to once a day and last about one to three hours. Don't let your toddler nap in the afternoon or close to bedtime, as it will cause them to stay up later at night.

This is a tough age for sleep. They are gaining more and more independence and enjoy their playtime, and they may not want to stop having fun in the name of bedtime. This is also the age when nighttime fears and nightmares become common. Daytime sleepiness and a moody, uncooperative child can be signs of a sleep problem or not enough sleep. Toddlers also need a consistent bedtime routine and environment to sleep in. Communicate your expectations and be consistent when enforcing rules. Security objects like a favorite blanket or stuffed animal can be a big help.

Preschoolers

Children from three to five years typically sleep eleven to thirteen hours each night and most do not nap after five years of age. As with toddlers, difficulty falling asleep and waking up during the night are common. With further development of imagination, preschoolers commonly experience nighttime fears and nightmares. In addition, sleepwalking and night terrors peak during preschool years.

Night terrors can be just as terrifying for a parent. You'll hear your child screaming in the night, but you'll find that even though he seems to be awake, he isn't, and you actually cannot wake him up. After a few minutes, he'll go back to sleep and he probably won't have any memory of the episode in the morning. Night terrors are usually an inherited problem and occur in about 2 percent of children. It seems as if the child is having a bad dream and cannot wake up. Night terrors are not caused by psychological stress, but they seem to be associated with being overtired, and most children outgrow them by age twelve.

If your child is having a night terror, do not try to wake him up. Turn on lights so he won't be further frightened or confused by shadows in the room. Remain calm and speak in a soothing tone. Tell him that he's okay, that he's in his own room, and that he's safe and can go back to sleep. You can try holding or snuggling, but if he pulls away, don't persist. Don't try to wake him by shouting or shaking him, as this may only worsen or prolong the episode.

If your child wanders during these night terrors, try to keep him away from stairs, windows, and sharp objects and gently direct him back to his bed. You should also consider removing possible hazards from his bedroom until these episodes subside. Be sure to warn babysitters, family members, or any caregivers and tell them what to do in the case of an attack so they don't overreact. It can be very unnerving.

School-Age Children

Children ages five to twelve need ten to eleven hours of sleep. At the same time, there is an increasing demand on their time from school, homework, sports, and other extracurricular and social activities. In addition, school-age children become more interested in TV, computers, the media, and the Internet as well as caffeine products—all of which can lead to difficulty falling asleep, nightmares, and disruptions to their sleep.

Bedrooms are not the place for computers, TVs, and other electronics. Any light in the room (even small LED lights from clock radios and electronic equipment) can hinder a good night's sleep. Sleep problems are very common at this age, so make it a priority to teach your children healthy sleep habits.

Assessing Sleep Problems in Children

Over the long term, lack of sleep has been associated with a slew of problems: obesity and diabetes, anxiety and depression, a hindered immune system, impeded physical development, and lessened response to vaccines. So it's important to detect and correct sleep difficulties. If you think your child may have a sleep problem, Amy Bellows, Ph.D., says you should ask yourself these five questions:

- **Bedtime.** Does my child have problems going to bed or falling asleep?
- **Excessive daytime sleepiness.** Does my child seem sleepy or overtired during the day? Is he or she difficult to get up in the morning?
- **Awakenings.** Does my child awaken frequently during the night or have trouble getting back to sleep?

- **Regularity and duration of sleep.** What time does my child go to bed and get up on weekdays? Weekends? How much sleep does he or she get? Need?
- **Snoring.** Does my child snore loudly? Does he or she seem to have breathing problems at night?

Naps

From Sara

Naps are an important part of your young child's sleep needs. Most children will transition from two naps a day to one longer nap at around twelve to eighteen months old. Pediatricians will tell you that most children will nap until age four, some until age six. But every child is different. My daughter took naps until almost age four, but my son gave them up at age two. Actually, he wouldn't take a nap until four in the afternoon, and if I let him nap, he'd sleep until dinnertime and be up until 10:00 P.M.! One mom of two toddlers has a rule in her house: if you don't nap by 3:00 P.M., you don't nap. Of course, Cade became horribly crabby for a while every day around 4:00 or 5:00 P.M., but he was in bed by 7:30 or 8:00 and got a good twelve hours of sleep. I nearly cried when I realized he wasn't going to nap anymore, but we got through it. And it was better than having him up trying to watch *The Sopranos* with us at night. If your child does give up naps, it's okay as long as he is getting the sleep he needs during the night hours.

Although you can't force your children to nap, you can give them some quiet time in their rooms to rest or look at a book. Even if they don't fall asleep, this quiet time can help them decompress, and give you a little bit of quiet time for yourself!

Just like nighttime sleeping, it's important to establish a routine for napping. Keep a consistent schedule and put your child down for a nap at the same time every day. Create a restful environment by darkening the shades and keeping the noise level to a minimum. Some children fall asleep easier with lullabies playing softly in the room. If you make this part of the routine, the music also signifies that it is time to nap.

Remember that it's typical for toddlers (and even babies) to resist their naps. This can happen for a number of reasons—and most of the time their resistance doesn't mean they need less sleep. When older babies start crawling they often are too interested in exploring to stop and rest. Toddlers will fight their naps when they start to realize that they might miss out on something if they go to sleep. When children are really ready to stop napping because they need less sleep, their naps tend to get shorter and shorter before they start skipping them altogether.

Bed-wetting

The medical term for bed-wetting is *enuresis,* and it is fairly common, with about five million to seven million kids affected. Bed-wetting is often inherited. According to pedi-

More Useful Sleep Tips

For most kids, sleeping comes pretty naturally. Here are some tips from www.kidshealth.org to help your kids catch all the ZZZs they need:

- Try to have your child go to bed at the same time every night; this helps her body get into a routine.
- Follow a bedtime routine that is calming, such as taking a warm bath or reading.
- Limit foods and drinks that contain caffeine. These include some sodas and other drinks, like iced tea.
- Don't have a TV in your child's room. Research shows that kids who have TVs in their rooms sleep less. If he does have a TV, turn it off when it's time to sleep.
- Don't let your child watch scary TV shows or movies close to bedtime because these can sometimes make it hard to fall asleep.
- Don't let your child exercise just before going to bed. Do make sure she gets some exercise earlier in the day—it helps a person sleep better.
- The child's bed should be just for sleeping—not doing homework, reading, playing games, or talking on the phone. That way, he'll train his body to associate the bed with sleep.

atrician Alan Greene (www.drgreene.com), if both parents were bed-wetters, then 77 percent of their children will be. Most kids who wet the bed fall into the category of "primary nocturnal enuresis" (PNE), which means their bed-wetting is due to delayed maturation of the central nervous system and not an emotional problem. Kids with primary nocturnal enuresis have never been consistently dry at night. Most kids will outgrow PNE by age five, and the remaining small percentage generally stop bed-wetting by age six. Surprisingly, getting a little more sleep (as little as half an hour more) can help some kids stop wetting the bed.

However, if your child has been consistently dry for at least six months and then begins to wet the bed, the problem may be the result of psychological stress brought on by a move, divorce, or other major change in the child's life. Or it could be brought on by physical problems such as a urinary tract infection or diabetes.

Moms and Sleep

From Stephanie

We certainly can't write a chapter about sleep without mentioning our fellow moms. If you're like me, you probably never realized how important sleep was until you became a parent. I tell people that I've been sleep-deprived for about seven years (ever since the birth of my first child). It's not that my kids are doing anything wrong; it's just that, as a mom, I think there's a part of me that's always on alert—even when I'm sleeping. How else can you explain how I can respond to gagging noises in the middle of the night in time to get a trash can under my son's face in the nick of time? Even when my children were babies, I would find myself waking just moments before they did. It is my own personal belief that you sleep differently after becoming a mom.

Think about it—how many moms do you know who have trouble sleeping? I know plenty of them. We discuss it a lot: what pills work, whether that glass of wine before bed actually helps or not, how we lie awake all night watching the clock tick the hours away. Every mom I know yearns for the kind of sleep she had before the babies arrived.

The National Sleep Foundation conducted a poll that focused on the sleep habits of American women ages eighteen to sixty-four. The study revealed that American women are overworked, stressed out, and significantly sleepy. The poll also showed that pregnancy and motherhood can increase a woman's risk of sleep problems and that whether you are a stay-at-home mom or a mom who works full-time or part-time, there are specific sleep challenges you face. You can take a quiz on the foundation's website to find out if, like most American moms, you need help sleeping better (as if you need a quiz to tell you that).

The reason many of us are up at night is that we're worrying. Our busy mind just won't let us get any rest. A great way to solve this problem is to keep a notepad and pen by your bed. Before you go to bed at night, jot down a list of all the things you want to accomplish the next day. Be realistic—you're only one person and there's only so much you can do in a day. If you wake in the night worrying about something that you might forget, jot it down. Having a plan will help reduce anxiety.

According to the National Institutes of Health, "at least 40 million Americans each year suffer from chronic, long-term sleep disorders, and an additional 20 million experience occasional sleeping problems. These disorders and the resulting sleep deprivation interfere with work, driving and social activities." If you are having trouble sleeping, please talk to your doctor. The reason could be simply a few bad habits, or it could truly be a medical problem. Seeking your doctor's advice will help you determine what's going on and how to fix it.

Clutter-Busting Resources

WEBSITES

www.sleepforkids.org
www.sleepfoundation.org
www.kidshealth.org
www.drgreene.com

BOOKS

Healthy Sleep Habits, Happy Child
by Marc Weissbluth, M.D.

Sleep: The Brazelton Way
by T. Berry Brazelton, M.D., and Joshua D. Sparrow, M.D.

22

Kids and Role Models

From Sara

NBA star Charles Barkley once made this statement in a Nike commercial: "I am not a role model." He said parents, not athletes, should be role models. But the reality is that parents are not the only influence on a child's life. Kids are inundated with images of wealthy athletes, glamorous movie stars, and young performers wearing too much makeup and too little clothing. If Charles Barkley is right, how can we parents influence our kids' decisions about role models?

Actually, Sir Charles is pretty on-target with his message. Study after study shows that children name their parents as role models more than anyone else. Although kids do identify with those they see in the media, ultimately parents wield the greatest influence over our children's behavior. That can be a little overwhelming when you think about it. Are you a good role model? It's a job we can all probably do better. It's okay to fall back on the old "Do as I say, not as I do" statement once in a while, but it is important to remember that our children learn by imitating us. Here's what the experts say we can do to be good role models.

How to Be a Good Role Model

Practice Empathy and Respect

If your child hears you talking down to your husband, she'll probably do the same thing to her little brother. Of course, it's impossible to agree 100 percent of the time, but try to show your children that even when you disagree, you can do so respectfully and calmly. (We're working on this one ourselves.)

Use Your Time Wisely

If you don't want your child to spend his afternoons channel surfing, then don't be a couch potato yourself. Go for a bike ride, read a book or the newspaper, or spend time reconnecting with your child.

Make a Difference

Show your child that our actions matter in the world by volunteering at school, a soup kitchen, or an animal shelter. A great way to teach your children about making a difference is by sponsoring an impoverished child through an organization such as World Vision (see page 144, as well as "Clutter-Busting Resources" at the end of this chapter). You and your child will be able to correspond with the child or family and see the impact your help is making in their lives. Stephanie's play group made Christmas ornaments and took them to a nursing home in December. It took only a phone call to schedule it, and it taught the kids the importance of giving back to their community. In November, ask your children to bag up some of their old toys and explain that it's for children who won't be getting many toys this Christmas. You'll be teaching them to give *and* making space in your toy room for the new gifts.

Be True to Your Word

When you tell your child you are going to do something, do it. Your child will know she can trust you and will strive to be trustworthy herself. If circumstances beyond your control prevent you from keeping your word, explain this as clearly as you can to your child and find a way to make it up to her.

Counteract Materialism

Instead of rewarding your child with a trip to the mall or the toy store, use trips to the library or one-on-one mommy time as rewards. Make cookies or dinner together. Give handmade coupons redeemable for a mother-daughter day or a walk together. Play baseball in the front yard. Take your bikes to a new park to ride together. Kids find rewards in spending time with you or doing their favorite activities.

Make Sure Your Child Is Watching

Be obvious about the habits and values you want to pass down. You may be an avid reader, but your kids won't know it if you only curl up with a book after they're asleep.

Clean Up Your Act

You really can't expect your kids to eat healthfully and be polite when you down Big Macs and burp at the dinner table. Having a child makes most of us want to be better people. Build on that desire by being conscious of your behavior—good and bad—and replacing bad habits with good ones.

Have Dad Clean Up His Act Too

Like it or not, girls tend to emulate Mom's behavior, while boys want to be like Dad. It's important for both parents to strive to set good examples for the entire family. When the kids aren't around, talk with your partner about the impact your behavior as parents has on the children and ways you can do better. If slip-ups happen in front of the kids, a reminder like "Daddy, use your good manners, please" usually does the trick.

Be Sneaky About Your Vices

If there's a bad habit you just can't give up, indulge discreetly. Swear at the top of your lungs or burp loudly when you're in the car alone. Watch trashy television after kids are asleep in bed. But beware: kids notice a lot more than you think, and it's pretty embarrassing when you get busted.

If you do get caught—if, for instance, your child is the one to point out that you just said a bad word—admit your mistake and say that you realize you need to be more careful. These admissions help kids learn honesty, remorse, and a willingness to accept criticism.

From Stephanie

On a lighter note, a dad once told me that if you let a curse word slip in front of your children, immediately shout "Barney" right after it, and the name of their favorite purple dinosaur will totally erase the word that came before it. I laughed when he told me this. But not long after our conversation, I was driving and became irritated by another driver, and sure enough, a not-so-nice word slipped out. I remembered my friend's advice and immediately shouted "Barney!" Both kids began giggling and singing a song from the show. Of course, this only works when your kids are young, and you'll need to insert the name of your child's favorite TV character if it's not Barney, but trust me, it works. Kids will remember swear words much faster than they learn anything else, and I think it's because we say them with such emotion—it just makes them more memorable.

Remember You Are a Grown-up

It's okay for kids to see that you live by some different rules than they do. Your children can understand that you can have Diet Coke because your body is finished growing, but they have to have milk or juice because theirs hasn't.

From Stephanie

I think the "Because I'm an adult" line is very useful in explaining why you are allowed to do things that aren't appropriate for them. They may need a little deeper explanation of what "adult" means, though. For example, "Adults have already graduated from high school and college. We earn money so we can pay for our house and to keep the TV and lights working. Adults have lots of responsibilities, like cooking meals and keeping everyone's clothes clean and taking care of our children. Adults work very hard." I think it's healthy for children to understand that adults have a lot of responsibilities in return for their freedom. If they can grasp even a small piece of this concept, it will help them understand why kids should be respectful to adults.

Helping Your Kids Find Good Role Models

As our children get older and go to school, we parents are less in control of the influences they are exposed to. But there are steps you can take to ensure your child makes positive friendships and interacts with good role models.

Know Your Child's Friends

It doesn't matter how old your children are; you need to know their friends, and their friends' parents if at all possible.

Set Aside Time for Your Kids

Give your kids the attention they want and need so they won't feel the need to look for it in a less positive atmosphere.

Listen

From Sara

Turn off the television, the computer, the BlackBerry, and the cell phone and really listen. I'm writing these words for myself as much as anyone. I have a bad habit of constantly trying to get things done. Often when my seven-year-old is trying to tell me something, I'm looking at my BlackBerry or folding laundry or taking out the trash. Then I realize I heard her talking, but I really don't know what she said. Not only that, but I've sent her the message that whatever she had to say wasn't worth my undivided attention. We moms get so busy with our to-do list that it's easy to get into this habit. But stop what you're doing for just a minute and listen to what your child is saying to you. Spend time connecting with your children every day. We've found dinnertime and bedtime are great for talking. We have a no-television and no-phone-calls rule during dinner. Sitting down together gives us the time to find out what's going on in our children's lives, with no distractions preventing us from hearing what they say.

Choose Activities That Support Your Beliefs

From Sara

My daughter is involved in Girl Scouts. She's not old enough to be a Scout yet, so she's a Brownie. Girl Scouts is an excellent organization that promotes values important to me. Their slogan is: "Building girls of courage, confidence and character, who make the world a better place." Through Girl Scouts my daughter gets to become friends with other girls whose parents support these values as well. With her Brownie troop, she gets to enjoy fun activities in an environment that encourages positive behavior.

Getting your child involved in an organization like Girl Scouts, Boy Scouts, or 4-H is a great way to provide opportunities for positive friendships and role models. (See "Clutter-Busting Resources" for contact information.)

When Your Child Has a Role Model You Don't Approve Of

Despite our best efforts, sometimes our children develop friendships with kids we'd rather they didn't. Or they want to be just like Britney Spears. What's a mom to do? First of all, talk to your child about what it is they like about this friend. If you see them emulating negative behavior, explain to them that you don't approve of that behavior and why. Talk about positive role models—friends or stars you do approve of—and explain why you like them.

If a friend is having a negative impact on your child's behavior, you may have to limit their time together. Host play dates at your home so you can see the behavior firsthand. It's okay to tell the other child, "We don't use that word in our house." If it's your home, you set the rules.

The Role of Television

For every TV show that's appropriate for children, there are at least twenty that aren't. You simply must be vigilant about what your child is seeing on television. There's no other way around it. Children should watch television in a "public" part of the house. This goes for computer access too. Don't allow a television or a computer in your child's room. Set clear rules about what channels they are allowed to watch and those that are off-limits. And before you give the okay to certain shows, watch them with your kids. Just because other kids are watching a show doesn't mean you'll approve of your kids viewing it.

Clutter-Busting Resources

SPONSOR AN IMPOVERISHED CHILD

www.worldvision.org
www.christianchildrensfund.org

(See "Clutter-Busting Resources" in Chapter 16 as well.)

ORGANIZATIONS

Girl Scouts
www.girlscouts.org

Boy Scouts of America
www.scouting.org

4-H
www.4husa.org
301-961-2800

23

Kids and Sports

More than twenty million kids register each year to play soccer, baseball, football, hockey, and other team sports. But the National Alliance for Sports reports that 70 percent of these athletes quit by age thirteen and never return to play the sport again. There's a very simple reason for this: it's because it stopped being *fun*. And what's the main reason a sport stops being fun? Because of *us*—their insane parents! We start them too early and they burn out. Or we have unrealistic expectations for them. We yell and criticize more than we praise them, and we ruin it for them.

What Age? What Sport?

As parents, we all feel pressured to get our kids involved in activities that we think will help make their future easier. We've all heard the stories about Tiger Woods starting to play golf at age three, and we are convinced that they can't be good unless we start them very young. Some of us hope for college scholarships or even multimillion-dollar professional sports careers. If that's what you're thinking, here's a little reality for you: fewer than 5 percent of kids ever get an athletic scholarship, and it's just plain crazy to think that starting them out at age three is going to influence that. The mentality of "the younger, the better" is not necessarily true.

Bob Bigelow, former NBA basketball player and author of *Just Let the Kids Play,* told us that "pre-pubescent athletic ability is a meaningless indicator of post-pubescent ability." In other words, your child's body will change so much during puberty that starting her early is not going to make much of an impact on her athletic ability. There are only a few individual sports (such as gymnastics, tennis, and golf) that can give you a boost by starting out at an earlier age.

Passion, confidence, and body maturity don't come until much later, so starting kids too early can actually hurt their confidence and turn them against a sport that they may have flourished at if they had started later. Many kids lose their passion for a sport because they feel they can't live up to their parents' and coaches' expectations. The other trap that parents fall into is keeping up with the Joneses. We're worried that our kids won't be able to compete if they don't start now. This is the easiest trap to get sucked into. Just remember that most athletes who start too early simply burn out or get tired of the repetition by the time they're twelve.

The key for young children is to make the game fun. The focus should not be on winning or losing, or on keeping score. If you want your child to be an athlete, then your job is to make them love the sport. And give them the chance to try different things. Trying different sports develops different muscles and skills and helps them realize where their natural ability and enjoyment lie. Just because you were a tennis star doesn't mean your child will excel at tennis. Your child's natural talent or interest may turn out to be baseball. But if you don't let him try, you'll never know. A good rule of thumb is to allow them to try out at least three team and three individual sports before age twelve. Of course they're exposed to some sports in school, but this interaction is very different from an actual team commitment that requires discipline, training, and learning how to function as a team player.

When choosing a sports program for your child, other parents are your best resource. They can tell you which programs are more competitive and help you decide where your child will best fit in. The main problem with sports programs is that they are designed by adults, and adults are wired to win. Too many of them are designed based on the professional sports we watch on television. Youth athletic programs should be based on what kids can accomplish at their different developmental levels, both physically and emotionally.

At the Game

It's really hard not to get excited and yell when you're at your child's game. Just remember that you are a guest at your child's athletic event. Unless you are adding something positive, keep your mouth shut.

For younger children, don't worry about their shortcomings. It's perfectly normal for a five-year-old boy to stand in the outfield at a baseball game and pick up rocks instead of paying attention. And after the game, he'll tell you just how good a ballplayer he is, and your job is to just agree with him. Let him enjoy it and feel good about it.

For older athletes, never talk about your child's shortcomings right after the game. Talk about the game together. Instead of pointing out your child's mistakes, ask, "What do you think you did well?" and "What do you think you could improve on?" Remember that the process of the game and how your child is reacting to it are more important than who won.

Stephanie's Experience

So, now that I've told you what the experts and the rational-thinking people have to say, I'd like to share my own experience with you. My daughter, Sara, began cheerleading at age five. She was taking the one-hour-a-week class and was really enjoying it, but I didn't see that she was very challenged by it. We were at the gym during a holiday event when the all-star cheerleading team presented their routine, and Sara was so excited by the uniforms and the music and the stunts, she begged me to let her join the team. Tryouts were coming up for the all-star team, which was a competitive travel team, and her coach recommended she give it a shot. She did, and made the peewee squad. I had no idea what I was getting myself into: three two-hour practices per week, an expense of over $2,000 per year, eight competitions per year (some of which were out of town), and a serious commitment to not miss any practices.

During the first year, it was one of the best experiences our family could have asked for! I watched my very shy six-year-old bond with her teammates and shine onstage. She danced, she smiled, she learned commitment and teamwork, and she gained strength and flexibility. With childhood obesity on the rise, I think it's awesome that she's in a gym exercising six hours per week. And above all, she loved it. The competitions, although pricey, were a great opportunity for our family to spend the weekend together away from the usual duties that home ownership demands. And during that two and a half minutes that she was onstage competing with her team, it was like the world stopped rotating. We cheered for her, we shook pom-poms and cowbells, and when she came off the stage we grabbed her and threw her in the air and gave her high fives and told her how wonderful she was. She won national championships and received medals and trophies and it was a great experience.

Now that I've shared the good stuff, I must tell you that if you're dedicated enough to enroll your child on a competitive travel team, you're in for a challenging ride. As I described above, we both loved the first year of it, despite its demands on our time and resources. Some of the competitions required us to get up at 4:00 in the morning in order to get her dressed and get to the convention center on time, and then we would be required to stay and support the other teams from our gym until as late as 6:00 P.M. (which isn't easy for a six-year-old or her younger brother). The financial commitment was enormous—on top of the cost of the coaching, there were travel expenses, uniform expenses, shoes, makeup, photographs, and spirit gifts, plus all the adorable cheer stuff you could buy at the competitions. The time required was also challenging, with six hours of practice per week and a few private lessons or classes along the way. Many of my friends told me I was nuts. The long hours, the rules, trying to make sure she was wearing the correct practice uniform on the designated day (there was a different outfit for each practice), and just having your entire life revolve around a competition and practice schedule is too much for most sane parents. After all, she was only six. But I was willing to put up with the demands because I saw the benefits.

The second year, however, proved to be just too much for Sara and especially for me. Going to practice started to become a drag. Sara loved the competitions, but the team began practicing in April for a competition season that didn't begin until October, and she got bored. During her second year, Sara got promoted to the position of "flyer," which means she's the one they lift up in the air during stunts and pyramids. To my surprise, this is a highly coveted position, even for seven-year-olds, and some of the parents began treating us differently. There was jealousy and catty behavior. One of the parents accused my daughter of kicking another girl during a stunt and not apologizing because, as she put it, "Sara thought she was so deserving to be a flyer that it didn't matter if she kicked someone." Can you believe adults would say things like that? If you ever met my daughter, you'd know that she has never had an attitude like that, and she would feel bad for kicking someone and certainly apologize if she was aware of it. My guess is that she was concentrating so hard to keep from falling, she probably didn't realize she had kicked anyone. I'm telling you this because it backs up the research. Kids quit sports because parents become insane.

Along with some difficult personalities among the parents, there were some changes within the coaching staff. Just last week, we arrived at practice late because I had a work meeting, and even though I'd contacted the coaches ahead of time to let them know, they still made my daughter stay after practice and do what they call "conditioning" (exercises like jumping jacks, push-ups, frog jumps, etc.) as punishment for being late. It wasn't her fault, and my job is certainly a higher priority than cheerleading. One of the little girls on her team was being "conditioned" because she didn't wear the right color shirt and shoes to practice that day. She was in tears by the time her mother came in from the parking lot to see why she wasn't coming out of the gym. That night was the last straw for me. That was the night that all the demands and rules began to overshadow the benefits.

I share this story with you because if you choose something as challenging as a competitive travel team, you need to know what you're getting yourself into. My experience is not uncommon. You will have to pick your battles with coaches and other parents. You'll need lots of patience and lots of organization and discipline to be able to follow all the rules. And you'll have to be able to swallow the fact that college-age coaches who don't understand the demands of parenting may be setting most of the rules. Discipline is imperative in these teams, and they will do whatever they have to in order to enforce it. The fact that you're the one paying isn't really a factor to these coaches, who are out to win. In our case, there was no consideration for the fact that these girls were much younger than the senior teams—everyone was treated the same whether they were kindergartners or high school seniors.

Now, my son started playing coach-pitched baseball at age five. This was much less of a commitment than cheerleading and didn't turn out to be as beneficial. In fact, its biggest payoff was the great entertainment value! It's impossible for five-year-olds to grasp the concept of baseball. We smiled as we watched him stand in the outfield and play with rocks; we chuckled as he played first base when he was actually the second baseman; we laughed as he hit the ball and ran straight to third base; and we doubled over in laughter as he strolled to home plate, bat in hand, and gave us a thumbs-up and a confident wink. We enrolled him because we felt bad that he spent so much time being dragged to all his sister's activities and we felt he needed a sport of his own. But it was like pulling teeth to get him ready for the games, and he just wasn't enthusiastic about it. The dilemma is that he's not really interested in doing anything that doesn't involve SpongeBob or the backyard. So, what's a parent to do?

My point is, every child is different and you have to constantly be aware of your child's needs, how your child is responding to the activity, and the level of commitment required. I have a friend who was a huge football star when he was young, and I was shocked to find out that his young boys were not playing football. The mother explained to me that they'd discussed it and felt that it takes a certain personality for a child to be

Clutter-Busting Resources

WEBSITES

Sportsmanship checklist for kids
www.printablechecklists.com/checklist38b.shtml

Sports parent code of conduct
www.nyssf.org/sportparentcodeofconduct.html

Could a sex offender be coaching your kid? Questions to ask
http://childcare.about.com/od/childsafe2/qt/criminal.htm

Top ten issues for sports parents
www.sportsparenting.org/csp/csp_wolff.html#parents

Sports parenting
www.sportsparenting.org/csp/csp_wolff.html

Age-appropriate tips for kids
http://life.familyeducation.com/sports/29512.html

Our expert, Bob Bigelow, former NBA player, author, and speaker
www.bobbigelow.com

BOOKS

Just Let the Kids Play: How to Stop Other Adults from Ruining Your Child's Fun and Success in Youth Sports
by Bob Bigelow

knocked down and be able to get back up again, and they didn't feel that their sons were at an age where they were ready for that kind of challenge. I was very much impressed by that insight, and it made me think a lot about how my own son would react to that kind of physical challenge. So once again, my advice to you is that despite what the experts say, you know what's best for your child. Just make sure you don't let baggage from your own athletic career—or lack of one—get in the way.

24

We're Going to Disney World!

It's inevitable. Sooner or later, becoming a parent leads to the question: should we take the kids to Disney? Or if you're like Stephanie and me, the question is: how soon can we take the kids to Disney? We've both learned that this question soon leads to scores of others, like "What's the best age?" or "Should we stay inside the park or outside?" Disney is a serious marketing machine, and as a result, there are options galore. And those options can get overwhelming very fast. We knew right away that Disney was a topic we wanted to cover in this book, because for many parents it's a milestone, a rite of passage right up there with learning to ride a bike. So here's what we've learned, our advice, and a few helpful tips to make your trip the best possible without completely blowing your budget or your mind.

It Takes More Than Fairy Dust

From Sara

If only it took just the wave of a magic wand to create a memorable trip to Disney World for your family. But alas, it takes more than fairy dust to give your family a trip to the happiest place on earth. And knowing that this would probably be the only Disney trip I would get my miserly husband to agree to in this decade, I figured I had one shot to give my kids the best Disney experience possible. (No pressure!)

My husband, David, and I had decided to invite the grandparents along. First, we thought they'd enjoy the trip, and second (though just as important), we thought they might help pay for a lot of it. It didn't exactly pan out that way. Of course, they were helpful to have along anyway, but now I not only needed to plan a great trip for our kids but also had to get each group (some would call them rival factions) to agree on each decision along the way. I was sure this was going to turn into one of those death-by-committee experiences.

Fortunately, I have the wonderful advantage of having a sister who's a travel agent. She wisely advised me to book early and plan ahead. Boy, was she right. We set a tentative trip date for late February or early March, and we started planning in August. Our first big committee decision was where to stay. Part one of that decision is whether to stay inside the park or outside the park. (For the uninitiated, I'm using the term *inside the park* to refer to any of the Disney resorts within Walt Disney World, which includes four theme parks: the Magic Kingdom, Epcot, Hollywood Studios, and Animal Kingdom.) Staying at a Disney resort offers lots of benefits, such as simpler and more accessible transportation and special park access hours—plus the housekeeping staff make really cool animals out of the bath towels and put them on your bed. However, Disney resorts can be a bit pricey, and many budget-conscious travelers choose to stay in a resort just outside of Walt Disney World to save some cash. I figured David was soon going to be lobbying hard for accommodations outside the park.

One day, after a few cocktails, my father-in-law matter-of-factly stated that he absolutely did not want to stay "outside the park." I secretly sighed with relief because I knew (and maybe my father-in-law did too) that those words were going to fall a lot easier on my husband's ears coming from his dad than coming from me.

Okay. Now on to step two: where to stay? I voted for the Polynesian. After all, what more purely represents Disney than the Polynesian? The South Pacific–themed resort is labeled "deluxe," meaning it has every conceivable amenity. There's a monorail stop right at the hotel, so it's extremely convenient, and it is one of the original Walt Disney World resorts, so it has the nostalgia factor. Unfortunately, I soon learned that unless I plan on being one of Donald Trump's next wives (and Lord knows I'm way too old to qualify for that job), the Polynesian was way, way, way out of my family's price range. Step back and punt. I turned the page in my Disney resorts guide to the "moderate" section. We came to the Port Orleans resort for many reasons, but mainly I think we stayed there because my daughter, Anna, loved the dragon water slide at the pool. It turned out to be a great decision, even if it was made by a five-year-old. The resort was clean and quiet, and it had a great little restaurant for breakfast.

Now, next committee meeting topic: the Disney Dining Plan. My sister the travel agent highly recommended we purchase the dining plan, which covers one counter-service meal, one table-service meal, and one snack per day for each guest in your party. It cost more money up front, so naturally my husband was skeptical. Once again, the voice of the grandparents was a boon. They voted yes. David had no choice but to acquiesce. This grandparent thing was working out way better than expected.

With these major decisions made, the only other important matters to be addressed

The Disney Dining Plan

Disney offers a dining plan that you can purchase up front and use in over one hundred participating Disney restaurants throughout the theme parks. Not all restaurants within Walt Disney World are included, but the majority are. You can purchase the Disney Dining Plan on its own or add it to your Disney vacation package (such as the Magic Your Way package—see www.disney.com for complete details). Your dining plan package will be added to your card (the one that gets you into the parks and into your room) so you don't have to worry about taking a lot of cash or credit cards with you in the theme parks each day. Paying up front means less stress about mounting credit card charges for meals out while you are on vacation. You've already paid for it, which makes it easier to enjoy.

Here is what the Disney Dining Plan includes. For each night of your package stay you will enjoy:

- One table-service meal (at a sit-down restaurant with wait staff), including appetizer, entrée, and dessert (*or* full buffet), nonalcoholic beverage, and gratuity/service charge
- One counter-service meal (at an à la carte, carry-your-tray restaurant), including entrée, dessert, and single-serving nonalcoholic beverage *or* one complete combo meal, dessert, and single-serving nonalcoholic beverage
- One snack choice (frozen ice cream novelty or fruit bar, *or* single-serve popcorn, *or* single piece of whole fruit, *or* single-serve Grab Bag of Frito-Lay chips, *or* 20 oz. bottle of Coke, Diet Coke, Sprite or 24 oz. bottle of Dasani water, *or* medium-size fountain drink, *or* apple juice

You may also exchange two table-service meals for one of the character meals.

in advance were the character meals. We decided to book a Cinderella breakfast at the castle and a breakfast at Chef Mickey's at the Contemporary Resort (which is easy to get to from just about anywhere via the monorail). Cinderella would cover Anna; Chef Mickey would cover Cade.

Disney's rule on character dining used to let you book these meals only ninety days in advance, but that recently changed to allow reservations six months in advance. I had heard talk among other moms that these coveted dining experiences booked up insanely fast. It's true. When my sister sent me the confirmation numbers, I breathed a huge sigh of relief. We were in.

When the time rolled around for our trip, we all piled into the car, brimming with anticipation. I also had a little bit of dread mixed in. Stephanie is a complete Disney freak; she cries every time she sees Cinderella's castle and has already taken her young children to Disney more times than most kids will get to go in their entire lives. I, on the other hand, fully expected to be "over" Disney in a couple of days' time. Sightseeing non-stop, in-laws, kids, crowds . . . I mean, honestly, how much fun could the happiest place on earth really be? But the truth is, it was incredibly fun. I am as shocked as anyone to tell you, but I would go back tomorrow. I wasn't ready to leave, even after six nights.

And here's the key to having fun: you have to make a plan. Now, I know the words *plan* and *fun* sound contradictory to a lot of people, me included. But at Disney, you *have* to plan. The first night we were there, I wrote out a schedule based on the hours of the various parks and show times. Then we made reservations for dinner for each night at the appropriate park. You simply must make dinner reservations at Disney or you won't eat until 10:00 P.M., which is a recipe for a meltdown with overtired, overstimulated kids. Without reservations you'll probably wind up eating fast food every night, because that's the only thing you can get at an hour that is even close to your kids' dinnertime. So make reservations. The 407-WDW-DINE phone number allows you to make reservations at any restaurant within Disney World. This number should become etched into your cerebral cortex within twenty-four hours after arriving in the park.

The character meals were one of the best decisions we made. Both the Cinderella breakfast and Chef Mickey's were terrific experiences—well, at least until Cade poked Goofy in the butt with his Power Rangers sword. (Good thing Cade is so little and hard to catch that he can run between people's knees in a crowd.) The beauty of character meals is that you can spend lots of time taking pictures with the characters (you can even let the kids pose with them) while eating a surprisingly good meal, then go enjoy the park without searching for characters or waiting in line when you find one.

The dining plan also turned out to be a great decision for our particular group (nah-neh-nah to David). Although there was a little confusion about how it worked at first, we quickly figured out the system. The best part of the dining plan was that you weren't looking at another credit card charge every time you sat down for a meal. You'd already paid for each meal in advance. With my husband, that really dialed down the stress level of the trip. Although I must warn you: you will eat more with the dining plan. If your family is like mine, then, by God, if we paid for this meal plan, we were going to eat every last morsel of food we had coming to us. The last day of our trip, as we were walking through the Magic Kingdom, my husband announced to everyone, "We have eight snacks left on the card. Everybody get a snack, now!"

Ultimately, the moral of my Disney story is this: you have to plan, and you have to go in with the right attitude. Expect to wait in line. Expect to wait for buses, boats, and trains. Count on some extra time in your schedule to allow for this, or else you're likely to go postal on someone, which will get you forcibly removed from the premises (although at least you might get a glimpse of the infamous Disney tunnel system, which Stephanie's always wanted to see). And try to remember that if you paid separately for every show, ride, and attraction that you went to in the Disney parks, it would cost a fortune. So even though the initial Disney bill seems like a lot, you really do get a heck of a lot of fun and entertainment for your money. And your kids get to experience the magic of the happiest place on earth.

From Stephanie

Okay, I admit it. Like Sara said, I'm one of those Disney fanatics who start crying on the monorail at the sight of Cinderella's castle. I can't help myself. I'm a creative person who appreciates the detail and the thought and the planning that go into any production. So the Disney parks are just plain overstimulating for me. I'm like a toddler with a bowl of sugary cereal and a new *Barney* episode. I notice every detail, every performer, every costume, and I'm dying to get a behind-the-scenes tour of the underground tunnels that only Disney cast members get to use. Walt Disney is my hero. I've read every book about him. I have photos of him all over my office (Sara makes fun of me for that). His life and his unwavering determination and creativity are so inspiring to me. And there's no place on earth that makes me feel like a kid again the way Disney does. So you can imagine how excited I am now that I can be a kid *with* my own kids. It's the best. We've taken our kids every year since they were eighteen months old. Here are some of our tips and ideas for making your visit go smoothly (or at least as smoothly as it can be with small children).

Before You Make Reservations

Go to www.disney.com and request an information and planning DVD. You'll get lots of great information about Disney and a sneak peak at all the resorts, which will help you greatly in your planning. And it's highly entertaining for the kids—this DVD is exactly how Anna knew that the Port Orleans had that cool dragon water slide.

Avail yourself of these great planning resources:

- **Birnbaum's Guide to Disney.** A new edition of this book comes out each year, and we highly recommend purchasing a copy. *Birnbaum's* gives you a chart of all the resorts and categorizes them by price, amenities, kid-friendliness, and access to transportation. The editors also designate certain rides and attractions with the "Birnbaum's Best" award, and they're pretty much right on.
- **www.allearsnet.com.** AllEarsNet is a terrific, comprehensive website that offers in-depth information on everything Disney, right down to menus at resorts and restaurants. You can even find customer reviews on resorts, restaurants, and guest rooms. This is the very best resource for inside information from our fellow Disney fanatics. You'll learn all the ins and outs.
- **www.disney.com.** The official Disney website.
- **407-WDW-DINE.** The number to call *far* in advance to make character dining reservations, as well as reservations for restaurants once you arrive at Disney. (We recommend tattooing this number on your forearm before you leave home. Just kidding . . . sort of.)

Walt's Secret

After the success of Disneyland in California, Walt Disney knew that if word was to get out about his plans to open a new theme park in Florida, the price of the land would skyrocket. So he hired lawyers to secretly purchase properties in Florida, and he disguised himself when he visited the area. Walt and his team purchased 27,443 acres (43 square miles) in central Florida at a cost of just over $5 million (which is about $145 per acre). Today, that land would cost somewhere in the neighborhood of $45 million.

Disney Parks

Let's clarify some of the lingo so we don't confuse anyone. When we say "park," we're referring to one of the Disney theme parks: Magic Kingdom, Hollywood Studios, Epcot, Animal Kingdom. And then there are the water parks: Blizzard Beach and Typhoon Lagoon. All of these parks, as well as shopping centers, hotels, golf courses, time-share resorts, and entertainment areas, make up the twenty-seven thousand acres of property Walt Disney secretly purchased back in the 1960s.

Logistics

What to Bring

Unless your kids are old enough to have a driver's license, you'll definitely want a stroller at Disney World. You can rent a Disney stroller in each park, or you can bring your own. We brought our own and it worked great (Disney strollers are rather large and you have to rent them at each individual park, i.e., Animal Kingdom, Magic Kingdom . . .). There is a lot of walking to be done between the bus stops and park entrances, so having your own stroller in hand (prior to even entering the park) is a necessity with little ones. But you'll want to bring an inexpensive, collapsible stroller (like the $20 umbrella stroller we list in Chapter 27, "Products We Love") that you can easily fold up or down when you get on and off the various forms of transportation around the parks.

Be sure to pack sweatshirts or windbreakers for the kids, as it can get cool at night during certain times of the year. You also want to prepare for the possibility of rain. And don't forget swimsuits and sunscreen for everyone.

Take a cell phone with you to the theme parks each day in case you need to make or change a dinner reservation. If you are traveling with more than just your immediate family and some of you will want to split up for different attractions, cell phones are vital for reconvening.

A small backpack is extremely helpful to take with you to the various theme parks.

You can stash your phone, room key card, sunglasses, brochures, and even a light windbreaker in the backpack and keep your hands free.

Getting There

Traffic around Disney World is a nightmare. You might as well expect it, accept it, and prepare for it. If you've traveled by car, you'll already be excited to see the signs announcing your entrance into Orlando, Florida, but the reality is that you'll still probably have another hour behind the wheel.

We've found that one of the best ideas for long car trips is to pack the kids' backpacks with little goodies from the dollar store. When they get in the car in the morning, they find a backpack full of little surprises and snacks to entertain them during the ride. The surprises don't have to be new, either. Stash away some toys and books the kids haven't played with in a while and bring them out for the trip. They're like new toys all over again.

Instead of filling backpacks with surprises, you can also keep a goodie bag in your possession. One mother I know makes a game out of her kids earning treats out of the bag. The kids earn their reward by doing things like counting to ten in Spanish or saying their ABCs. You can pick challenging, age-appropriate games for your kids that will help the time in the car pass quickly.

When to Go

Each year, Disney's official calendar lists peak and off-peak times for visiting the parks. *Birnbaum's* also offers these guides. It's a good idea not to go during major school holidays like spring break or Easter. Try to find a balance of good weather and off-peak timing. If you are able to stay for at least five or six days, you will build in some cushion time for bad weather days. Disney is simply more pleasant when the crowds are smaller. The lines are shorter and you spend more time riding rides and seeing shows than standing in line.

Age of the Kids

From Sara

This is a big debate among parents: what is the best age to tackle Disney? This depends on a number of factors. How many kids are in the family? Is anyone else going with you on the trip? For me, it came down to one thing: magic. I wanted to take my kids for the first time when they were still young enough to believe in the magic of Disney. I wanted them to go before every character was just a person in costume. When we walked into Cinderella's Castle for the first time, Anna looked at every door and imagined which princess's bedroom was behind it. I figure that we'll take the kids back again to Disney World when they are older and are more interested in Epcot and Hollywood Studios, but for our first trip, it was all about believing in the magic.

Where to Stay

The first decision you'll need to make regarding accommodations is whether to stay inside the Disney property or out. Staying at one of the twenty Disney resorts is more convenient, and they offer all sorts of perks to visitors who stay at their resorts. Then again, it can be more expensive. But you'll likely never have to get in your car while you're there, so the benefits of staying on the Disney property may outweigh the extra cost.

One very cool extra perk of staying at a Disney resort is called "Extra Magic Hours." Each morning and night, one of the theme parks opens an hour early or stays open an hour later for Disney resort guests. That means fewer people are in the park, the lines are shorter, and you can get a chance to ride some of the cool rides that had long lines all day.

Another bonus of staying inside the park is that you only need one card for everything. Your room key card not only opens your door but also gets you into the park (because your admittance charge is generally included on your card for the duration of your trip, although this depends on which Disney package you choose) and serves as your dining plan card. You can even use it to charge purchases. This is a real perk for parents who certainly don't need one more thing to carry around Disney all day. Just slip your card in your pocket and you're ready to roll.

Sara's Disney Money Tip

It's no fun to go to Disney if your kids are constantly squabbling over who gets to buy what and begging you for every item they see in the plethora of gift shops. The solution? Give them each a piggy bank, peanut can, or glass jar months in advance of the trip (again, this is where planning comes in) and designate it their Disney spending money. The kids can even decorate it with Disney stickers. Every cent they get should go into that jar. My kids made their grandparents well aware that they were saving for Disney, so Grandma and Grandpa often passed along a five-dollar bill or even a ten whenever they came to visit. My husband would give them the change from his pockets almost every day. They saved every single penny that came their way. The week before our trip, the kids and I took their loot to the bank. After we counted out all the change and the paper money, they had accumulated over $100 each. Those nickels and dimes really add up!

The real beauty of this system is that it eliminated any fighting or whining. Purchases were their decisions, not ours. David and I weren't constantly saying no to them. And when one child's money was gone but the other still had some left, it didn't cause a problem. No complaining, no whining, no pouting. Even among the kids. Beautiful.

At the Parks

As soon as you arrive at each theme park, pick up a Times Guide and New Information sheet. They have them at the entrance of each park and they list times for all the attractions, character greetings, parades, fireworks, and park hours. Times Guides are updated weekly. You can plan your visits to the parks once you have all this information at your fingertips.

Also be sure to pick up a map of the park you're entering at the gate. These detailed maps are essential for finding rides, attractions, and—of course—restrooms.

The Best Seat on the Monorail

Even if you don't stay at a resort that has monorail access, you just have to give your kids the experience of riding on one of Disney's transportation pride and joys. Take the monorail from the Magic Kingdom to Epcot, or the one between the Grand Floridian, Polynesian, and Contemporary resorts. Riding at night is a great way to get a spectacular view of Cinderella's Castle illuminated by the nightly fireworks. But the absolute best seat on the monorail is right up front where the driver is located. And yes, you can sit there too. Just ask the driver at one of the stops, and he or she will give you the next available opportunity to sit up front (usually only four people at a time). Now that's an incredible view!

Schedule a Pool Day

We always recommend staying for as long as you can afford at Disney, especially with young children. A longer trip allows you to build in a pool day, preferably in the middle of your week, to give the kids a break from the theme parks and a chance to relax and play.

Bedtime Stories

This is just about one of the coolest ideas we've ever heard. If you stay in a Disney resort, you can turn the television in your room to a certain channel at night and a princess will read your kids a bedtime story! Isn't that awesome? Check to make sure this is available at your hotel when you make your reservation.

Autographed Postcards

Don't you just wish you could take something back for everyone waiting for you at home? You can if you're related to the Hiltons. But let's face it: most of us just don't have the budget. So here's a cute and inexpensive way to send something really special back to a few of your friends waiting at home. Buy some of the character postcards from the gift shop and ask the characters that you meet to sign the cards for your friends. It makes them extraspecial when you mail them back home. The characters have to be careful to manage their time, so don't get too greedy, but they usually don't mind signing an extra postcard or two. Little Sara's friends were beyond excited to get a postcard signed by the *real* Cinderella.

Little Bladders and Long Lines

From Stephanie

Make it a policy to visit the potty before you get in line for the rides. The lines are really long and little ones just can't wait—and we all know that they wait until it's an emergency before they tell you. This seems like a simple instruction, but it's so easy to get caught up in the excitement and forget.

Here's a cautionary tale to help you remember. On one of our trips to Disney, we went to the Arabian Nights dinner show—an attraction that, by the way, I can only recommend if you like horses. I don't know why a germ freak and restaurant snob like myself suddenly felt perfectly comfortable eating chopped steak and a salad in a horse arena. Maybe it was the bad wine, but we did have a blast.

As exciting as it was, my son, Timmy, was just under two and he fell asleep. At the end of the show, they allow you to pet the horses and my daughter really wanted to have a turn (and so did I). As I was standing there waiting for our turn, balancing Timmy's sleeping body on my hip, his bladder fully relaxed and he began to pee all over me. There was so much volume and force that the urine even splashed onto the people behind me. (And some people are worried about their children *crying* in public.) Now, you may be wondering what to do in a situation like this. And this is the best way I can explain it. You know when someone is flatulent in public and everyone just pretends that nothing happened? Well, that's what you do when your child pees on someone in public, too. It's the same rule. We all looked down, realized what was happening, and then continued about our business. If I had been holding a glass of water or the aforementioned bad wine, I might have spun it as if there were a spill. But no such luck. Just smile and watch the

Stephanie's Stroller Tip

If possible, leave your husband at home. Give a man a stroller, put him in a crowd, and it renders him totally defenseless. I can't figure out if it's that "don't hit girls" thing, but most men are just incapable of pushing a stroller through a crowd. In any case, attach a cargo bag to the back of a lightweight stroller for all your belongings. It will serve you better than the big, heavy, fancy variety when you have to lug it onto the monorail or parking tram.

horses, and maybe no one will notice the warm liquid expanding on their newly purchased Bermuda shorts.

And then it almost happened again at Epcot as we were standing in line for the Soarin' ride. Fortunately, I was near an emergency exit. Tim and Sara got to enjoy the ride, and I sprinted to the bathroom to make sure Timmy didn't mark his territory again. By the way, I definitely belong to him now—I've been marked.

Photo Pass

From Stephanie

Once again, Disney has outdone itself when it comes to photo memories. There are plenty of Kodak moments at Disney, and they have photographers all over the parks ready and willing to snap a photo for you and your family. When you have a photo taken at the Disney parks, you'll be given a little plastic card with an account number, which is used to group all your photos together. Every time you have a photo taken, give the photographer your card. At the end of the day, you can go to one of the photo shops at the park and view all your proofs, print them out, and take them home with you. Or you can skip the lines and go to the website listed on the card and order them via the Internet. In fact, the proofs will be available online by the time you get back to your hotel, and you can even e-mail your photos to friends and family before you get home, for free, like a digital postcard. Another really fun thing to look for is a photo with a Disney character superimposed onto your picture. One photographer at the Magic Kingdom asked us to all stand holding our hands palm up. When we got the proof, Tinker Bell was sitting in our hands! (As if I'm not going to buy *that*!) They think of everything!

Stephanie's Money-Saving Tips

- There's no better place to enjoy your stay than one of Disney's many resorts. However, on many of our Disney adventures, we've opted to stay off-property to ease the cost. There are plenty of inexpensive choices for hotels and time-shares near the parks. It means you'll have to have your own car, but Disney makes parking easy with the parking lot trams. Just remember it's one more time you'll have to be ready to collapse and juggle the stroller.
- If you're really trying to be cost-conscious, pack a lunch. It's a little extra effort, but it does save money when you're traveling with little ones who are picky eaters. Bring their favorite lunch, snacks, and juice in your own cooler. We've saved big bucks with this strategy. Note that all bags are checked by security when you enter the parks, so be prepared.

Disney's Water Parks

If you want to take a break from the parks, try one of Disney's water parks: Blizzard Beach or the one we chose, Typhoon Lagoon. It had a fantastic area for smaller children that included water cannons, squirting fountains, and even their own miniature lazy river where you can float on little rafts in a small circle. The kids loved it! Some of the family rides worked out well, too. And the huge wave pool was a blast. It even offers a chance to scuba-dive with tropical fish. Older kids love Blizzard Beach because of the thrilling slides, but Typhoon Lagoon does a great job of offering fun and safe activities for little ones.

Sara's Must-Sees

Cinderellabration: Magic Kingdom

If there's a little princess in your family, this is a must. This is Cinderella's coronation ceremony in front of the castle. All the princesses and princes come to join Cinderella with music and dancing and even fireworks. It's a great way to see a lot of princesses in one place. There's a sign posted at the front of the castle listing performance times.

Ariel's Grotto: Magic Kingdom

Just behind the Flying Dumbo ride, you'll find a sign for Ariel's Grotto. There's usually a line, but it moves fast. Down in the grotto, you'll find Ariel sitting on a rock combing her hair (all the characters are amazing at using the exact mannerisms from the films). This is the only way to see Ariel, so if there's a fan in your crew, you don't want to miss this stop!

Goofy's Barnstormer Roller Coaster: Magic Kingdom

My three-year-old wasn't tall enough to ride Thunder Mountain the Big Railroad (which his older sister reminded him of every chance she got), but he was able to ride Goofy's Barnstormer. All four of us had a ball riding this small but very fun coaster. It was great to find a roller coaster we could *all* ride.

Beauty and the Beast Onstage: Hollywood Studios

What a fabulous show! Even very young girls and boys will love this performance, as will adults. The music, costumes, and choreography are simply great.

Interactive Crush the Turtle: Epcot (Living Seas)

This is one of the coolest shows for kids and for adults. Crush, the surfer dude sea turtle from *Finding Nemo*, appears (or actually crashes) on-screen and takes questions from the audience. I have no idea how they do it. It wasn't canned or staged—Crush actually responds to questions from the kids in the audience. Don't miss it!

Soarin': Epcot

Both of my kids loved this ride—even my three-year-old. It simulates hang-gliding over famous American landscapes. You have to be careful with young children, because your seat does actually lift off the floor several feet or more, but you'll feel as if you're soaring high above the land.

The Lion King Show: Animal Kingdom

Costumes, acrobatics, fire, dancing—this show has everything, all set to the inspiring music from the movie. Everyone in your family will enjoy it!

Stephanie's Must-Sees

The Parades

You can have Macy's, the Rose Parade—take 'em all. *Nobody* does a parade like Disney. Period. And the new fireworks show at the Magic Kingdom called "Wishes" is narrated by Jiminy Cricket and Julie Andrews and is nothing short of breathtaking. If you don't get weepy standing in front of that castle with a real, live Tinker Bell flying overhead and an amazing fireworks show set to music, then don't even bother getting out of bed, because there's nothing left to live for. That show is truly nothing short of *magical.* Both of my kids slept through the entire thing . . . but who needs kids to enjoy the Magic Kingdom anyway?

Fantasmic at Hollywood Studios

All I can say is, *wow*! This is one of the most amazing shows I've ever seen. Enter the amphitheater at least an hour before the show if you want a seat at all. For a good seat, find your spot an hour and a half prior to show time. Trust me, it's worth it. This show is the story of the triumph of the imagination. Mickey battles a fierce, fire-breathing dragon that ignites the entire lagoon. Favorite scenes from Disney movies are projected onto screens made of water. And the finale is amazing. (I cried again.) Please don't miss it.

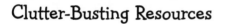

Clutter-Busting Resources

WEBSITES

Help with planning

www.allearsnet.com
www.disney.com

For reservations in Disney World

407-WDW-DINE

BOOKS

Birnbaum's Guide to Walt Disney World

(There's a new edition each year, so make sure to get the latest.)

25

You Don't Have to Be Perfect

From Stephanie

As bad as my children were in Wal-Mart one day, they were equally as good at the pediatrician's office the next. It was Timmy's three-year-old checkup. I have to admit, I was a little late scheduling his well-child visit—I was so busy planning his pirate birthday party that I totally forgot that he was supposed to go to the doctor on his birthday too.

Timmy was quiet in the waiting room. He giggled adorably, dimples showing and blue eyes beaming, when the nurse teased him. He answered all their questions politely with an impressive vocabulary for a three-year-old. He peed in the cup with no complaints or complications (we're experts in the bathroom arena, so that was a given). He said "Yes ma'am" and "No ma'am." And when it was time for the doctor to remove a pesky splinter from the ball of his foot, he sat on the table, eating his blue Popsicle (brilliant on their part, by the way) and didn't make a peep except to lean over to me just once and whisper, "Mommy, that hurts." He was amazing. He thanked them all when we were leaving. I could almost hear harps playing in the background as the doctor and nurse looked at him lovingly and said, "Thank you for being *such* a good little boy." As I paid the bill, he politely asked for the customary lollipop and sticker, and asked if he could take a sticker home to his sister, which earned him even more accolades from the reception desk. As we walked out to the car, I could feel the glow all around us, the perfect mother and her perfect child. I could imagine the staff talking behind my back: "No wonder she wrote a parenting book." The universe was finally in alignment. I was at the height of my parenting career. And then as I leaned over to put him into his car seat . . . it was like that needle-scratching-across-a-record sound they always use on TV when something goes terribly wrong. The harps stopped. The glow extinguished. I realized, standing there in the parking lot, that my fly was open.

Being one of those silly, old-fashioned people who think they should dress nicely to go to the doctor's office, I was all decked out in my white summer capris and my spaghetti-strapped navy blue sweater, the one that makes my arms look really skinny, my best hair and makeup. And I was crushed. Mortified. There was *no* way they hadn't noticed. During the fifteen minutes it took to remove the splinter, I'd been sitting in a chair holding Timmy's foot while the doctor stood over me, in direct alignment with my zipper!

It must have been the pee-pee-in-the-cup-for-the-first-time session in the bathroom. Just as I was standing up from going potty myself (hey, I was already there), Timmy grabbed his full cup before I could put the top on. And as I hurriedly grabbed it from his hands, I must have forgotten to go back and finish zipping. Damn, the bathrooms—they get me every time. I just stood there in the pediatrician's parking lot laughing at myself and shaking my head.

That's one of the great things about kids. Just about the time you get a little full of yourself, they have a way of putting everything into perspective again.

Why Do We Try So Hard to Be Perfect?

We're all so caught up in making our children successful. Do we really think they're going to get a sports scholarship or that we're grooming a future president? Recent studies show that success and even wealth do not necessarily determine happiness.

In fact, research reveals that "the happiest people surround themselves with family and friends, don't care about keeping up with the Joneses next door, lose themselves in daily activities and, most importantly, forgive easily," writes Marilyn Elias.

"The happiest people spend the least time alone. They pursue personal growth and intimacy; they judge themselves by their own yardsticks, never against what others do or have.

" 'Materialism is toxic for happiness,' says University of Illinois psychologist Ed Diener. Even rich materialists aren't as happy as those who have lower incomes and care less about getting and spending."

Happiness Is a Dung-Plastered Hut

On a scale of 1 to 7, where 1 means "not at all satisfied with my life" and 7 means "completely satisfied," the people on *Forbes* magazine's list of the 400 richest Americans average 5.8—the same as the Inuit people in Greenland and the cattleherding Masai of Kenya, who live in dung-plastered stick huts with no electricity or running water. Calcutta's slum dwellers score only a little lower, at 4.6.

Another study, reported in the *Journal of Personality and Social Psychology*, states, "Topping the list of needs that appear to bring happiness are autonomy (feeling that your activities are self-chosen and self-endorsed), competence (feeling that you are effective in your activities), relatedness (feeling a sense of closeness with others) and self-esteem."

When you consider findings like these, doesn't it make you wonder why we're all trying so hard to make our kids the brightest and best? Are we making ourselves and our kids miserable in our quest for having extraordinary children? Shouldn't our goal really be to guide our children to have happy lives?

The following is an article we found by a fellow writer-mom, Tracy Line, and we thought she said it so well we wanted to share some of it with you.

In Praise of the Average Child

Guess what? My children are not brilliant. They're not in the accelerated program at school, they do not excel in sports, and they do not have any particularly amazing talents. They are just plain, ordinary, good old American kids; I am very proud of them.

In our country, it is generally agreed that the top 2 to 5 percent of all students are gifted. Thus, 98 to 95 percent, like mine, are not. In this day and age there is much admiration for that upper 2 to 5 percent. While being gifted and/or highly talented is undoubtedly something to be proud of, it is important to remember that all children are something to be proud of. In other words, gifted and talented does not equate to better.

In this land of opportunity, we adults are quick to note intelligence and achievement. Research and technology have taught us the recipe for giving our children the best environment in which to succeed. We know what to feed our kids, what music to play while they look at their flash cards, and what "super-baby" videos will stimulate their brains. We are very proud of their abilities.

Beyond the home, there is a multitude of enrichment activities for our highly accomplished youth. Even the youngest child can take ballet, art, pottery, or learn a foreign language. The older the child is, the more the possibilities. As we want our own children to achieve, we are quick to do what we've been programmed to believe is best for them. The question is: What is best?

Not every child is academically gifted or highly talented. The spectrum for intelligence is a broad one. Yet all children are unique beings gifted with individual talents and abilities, many of which will never show up on tests or on the soccer field. Our children will develop strengths and interests different from our own, and in their own time. To expect them to be something they are not will leave them feeling as if they never measure up. This can be damaging to the ego and is also a useless effort. It's like trying to ski uphill. To encourage instead of push, to accept children as is, faults and all, this is what is best.

The world is full of average children who have grown up to excellence. After graduating near the bottom of his class, Michael Landon later became a hugely successful actor, writer, director, and producer. The son of a mechanic and a bank teller who was once cut from his high school basketball team grew up to be Michael Jordan. Steven Spielberg and Bill Gates both chose to drop out of college to pursue their dreams. Class clown David Letterman is still making millions laugh.

What made these individuals successful? It's hard to say what complex sequence of events and personality traits led these people to their place in the world. One thing seems obvious though; academic strength is not the sole predictor of success. It is just one of a plethora of talents. Personality, creativity, moral values, work ethic, and tenacity—these and other traits combined to make us who we are. We are not and should not be defined by our test scores.

So why are parents so aggressive in wanting their children to excel academically and otherwise? Because we want our children to grow up and lead successful, productive lives. We want a happy childhood to lead them to the spouse, the house, the 2.5 kids, and the white picket fence. The world has changed but the American dream hasn't. Even as dreams vary a bit among us, essentially, at the heart of it all, what we really want most for our children is for them to be happy.

Being happy, interestingly enough, doesn't have much to do with brainpower. In a recent study of intelligence and happiness, researchers Furnham, Adrian, and Petrides found little evidence to support that cognitive intelligence is in any way related to happiness ("Trait Emotional Intelligence and Happiness," *Social Behavior and Personality*, 2003). Hmmm . . . remember Forrest Gump?

Furthermore, life coach Susan Dunn writes in her article "Emotional Intelligence Versus Cognitive Intelligence" that one's emotional intelligence, or ability to understand and manage emotions and get along with others, accounts for more success and happiness in life than the strength of one's intellect (see www.susandunn.cc for more information). I believe we're better off to teach our children the golden rule rather than worry about which videos they watch, how quickly they learn to read, or whether or not they are selected for the gifted program.

As children grow, their personal attributes will surface. They may or may not turn out to be what we wanted or expected. Some will do well in school while others will struggle. Yet it is the person, not the test scores, that matters. It is our job as parents to love, support, and accept our children for who they are. Even if what they are is average. In other words, focus on the gifts your child has instead of dwelling on what he doesn't.

Perhaps as parents we should relax. We can allow our children to grow and experience life as we teach them self-acceptance, moral values, and a strong work ethic. Hopefully if we do this, the end result will be happy, successful adults. Our offspring will make many mistakes, as do we. Failure though is necessary; if you never fall, you'll never learn how to get back up and try again.

If your child does well in school, it can only help him to succeed in life. If he doesn't, well then, maybe he'll turn out to be the next Letterman or Spielberg. And if he grows up to lead an average life, to get married, have a couple kids, and buy a nice house, well then, he'll fit right in with the rest of us. Be proud of him regardless.

Tracy Line is an Indianapolis-based freelance writer and the mother of three perfectly average and wonderful children. For writing or reprint information, see www.tracyline.com. This article first appeared in Indy's Child *magazine.*

From Stephanie

If you want your children to be successful, make them happy. Recently, scientists looked at 225 studies involving 275,000 people and found that chronically happy people are more successful in both their personal and professional lives. "When people feel happy, they tend to feel confident, optimistic, and energetic and others find them likable and sociable," said Sonja Lyubomirsky of the University of California, Riverside. "Happy people are thus able to benefit from these perceptions." The study showed that happy people are more likely than their less happy peers to have fulfilling marriages and relationships, higher incomes, superior work performance, community involvement, robust health, and even longer lives.

I think there are too many parents living vicariously through their children. Wanting your children to have a better life than you did isn't wrong, but don't get carried away. For many parents, our own self-worth lies in the accomplishments of our child. Being proud of your child is one thing, but letting your child's abilities affect your own self-image or self-worth is a little psychotic. If your child is the team captain or the winner of the spelling bee, it doesn't mean you're a better parent than anyone else. You might have focused a little more on something than another parent, and more than likely your child had a specific talent or interest that gave her a boost, but if you think your child's spot on the football team is a testament to your worth, then you're kidding yourself.

Let me give you an example. My older child, my daughter, was great at learning her sight words in kindergarten. I made playing cards with the sight words on them and we would play her favorite game, Go Fish. After about two or three rounds, she would know her words. It was simple. She quickly passed many of the other kids in her class and was reading very well by the time summer vacation rolled around. My son is one year behind her. Once again, I made Go Fish cards out of the sight word lists. But teaching these words to him has been like pulling teeth! I've spent much more time working with him than I did my daughter and getting far slower results. There are many reasons for this, and probably his level of maturity is more to blame than anything, but I can't help wondering if his teacher thinks I'm some kind of slacker—not spending enough time with him at home.

But the truth is, it's not my fault that my daughter learned her words quickly, and it's not my fault that it takes my son longer to learn the same words. There are many factors affecting why one child is better at something than another. There are plenty of things that my son can do better than my daughter. I don't think one is any smarter than the other; they each have a natural affinity for different things. And let's not forget that everything with children is a stage. Plenty of kids who are popular athletes in high school grow up to be complete losers. So don't be so quick to pat yourself on the back. The best thing you can do to create a happy and successful adult is to focus on their education and their happiness now.

Managing Your Household

26

An Organized Life

From Stephanie

Sara is the neat and organized one. My philosophy on household chores? Erma Bombeck summed it up best: "My theory on housework is, if the item doesn't multiply, smell, catch on fire or block the refrigerator door, let it be. No one cares. Why should you?" For the record, this quote is framed and hanging on my kitchen wall. And that's exactly why Sara is in charge of this chapter. If you're like me and you can live with a messy closet, then skip it. But, if you'd like to try to get a little more organized, then Sara is your girl. Her house is always neat and orderly. She could give people tours of her closets on any given day and not be at all embarrassed. For me, closets are primarily used for cramming things into just before people come over. In any case, this chapter will give you great, realistic tips for getting some organization back into your life.

From Sara

Having kids means having stuff. It starts from the moment they're born. You need a Pack 'n Play, a bassinet, a swing, a floor gym, an ExerSaucer, a Moses basket, a Jumperoo, a vibration seat . . . and before you know it you can't see your furniture anymore. As a mother, you're waging a constant war against clutter.

For me, all this stuff that comes into your household via kids is one of the great mental challenges of motherhood. I can't stand clutter. I've become very close friends with the guy who mans the Goodwill truck. With all the bags and boxes I've given to him, you'd think there'd be nothing left in my house. But the stuff multiplies faster than I can get rid of it.

Yes, I am the anal-retentive, organized one of this team. I lust over the serene minimalist photos in *Real Simple* magazine. I get excited about drawer dividers and storage bins. But I must confess that my house doesn't look as organized as I would like. In spite of my best efforts, I still spend entirely too much time looking for other people's shoes and I end up buying duplicate items at the grocery store. And I do have at least one closet that is exactly what Stephanie described. But the truth is, no one who has kids lives in a house that looks like the ones in the magazines. I always laugh at how the photographs have a board game out on the table or a few blocks scattered out on the floor while the rest of the room is pristine. *This* is supposed to illustrate family life? Where are the grape juice stains on the carpet? The forty-thousand-piece Lego set that has just been dumped upside down? The stray juice box? And look, there's a child's hairbrush on the kitchen counter and a kid's single tennis shoe on the dining room table. *That's* family life. I tell you all this so you know I am not removed from reality.

Having said that, I am a total believer in getting organized. Organization isn't just about having a neat and tidy house (although that is a perk); getting organized really can help make life easier and more enjoyable. Even if it's a two-steps-forward-one-step-back process getting there. Clutter and disorganization cost you valuable time and money—two things most moms are short on in the first place. Creating a system that works for you can give you time to do the things that nourish your soul, whether it's reading a great book, starting a business, or working on a scrapbook. I've scoured all the magazines, resource books, websites, and stores and have found some great methods and products for getting control of your household, your time, your money, and even your meals. There are tips on getting every member of your household to chip in, including the dog. (Okay, just kidding about the dog, but how cool would that be?)

I've divided this chapter into three main parts: "Clearing Out the Clutter," "Getting Organized," and "Managing Your Time." There's a lot of information here, so I recommend reading a little at a time and incorporating the tips in stages. If you try to do it all at once, it's just too overwhelming. However, no matter whose book you read on organization, they all tell you to start with the same first step: clear out the clutter. And boy, do we Americans have some clutter.

Clearing Out the Clutter

Our Cluttered Lives

If you're frustrated about the current condition of your household, you're not alone. Just look at the results of this survey by *Parenting* magazine.

- 1 in 5 moms says her house looks like a tornado just swept through.
- 16 percent say they spend at least an hour a week hunting for misplaced books, toys, keys, and other things.

- 53 percent of moms would rather be superorganized and a little stressed, as opposed to 47 percent who preferred to be relaxed but disorganized.

And you have to love this one:

- 26 percent say they can't even get organized enough to organize what they need to organize!

Ten Traits of an Organized Home

So what would an organized home look like? According to Barbara Myers at www.ineedmoretime.com, here are the ten traits of an organized home.

1. Lack of clutter because everything has a place. The Band-Aids are in the kitchen cabinet near the sink. All videos are stored near the VCR. Today's mail is sorted into baskets or folders.
2. Refrigerator, freezer, and pantry are stocked and organized. There's a planned menu for this week. A grocery-list-in-progress is posted near the fridge.
3. Clean laundry is put away. Dirty laundry is in hampers or is being laundered.
4. Family calendar is updated daily and color-coded by person.
5. Chore list is clearly posted. Everyone does his or her share as a member of the family.
6. There is a key rack, shoe rack, and pegs for jackets and backpacks near the door.
7. Toys are categorized into containers and can be put away quickly.
8. There is a portable file box into which bills and paperwork are organized.
9. Home appears adequately clean. Family has a daily system for picking up clutter and a weekly system for cleaning the house.
10. Family members have time for one another because their home is organized.

Ahhh . . . a home like that sounds like heaven, doesn't it? But right now you're probably wondering, how do you actually pull it off? Here's how to get started.

From Stephanie

Heaven? Sounds more like prison. Color-coded by person? Seriously? Oh my God . . . take a larger dose of OCD meds and get a life, will ya? I'm gonna go have a cocktail with my tennis team while you alphabetize your daughter's Barbie collection.

Declutter

Every organizational expert will tell you that decluttering is rule number one when it comes to getting your house in order. Purging your household and your life of all the stuff that bogs you down is the place to start. Why? The more stuff you have, the less time you have, that's why! Stuff breeds. The more you have, the more you need. One purchase often leads to another. You buy toys for the kids, so you need containers to put the toys in. You buy a digital camera, which leads to a photo printer, which leads to photo paper, ink cartridges, and photo albums. The more stuff you have, the more you have to clean and the more stuff you have to put away or look for when it's lost. So it makes sense to scale back and streamline every room in your house. Clearing out the clutter is the best first step to getting organized, no matter what part of your house you're talking about.

How do you know what to get rid of? If you don't use it, put it away, give it away, or throw it away. When you have children, it's absolutely essential to regularly do a sweep of your home and get rid of broken and unused toys, clothes that don't fit anymore, and so on. No one brings more clutter into a household than kids do: schoolwork, crafts, party treat bags, Happy Meal toys, treasure box toys, birthday gifts, holiday gifts, and on and on. There is a constant inflow, so there must be a constant outflow or you will be knee deep in clutter before you know it.

If you're like Stephanie, you're probably thinking, "Big deal. What's so bad about a little clutter?" The reality is, clutter affects you in more ways than you even realize. Here are six ways clutter costs you.

The Six Costs of Clutter

These ideas are from one of our favorite websites: www.mommysavers.com.

Cost 1: Hard-Earned Money

How many times have you come home from the store with more than you intended to buy? Did you really need those extra things? Often those impulse buys get cast aside after only a couple of uses. In other words, you just spent money to clutter your home.

If you catch yourself wanting to buy something that isn't on your shopping list, walk away for a while. If you still "need" it at the end of your shopping trip, then and only then go back and get it. Better yet, go home to think about it. If you still want the item the next time you go shopping, put it on that day's list of things to buy.

Cost 2: Cleaning Time

Once you bring something into your home, you will have to maintain it by dusting and cleaning. You're paying with your time. How long does it take you to clean the top of your refrigerator in its current condition? Don't remember because it's been so long since you've done it?

Imagine that nothing (absolutely nothing) is on top of the refrigerator. No cereal or potato chips. No unused small appliances. No knickknacks. It's completely empty.

Now how long will it take you to clean the top of the refrigerator? That theory holds true for all the horizontal surfaces in your house (tables, countertops, dressers, televisions, entertainment centers, even floors). Clear them off and you can cut your cleaning time down to almost nothing.

Cost 3: Happiness

If you don't like that bookshelf (dress, knickknack, etc.) anymore, get rid of it. It doesn't matter if that china clock was a gift from a special friend or if that huge desk has been in your family for five generations. If it doesn't make you happy, get rid of it. Trust me, you will feel lighter and liberated once you do. Put something that pleases you in that new space. Or leave the space open and simply enjoy the empty clean space.

Cost 4: Higher House Payments

All those extra things (those unused items that you're saving for whatever purpose) are taking up valuable space in your home. Or worse, perhaps you're renting a storage locker just so you can hang on to items you will never need or use. Every inch of space used for storage is one less inch of space that you can use for living. It doesn't matter if your clutter is limited to one closet or if you have stuff strewn from one end of the house to the other. You're paying for that space. What percentage of your home is occupied by clutter?

Do the math. Let's say you have a 2,000-square-foot house with a monthly mortgage/rent payment of $700. Even if you've limited your stuff to a 10-by-10-foot area (100 square feet), that clutter is taking up 5 percent of the space in your house (area of clutter divided by area of house). And 5 percent of your house payment is $35 every month (or $420 every year)!

Get rid of the excess stuff and you might very well be comfortable in a smaller home, with smaller monthly payments, smaller utility bills, and a smaller space to clean and maintain. Or getting rid of the stuff might save you from having to move to a bigger house, with bigger bills, etc.

Cost 5: Time and Frustration

If you've got a lot of stuff, you're bound to lose track of at least some of it. How much time do you spend looking for everyday items like car keys or the other shoe? What about items that you know you have but just can't find? Wrapping paper for a wedding present (she's getting married in an hour). Glue for your daughter's school project (sure, she's known about it for weeks, but it's due tomorrow morning). Or worse, your son is bleeding and you've managed to locate the bandages, but where is the antibiotic cream?

Even if you do know where something is, how much extra time do you waste moving other stuff out of the way just to get to it, and then again just to put it away? How many pots and pans do you own, and how many do you use regularly? If you got rid of just a few of those unused pots, putting away the ones you do keep will take less time.

Cost 6: Self-Esteem

Did you break out into a cold sweat the last time somebody dropped by unexpectedly? Or have you simply informed everyone to stay away from your house unless they give you two weeks' advance notice of their upcoming visit? When you do have guests, you can't relax and enjoy them if you're fretting about the dust bunnies lurking in the corner or trying to straighten the pile of mail on the coffee table. Imagine the freedom of saying, "Why don't you just drop by tonight?" without having to worry about all the things you have to do to make the house presentable.

Being ashamed of your home and frightened of anyone who might see it is a lousy way to live your life. Clear out the clutter and welcome your friends back into your life.

Getting the Kids Involved

Are you starting to get motivated to get your house in order? I am! So let's start by talking about what's realistic and setting the right expectations. Your house is probably never going to look pristine for long with small children around. That's just the reality. However, there are many things you can do to help get kids involved in the act of keeping the house in order and under control. Let's face it—you can't do this all on your own, because they can pull it out faster than you can pick it up. If you're going to get your house in order, it's going to have to be a team effort.

Every member of the family needs to contribute in order for the household to run smoothly (or at least as smoothly as possible). We moms tend to take on all the work ourselves, but the reality is when one person is carrying the whole load, it doesn't take long to burn out. By getting kids involved, you'll also be giving them invaluable skills they'll use for the rest of their lives. Try these tips for getting the rest of your crew on board.

Have a Family Meeting

Gather the entire family together and make it clear that you are willing to do your share of the housework, but everyone in the family needs to help. Explain that you would be a more relaxed person and easier to live with if everyone would simply select a few chores and do their share. Offer a list of the chores that you'd be interested in sharing so they can choose some chores right away. Post a schedule of chores for everyone—including yourself—as a reminder. I use responsibility charts for the chores I want my kids to help out with. They get a check each time they do the task and a reward once they have reached their "goal"—a total number of checks that I set each week.

Teach Your Kids to Help

When my daughter started kindergarten, I was amazed to see how self-sufficient she was after just a couple of weeks in the classroom. She and all the other children hung up their own coats and backpacks, filed their own work in the appropriate folders, cleaned tables, stacked chairs, picked up toys, and took care of their own assigned duties for the week. Of course, as soon as she got home it was like pulling teeth just to get her to hang up her backpack. We moms tend to coddle our kids, and that's understandable—after all, they're our babies. We want to take care of them, but sometimes in the process we forget to teach them some self-sufficiency. If they don't learn organizational and homekeeping skills from you, they'll have to learn it the hard way later on when they're on their own. So when they grumble, remember that you're giving them important life skills that will make life much easier down the road.

Make It Easy for Kids to Clean Up and Get Organized

What good are hooks for coats and backpacks if kids can't reach them? (I learned this lesson the hard way.) Place hooks, racks, bins, and hangers within kids' reach. If possible, put closet rods low enough for kids to hang up their own clothes. If this isn't possible, provide a sturdy, nonskid stepstool so they can hang up their own clothes. Put drawers, baskets, bins, and toy chests down on their level. Make sure there are no heavy lids that kids can't open on their own or, worse, that could smash little fingers.

Be Realistic

Remember that your children will not be able to perform tasks the same way you would. If your five-year-old can make her own bed, don't expect the covers to be perfectly smooth. Be careful not to complain that your child doesn't do it "right." If he hears criticism, he'll be less likely to help out willingly. Set realistic expectations too. Kids can only put away what's in reach in places that are easily accessible to them.

Let Them Learn

Don't do it for them! I learned this lesson when my daughter started school. Her teacher ran a tight ship and it was up to every child to do his or her part. They had to try doing things on their own so they could learn. This was so strange to me at first. I would go have lunch with Anna and start walking around the lunch table opening kids' milk cartons and ketchup packets for them. The teacher politely told me that the only way they would learn was by doing it themselves and practicing. As moms, we can easily slip into the habit of doing too much for our kids because it's easier in the short run. But we pay for it in the long run. Children are usually capable of doing much more than is asked of them. Obviously there are some things kids of certain ages can't do for themselves. But many of the simple tasks we moms perform every day can be done by the kids. Make sure to give lots of hugs, praise, and thank-yous, to build on their sense of accomplishment.

Make Cleaning Up Fun

Preschools often teach the "Clean Up" song. You may have even heard your preschooler singing it at home: "Clean up, clean up. Everybody do your share!" Sing along with the children as they clean up. Let them wear fun work hats and aprons. Have a race to see who can throw their toys into the baskets the fastest. When all the tasks are complete, reward them with a trip to the pool, a visit to the library, a picnic in the backyard, or some TV time. Give kids a "Job Well Done" sticker or simply lots of praise and hugs for helping out.

Make It Easy

I like to keep baskets in the living room as catch-alls for the endless Happy Meal toys and party favors that seem to come into my house. It's easy for kids to toss loose items into the baskets on their own. I tuck mine under end tables and in the corner for an uncluttered look.

Rotate Tasks

Be sure to give your child new and challenging tasks so he won't get bored doing the same chores over and over. Give him different jobs to do, and he'll learn a wide range of valuable and lasting skills.

Label Shelves, Baskets, or Boxes with Words or Pictures

Help children understand what goes where with labels. I like simple tie-on tags that you can write on (or paste a picture on for younger kids) because you can easily change them or replace them as your needs change. You can easily make these tags yourself with some construction paper, a hole punch, and some ribbon or string. At Target you can also find toy bins with a chalkboard on the side so you can write the label right on the bin.

Responsibility Charts

I bought responsibility charts for my kids from Leaps and Bounds, and I highly recommend using them in tandem with some type of responsibility and reward system. This has worked wonders with my kids and helped my sanity immensely. You can get these charts at lots of stores or you can make your own. The ones I got from Leaps and Bounds are magnetic, so they adhere easily to the fridge. I placed them low on the refrigerator door along with a magnetic dry-erase pen so the kids can check off their daily responsibilities and keep track of how many checks they have earned. I set a number of checks they have to earn in order to redeem a reward that we both agree on. Sometimes it may be a new (small) toy, but I try to make the rewards things that won't add to the clutter in my house. Sleepovers, a trip to the library, a play date, a trip to the park, or some special one-on-one time with Mommy or Daddy are just as motivating as toys.

The Leaps and Bounds charts have removable decals for daily and weekly chores. There's also a place for bonus checks. I love the bonus check feature for little tasks the kids can help out with as you need them. Almost every day I hear myself saying, "I'll give you a bonus check if you take the clothes out of the dryer" or "I'll give you a bonus check if you'll go get the mail out of the box." You get the idea. It's perfect for little unforeseen things you need the kids to help out with that aren't part of their regular responsibilities.

You can tailor these charts based on the age of the child. My five-year-old isn't quite ready to make up his own bed yet, but my seven-year-old can. You can also increase the number of checks or points needed to receive a reward as the children become more proficient at their tasks.

Work Together

Working alongside your child is a great way to gain insight into how he or she does things. Children aren't going to do everything the way you do. Sometimes good enough really is enough. Stephanie has a great saying: "Don't let perfect get in the way of good."

The Butler Box

Teach your kids to do a complete cleanup by bringing out the "butler box" (or bag) after they've had time to pick up their toys. Anything not put away gets added to the butler box. Your kids can redeem their items by doing extra chores around the house. Explain to them that this isn't punishment, it's an exchange of labor. Since you had to pick up their stuff, now they have to do something for you.

Make Sure Your Child Is Able to Do What You Ask

A toy box lid that is too heavy, shelves that are too deep, and clothes poles that are out of a child's reach all make it hard, if not impossible, for kids to help. Low, shallow shelving units are found in many day care centers for a reason. It's one of the best ways to encourage children to put things away for themselves. If you had twenty children to manage, you'd almost immediately give up on the concept that it's easier to do it yourself. (Just ask a kindergarten teacher.) Besides, it may be easier to do it yourself right now, but the sooner you teach your kids to do tasks themselves, the sooner they can help share the load.

Give Specific Instructions

Just saying "Clean your room" or "Get ready to leave" is too vague for most children, as well as overwhelming. "Pick up all the blocks and put them in the block box" is more useful.

Break Big Jobs Down into Smaller Ones

Divide larger jobs into parts. Don't ask your six-year-old to clean up her room without first showing her the step-by-step process: in other words, how to sort toys into the right bins, make up her bed, put dirty clothes in the hamper, and so on.

Make Sure There Is Enough Storage Space

If you are helping your child clean his room and you get stuck trying to find a place for everything, you need to either get rid of some stuff, get more storage, or both. Maximize closet space by hanging shoe racks on the doors. Add Command hooks (see sidebar) for hats, belts, necklaces, tote bags, robes, and so on. If hangers and drawers are out of reach, keep a library stool in the room so kids can reach clothes, for cleanup and getting dressed. You can find library stools (just like the ones in public libraries) at TheContainerStore.com (see "Clutter-Busting Resources"). These nonslip stools are lightweight, safe, and perfect for kids.

Designate a Place for Your Kids' Crafts and Artwork

When your kids are in preschool and elementary school, it's important to designate a place (other than the refrigerator) to display their prized artwork and projects. I use

Command Hooks

This has to be one of the best inventions ever if you're a mom. These hooks have adhesive backs that adhere to wood, metal, walls, and just about anything else, yet they can be easily removed without damaging the surface. The hooks come in a variety of sizes and styles. Use them on the inside of closet doors for hats, coats, bags and more! See www.solutions.3m.com.

mounted clips on a low wall near my kitchen to hang my kids' creations up for everyone to see. The kids can reach the clips to hang up or take down their artwork. A bulletin board, either in their room, the playroom, or the kitchen, also works well. If you're worried about the potential hazards of thumbtacks, try mounting a magnetic board with large magnets that will even hold up poster-size artwork. A long ribbon or string hung along the wall with clothespins for attaching artwork is an easy and inexpensive way to display kids' masterpieces. You can also purchase frames with an opening on the back that makes it easy to slide artwork in and out for displaying various pieces. These are available at Pottery Barn. No matter what method works for you, be sure to use the revolving-door technique of rotating artwork so your display area doesn't get overloaded.

Purge Regularly

Go through your child's clothes, toys, and papers along with your child and discuss what she really wants to keep. Give clothes to a friend or neighbor with a younger child. My daughter loves seeing the younger girls enjoy the clothes she has outgrown. It's a lot easier to stay organized and keep rooms tidy when they aren't bursting at the seams with stuff!

Kids rarely want to part with their toys. And sometimes parents don't either. I've gotten just as attached to some of my kids' stuff as they have. Which means you'll have to dig deep for your most creative mom skills to help them realize they should part with something. For very young children, sometimes it's easiest to simply put an item away for a while, then get rid of it after the child has forgotten about it. This also helps sentimental parents because it's a two-step process. Somehow it's easier to get rid of something that has gathered dust in the basement for several months than if you take it straight out of your child's toy box. However, as kids get older, it's best to be up-front and honest about clearing out the clutter.

- Start with the easy stuff first: broken toys, puzzles with missing pieces, Happy Meal–type toys that have no sentimental value.
- Get them to give away toys by telling them it's a toy they've outgrown: "This toy is for really little kids. You're way too big for this now!"
- If it's something sentimental, give it to a younger cousin or close friend. That way you don't feel like you are discarding something important but sharing it with someone special.
- Tell them they can't get anything new until something is cleared out. You can structure this as a one-in, one-out rule, or whatever arrangement works for your family.
- Give the kids a bag to fill for less fortunate children.

Getting Organized

Keeping Stuff from Accumulating

Cluster Like Items

Put all the toy trains in one bin, all the Legos in their container, and all the dolls in one basket. Keep hats and gloves in one spot, batteries all in one drawer. You'll spend a lot less time looking for things and it's much easier for the kids to clean up their toys.

Make Things Convenient

Put frequently used items at the front of shelves within easy reach. Minimize the amount of steps it takes to access something that is frequently used. For example, if you use your toaster every morning, leave it out on the counter; don't store it in a cabinet, as it creates unnecessary steps to take it out and put it back every day. On the other hand, *don't* leave infrequently used appliances out on the counter. They'll just make your kitchen look cluttered and make it more difficult to clean.

Purge Regularly

Don't feel guilty about getting rid of gifts that you never used or didn't like. Remember, it's the thought that counts. And it is better to give the item to someone who is going to use and appreciate it rather than having it take up valuable space in your home.

Use the Revolving-Door Technique

For items such as books, use the revolving-door technique: for each new book that you purchase, remove a book from your home that you have already read (except for this one, of course) or do not like. Give it to a friend, donate it to a charity, or sell it in a secondhand shop.

Don't Keep It if You Can Find It Elsewhere

So much research is easily accessed on the Internet these days that much of the paperwork, forms, and documents we keep on file, we don't even need!

Follow the Thirty-Second Rule

If it takes thirty seconds or less to do a job, then do it immediately. This applies to things like putting the scissors (or whatever) back where you got them, hanging up the clothes you take off, putting away your shoes, etc.

Cleaning

Clean Top to Bottom, Left to Right

You'll save time and eliminate duplicate work by using this method. Don't mop the floors before you clean the counters or you'll likely have to at least get out the broom or the vacuum again. Working in an orderly pattern enables you to work faster and more efficiently.

Keep a Cleaning Caddy

Put all your needed cleaning items in a caddy and carry it with you from room to room. This saves you time searching for supplies all over the house and enables you to keep all your cleaning tools in one place. I keep a few plastic grocery bags in mine for emptying trash cans and throwing away disposable cleaning cloths.

Storage

Take Back Your Garage

In the garage, getting equipment off the floor allows you to actually park your car in there! Install a shelving system with large hooks and bins for hanging gardening equipment and storing sporting goods. Clean out toys and ride-ons your kids have outgrown and donate them to a nearby preschool or give them to Goodwill.

Label It

If you're storing items in the attic or on shelves in bins, label the bins and boxes so you won't have to search through ten to get to the one you are looking for. You can even label shelves so there is no mistaking what goes where.

Keep Closets Neat and Organized

Keep your closet organized by separating different clothing items. Create different sections for pants, blouses, suits, dresses, skirts, etc. Then arrange each section by color, from white to black and through the rainbow. These techniques will save you time when you're looking for something to wear.

Buying Tips

Avoid Impulse Purchases

Keep a wish list in your purse or wallet. When you see something you want (but don't really need), add it to the list. After waiting a week or so, look over your list. Decide if you truly need, love, or have to have anything on your list. If so, go get it and enjoy! If not, throw out your list and pat yourself on the back—you just prevented clutter and saved some of your hard-earned cash!

Choose Quality, Not Quantity

A great way to pare down is by purchasing the best. If you have one tool that works well all the time, you won't need to buy another one for a long time. If you need a vacuum cleaner, buy one that will do all the jobs you need it to. Don't buy a cheap one that won't fit the bill and then end up buying a second one. Buying a quality item first might not seem like you are saving money up front because you are spending more, but I have found that buying a good product in the first place really does save me money. It took two vacuum cleaners, but I did learn.

Create a Command Center

I just love the idea of a command center—a place for incoming and outgoing items, the family calendar, a cute little rack to hang my keys on . . . you should have seen the look Stephanie gave me when I told her I was including this in this chapter. She thinks I'm nuts. But if you're seriously interested in better ways to manage your everyday life, then read on.

Every busy household should have a command center—a place that is the hub of your family's activity and daily life. The command center should have a phone and a central place for writing down messages as well as uncluttered workspace. You'll also need wall space for a family calendar to keep track of everyone's schedules and a place for other information that needs to be posted regarding chores, schoolwork, and other to-do items. The command center should also house incoming and outgoing mail and car keys so they're always easy to find.

Obviously, this area should be tailored to your family needs. Ideally, it should be located in the same place you store your important documents, and it should contain a computer. A home office is ideal. If this isn't possible, a great place for a command center is a table or desk (even a set of shelves can work) near the busiest entrance of your home. This is a perfect spot to sort incoming mail, kids' school papers (and Lord knows there are a zillion of those), keys, cell phones, purses, backpacks, and sunglasses. You can also designate an area for videos that need to go back to the rental store, library books that need to be returned, or purchases that need to go back to the store.

I'm in the process of setting up a command center in my house, and after much hand-wringing on my part (I wasn't kidding when I said I was anal), I've decided the best option for me is to make the room my husband and I use as our home office our main command center, but to create another mini command center near the kitchen and back door, which everyone in our household uses. This is where I'll keep a monthly calendar posted as well as a bulletin board for birthday party invites, school lunch menus, and the like. I'll also store permission slips, order forms, and other to-do items here. I'll have a slot for outgoing mail, DVDs to be returned, and so on. Nearby in the laundry room is a place for the kids to store their backpacks and coats when they come home from school.

I also have an area for the kids to display their school projects and artwork. Every week or two I take out the ones I want to save for the scrapbook and place the others in the recycling bin. I always find it difficult to throw out anything my kids have brought home from school, but the reality is you just can't save everything. Having said that, I do err on the side of saving too much now, when they're little. Other moms have told me that you just don't save as much as they get older because it's just not as cute.

Specific Problem Areas

Scrapbooking

Most of the moms I know have given in to the scrapbooking craze, yet we soon learn it's a double-edged sword. We love the memory keeping and being able to create something so special for our kids and us to hold on to, but talk about clutter! In order to scrapbook you need some space to spread all your stuff out, and for most of us, that usually ends up being the dining room table. And I personally got really tired of not seeing the surface of mine or, worse, having someone spill juice or ice cream on a precious bit of artwork.

Do you have a closet or nook somewhere in your house that's underutilized? Or one that could be decluttered to free up some space? We recently finished a room in our basement and the double-door closet became my scrapbooking nook. I was tired of spreading everything out on the dining room table, working for an hour if I was lucky, then packing it all back up again. My husband and father-in-law (God bless them) installed a countertop, wire drawers, and shelves for me. I added a wire wastebasket for storing gift wrap, a small rod (that I attached to a shelf) for ribbon, and Command hooks for gift bags, cutting templates, scissors, etc. My workspace is at counter height in an effort to keep little hands out of my stuff. I bought an inexpensive stool that stores under the counter when not in use. This is one of the best ideas I've ever had for my house because I don't have to put anything away when I am in the middle of a project and can't finish. I simply close the doors. When I show other moms my closet, they nearly turn green with envy.

Photos

We moms take loads of photos. And it nearly kills us to get rid of any photo of our precious children, even if it's so blurry we can barely make out their facial features. But as with all organizing, clearing out the clutter is the first order of business.

- Purge before you print. Digital cameras lend themselves to lots of duplicate shots, "because I can always delete ones that aren't good." Just make sure you delete. There's no need to have eight different shots of your daughter's Brownie troop lined up together. Delete these right on the camera before you upload them to your computer.
- Sort through boxes and eliminate bad shots.
- Pass on duplicates to grandparents and aunts and uncles.
- Give away or toss photos that have little meaning to you.
- Keep negatives only if you think you'll need them for additional copies.
- Place negatives in an envelope and write a brief description on the outside of the negatives' envelope or store in a pocket inside the photo album where the pictures are placed. Another option is to keep these envelopes of negatives in a photo box or a binder with archival pages for storing negatives.
- An even better option is to have your old negatives (or photos) scanned and converted to digital photos. There are many online services as well as brick-and-mortar businesses that do this.
- Use an acid-free self-adhesive label on the back of the photo, or you can write gently on the back of the photo with an archival marker.
- Sort photos in chronological order or by categories, such as "Anna's Sixth Birthday." Creative Memories offers a great photo-sorting box with removable compartments that makes it easy to group and categorize photos this way. As soon as you get your developed photos, sort them into categories. It will make scrapbooking or organizing them into albums much easier when you are ready to do it.
- Use albums with acid-free paper. You can find these at Michael's or through a Creative Memories representative (see "Clutter-Busting Resources").
- Consider using three-ring albums, which allow you to add pages to them.

Paper Management

Files

- Don't keep entire magazines in a file—they are too big to store and you'll spend too much time later looking for what you saved it for in the first place. Cut or tear out important articles and file them. I use a binder with clear sheet protectors for decorating ideas and recipes.
- Store your valuable papers in a safe deposit box or fireproof box.
- Every quarter, go through your files and purge (shred and discard) outdated or unnecessary papers to free up space.

Business Cards

- Buy a business card binder to hold hundreds of business cards without taking up too much desk space. You can purchase a variety of sizes at places like Office Depot, OfficeMax, or Target. Then when you are looking for that guy who cleans gutters, you'll easily be able to find his card.
- Only keep business cards of people or businesses you can't easily find online.

Bills and Mail

- Sort your mail over the recycle bin, and throw out junk mail and flyers before they ever have a chance to enter the house.
- Handle paperwork once and handle it now. If you can't handle it now, then put it in a labeled tickler file. A good place to keep this file is at your command center (see page 238). Schedule time regularly to deal with these items.
- File bills as soon as they are paid and statements and other documents as soon as you open them, otherwise they are likely to get misplaced. If you can, switch to online banking and pay your bills online. It's much faster and more efficient and you'll save money on stamps!
- At my command center, I keep file folders labeled "Take Action," "File," and "Follow Up." Each family member also has a file with his or her name—sometimes there are items that don't require immediate action but do need to be saved (like the Brownie troop yearly schedule or information on an ongoing school project, for example), so I keep these items in the appropriate person's folder.

Taxes

- At the beginning of each year, place a file folder (labeled with the year) in a hanging file for your tax-related documents such as charitable contributions, property tax receipts, W-2s, 1099s, etc. If you own a business, also create a folder for business receipts. It's a great idea to create an Excel worksheet and enter business expenses before filing the receipt. When it's tax time, you'll have a record of all your business expenses.
- Most tax returns and documentation only need to be kept for seven years. Some businesses and professions need to maintain their records indefinitely, however. Check this out before tossing your tax records.

Check Register

- Opt for online banking and you won't have to worry as much about a check register because you won't write as many checks! You'll be able to check your balance and cleared checks anytime online.

- If you do prefer the old-fashioned way, on the outside of your check registers write the range of dates it includes and the range of check numbers it includes, for instance: "April 10, 2007 to September 12, 2007, check numbers 1312 to 1418."

Bank Statements and Canceled Checks

- Reconcile your statement every time you get one.
- Request that the bank keep a computerized record of your canceled checks so they are not sent to you in the mail every month. This cuts down on clutter and frees up room in your files you won't be using to store checks.
- If you ever need to document a payment by check, just ask your bank for a copy.
- If you do keep canceled checks, only save checks written for deductible expenses. Shred the rest.

Scheduling Paperwork

- Set aside at least one uninterrupted hour (which will likely be after the kids are in bed) every week for paperwork. Having regularly scheduled time for paperwork will help you stay on top of your finances and to-do list and keep you from becoming overwhelmed.
- Prioritize. Do the financial stuff first. Pay your bills, balance the checkbook, and reconcile any investment statements. Then take care of any paperwork that's left. Write a note to the teacher, fill out an application form, write thank-you notes, etc.
- File everything away immediately so you don't have to deal with it again. Remember the "handle it once" motto!

Taming the Paper Monster

- Reduce the number of credit cards you have to one card for personal use and one for business use.
- Cancel some of your more obscure magazine and newspaper subscriptions.
- Pay any bills you can by setting up an automatic draft from your checking account.
- Bank online!
- Sign up at www.catalogchoice.org and you can decline any catalogs you do not want to receive in the mail.
- You can stop junk mail by signing up at www.proquo.com. Enter your address and you'll see a list of junk mail currently being sent to you that you can decline. Some companies require that you notify them by mail, but the ProQuo website instantly creates a letter that you can print out, sign, and pop in the mail. You

can also write to the following address and ask them to remove you from their direct mail lists:

Mail Preference Service
Direct Marketing Association
P.O. Box 9008
Farmingdale, NY 11735-9008

Change Your Habits

- Take a little time each day to put things into their proper places. Get your kids to pitch in too! It's easier to stay on top of clutter than to play catch-up.
- File or pay bills right when you get them or place them in your holding spot to be paid during your next paperwork hour.
- Respond to invitations and notices as they arrive and mark any dates on a calendar immediately.
- Keep making those tough decisions about what to keep and what to throw away!
- Invest in an inexpensive shredder. Be sure to shred any documents with account numbers, credit card or bank information, social security numbers, etc. The time and effort are worth protecting your identity.

Organizing Your Kitchen

Spending a little time up front to organize your kitchen will save you time and energy in the long run. A well-organized kitchen will enable you to prepare meals faster because you won't waste time searching for a lost spatula or colander. You'll save money with an organized pantry by not buying groceries you don't need or already have.

Declutter

Again, start by clearing out the clutter:

- Get rid of old spices that are past their prime.
- Organize food storage so you know what you have and what you need.
- Throw out old, out-of-date items in your pantry and your fridge.
- Keep only kitchen tools that you use frequently. You'll be amazed how much easier it is to find things when you have less clutter in your drawers.
- Max out counter space. Keep out only appliances you use every day, like the coffeemaker or toaster oven.

Grocery Lists

I created a master grocery list on my computer. I keep blank lists attached to a clipboard that I've hung on the inside of my pantry door. A pencil is attached so that anyone can check items as we run out.

Try Meal Planning

There are lots of great websites that enable you to plan one or two weeks' worth of meals online—and the site will create a grocery list for you based on your choices! How cool is that? And you won't waste time wondering what to have for dinner. A couple of great sites we found are www.morethyme.com and www.allrecipes.com.

Switch from Plastic to Glass Storage Containers

I don't like to use plastic containers in the microwave, so I am constantly transferring leftovers from plastic containers to glass or ceramic containers before I reheat them in the microwave. I recently discovered Martha Stewart's line of glass storage containers at Kmart. Now my leftovers can go straight from the refrigerator to the microwave and I don't have to worry about chemicals leaching into my kids' mac and cheese. Plus these containers are long-lasting and heavy-duty.

Make Extra Portions and Freeze for Later

It doesn't add much time at all to make a little more of the meal you are already preparing. Put the extra in a glass freezable container and pop it in the freezer for later. When you're in a pinch, you have a meal that will be ready in minutes.

Are Plastics in the Microwave Dangerous?

That depends on whom you ask. The plastics industry (not surprisingly) says that plastics are safe in the microwave if you see the words "Safe for microwave use" on the bottom. The FDA says that chemicals used to make plastics can leach into foods but that no studies have shown high enough levels to cause concern. Some consumer groups disagree, saying that not enough studies have been done. One thing all sides agree on is that you should never use "one-time-use" containers such as butter tubs, whipped topping tubs, or take-out containers in the microwave. Chemicals can seep into food heated in these containers.

Tips for Safe Reheating in the Microwave, from the Food Safety Council

- Only use cookware that is specially manufactured for use in the microwave oven. Glass, ceramic containers, and all plastics should be labeled for microwave oven use.
- Plastic storage containers such as margarine tubs, take-out containers, whipped topping bowls, and other one-time-use containers should not be used in microwave ovens. These containers can warp or melt, possibly causing harmful chemicals to migrate into the food.
- Microwave plastic wraps, wax paper, cooking bags, parchment paper, and white microwave-safe paper towels should be safe to use. Do not let plastic wrap touch foods during microwaving.
- Never use thin plastic storage bags, brown paper or plastic grocery bags, newspapers, or aluminum foil in the microwave oven.

Clean as You Cook

Rinse bowls and utensils and place them in the dishwasher or a sink of soapy water as you go. There's nothing more overwhelming than a kitchen full of dirty dishes awaiting you after a meal.

Use Larger Mixing Bowls Than You Think You'll Need

With this one simple step you can eliminate messy spills and time spent cleaning up.

Organizing Your Car

It seems we moms spend half our lives in the car, on the way to school, play group, soccer practice, ballet, birthday parties, and so on. With kids in tow, it takes about two seconds for your car to look like a dumping ground on wheels. Although you're nearly always going to find month-old french fries under the seat, here are a few tips to help keep your car organized.

- Set a monthly appointment on your calendar to clean out and wash your car.
- Keep wipes within reach so you can clean up messes. Keep a portable trash can available as well. Empty trash into the gas station trash bin every time you fill up.
- Keep a Diaper Duck mini trash bag dispenser in your car (see "Clutter-Busting Resources").
- Place seat covers or even an old bath towel under child safety seats. When you do need to remove the child seat so an adult can ride there, you'll save yourself

the time and embarrassment of having to clean up the sticky mess underneath.

- Every day when you exit your car, bring in an armful of car clutter.
- Use one of the many types of over-the-seat organizers to keep maps, umbrellas, gloves, antibacterial gel, and other essentials at hand.
- Keep DVDs and CDs organized in their own holder in the glove compartment or over the visor.
- Use your iPod in the car with an adapter like Griffin's iTrip (see "Clutter-Busting Resources") and you'll eliminate the need for any CDs taking up space in your car.
- Consider crates, boxes, or other car organizers to keep your trunk's contents organized by type. Organizers that roll out and fold down are the most useful.
- Put in a hands-free unit if you use a cell phone in the car.
- Make sure nothing can roll around while you are driving by keeping things tidy and in containers.

From Stephanie

All this organized stuff sounds so great, doesn't it? I have to admit, I love opening one of my closets without having to shield myself from falling debris. However, all this neat and tidy stuff comes very naturally for Sara. I, on the other hand, have to work at it constantly. She reads *Real Simple* and other organizational and decorating magazines as a hobby. That's about as much fun for me as reading a book on calculus. And while I must admit that she's sold me on the idea that I can actually *save* time by taking the time to put things in their proper spots in the first place, I just can't seem to find the time to be as exceptionally organized as she is. She has actually made that "command center" idea come to life. The last time I was at her house I was in awe of it. There were no loose cell phone chargers, no crumbs, no jumbled-up bulletin boards. It was neat and organized, and she even found a way to make all this stuff look pretty. But for me, it's forced, and therefore more time-consuming. I don't want to spend money on baskets and containers and shelves. I have a master plan and I know where everything is (for the most part); it just may not look as pretty as hers.

And I have to remind you too that spending time with your children is far more important than having perfectly organized closets. If you must choose between alphabetizing your toy room and going outside to blow bubbles in the backyard with your kids, choose the backyard. I know Sara would agree. She shares these organizing tips with you to help you have more time with your family. If all this information helps you, great. But if you're like me and all this just seems overwhelming, then do what you can and don't fret. All moms know what a challenge it is to keep your house neat and organized with children running around. Most of your fellow moms understand, and if they don't, then remove them from your Christmas card list immediately because they're not true friends. My girlfriends who have messy houses know that I don't care. I love them for far greater reasons than what their kitchen countertops look like. After the kids go to college, you'll have more than enough time to devote to a spotless home. While they're here with you spend every minute with them that you possibly can stand. Your kids are not going to remember how clean your house was, but they will remember that you played games with them in the afternoons. So take what you want from this section, but remember that we both believe that spending time with your family is the best thing you can do for them.

Managing Your Time

Every mom we know could use more time. But, alas, we can't make more of it. There are only twenty-four hours in a day. It's how you use and enjoy those hours that matters. Although no mom is probably ever going to feel like a lady of leisure (unless your kids are in college . . . maybe), here are some tips to help you get the most out of your day without losing your mind.

Plan Ahead

Don't forget to plan! Schedule ten to fifteen minutes every morning to plan your day. If the morning doesn't work well for you, spend a little time at night before you go to bed in order to plan the next day. Being prepared will help you stay on time and on track. Nothing is more crucial to maximizing your time than this brief planning period each day.

Prioritize

Jot down everything you would like to accomplish for the week or month on a master list. Go over the list and highlight the three most important items. Put those on your to-do list for today and write the number *1* beside each item. These are your number one priorities of the day. Go back to the master list and highlight the next three most important items. Add these on today's list with the number *2* written beside each item. Try to accomplish the first three items on your list. Cross them off both your daily list and your master list when you are done. Do the same for your number two priority items. If you don't accomplish these tasks, simply move them to the next day in your planner and mark them as the highest priority. Go back to your master list and add three more items as number two priority tasks.

Make a Date with Your Child

Keeping the house straight and getting the kids to preschool, ballet, and swim team practice are common everyday stresses for moms. But what hits us when we finally collapse

How to Have More Family Time on the Weekend, from *Parenting* Magazine

- **Attend only one big event per weekend day.** Limit birthday parties, plays, museums, and soccer games to one per day on the weekend. More time for playing catch in the yard!
- **Honor naptime.** Don't let naps go by the wayside on weekends—a nap or just a little downtime gives kids time to settle down and unwind, and gives Mom and Dad some peace and quiet to recharge their batteries.
- **Take care of more chores during the week.** Don't leave a week's worth of cleaning for Saturday or Sunday. Try to stay on top of laundry, picking up, and cleaning by doing little chunks throughout the week.
- **Set aside unscheduled family time.** Leave some time blank on the calendar during the weekends for time to just hang out together as a family.
- **Cut down on your kids' weekend activities.** This can be tough, especially if your kids are into sports that take place on the weekends, but try to keep activities to a minimum.
- **Leave work at work.** Turn off the BlackBerry, the cell phone, the pager. Unless you're a surgeon, your co-workers probably don't need to reach you while you're at the zoo.

in bed at night is that nagging question: "Did I spend quality time with my children today?" Here's a great way to ensure that you do.

Block off some one-on-one time with each of your kids and write it on the calendar, write it in your planner, or enter it on your BlackBerry. It doesn't matter how you spend the time; it can be as simple as going for a walk or having a special lunch together, or something more involved like a camping trip or special vacation. My daughter and I love to have what we call our "girl time." We go to the mall (of course), do a little shopping, eat lunch together, and sometimes see a movie. It doesn't matter what you do—the point is to spend time together. Schedule it. Don't wait for a spur-of-the-moment opportunity or until your to-do list is empty because it won't happen.

Delegate or Outsource

Is there something on your list you can hire out to a contractor, housekeeper, dog groomer, landscaper, accountant, or entrepreneurially minded neighborhood kid? If you're really pushed for time, it may be worth it. Look at whether outsourcing will give you more family time. And think about what your time is worth in dollars; if the cost of your time is too high, hire out the work.

Say No

For some reason, we females are genetically programmed to take care of everyone and everything, so it goes against the grain for us to say no. This is where I think men have a leg up on us gals (and believe me, I don't say that often). We hesitate to say no because we worry what everyone else will think about us. If we do say no, we feel guilty about it and agonize over it for days. Men don't do that; they just say no and forget it.

We women say yes to far too much and end up overextended, which costs us and our families. Saying no may seem unnatural, but that is exactly what we should do in order to regain control of our lives, have the family time we crave, and keep stress to a minimum. Say yes only to the activities and commitments you feel completely passionate about. If you find yourself saying yes just because it's too uncomfortable to say no, that's a red flag that you are agreeing to something you really shouldn't be.

Optimize Your Time

After a couple of hours at the pool, my kids are often ready for some serious downtime or even a nap. If there's something important you need to accomplish, do it at a time like this. Don't squander your time by checking e-mails, answering the phone, or getting caught up in another trivial task that eats up your time. Ask yourself, "What's important now?" and get it done.

Clutter-Busting Resources

ORGANIZATION RESOURCES
www.orderperiod.com
www.mommysavers.com
www.flylady.net
www.myorganizedlife.com

STOPPING JUNK MAIL
www.catalogchoice.org
www.proquo.com

PRODUCTS
Go Mom!
Planners and great advice on managing your busy life
www.gomominc.com

Truly Mom
Adorable planners, calendars, stationery, and more for moms
www.trulymom.com

Responsibility charts
www.leapsandbounds.com

Diaper Duck
www.target.com

Griffin iTrip
www.amazon.com

The Container Store
Library stools, bins, and nearly everything you need to get organized
www.thecontainerstore.com

MORE GREAT PRODUCTS
www.seejanework.com
www.russellandhazel.com
www.organize.com
www.themacbethcollection.com
www.creativememories.com
www.michaels.com

MEAL PLANNING
http://allrecipes.com
www.mealmixer.com

Sara's grocery list
www.saraandstephanie.com

BOOKS
The Complete Idiot's Guide to Organizing Your Life
by Georgene Lockwood

Give It Up! My Year of Living with Less
by Mary Carlomagno

Real Simple: The Organized Home

Clutter's Last Stand: It's Time to De-Junk Your Life
by Don Aslett

27

Products We Love

From Sara

One thing you learn practically the moment you conceive is that being a mom means you are going to need gear—and lots of it. I remember the first time David and I set foot in a Babies R Us store. We were there to register for our first baby shower. As we walked along the aisles we suddenly realized we were utterly clueless about strollers, Pack 'n Plays, high chairs, cribs, crib mattresses, car seats, even diapers! There were so many options, it was overwhelming. There must have been twenty different strollers to choose from—we had no idea which one to pick. The same was true of everything else right down to nail clippers. (Do you go with the cute clippers that look like a bee and have a safety guard, or the regular kind that allows you to actually see baby's nails better as you trim them? And what about those nail scissors? Arghhh!) We made a frantic cell-phone call from the store to a few of our seasoned parent friends and asked them for help. One mom friend gave excellent advice regarding strollers, which was to take each one down and push it around, collapse it, and set it up—right in the store—to figure out which one worked best for us. It was a great tip, but unfortunately you can't take most products for a test drive before purchasing them. There are more options than ever these days—our mothers didn't even have car seats when we were babies. (My mom said she used to put me in a netted sling-type contraption in the front passenger seat of the car—I guess I would have been slingshotted right through the windshield if she had ever been rear-ended.) It's great to have all these options, but it's also mind-boggling. So Stephanie and I have tried to take some of the trial and error out of gearing up for parenthood. Here are some really useful products we've found and our trusted friends have told us about—and no, we don't get paid for our recommendations.

(However, if anyone would like to pay us retroactively, I could sure use a few new pairs of shoes!) Seriously, here are some great products that made our lives easier and our days a little more manageable.

Mommy and Kid Gear We Couldn't Live Without

- **Especially for Baby car seat mat.** This mat for under your baby's car seat works much better than the old bath towels we used to put under ours. It will protect the seats in your car from the inevitable spills, vomits, and accidents that will happen during the baby and toddler years. On that note, yes, it is machine washable.
- **Kolcraft umbrella stroller.** This may be the most useful twenty bucks you'll ever spend as a mom. You won't be able to use this stroller until your baby is at least four or five months old, but you'll use it for years thereafter. You'll find that your umbrella stroller folds up and down easily, takes up very little space in your car, and easily navigates narrow aisles in shops. We recommend spending a few dollars extra and getting one with a cup holder. Available at Babies R Us.
- **Bella Tunno baby basics.** The cutest bibs, burp cloths, pacifier holders, and changing pads you've ever seen. Check out the "Designer Diner"—a wipe-clean place mat on one side and a chalk mat on the other. Available at www.bellatunno.com.
- **Diaper Duck by Munchkin.** There are different brands, but these little cylinders that hold small trash bags are extremely handy when baby makes a smelly poopy and there's no Diaper Genie handy. These little bag caddies contain dirty diapers and bad smells until you can get to a proper poop receptacle. Available at Target stores.
- **Pee Wees disposable diaper changing pads.** A must-have for your diaper bag! These disposable paper pads are great for covering those plastic diaper-changing stations in public bathrooms. They're called pads, but Pee Wees are thin and made of paper. They won't give your baby any extra cushion, but they will provide a sanitary barrier between your baby and the germs lurking on the changing station. Pee Wees come in packs of thirty-six and are available at Target and Babies R Us.
- **Boppy pillow.** These U-shaped pillows are the best and have a long useful life too. They are great for Mom during breast-feeding and bottle-feeding. You put the Boppy around your waist and it helps support baby during feeding and saves strain on Mom's back and shoulders. Boppies also work great for tummy time, and they are super for propping baby and supporting little backs when baby starts learning how to sit up. The Boppy company has expanded its product line to include many variations of the Boppy as well as other items for Mom and

baby. There are now versions available with removable slipcovers, which is a really good idea. Check out www.boppy.com.

- **My Brest Friend.** Many breast-feeding moms prefer the My Brest Friend pillow to the Boppy for nursing. It's much firmer, and less like a pillow than a Boppy. It has a foam core and also provides support for Mom's back. It has an adjustable strap and little pockets on the sides for storing toys or supplies.
- **Similac Singles formula pouches.** These little bags of formula powder contain the precise amount to make a four-ounce bottle. They're great for traveling or going out to dinner. Pack a couple of bottles filled with room-temperature water and add the formula powder when you need it. Just put the top on and shake to mix. No heating needed. Love it!
- **The Snack Trap cup.** This handy little cup is great for babies and toddlers who love to snack on Cheerios and Goldfish. The cup has two handles and a plastic lid with slits in it so that chubby little hands can pull a single Cheerio out but can't dump the entire contents onto the floor. These are great for the car or when you are out and about. Although be advised: as baby becomes a toddler she may figure out how to get the plastic lid off.
- **Boogie Wipes.** Designed by a couple of moms (who call themselves Boogie Moms), these are not your average baby wipe. They contain saline—perfect not just for wiping noses but for removing that cement-like residue that builds up under kids' noses. No more chiseling it off with your fingernail while your child screams in pain. These little wipes take away the mess—they're brilliant. Find them at www.boogiewipes.com.
- **Johnson's Buddies Sudzing Bath Bar.** This is a brilliantly simple idea that makes bath time much easier for kids. The Sudzing Bar is a bar of soap inside a sealed soft pouch that has the same effect as wrapping a small washcloth around the soap. Kids can hold on to the soap without it constantly slipping out of their hands and it makes a terrific lather. Kids love washing themselves with these, which means less work for Mom! At only $1 each, these are a no-brainer in our book.

Great Cleaning Products for Moms

- **Shark cordless vacuum (by Euro-Pro).** We often joke that every mom should leave the hospital with one of these. The Shark vacuum looks like a floor sweeper except that it's electric, so it's great for cleaning up the daily messes that you find on your kitchen floor: cereal, peanuts, pet hair, cream of wheat, and even wet messes like macaroni and cheese. You may not even yell at your kids for spilling anymore, because this makes cleaning up messy messes really fast and simple. And it's cordless—so it's so easy to give the floor a quick once-over without dragging out your twenty-five-pound electric vacuum. It works on carpets too. We don't know exactly how it works, but it has a round brush that picks up debris and puts it in a removable cup that you empty when you're done. It's lightweight and is rechargeable between uses.

- **Mr. Clean Magic Eraser.** This has to be one of the best cleaning inventions ever. It looks like a white sponge but it does so much more than a plain old sponge ever could. Just wet it and squeeze out the excess water and you can get crayon marks off the wall, stains off furniture, you name it. It really is like magic. Just be careful—if you scrub too hard or too long, you can also take the paint off your walls (yeah, we know from experience).

Around the House

- **Plantronics telephone headset.** This may be the best piece of equipment a new mom can buy. These hands-free headsets for your phone are invaluable! We love the ones that attach to your belt, so you can cook, breast-feed, potty-train, and move freely around your house without giving up your only tie to the outside world—a good phone conversation.

In the Nursery

- **Prince Lionheart Wipes Warmer.** This was one of those items that all the "money-saving" books told us we didn't need. We both loved having warm wipes for our little babies' sensitive tushies. It sure was nice not to have to wake them with a cold wipe against their skin during those late-night diaper changes.
- **Lansinoh Breast-feeding Cream.** This is the best stuff ever invented for breast-feeding moms. The problem is, it can be hard to find. You can usually find it at Target, Wal-Mart, and some drugstores. Lansinoh is the leader in topical nipple treatment, and the La Leche League endorses it. Sore nipples are one of the main reasons mothers quit breast-feeding. You put it on after every feeding, and you don't have to wash it off before baby's next feeding. It soothes and helps to repair sore nipples. Lansinoh is the only brand of lanolin available that contains no preservatives or additives of any kind, which is why it doesn't have to be removed before breast-feeding. See more at www.lansinoh.com.
- **Waterproof lap and mattress pads.** The inexpensive waterproof pads called "lap pads" are small, but don't let their small size lead you to believe they aren't useful. Try layering two lap pads on top of your diaper-changing pad—if they get soiled, you can just wash the pads instead of taking off the entire changing pad cover. Because they are small, you can also use them in a baby swing, or in a car

seat. The larger, flat mattress pads are great to put under a fitted crib sheet, and you can use them as your child gets older. You can continue to use one (strategically placed) on your toddler or preschooler's bed in case of accidents. These are also great to use as changing pads on a couch or floor. Perfect for traveling! The Circo brand is available at Target; the Gerber and Carter's brands are available at Babies R Us.

Entertainment

- **Baby Einstein videos.** All of our babies loved Baby Einstein videos! We have many, as we kept adding to our collection depending on our child's age. Baby Mozart, Baby Bach, Baby Van Gogh, and the Neighborhood Animals are a few of our favorites. They love the puppets, colors, and music, and it bought us a few minutes to grab a shower or empty the dishwasher.
- **Whoonu game from Cranium.** It says age eight and above, but we've had loads of family fun and laughs with this game even before our kids could read. The game requires you to choose your family's favorite things, like "What does Mommy like better: sand castles or snowmen?" We laugh out loud over the choices the kids make for us and for their friends. It's one of the few kid games that we actually have as much fun playing as they do.

Technology

- **TiVo (or similar digital recording services or devices).** You'll get to watch plenty of TV when your baby is a baby. But once they can repeat the four-letter words they hear on *Entourage,* it's time to alter your television viewing habits. Thank goodness for the inventors of TiVo. With this or any other digital recording service or device, you can record your favorite shows and watch them when Junior is asleep or at Grandma's. It's also great for rewinding purposes because somehow kids always start shouting during the final two minutes of the movie you've been watching for the last hour and a half. When you can rewind and listen to the line you missed, you won't have to get mad at your kids for making you miss the part you've been waiting for.
- **iPod.** It's unlikely the iPod was invented with moms in mind, but most moms we know have one. We use ours in the car to listen to the music we want to hear while the kids are otherwise occupied with a movie or other activity (just keep the volume turned down low for safety). You can download all sorts of podcasts on iTunes.com (including the wonderful *Mommy Chronicles* podcast). The concept of podcasting is similar to TiVo: you can listen to radio and television shows when your schedule allows.

- **Griffin iTrip.** This handy little adapter cord allows you to plug your iPod into the cigarette lighter in your car and listen to anything stored on your iPod through your car stereo speakers without needing headphones.

Stores

- **Portrait Innovations.** We've both been thrilled with the results when we've had our kids' photos taken here. The great thing about Portrait Innovations (www.portraitinnovations.com) is that your proofs are ready immediately after your session, and the photos are ready within twenty minutes! (Instant gratification!) And the photos are much nicer than those you'd get at a department store. Best of all, there is much less pain in selecting which photos of your child you want to keep because you can keep them all. Portrait Innovations will give you a CD of your child's proofs from the entire photo session, even the ones you didn't purchase. You won't be able to print high-resolution photos at home, of course, but if you decide you want to purchase additional proofs from that session, all you have to do is take the disk back to the store and they will print the ones you want for a fee. It's so nice to know that photos of your precious, will-never-be-this-age-again child are not being thrown into a digital trash can never to be retrieved again. They are right there on the disk if you want them.
- **Shutterfly.com.** With the advent of digital cameras and wonderful online developing services, there's no more schlepping your baby in her forty-pound infant seat to the drugstore to get photos developed for the grandparents. Upload your digital pictures and share them with friends and family (who can choose and order their own photos, thank you very much!). Shutterfly's system is easy to use and helps you keep your photos organized into albums. Loads of great photo-related products are available. One of our favorites is the photo calendar, a beautifully printed one-year calendar personalized with photos you choose from your online albums. They make a great personalized gift that takes very little time and effort. These were a big hit with our kids' grandparents!
- **The Container Store.** Whatever you need to organize, from toys to kitchen utensils to scrapbook supplies, can be found at the Container Store. If you aren't lucky enough to have one of these stores in your city, visit www.containerstore.com. The site is easy to navigate and you'll find amazingly good ideas to make your life as a mom much simpler.
- **Barnes & Noble.** We love them for their comfortable chairs, their plethora of caffeinated beverages, and their clean, spacious bathrooms that offer changing tables in both the men's and women's. (No excuses, Dad!) Also online at www.bn.com.

Health and Well-Being

28

Food and Kids

From Sara

When my mom was diagnosed with breast cancer several years ago, I read everything I could get my hands on about breast cancer research. I learned that hormones play a role in many breast cancers, including my mother's. I suddenly began to think about the hormones I was putting into my body and my children's through the foods we eat. That's when I began buying organic milk and other dairy products—as much as I could afford anyway.

Then I was diagnosed with Hodgkin's lymphoma, a cancer of the lymphatic system. Researchers don't know what causes Hodgkin's, but as is the case with many cancers, they suspect exposure to environmental toxins has something to do with it. So you can understand why I really worry about this stuff.

I began to think about all the pesticides on the fruits and vegetables our family eats, the toxins in the weed killer we put on the yard (we don't do that anymore!), and even in the cleaners I use around the house. I was shocked to learn that nearly all Americans have chemicals coursing through their blood: fire retardants, pesticides, even banned chemicals such as DDT and chlordane. They've even been found in umbilical cord blood.

The reality is, we live in a chemical-filled environment. And though I realize it is impossible to completely eliminate our exposure to these toxins, I try to control what I can. To me, buying organic foods was a good place to start. I figure limiting the chemicals my family actually ingests is priority number one.

But I have to be practical too. I simply can't afford to go 100 percent organic. So I wanted to know what is really worth spending the extra money on—where I can get the most bang for my organic buck. I imagine you'll be as happy as I was to learn that you don't have to go all-out organic to reap most of the benefits. And that you can find healthy food for your kids that's also convenient. We've got lots more useful information and practical tips on this subject to share with you too. So before you make dinner tonight, read this chapter. It'll be good for your health, I promise.

Organic vs. Non-organic

Organic food is one of the fastest-growing trends in the food industry. In recent years, American shoppers spent more than $51 billion on natural and organic products, and it is forecasted that by 2025, the everyday use of organic products of all kinds will be both accepted and routine. But if you buy organic, you know it can add up fast on your grocery bill—you'll shell out 50 to 100 percent more for organic. So we asked the question many moms are asking: "Is it worth it to buy organic?" The short answer is "Sometimes." Clear as mud, right? We thought so too, but the reality is, some things are worth paying more for to get organic quality, while others are simply less important. Read on to find out what organic products are worth spending money on and which aren't. But first, let's talk about why you might consider organic foods in the first place.

Research has yet to formally prove an adverse health effect from consuming the low levels of pesticides commonly found in U.S. food. But a growing number of studies show that pesticides and other contaminants are more prevalent in the foods we eat, in our bodies, and in the environment than previously thought. Pesticides are powerful chemicals. On its website, the Environmental Protection Agency (EPA) states, "By their very nature, most pesticides create some risk of harm. Pesticides can cause harm to humans, animals, or the environment because they are designed to kill or otherwise adversely affect living organisms." However, the EPA does impose strict rules to limit the amount of pesticide exposure to humans.

Research has shown that by eating organic foods, you can reduce your exposure to the potential health risks associated with those chemicals. A recent such study at Emory University in Atlanta included twenty-three children ages three to eleven. The kids took daily urine tests for about two weeks. The urine samples were checked for traces of two pesticides, malathion and chlorpyrifos. (Foods treated with malathion and chlorpyrifos are considered safe to consume by the EPA.)

The kids ate their normal diets for three days. Then they switched to a mainly organic diet for five days. Lastly, the children resumed their normal conventional diet. Researchers purchased the organic foods at a local store. They simply chose organic versions of foods the kids typically ate. The organic grocery list included fresh fruits and vegetables, juices, processed fruit or vegetable items (such as salsa), and wheat- or corn-based items (such as pasta, cereal, popcorn, or chips). Organic meats and dairy products weren't provided since they aren't regularly found to contain the type of pesticides being studied.

When the kids started eating the organic foods, traces of the two pesticides immediately vanished from most of their urine samples. The study showed that those pesticide levels remained undetectable until the children resumed their conventional diets.

When it comes to fruits and vegetables that carry the heaviest pesticide load, going organic is especially important for children and pregnant or breast-feeding women. That's because high doses of pesticides can cause neurological or reproductive damage. With the reproductive organs still forming in the fetuses of expectant mothers, the brain developing in children through age twelve, and young livers and immune systems less able to rid bodies of contaminants, eating organic is important for these groups.

Additionally, children may be exposed more to certain pesticides because often they eat different foods than adults. For instance, children typically consume larger quantities of milk, applesauce, apple juice, and orange juice per pound of body weight than adults. Children's behaviors, such as playing on the floor or on the lawn (where pesticides are commonly applied) or putting objects in their mouths, also increase their chances of exposure to these chemicals.

So which fruits and vegetables contain the most pesticides? The U.S. Department of Agriculture found that even after washing, some fruits and vegetables consistently carry much higher levels of pesticide residue than others. Based on an analysis of more than a hundred thousand U.S. government pesticide test results, researchers at the Environmental Working Group, a well-respected research and advocacy organization based in Washington, D.C., have developed a list of the "dirty dozen" fruits and vegetables that they say you should always buy organic, if possible, because their conventionally grown counterparts tend to be laden with pesticides.

The Dirty Dozen (always buy organic if possible)

- Apples
- Cherries
- Grapes, imported (Chile)
- Nectarines
- Peaches
- Pears
- Raspberries
- Strawberries
- Bell peppers
- Celery
- Potatoes
- Spinach

Consumer Reports also suggests looking for fresh organic fruits and vegetables that aren't placed too close to non-organic produce in grocery stores, since misting could let pesticide residue run.

What About Meat?

Although nearly half of the produce sampled by the USDA in 2002 had detectable pesticide residues, only 16 percent of grains and 15 percent of meat tested did. Most of the residues found in meat (almost always in the fat) were from long-banned chemicals like DDT, which remain in the environment and unfortunately are not removed by organic farming methods.

But when it comes to meat, poultry, and dairy, it's not just pesticides you have to worry about. Many consumers are choosing to buy organic because of widespread antibiotic and growth hormone use in livestock. Giving animals antibiotics helps prevent disease but also helps promote antibiotic-resistant strains of bacteria. Although the U.S. Food and Drug Administration says the growth hormone used in cattle is virtually identical to what cows naturally produce, consumer groups such as Consumers Union argue that milk from cows treated with rBST (recombinant bovine somatotropin, a growth hormone) has higher levels of a growth factor linked to increased cancer risk. *Consumer Reports* also states that synthetic growth hormones (which are banned for poultry and organic animals) could cause cancer or speed up puberty in girls.

The National Dairy Council begs to differ, however. It states that American milk and dairy products are among the safest and most highly regulated in the world. The council also asserts that milk from hormone-treated cows has repeatedly been shown to be safe for human consumption.

Another, more recent concern regarding meat safety is bovine spongiform encephalopathy, or mad cow disease. The disease spreads when cows ingest animal feed made with parts from dead animals. The human form of the illness, variant Creutzfeldt-Jakob disease (CJD), is caused by eating contaminated beef. It is always fatal. The risk of contracting the disease, however, is low. The United States has had only one confirmed case of mad cow disease in animals, and the only American case of variant CJD involved a woman who contracted it in Great Britain.

Ultimately, whether to shell out more for organic meats will depend on your budget (organic meats often cost double what conventional meats do) and your personal level of concern for food quality. You can also lower the odds of eating unsafe meat by avoiding processed meats such as hot dogs and pre-ground hamburger that might contain brain or spinal cord matter. It's also a good idea to avoid cuts sold with the bone. There are also more and more meats available that, while not organic, are antibiotic- and hormone-free.

Most of us can't afford to purchase all organic all the time. What's worth the extra money and what's not? *Consumer Reports* magazine recently issued their own list of items definitely worth the money and those you should only buy if your budget allows.

- **Organic items worth buying as often as possible:** apples, baby food, bell peppers, celery, cherries, dairy, eggs, imported grapes, meat, nectarines, peaches, pears, poultry, potatoes, red raspberries, spinach, and strawberries.
- **Organic items worth buying if money is no object:** asparagus, avocados, bananas, bread, broccoli, cauliflower, cereals, sweet corn, kiwi, mangos, oils, onions,

Removing Pesticides from Food

- Wash and scrub all fresh fruits and vegetables under running water.
- Soaking produce isn't the same. It doesn't have the abrasive effect of running water.
- Do *not* use detergent or soap to wash produce. The Food and Drug Administration advises against using soap or commercial produce washes because they haven't evaluated the safety of residues that could be left on produce and because the effectiveness of produce washes is not standardized. They recommend washing all produce thoroughly in cold water. Not all pesticide residues can be removed by washing. Washing produce (including fresh organic fruits and vegetables) will also help reduce dirt and bacteria.
- Peel fruits and vegetables when possible.
- Discard the outer leaves of leafy vegetables.
- Trim fat from meat and skin from poultry. Some pesticide residues collect in fat.
- Eat a variety of foods from a variety of sources. Doing so will provide a better mix of nutrients and reduce the likelihood of exposure to a single pesticide.
- Choose skim or low-fat milk and lean meats whenever possible. Pesticides and pollutants such as dioxin (which is also found in organics) tend to be concentrated in fat.

papaya, pasta, pineapples, potato chips, and sweet peas. Also included are packaged products such as canned vegetables and dried fruit.

- **Organic items not worth buying:** seafood. There's no such thing as organic fish, but you can lower your exposure to toxins by removing skin and draining fat. If your kids like tuna, stick to "light" canned tuna, rather than albacore, or "white," which has more mercury.

What Does the Label "Organic" Really Mean?

But what does the word *organic* mean when you see it on a package? Food certified under U.S. Department of Agriculture regulations as organic must be produced without most synthetic pesticides and fertilizers. Antibiotics, growth hormones, and feed made from animal parts are also banned. Look for the "USDA Organic" label.

A Guide to Label Lingo from *Consumer Reports*

"100% organic": No synthetic ingredients are allowed by law.

"Organic": At least 95 percent of ingredients are organically produced.

"Made with organic ingredients": At least 70 percent of ingredients are organic; the other 30 percent are from a list approved by the USDA.

"Free-range" or "free-roaming": Animals had an undetermined amount of daily outdoor access. This label does not provide much information about the product.

"Natural" or "all natural": Doesn't mean organic. No standard definition, except for meat and poultry products, which may not contain any artificial flavoring, colors, chemical preservatives, or synthetic ingredients. Claims aren't checked.

Health Off the Shelf

It's easy for kids (and moms) to fall into the habit of eating junk food. Fast food is almost the only option when you're on the go—most moms we know don't have time to stop and eat at a more healthful restaurant when you're busy running errands or trying to get the kids to soccer practice on time. Packaged foods and fast food taste good to kids (often because they are full of sugar, salt, or fat) and they come in those cute containers with a toy surprise. It all makes eating healthy when you're in a hurry a challenge to say the least. Some food manufacturers have sensed our frustration in fighting the snack wars and as a result are finally putting better choices on grocery store shelves and menus. Here are a few of our favorite healthy foods you can grab right off the shelf or at the drive-through window.

Clif ZBar. This organic bar tastes just like a cookie and has as much calcium as a glass of milk, plus three grams of fiber and zero trans fat. Flavors include Peanut Butter, Chocolate Brownie, and Caramel Apple. Find out more at www.clifbar.com.

McDonald's Apple Dippers. If you have to hit the drive-through, at least skip the fries and opt for McDonalds's Apple Dippers. They only have 35 calories (compared to 230 for a small order of fries) and have no fat, while McDonald's fries have 11 grams of fat. The yummy caramel dipping sauce makes Apple Dippers appealing for even picky eaters and only adds about 70 calories.

McDonald's Fruit 'n Yogurt Parfait. As Donkey says in the movie *Shrek*, "Everybody loves a parfait." That includes moms at McDonald's because this treat sure beats fat- and calorie-laden ice cream for a healthy treat. The parfait only has 160 calories and 2 grams of fat. Compare that with 330 calories, 10 grams of fat, and 25 milligrams of cholesterol for a hot fudge sundae. For an Oreo McFlurry, you're looking at 550 calories and 50 milligrams of cholesterol.

Save Money on Organic Foods

- Comparison-shop.
- Buy locally produced organic foods (check farmers' markets).
- Buy a share in a community-supported organic farm to get a regular supply of seasonal organic produce.
- Order by mail.

Yoplait Go-Gurt Smoothies. Only 120 calories and almost completely fat-free, these tasty yogurt drinks are loaded with calcium. See www.yoplait.com.

Stonyfield Farm YoKids Squeezers. Organic, lowfat yogurt in a fun squeeze tube that kids love. Great to pack in lunches or grab on the go. You can even freeze them for a cooler treat. They're a great source of calcium and protein too. See www.stonyfieldfarm.com.

Nabisco KidSense Fun Packs. (six-pouch box featuring one of the following: Teddy Grahams Cubs, Kraft Cheese Nips Sport Crisps, or Smilin' Ritz Bits). These snacks are fortified with calcium and contain no artificial flavors or trans fat. Just 100 calories per pouch. Info at www.nabisco.com.

Whole Foods Whole Catch Lightly Breaded Fish Sticks. These sticks are crunchy, the way kids like 'em, and they're about 30 percent lower in fat (with less than a gram of saturated fat and no trans fat) than most brands. Another attractive quality is that they're cut from a whole fish, not made of minced, processed pieces (yuk). Available at Whole Foods Markets, www.wholefoods market.com.

Kashi Mighty Bites and Kellogg's Tiger Power Cereal. These are fortified, whole-grain cereals (kids need three servings of whole grains every day). They are lightly sweetened and come in fun shapes so kids actually like them. Check out www.kashi.com or www.kelloggs.com.

Thomas' 100% Whole Wheat Mini Bagels. With 2.5 grams of fiber each (that's 10–20 percent of the recommended daily allowance), these bagels offer whole-grain goodness, but kids can't tell by the taste. Toast with cheddar cheese or spread on cream cheese for added calcium. Find out more at http://thomas .gwbakeries.com.

Flat Out bread/wraps. Kids love these flat breads when you roll them up with turkey, cheese, veggies, or even peanut butter and jelly. These breads contain no hydrogenated oils (so no artery-clogging trans fats) and they have 3 grams of fiber and 7 grams of protein! Find recipes at www.flatoutbread.com.

Ready Pac Ready-to-Go Snack Cups with Savory Dips. Single-serving packages are perfect for lunch boxes and after-school snacks. Flavors include Celery & Peanut Butter Dip, Apples & Peanut Butter Dip, and Veggie Snack Tray & Light Ranch Dip. The website is www.readypac.com.

Annie's Organic P'sghetti Loops (with soy meatballs). These are a great alternative to traditional SpaghettiOs and meatballs. (Who knows what's in those meatballs anyway?) The soy meatballs do have a softer texture, which may take some getting used to. But Annie's (www.annies.com) offers many other canned pasta loops and raviolis as well. They also offer organic boxed mac and cheese.

Back to Nature Cinnamon Graham Sticks. Yummy graham crackers with a hint of cinnamon, but no trans fat, saturated fat, or artificial flavors and preservatives. Only nine grams of sugar. Check out www.backtonaturefoods.com.

Skippy Natural Peanut Butter. This peanut butter contains no hydrogenated oils like most peanut butters, but you'd never know it from the texture or taste. (There's no oil on top to stir in and you don't have to refrigerate it.) This peanut butter tastes just like conventional peanut butters but has no trans fats and provides 7 grams of protein per serving. There's more information at www.peanut butter.com.

Nature's Own Double Fiber Sliced Bread. This bread is 100 percent whole wheat with 5 grams of fiber per slice, yet kids will love the taste. Nature's Own, at www.naturesownbread.com, uses no artificial colors, flavors, or preservatives, and contains omega-3s.

Morningstar Farms Chik'n Nuggets. These soy-based veggie nuggets are an equally delicious alternative to the greasy chicken variety—and they are packed with protein, important B vitamins, iron, and fiber as well. We've yet to meet a kid who didn't love these! Take a look at www.seeveggiesdifferently.com for all the Morningstar Farms products.

Morningstar Farms Veggie Corn Dogs. Veggie hot dogs often are not palatable, but these corn dogs are tasty for both kids and adults. And they're much healthier without all the nitrates and processed meats in regular corn dogs. Plus each packs 7 grams of protein. This is a great way to trick your kids into eating vegetables. Just think of it—they're eating corn dogs and you don't have any guilt.

Morningstar Farms Grillers Prime. As far as veggie burgers go, these are the closest to tasting like a real burger we've found. Our kids love them, and with no trans fat and 17 grams of protein, what's not to love?

Muir Glen Organic Garden Vegetable Pasta Sauce. With only 1 gram of fat, this pasta sauce offers healthy doses of both vitamin A and vitamin C. Serve it with fortified pasta and the kids will lap up a healthy meal with smiles on their faces. Sprinkle on some low-fat parmesan cheese for added calcium. The company website is www.muirglen.com.

Hodgson Mill Organic Whole Wheat Spaghetti. Tastes great with pasta sauces for a full meal, or simply toss with a little butter for a nutritious side dish. Info at www.hodgsonmill.com.

If You *Have* to Eat Fast Food

Let's face it, moms, sometimes you just don't have a choice—you have to hit that drive-through line. Stephanie knew it was time to take a break from the drive-through when she pulled up to the drive-through window at the bank and her three-year-old started ordering into the speaker, "Ahem, yes, I'd like some chicken and fries."

So what are some healthy fast-food choices? Fortunately, fast-food restaurants have added many new healthful options. Most now offer a fruit cup or sliced apples as an alternative to fries. You can also find nutritional information about their food offerings on their websites. It's a good idea to visit some of the sites ahead of time if you can. That way, you can make informed choices when it's time for you and your kids to order. If you decide what you can and should order before you arrive (and discuss the rules with your kids in advance) it will make it easier to avoid the less nutritious, higher-calorie options. (It's a lot easier to skip that Oreo McFlurry when you know it packs 550 calories.)

Children love to eat out, and the growing numbers of overweight and obese children means that adults need to take more responsibility for proper nutrition and help their kids make good choices. Nearly one-third of children in this country eat fast food every day, and it's no surprise that those who do eat it tend to consume more calories on a daily basis. These increased calories lead to increased pounds and add to the child's risk of becoming overweight. It's important to keep this in mind when you're thinking about taking your children out to eat with you.

Even sit-down restaurants are typically sorely lacking in what they offer on their kids' menus. The vast majority of the time you'll find the standard chicken fingers, grilled cheese, and hamburger as the only offerings for your children. The lack of options makes it even more difficult to persuade your child to eat healthfully, but you can steer them toward more nutritious options. Below are some important things to remember about fast-food and restaurant dining for kids.

From Stephanie

- Soda is highly caloric and not nutritious (they call those "empty calories"). Kids should have water or milk instead. Not to mention what liquid sugar does to your kids' teeth. Every time my kids ask me for soda (or gum) I ask them back, "Would you like the dentist to drill holes in your teeth?" "No." "Well then, you can't have soda." Plus, studies show that caffeine is bad for kids, particularly when it comes to brain development. Choose bottled water or fruit juice when you can. Once your kids are hooked on the great taste of carbonated liquids, it's a hard habit to break.
- Avoid chicken nuggets. Fried nuggets are often more like mystery meat than real chicken. And don't kid yourself, there just isn't much nutritious in a chicken nugget.
- Skip the fries. Consider taking along a bag of mini carrots, grapes, or other fruits and vegetables to have instead. This will add vitamins and fiber to the meal.
- Order the kid's meal with some substitutions. Children often love the kid's meal more for the fun box and toys than for the food. Let them order the kid's meal,

but ask to make substitutions for the soda and the fries if possible. Many restaurants are making it easier to substitute and all usually have water and milk available as beverage options. In sit-down restaurants, help them opt for chicken and vegetables or spaghetti with tomato sauce rather than a big plate of macaroni and cheese.

- If vegetables are not listed as a side dish on the kids' menu, ask your server if you can substitute with some of the "adult" vegetables or applesauce instead of fries.

Chicken Nuggets Could Be Your Worst Enemy

From Stephanie

Too many parents think that feeding their kids chicken nuggets is nutritious. Sure, it might be slightly healthier than potato chips and burgers—but not much. I've even seen parents come to visit their kids during the school day and bring in fast food instead of eating nutritious school meals—what kind of message does that teach your children? Let's take a closer look at a kid's meal from McDonald's: As of this writing the McDonald's website states that a six-nugget kid's meal with fries and a small Sprite has over 650 calories, 29 grams of fat, 40 milligrams of cholesterol, 800 milligrams of sodium, 84 grams of carbs, and 39 grams of sugar. (Remember that active kids only need between 1,600 and 2,500 calories per day.)

Is there anything good about chicken nuggets? Not much, and what little nutrition is present is pretty much wiped out by fat, calories, and chemicals. Chicken nuggets are *not* a healthy alternative to junk food. The popularity of high-fat, highly processed foods like chicken nuggets is one reason the percentage of overweight kids has tripled in the past twenty years. And experts now know that heart disease, which is linked with obesity, can begin in early childhood. That means that there's a good chance that the consequences of these kinds of food choices in childhood are going to show up later in life.

McDonald's says their six-piece chicken nuggets meal described above has 3 grams of fiber, 17 grams of protein, 25 milligrams of calcium, 1.5 milligrams of iron, and 6 milligrams of vitamin C. And for the record, don't assume that baking frozen chicken nuggets at home makes them healthier. Most of the fat and sodium is in the meat mixture and the coating, not because of deep-frying.

You should also know that calling it "chicken" is a bit of a stretch. True, chicken is the first ingredient and therefore the largest by weight, but once it's turned into a nugget, it's so loaded with fillers, breading, and fats, it's hardly chicken anymore. Fifty to 60 percent of the calories in most nuggets come from fat. Unless the label specifically states that it's made with all white meat, it's usually a combination of white meat, dark meat, and a lot of skin. Dark meat and skin contain much higher amounts of fat and fewer nutrients.

Most chicken nuggets are not whole pieces of chicken. They are bits and pieces that are chopped and "comminuted," which means the meat and skin are ground into a concoction much like paste. Binders (such as sodium phosphate) are added to make it stick together, and it's then pressed into "fun" shapes. And as if that isn't bad enough, then they're fried.

Some parents complain, "That's all I can get her to eat." Don't kid yourself . . . children develop a taste for what they're served. The more unhealthy food they eat now, the more they will crave as they get older. You can start by trying to scale back on the number of times you're hitting the drive-through each week and substitute healthier foods like veggie pizza. If you do have to serve nuggets, make wiser choices like Morningstar Farms nuggets that are made of vegetables (your kids will never know the difference).

Avoiding the drive-through takes planning. Make some turkey and cheese roll-ups from tortillas or honey-wheat bread. There are plenty of quick and easy choices that you can take with you in the car—and just think of the money you'll save and how healthy your kids will become.

Healthier Chicken Nuggets

These "oven-fried" nuggets are crisp and golden. But they don't have that extra fat you get from deep-frying.

1¾ cups herb-seasoned crumb stuffing mix
¼ cup grated parmesan cheese
3 tablespoons trans-fat-free margarine or butter
¼ cup low-fat buttermilk
¼ teaspoon ground black pepper
2 boneless, skinless chicken breasts (approximately 1 pound)

1. Preheat oven to 450 degrees F.

2. Measure stuffing mix into zip-top bag. Seal bag and place on flat surface. Crush crumbs by rolling and pressing rolling pin over bag.

3. Open bag and add parmesan cheese. Reseal bag and shake to mix thoroughly.

5. Melt margarine, and add buttermilk and pepper in medium shallow bowl. Stir well with spoon. Set aside.

6. Rinse chicken breasts and pat dry with paper towels.

7. Place chicken breasts on cutting board. Cut chicken with small, sharp knife into sixteen chunks of the same size.

8. Dip each chicken chunk into buttermilk mixture, covering all sides. Let extra buttermilk mixture drip off. Place a few chunks into the bag of crumbs and shake until chicken pieces are evenly coated with crumbs.

9. Place coated nuggets on an ungreased baking sheet.

10. Place baking sheet in oven. Bake nuggets 4 minutes. Turn over each nugget and return to oven and bake 4 to 5 minutes, or until medium golden brown.

Serve with your favorite dipping sauce. You can also make a lot of these at once and then freeze them for quick meals later.

Helping Your Child Form Healthy Eating Habits

One of the smartest moves you can make when it comes to forming healthy eating habits is to start early. It's much easier to create healthy habits from the start than to change bad ones down the road. So don't wait; start instilling a taste for good nutrition in your kids now. It's also important to talk to your kids about being healthy. Every kid we've ever known is anxious to grow, to run faster, to move from a car seat to a booster. Use their goals to start a conversation about choosing foods that build strong bones and muscles. Reward them for trying new fruits and veggies and making good snack choices.

What you eat is also important. Kids model their behavior on ours much more than they'll ever admit, so it's important for them to see your plate is filled with a variety of nutritious foods. Make sure not to plant any preconceived notions in their heads, either. If kids hear you talking about how much you hate tomatoes, they'll assume they hate them too, even if they've never tasted one!

Another tactic is to make healthy choices appealing. Cut fruits and vegetables into fun shapes and serve with low-fat dips. Combine bananas, strawberries, vanilla yogurt, and ice in a blender to make a smoothie kids love to slurp through a straw (even more when it's served in a fun glass). If they're old enough to help, kids are often more likely to try new foods they've helped prepare. Keep healthy snacks such as cut fruit, whole-grain crackers, and granola bars on hand so it's easy for kids to find healthy snacks at home.

Tips for Healthy Family Eating

- **Reward kids for trying new foods.** Often the toughest part is just getting kids to even try new foods. Reward them for it with an extra story at bedtime, an extra check on their responsibility chart, or just about anything else that's appropriate, except candy!
- **Have regular family meals.** Try to sit down together for as many meals as possible. The routine helps establish healthy habits, plus it's easier to monitor what your kids are eating when they're sitting next to you. Also, it's a great time to talk!
- **Eat at home as much as possible.** You'll have more control over your choices and consume less salt, sugar, and fat than if you eat out.
- **Get kids involved.** Children enjoy helping adults grocery-shop, selecting what goes in their lunch box, and preparing dinner. It's also a chance for you to teach them about the nutritional values of different foods, and (for older children) how to read food labels.
- **Make a variety of healthy foods available.** Keep plenty of fruits, vegetables, whole-grain snacks, yogurt, peanut butter, raisins, and healthful beverages

(water, milk, occasional fruit juice) around and easily accessible so kids become used to reaching for them when they're hungry.

- **Serve lean meats and other good sources of protein, such as eggs and nuts.**
- **Choose whole-grain breads and cereals so your child gets more fiber.**
- **Limit fat intake.** Contrary to what many parents believe, kids don't need large amounts of fat because they're "burning it off" by being active. But the *kind* of fat they're eating does matter. Butter on vegetables, avocados, corn chips (made with sunflower or safflower oil), pecans, or walnuts are far preferable to the fat contained in french fries, doughnuts, candy bars, or cheeseburgers. Avoid deep-fried foods and choose healthier cooking methods, such as broiling, grilling, roasting, and steaming.
- **Limit foods with hydrogenated and partially hydrogenated oils.** These oils are used to prolong the shelf life of foods but contain trans fats, which, unlike regular fats, are not necessary to health and have been linked to heart disease. Fast-food restaurants have used these kinds of oils for years, but recently some chains, including Wendy's, Chick-Fil-A, and McDonald's, have switched to healthier oils for frying. But many crackers, cookies, and other snacks on grocery store shelves are loaded with hydrogenated oils, so be sure to check the nutritional information on the box.
- **Limit fast food and other low-nutrient snacks.** We're talking about chips and candy here. But you don't have to go completely cold turkey on these treats. Instead, eat them only every now and then.
- **Let them choose.** Don't make mealtimes a battleground by insisting a child clean the plate, and never use food as a reward or bribe.
- **Be a role model by eating healthy yourself.** Monkey see, monkey do. You have to walk the walk yourself when it comes to eating healthy.
- **Work fruits and vegetables into the daily routine.** Aim for five servings a day.
- **Limit sugary drinks.** Keep soda and fruit-flavored drinks to a minimum. Serve water and milk instead.

Sneaking Veggies into Meals

From Sara

One day while watching the *Today* show, I felt like Jessica Seinfeld had just slapped me on the forehead. Let me explain. She was there promoting her book, *Deceptively Delicious,* which shows parents how they can puree vegetables and sneak them into their kids' meals. After all these years of struggling to get my kids to eat cauliflower and sweet potatoes and spinach, when I could have been sneaking it in all along! It was an "Oh my gosh, I can't believe I never thought of doing that" moment. Of course, I ran right out and bought *Deceptively Delicious,* along with a similar book, *The Sneaky Chef,* and I have been a pureeing fool ever since. I sneak cauliflower into mac and cheese and mashed potatoes. And I stir sweet potatoes and carrots into spaghetti sauce and spinach into pizza sauce.

Apparently (based on her baby-food-making skills) Stephanie has been wise to this whole food-pureeing business for a long time. Would have been nice if she had shared some of that info with me, but she obviously assumed I already had heard of it or figured it out for myself. However, as she of all people should know by now, I can occasionally be a little slow to catch on to these things.

But I digress. I have found these books to be very helpful and have used many of the recipes in both. I've even started branching out on my own and stirring pureed beans and veggies into my old standby recipes. At first the kids noticed a difference in the taste. That's when I realized that I was going a little overboard with the amount I was stirring in and I needed to scale back. I started with small portions so the taste was nearly undetectable. Then I gradually increased the amounts. And my kids have unknowingly developed a liking for the new taste.

The best part is how wonderful I feel knowing my kids have gotten two or three servings of veggies in a meal. Nothing makes me happier than knowing my kids have gotten a healthy, balanced dinner. And I figure it can't hurt David and me either.

Should My Child Take Vitamins?

As is often the case on issues like this, experts disagree on whether a daily multivitamin is necessary for all children. Like most moms, you're probably worried that your child isn't getting all the vitamins and minerals she needs in her daily diet. But even if you have a picky eater on your hands, that doesn't necessarily mean your child will develop a vitamin or mineral deficiency. Children don't need large amounts of vitamins and minerals, and besides, many foods that children eat are fortified with the important ones, so your child may be getting more vitamins and minerals than you think.

So when is a multivitamin necessary? Talk to your child's doctor. If your pediatrician is concerned that your child isn't getting the recommended amounts of vitamins and minerals, he or she may suggest a daily multivitamin. Just remember that giving your child a multivitamin can't replace proper nutrition.

It's also important to keep in mind that certain vitamins and minerals can be toxic if taken in large amounts. To prevent your child from getting too much of any one vitamin or mineral, choose a multivitamin specifically made for children, not for adults. Also, keep multivitamins out of reach of children. (Don't let your child find the bottle of Flintstones vitamins and eat several handfuls before you catch him, like Sara's son, Cade, did. He's okay, by the way.)

Since children's multivitamins are made to look and taste like gum or candy, it's important to teach your child that a multivitamin is real medicine and that it can make them very sick if they take too much of it.

One vitamin that has been getting a lot of press lately is vitamin D. According to the Mayo Clinic, some research shows that vitamin D deficiency is not uncommon in the United States, and vitamin D deficiency has a very negative impact on bone development in children. As a result, the American Academy of Pediatrics recommends a daily multivitamin with at least 200 international units (IUs) of vitamin D if a child:

- Does not get regular exposure to sunlight
- Does not drink at least 17 ounces (a little over two cups) of vitamin D–fortified milk, juice, or soy milk daily
- Follows a vegetarian diet

In general, a children's chewable multivitamin is a good basic dietary supplement program. However, talk to your pediatrician first before giving your child any supplements. Some kids with health problems may need more complex dietary supplementation, which should be determined by a doctor, nutritionist, or dietitian.

Making Your Own Baby Food

From Stephanie

I admit it, I don't know what possessed me, as a working mom, to decide to make my own baby food. Maybe *Oprah* or the *Today* show had a segment on the dangers of the preservatives, or perhaps I was trying to impress someone—I'm not sure. But for a brief period of my baby's life, I did make my own baby food, and it really wasn't that hard. What I will warn you about is that you can't do this alone—you need a book or a website with recipes to guide you because there are things you need to know, like what baby can digest at what age. I used a book called *The Healthy Baby Meal Planner* by Annabel Karmel. The author was trained at the Cordon Bleu school and this book is a great reference for not only baby food but also ideas and recipes for feeding your baby and toddler.

So why should you even consider going to all the effort of making fresh baby food when the grocery store is stacked full of tasty little jars of perfectly healthy food that babies have eaten for years? One reason is that fresh foods taste, smell, and look better and are just plain better for your baby. Many important nutrients are lost in the processing of baby food. Also, there's much more variety for your baby when you're making your own, which means there's a better chance that your baby won't be such a picky eater in years to come. Most of the commercially prepared foods taste the same and are the same bland consistency, so it may be difficult to convince your baby to accept food that is a different texture (texture is a big deal for babies). Making your own baby food teaches your child to prefer fresh and real food rather than sugary, processed foods. You will save money—it's much cheaper to make your own.

Here are a few pointers to get you started:

- Fruits and vegetables lose valuable nutrients when they are cooked, so it's always wise to serve a mix of raw and cooked veggies in baby's diet. The problem is that babies can't digest raw veggies until they are at least six months old. Bananas, peaches, avocados, and nectarines are okay to eat raw before then.
- As your baby's teeth come in and baby gets older, fruits and veggies can be cooked lightly (not overcooked) to help retain nutrients.
- It is very important that you sterilize baby food containers properly. Once baby is a year old, you can ease up on your sterilizing methods. By that time baby is crawling and putting everything that's not nailed down into his mouth anyway.
- Designate one cutting board in your kitchen for meat products and another one for fruits and veggies. Plastic or glass boards are best (wooden ones tend to harbor bacteria).
- Save time and effort by making more baby food than needed and immediately freezing the remainder in ice-cube trays for future meals. This is key because in just a couple of hours, you can make a month's worth of baby food. For babies under six months of age, be sure to sterilize those ice cube trays and place them in sterilized plastic freezer bags.
- Be sure to label all freezer bags with the ingredients and the date. Freeze baby food within two hours of making it to prevent the growth of bacteria. To thaw one meal, remove the appropriate number of cubes from the tray, cover, and leave at room temperature for one hour. Then you can heat it and serve it.
- When using a microwave to defrost baby food, always stir and test the temperature of the food to prevent burns.
- Never refreeze meals that have been frozen already, and you really shouldn't reheat them more than once.

Freezer Storage Times from *The Healthy Baby Meal Planner*

Fruits	6 months
Vegetables	6 months
Purees that include milk	4–6 weeks
Fish	10 weeks
Red meat and chicken	10 weeks

When to Start

Many moms feel pressured to get their baby started on baby food as early as three months of age. Once again, this is a little bit like the "Baby Olympics"—the same train of thought that makes us race to get them sleeping through the night on their own—and it's crazy. Your baby can safely drink only breast milk for up to five or six months of age. Every baby is different, and when your baby is still hungry after a feeding, or if feedings are happening more frequently, you'll know it's time to add some baby food to his diet. When you introduce a new food to baby, be sure to try one new food at a time and stick to it for about three days. This is the only way to be sure that baby can tolerate (and not be allergic to) a new food.

Baby Food Recipes for Ages Four to Five Months

BANANAS

Bananas very rarely cause allergies. They are the perfect baby food—easy to digest, easy to prepare, and sweet (babies like sweets because breast milk is sweet). Simply mash it with a fork or potato masher. Add a little baby milk or boiled water to thin it if needed. Do not freeze bananas.

CARROTS

Small, thin carrots are the sweetest. Peel and slice two carrots. Place them in boiling water and simmer for about 25 minutes or until the carrots are very tender. Drain the carrots but reserve the liquid. Puree the cooked carrots and add the liquid as needed to make it smooth. Once your baby has teeth and can chew, you can reduce the cooking time to preserve vitamins and keep the carrots a little crisper.

SWEET POTATOES

Experts have rated sweet potatoes as the number one healthiest food we can eat (for us and our babies). They are loaded with vitamins and minerals, and babies love them because of their sweet taste. Sweet potatoes can be baked, boiled, steamed, and even microwaved. Here's how:

Boiling: Peel the potato and cut it into chunks. Use just enough water in the pan to cover the potato and bring it to a boil. Reduce heat and simmer until tender. Drain and mash.

Baking: Scrub the potato, prick it with a fork a few times, and bake at 375 degrees F for about 45 minutes or until it feels soft. Split the skin, scoop out the mushy potato, and serve or freeze.

Steaming: Peel and cube and place on a steamer rack over a pan containing about 1 inch of water. Cover and bring the water to a boil. Steam for about 10–12 minutes.

Microwave: Prick with a fork, place on a paper towel, and microwave on high for about 5–6 minutes. Let the potato stand before serving—it continues to cook during this time and will also get softer.

Sweet potatoes are one of the very best first foods you can give your baby. In addition to being rich in nutrients, they are easy to digest and not associated with constipation (sometimes found with newly introduced solids). My daughter ate so many sweet potatoes, she began to turn orange . . . seriously. Your baby's body will only use as much beta-carotene as it needs and the rest is deposited in his skin. So if your baby eats sweet potatoes frequently, you may notice a yellow or orange tint to his skin (often seen around the nose). This side effect is completely harmless and will fade as your baby begins to enjoy a wider variety of foods. If the whites of your baby's eyes appear yellow, consult your doctor; otherwise don't worry—it just means that baby is getting plenty of vitamins and minerals from orange and yellow veggies.

The recipes that follow are from www.homemade-baby-food-recipes.com.

Baby Food Recipes for Ages Six to Nine Months

CHEESE AND VEGGIES

5 teaspoons milk
4 ounces cottage cheese
3 ounces cream cheese
1 ounce finely grated mild cheddar
1 ounce cooked carrots
2 ounces cooked peas
Parmesan cheese

Mix the cottage cheese, cream cheese, cheddar, and milk together until well blended. Stir in the hot, cooked vegetables. Sprinkle with parmesan cheese.

ZUCCHINI AND BANANA PUREE

Sounds like a crazy combination—but they complement each other nicely.

1 small zucchini, washed, trimmed, and sliced
½ banana, peeled and sliced

Steam the zucchini slices for 8 minutes and puree with the banana.

PEACHES AND RICE

1 tablespoon flaked brown rice
⅝ cup milk
1 ripe peach, skinned, pitted, and chopped

Put the rice and milk in a small pan and stir over low heat for about 5 minutes or until it boils and starts to thicken. Simmer for 5 more minutes, then stir in the chopped peach. This can be pureed for younger babies.

TWICE-BAKED POTATOES

1 large baking potato (I prefer to use red-skinned potatoes—they have a creamier texture)
2 tablespoons butter
¼ cup milk
3 ounces grated mild cheddar

Wash the potato, prick with a fork, then bake at 350 degrees for about 1½ hours, until the potato feels soft. Remove from the oven and cut in half. Scoop out the potato and place in a bowl, along with the butter, milk, and most of the cheese. Mash well. Return the potato mixture to the skins, place on a cooking sheet, and top with the remaining cheese. Return to the oven and cook for a further 10–15 minutes, until the cheese has melted and is golden in color. Serve in small pieces for baby. If your child isn't able to chew table foods yet, simply serve him the mashed portion.

CHEESY CAULIFLOWER

6 ounces cauliflower
1 tablespoon cornstarch
1 tablespoon butter
¾ cup milk
2 ounces grated cheese

Steam the cauliflower until tender (about 10 minutes). To make the cheese sauce, melt the butter in a small saucepan. Stir in the cornstarch and cook briefly. Add the milk slowly, stirring well. Continue to cook, stirring, until sauce thickens. Remove from the heat and stir in the grated cheese. Finally, add the cooked cauliflower.

CREAMY PASTA SAUCE

This can be used by itself over pasta, with grated cheese, or over pureed vegetables.

1 inch celery, chopped
1 inch carrot, chopped
Small piece of onion
½ bay leaf
Pepper
¾ cup milk
1 tablespoon butter
1 tablespoon all-purpose flour

Add the veggies, bay leaf, and pepper to the milk in a saucepan and bring to a boil. Remove from heat and allow to infuse for 30 minutes. Strain the milk. Melt the butter and mix in the flour to make a paste. Gradually stir in the flavored milk. Bring to a boil over low heat, stirring to make a thick white sauce. Remove bay leaf before serving.

CREAMY FISH WITH CHEESE AND CORNFLAKES

Teach your child to eat fish early—it's a very healthy habit to start!

4 ounces white fish, filleted and skinned (use a mild fish like tilapia, grouper, or flounder)
Milk
¾ cup Creamy Pasta Sauce (above)
¼ cup grated cheddar
½ cup crushed cornflakes (I put them in a zip-top bag and roll over them with a rolling pin)

Put the fish in an ovenproof dish with just enough milk to barely cover it. Bake at 350 degrees for 20 minutes. Drain off the liquid. Add the sauce, sprinkle with cheese and cornflake crumbs, and return to the oven for about 8 minutes.

Baby Food for Ages Nine to Twelve Months

You should note that baby's growth slows a little during this time, so he may not have as many growth spurts and simply not feel as hungry as before. He's also more interested in his environment, so he may be less interested about what's on his plate and much more interested in what's on your plate. Or he may just be getting picky—babies begin to form likes and dislikes around this age. This is also the time to start providing more texture in baby's diet. Leave the lumps in his food—he needs to learn to chew. Most babies can begin to successfully use a spoon around ten months old. Granted, don't expect accuracy, but practice makes perfect.

This is the time to give your child the opportunity to use his motor skills by using his fingers to pick up foods. However, never give a nine-month-old food that may cause choking, such as grapes, hot dogs, popcorn, peanuts, whole or baby carrots, celery, raisins, hard candy, large pieces of raw veggies, or tough meat. Always supervise your child when he or she is eating.

Here are some great ideas for finger foods that are appropriate for a 9–12 month old:

Fruit: all kinds of berries, oranges, kiwifruit, sliced apples, melons, bananas, dried fruit, peaches, plums, avocados. Serve them plain or with a yogurt dip.

Vegetables: tomatoes (cut cherry tomatoes in half), cucumber wedges, carrots, pumpkin, potatoes, parsnips, broccoli. Boil or steam to soften slightly. Or grate or bake wedges or cubes.

Breads and cereals: sandwiches with smooth peanut butter, mini muffins, plain biscuits, bagels cut into small pieces, crackers, and cooked pasta.

Meat and fish: cook well and cut into very small pieces.

Milk products: cheese—grated, cubed, slices.

There are thousands upon thousands of great baby food recipes out there! Just get online or visit your local bookstore to learn more about proper storage and preparation.

Tips for Finger Foods

Here are some ideas from www.homemade-baby-food-recipes.com.

- Introduce finger foods one at a time and slowly add new ones. Offer a variety of colors and textures.
- Your baby will want to touch, smell, taste, and play with his food . . . stay relaxed about the mess and let him experiment.
- Make sure your child is sitting still when eating, as most choking occurs when toddlers are crawling or running around while eating.
- To keep mess to a minimum, only give your baby two or three pieces of food at a time—any more will probably end up on the floor! Put the food in a suction-type bowl that will stick to the table or straight onto the high chair tray itself.
- Coat slippery foods, like banana or avocado, in finely crushed cereal powder or nutritious wheat germ—it makes them easier to pick up.
- If your baby doesn't like a certain type of food, try it again a few weeks later—babies' tastes change all the time. If he refuses all finger foods, be patient and keep trying. You're sure to offer him something to catch his interest eventually!
- Baby finger foods make perfect snacks between meals, to tide your baby over. But be careful not to allow your baby more snacks than he really needs, as he may become less interested at mealtimes.
- If your baby is teething, offer him cold finger foods to soothe his gums. Try freezing pieces of melon or banana for the ultimate in gum relief!
- Pack some healthy travel snacks for baby wherever you go. It will keep him occupied and makes life a lot easier, particularly if you go out for a meal.
- *Always* supervise your baby and *never* leave him to feed himself alone.

Clutter-Busting Resources

WEBSITES

Adventures in Healthy Eating from the *Family Fun* Guide
http://familyfun.go.com/recipes/family/feature/famf0600healthy/famf0600healthy.html

Food News
www.foodnews.org (part of the Environmental Working Group)

Helpguide.org (healthy eating)
www.helpguide.org/life/healthy_eating_diet.htm

Morningstar Farms product information
www.seeveggiesdifferently.com

The Food Guide Pyramid
www.kidshealth.org/kid/stay_healthy/food/pyramid.html

Healthy Children, Healthy Choices from the Centers for Disease Control
www.cdc.gov/nccdphp/dnpa/nutrition/nutrition_for_everyone/quick_tips/healthy_children.htm

Homemade Baby Food
www.homemade-baby-food-recipes.com

BOOKS

The Sneaky Chef: Simple Strategies for Hiding Healthy Foods in Kids' Favorite Meals
by Missy Chase Lapine
www.thesneakychef.com

Deceptively Delicious: Simple Secrets for Getting Your Kids to Eat Good Food
by Jessica Seinfeld
www.deceptivelydelicious.com

The Healthy Baby Meal Planner: Mom-Tested, Child-Approved Recipes for Your Baby and Toddler
by Annabel Karmel

29

Germs and Kids

From Sara

I hate germs as much as anybody, but Stephanie is the real militant germophobe of the two of us. I figure a little dog hair and dirt is good for kids. It builds up their immunity. But you don't want your kids sick all the time either, so there are some real, practical ways you can limit your child's exposure. Take it away, Steph.

From Stephanie

Nothing freaks moms out like a common public toilet seat. Trying to make kids understand the importance of touching *nothing* in a public restroom is about as difficult as the first mission to the moon. They cannot comprehend what a germ is or how it can hurt them, nor do they care. In fact, if your children are anything like mine, it's astonishing to watch just how many surfaces they are actually capable of touching in a mere five-minute period. Some of the most frustrated, freaked-out mothers I've ever encountered have been voices from the other side of the bathroom stall. In this chapter, we're going to educate you and therefore make your bathroom experience a little more pleasant for you and your children. Because as it turns out, the public toilet really isn't so bad after all.

The Dreaded Public Toilet Seat

Okay—are you sitting down? (No pun intended.) The toilet seat should not be your biggest worry when it comes to public restrooms. This is shocking news, I know. But science tells us that there just aren't many disease-causing organisms (in the United States) that are capable of entering our system directly through our skin. Did you know that our skin is actually considered part of our immune system?

Even if you sit on a toilet seat immediately after someone who has a sexually transmitted disease, it's virtually impossible to become infected (hence the name "sexually transmitted"). And remember that urine is actually sterile, so just drying the seat off with toilet paper is as effective as using a paper toilet seat liner.

Now, there are skin infections that could be caught from a toilet seat, like pubic lice, scabies, and *E. coli* and staph infections. But these are extremely rare. Pubic lice cannot survive away from the human body for more than twenty-four hours. Almost nothing can be contracted through the skin of your thighs and buttocks.

The transmission of the really disgusting germs isn't from using the toilets; it's actually from touching objects that other people touched who didn't wash their hands after using the toilet, and then eating without washing your own hands. People who think they don't need to wash their hands after using the restroom "because they didn't touch anything" are just plain ignorant. Unless they have telekinetic powers, they've had to touch door handles and toilet paper holders, and they've come into contact with tens of thousands of germs just floating around in the air due to flushing toilets. Those are the people who cause the spread of epidemics and make the rest of us sick. Please feel free to politely ask them to wash their hands.

Faucet handles in public restrooms can hold up to 50,000 germs per square inch, but a thorough hand washing with plain soap and water will remove up to 95 percent of bacteria and viruses (almost the same as using antibacterial soap or hand sanitizer). Be aware of wet bar soap, since stagnant water breeds bacteria. Simply rinse the bar under water for thirty seconds before using it.

Another one of the germiest places in the restroom is the tampon bins and lids (this is due to people's hands touching them, not menstrual blood). Kids love these little boxes—they can't wait to see what's inside. One of the best tricks I've learned for public restrooms is bringing in a favorite game or toy. That way little hands stay occupied instead of amusing themselves by touching everything. I've also learned to play a little game with my kids where they fold their hands together and keep them folded—like the little game where you interlock fingers and play "here is the church, here is the steeple, open it up and see all the people." You can also sing songs that have hand movements to prevent them from exploring the bathroom stall. And remind them constantly about not touching the floor. The floor of the bathroom is still one of the dirtiest surfaces on earth.

Another shocker you should know about the restroom is that the hand blowers (designed to prevent the spread of germs from paper towels) are actually quite disgusting. They trap all the infected air in the bathroom, concentrate it, and blow it directly onto your freshly washed hands. So avoid them.

Never put your purse or bags on the floor. Fecal bacteria abounds on the floor of restrooms, and many women transfer this bacteria from the floor to the sink when they set their purses down to wash their hands. Actually, studies found that the cleanest places in the public restroom were the toilet seat and the door handle (because people are so paranoid about door handles that they avoid them).

Yet another shocking piece of scientific information is that most men's rooms actually tested cleaner than most women's rooms. By cleaner, I mean less bacteria—and the reason for that is probably because there are fewer children visiting men's rooms, and we spend a lot more time in the bathroom than men do.

Here are a few more tips to help arm you in your battle against public toilets:

- Use the roll of toilet paper inside the dispenser. This roll has been covered by the plastic dispenser and has not been exposed to as many germs.
- Lower the seat lid before flushing. Toilets spray fecal-infected droplets of water into the air every time they're flushed. (That holds true for the toilet waiting for you at home too—so be sure to store toothbrushes far away from the toilet.)
- Proper hand washing means that you lather up with soap and scrub for at least fifteen seconds. (Sing the ABC song with your kids, or the "Happy Birthday" song twice.)
- Paper towels from an enclosed holder are much safer than air dryers.
- If you suffer from bathroom insanity like me, perhaps you've wondered which stall is best to use. I'm pleased to tell you that I have found the answer: use the first stall in the row. Studies show they get the least use because people are often looking for privacy and head to the rear of the bathroom.

Now, if this scientific information still doesn't move you, then we recommend you purchase toilet seat covers from Tabletopper.com. They have adhesive on the back so they don't slip during use, and they come in a convenient travel size package. They're a mere $19 for a forty-count jumbo pack, which is a pretty good price for peace of mind.

The Most Germ-Ridden Place in Your House: Your Kitchen

It's hard to believe, but it's true: the average kitchen countertop contains ten times more bacteria than a toilet seat! It's mostly because people don't wash their hands properly after working with raw meat or using the restroom. Unwashed hands are the number one carriers of germs like *E. coli*, salmonella, and plenty of their scary relatives.

One of the germiest places in the kitchen is often the tray on a baby's high chair. A staggering 60 percent of baby high chair trays were tested and found to be contaminated with coliform bacteria, which comes from fecal matter, raw meat, dirt, and unwashed veggies.

When we did the research for our radio show about keeping kids germ-free, we were amazed at how many things we do wrong in the course of a day that basically turn our entire houses into a germ party. Our goal is to help you spend time doing the things that matter when it comes to cleaning your house, not adding to your already daunting list of household chores. Straightening your toy room twice a day isn't going to keep your house free from germs that make your family sick. So do the stuff that counts.

Horizontal countertops and moist kitchen sponges are the perfect breeding ground for germs. And remember that one single bacterium can become more than 8 million bacteria in less than twenty-four hours! It can take anywhere from as few as ten to as many as millions of bacteria to make your family sick, depending on the kind present.

Your Kitchen Sponge

If you're like me and love your kitchen sponge, there's good news and bad news. The bad news is that kitchen sponges are the number one source of germs in your whole entire house. Those moist little crevices make it the perfect home for germs. When you wipe your counters and dishes with a dirty sponge, you're simply moving the bacteria around (even if you're using a disinfectant cleaner). But the good news is that if you wet your sponge and pop it into the microwave for two minutes, it will eliminate all the germs inside the crevices. So get into the habit of nuking your sponge a couple of times a day, every day.

And as for you dishcloth users who are snubbing us sponge users . . . don't judge too quickly. Dishrags are no better than sponges, and just washing them isn't enough to kill all the germs.

The only effective way to eliminate germs in your kitchen is to use a disinfectant and paper towels that can be thrown away after each surface. And don't forget to disinfect faucet handles, refrigerator door handles, telephones, doorknobs, stove handles, trash cans, and anything that you touch with your hands. Make sure the cleaner you're using is labeled as a disinfectant—they kill germs on contact. Do this as often as time allows.

Other Target Areas

- **Cutting boards.** Cracks and crevices in your cutting board are another favorite hiding place for harmful bacteria. We read one study that showed that the average cutting board has about 200 percent more fecal bacteria than the average toilet seat. People don't disinfect cutting boards well enough. Never cut up raw chicken or any other kind of meat and then use the same cutting board for salad. It's best to designate one cutting board for meats and one for produce.
- **Drains.** This is an area we never think about but drains in both your kitchen and your bathroom provide another perfect, moist hideout for germs and bacteria. Make it a habit to disinfect drains each week when you clean. You can use bak-

ing soda and an old toothbrush to get rid of stains, grit, and grime around your drains.

- **Bedsheets.** Changing your bedsheets weekly can help in keeping your family healthy. Germs like your bed as much as you do. If your child gets sick, be sure to change his sheets more often. And if your children share a bedroom, let the well child camp out in another room for a few nights to reduce the number of germs she is exposed to. And keep your dog off the bed. Furry coats are great hiding places for germs and allergens.
- **Floors.** The next time you mop your floor, know that cleaning your floor is a very effective way to eliminate germs from your house. I never think about germs when I mop; I'm just thinking about how nice it will be to not have anything stick to my bare feet when I walk. But mopping actually removes dust, dirt, mold, and germs and will make a big difference in keeping your family healthy.

Hand Washing

Antibacterial Soaps

Antibacterial soaps really aren't any better than regular soap. All soaps kill bacteria. What's most important is *how* and *when* you wash your hands. You must wash for at least fifteen seconds to ensure that you're killing all the bacteria. And above all, make sure your kids wash their hands before they eat anything (even snacks and candy). The Centers for Disease Control recommends that you teach your kids to sing the "Happy Birthday" song twice (or the ABC song once) to ensure that they are washing their hands long enough. It's also smart to have your kids wash their hands as soon as they come home from school or wherever else they've been, so they don't bring unwanted germs into your home. Also, be sure to wash your kids' hands as soon as you leave a store—I keep a bottle of hand sanitizer in my car cup holder.

I got a kick out of the website www.drgreene.com when I was researching this topic. Dr. Greene gave the best example I could find for why antibacterial soaps aren't so great. He said that a kids' science fair last year did an experiment where they used four test tubes. In the first tube, they put a few drops of antibacterial soap. In the second tube, they diluted the soap with water by ten times; in the third, they diluted the soap a hundred times; and in the fourth tube, they diluted the soap a thousand times. Then they put normal bacteria from their hands in each tube. The interesting part is that all the bacteria in the first three tubes were killed. But in the tube where the soap was most diluted, some of the bacteria survived. (That's what happens when you don't wash your hands long enough.) They kept those surviving cells and grew them in an incubator and repeated the experiment. This time, the bacteria were able to survive in *two* of the test tubes. So basically, they were breeding increasingly hardy bacteria. Antibacterial soap can cause the exact same reaction. We're actually breeding more resistant bacteria. The bottom line is, antibacterial soap is pretty much just a marketing ploy that may actually *increase* your chances of getting sick.

From Sara

Zzzzzzz . . .

Hand Sanitizers

Remember that most infections are "caught" when the germs on our hands get into those nice, warm, moist membranes that germs love: our eyes, nose, and mouth. Hand sanitizers like Purell and Germ-X do a great job at keeping your kids healthy. They kill about 99.9 percent of germs, and remember, they're an antiseptic, which means they kill germs using alcohols (which also makes them dangerous if ingested). We've found great ones from Bath and Body Works (www.bathandbodyworks.com) that come in kid-friendly scents like grape, apple, and banana and cost about $4 per bottle. We've also learned that these don't sting boo-boos as badly as Purell. If your kid's teacher doesn't have a few bottles of hand sanitizer around the classroom, bring some in for her and ask her to spread them around the room.

Ten Tips for Fighting Germs at School

Children catch about eight colds a year. Combined, children in our country lose nearly twenty-two million school days due to just the common cold. There's nothing worse than having a sick child—all mothers agree about that. So here are a few things that will help keep your child well when he or she isn't at home with you.

1. **Buy mechanical pencils.** Studies have shown that the dirtiest thing in any classroom is the community pencil sharpener. Using a mechanical pencil means your child won't have to share with everyone else.
2. **Teach your child to wash hands before school lunch.** This is extremely important, and your teacher should be making this a priority. (In my experience, most teachers do.)
3. **Teach your child to hang up her backpack when using the restroom.** Women's purses have been found with huge amounts of fecal bacteria from placing them on the floor in the restroom. Wash your child's backpack as often as you can.
4. **Don't borrow crayons and art supplies.** Make sure your child has his own supplies. Anything that passes from one person to another can be carrying germs. So this time, it's okay *not* to share.

5. Pack two juice boxes. Teach your kids not to share drinks or take a sip from anyone else's cup. During flu season, put an extra juice box into your children's lunchboxes so they don't have to share.

6. Teach your kids not to share their food. If your child is really into sharing, then cut the food into shareable-size bites.

7. Concentrate on packing a healthy lunch. Studies show that kids who eat poorly don't get enough calories and have weaker immune systems. Avoid foods with empty calories like chips, crackers and processed meats and go for peanut butter, cheese, fruit, and turkey instead.

8. For example, don't pack your kid's lunch while doing the laundry. We moms are famous for multitasking, but this is a bad combination. Washing machines don't necessarily kill germs, so you might unknowingly contaminate food from soiled laundry. Wash your hands before packing lunches.

9. Teach your child about the dangers of common surfaces like drinking fountain handles, light switches, computer keyboards and mouses, and water faucets. Send disinfecting wipes to school with your kids and show them how to take a few seconds to wipe down desk surfaces and computer mouses before using them, and how to wash their hands after using them (with travel-size hand sanitizer that you keep in their backpack). Yes, they might be la-

Tips for Moms with Preschoolers

- Limit play dates during flu season. This may seem a little over the top, but consider that an infected child can spread cold or flu symptoms twenty-four hours before any symptoms appear. Kids touch each other's toys and cups and hands, and little kids especially tend to exchange too much bodily fluid during normal play by slobbering and putting their hands in their mouths and then touching things.
- Make sure toys are clean before and after a play date at your house. Kids this age love to put toys in their mouths, so it's important to take a few steps to keep your house safe. You can wash most stuffed animals in the washing machine weekly. Plastic toys like Legos can be washed with soap and water; disinfecting wipes work great too. I always sprayed Lysol heavily over the entire toy room, toys, bathrooms, furniture, and rugs as soon as playtime was over. For something a bit gentler than Lysol, you can try Clorox's Anywhere Hard Surface Sanitizing Spray. It kills 99 percent of common household bacteria but is "as safe as water," according to their ads.
- Ask your day care facility to talk to you about their hand-washing policy. They should be able to recite it to you and there should be plenty of sinks available. It's okay to remind them of the need for extra hand washing during cold and flu season.

beled as nerds, but depending on how often they get sick, they may decide it's worth it.

10. Antiviral tissues really do help. Teach your kids to throw their tissues away immediately after using them. And teach your kid to sneeze and cough into their elbow instead of their hands. (This gets confusing: "No, honey, you shouldn't wipe your mouth on your sleeve, but you can sneeze into it.") When you cough or sneeze into your hands, it just puts germs in your hands that you can spread to anything you touch and then to everyone else.

During cold and flu season, or if there is a sick family member in your home, you might try putting away your drinking glasses and changing to disposable paper cups for a while. Make sure that everyone in the house has a different cup so you're not spreading germs to each other. Yes, most dishwashers get hot enough to kill germs, but glasses sitting around or being touched (even to put them away) can spread germs. Too many times viruses spread through entire families because symptoms don't show up until it's too late. And try putting paper towels in your bathrooms instead of sharing hand towels.

The number one way to keep your family healthy is by simply having everybody wash their hands often, especially before eating. People who wash their hands seven times a day have about 40 percent fewer colds than the average person.

Boosting Your Immune System

Like we always say, mommies don't get sick days. So let's talk about how to boost your own immunity.

Plenty of Sleep

Experts say that not only does prolonged sleep deprivation wear down your immunity, but getting adequate rest can help boost your defenses as well. Be sure to get at least seven to eight hours of sleep every night.

Moderate Exercise

Moderate exercise—like a brisk thirty-minute walk three or four times a week—has been shown to increase your immunity to disease. Working out too hard can actually run down your immune system and make you more susceptible to illness. While moderate exercise is important, we must warn you to watch out for germs in the gym. Gyms are breeding grounds for germs, so wash your hands frequently and don't use machines that are damp with sweat.

Moderate Alcohol Intake

Good news, girls! You have a solid excuse for that glass of wine every night (well, almost every night). Studies show that moderate alcohol intake releases opioid peptides and raises IgA levels. IgA is a protein from the immune system that helps fight infection and plays a critical role in keeping pathogens from entering your body. Opioid peptides are happy little brain chemicals that boost the production of IgA. However, too much alcohol can damage your immunity, so stick to fewer than four glasses per week.

Sex

Yes, it's true, sex can help boost your immunity. Having sex boosts IgA and opioid peptides too. But it's not just sex—a loving touch can release those things too. A study done in the early 1960s at the University of California at Berkeley showed that having a social support system (especially one that involved frequent physical touching such as hugs and handshakes) was more predictive of long life than age, medical status, or even smoking.

Reducing Stress

There is overwhelming evidence that stress has an immense impact on our ability to remain healthy. Your body simply cannot react to infection when you are overstressed. People who have less stress are healthier.

Chicken Soup

You probably thought it was an old wives' tale, but it's true. Chicken soup not only can pump up immune power but also help colds go away faster. Chicken soup helps relieve cold and flu symptoms in two ways. First, it acts as an anti-inflammatory by inhibiting the movement of immune system cells that participate in the body's inflammatory response. Second, it temporarily speeds up the movement of mucus through the nose, helping relieve congestion and limiting the amount of time viruses are in contact with the nose lining. And it's giving your body more of those fluids it so desperately needs when it's fighting off a bug. So which is better, homemade or canned? Researchers at the University of Nebraska compared homemade chicken soup with canned versions and found that many, though not all, canned chicken soups worked just as well as soups made from scratch. For some reason, chicken soup seems to have more healing ingredients than other soups.

Good Diet

A diet that is low in red meat and high in fish, fruits, and vegetables makes for an unbeatable immune system. Choose "superfoods" like blueberries and broccoli that pack an extreme nutrient and antioxidant punch. Green tea is also effective in assisting the immune system. And dark teas (like orange pekoe, English breakfast, and Earl Grey) also have antioxidants that keep immune systems strong.

Sooner or later your kids (and you) are going to get sick. And if you're like me, you'll probably find yourself in a *CSI*-like episode, trying to retrace your steps and the people you came in contact with to determine where your war on germs went awry. There have been plenty of times when my whole family was sick, and I kept repeating, "But I used hand sanitizer religiously! After every store! I even wiped down the cart at the grocery store! What did I miss?" Sometimes there's nothing you can do. It's not your fault. Kids are germ magnets and they will get sick despite your best efforts.

Be sure not to forget to take extra good care of yourself when your children are sick. It's ironic because we're so busy when our kids are sick. At the very time that we need the most rest and the most nutritious food, we're tired from sitting up with them, and we're running around washing sheets, driving to the pharmacy, cleaning toilets, and forgetting to eat. Wash your hands often when your kids are sick. Cancel daytime appointments or ask Dad to take over so you can catch up on some sleep. There's nothing worse than being sick at the same time your kids are sick. They need their mommy, and they don't care if she has to stop and vomit on the way to the kitchen to get their favorite juice. Mommies don't get sick days, so make the time to take care of yourself and it'll make taking care of your family much easier on you.

Clutter-Busting Resources

Bath & Body Works
www.bathandbodyworks.com

Clorox Anywhere Daily Sanitizing Spray
www.clorox.com/products

Purell
www.pfizerch.com/brand.aspx?id=310

Germ-X
www.germx.com

30

Potty Training

From Sara

My pediatrician, a father of four, gave me the potty-training method I used on both my children. He told me to let them go without any bottoms on around the house for a week. He said that after a couple of days I would curse him (and I did), but that it would work. In a week they would have the concept down. He was right. They did get the concept within a week. It was being able to act on the concept that seemed to take about six months to master.

The reasoning behind the good doctor's method is that without a diaper or even pants, toddlers become much more aware of their need to go to the bathroom. It also means they'll do a number (literally) on your rugs and carpets. No, it's not pretty, but you'll get through it. When you do decide your child is ready, be prepared to stay close to home for a week or so to really work with them. It's much harder to potty-train when you are running errands.

Most of all, be patient and relax. Potty training takes time. It won't happen overnight. But try not to worry—your child is not going to go off to college wearing Pull-Ups.

Signs of Readiness

From Stephanie

Most children show signs of being ready to potty-train between the ages of eighteen months and three years, but it depends totally on the child. Let me just warn you that potty training is not fun. About three days into trying to potty-train my son, I had spent all morning up to my elbows in pee and poop and I said to myself, "What exactly is the benefit of this again?" I decided to put his diapers back on and give it a few more months. And my intuition was right. When he was ready, it was a breeze. So don't kill yourself trying to get this done. It will be easier when your child is ready, and there's not much you can do to force it. Besides, believe it or not, diapers mean you're in control, and that's much easier. Taking a child who's being potty-trained out of the house is no fun at all.

If your child shows these signs, he may be ready:

- Being able to stay dry for at least 2 hours at a time
- Having regular bowel movements
- Being able to follow simple instructions
- Feeling uncomfortable with dirty diapers and wanting them to be changed
- Asking to use the potty chair, or asking to wear regular underwear
- Being able to walk well (to and from the bathroom) and to get on and off the toilet or potty chair fairly easily
- Being able to pull pants up and down independently

When You Start Training

Don't let potty training turn into punishment. Only keep your child seated for a few minutes at a time. And please realize that this is no easy task; you may decide to give up and wait another few months before trying again.

Try emptying your child's poopy diapers into the toilet or potty seat to demonstrate what you want him to do. (Ah yes, the joys of motherhood.)

Never start trying to potty-train during a stressful time in your household or during a time of transition. Things need to be calm and stable. You need to be prepared to exert more patience than you ever knew you had.

Discuss using the toilet. Explain what you want your child to do. Let him see you or his friends using the toilet. Watch videos and read books (like *Once Upon a Potty*—see "Clutter-Busting Resources") about potty training. The more he understands, the better his chance for success.

Dress kids in loose clothes that they can easily take off by themselves—this is all about letting them do as much as possible independently.

Equipment

All kinds of potty-training merchandise are on the market nowadays. It's kinda crazy because all you really need is a kid and a potty. Avoid the pricey kits that come with a doll and potty seat for the doll and the kits that claim you can potty-train in a day. That's highly unlikely.

What you will need is a potty chair, washable training pants, disposable training pants (like Huggies Pull-Ups or Pampers Easy Ups), extra pairs of underwear, and lots and lots of resolve (both the carpet cleaning variety and the kind that gives you the strength to finish the job).

There are several potty chairs out there. You needn't spend a fortune on one, but:

- Make sure that it is sturdy. The last thing you want is for it to collapse while your child is sitting on it!
- Make sure the "pot" part (where the pee and poop end up) of the chair is secure and empties easily for easy cleaning and minimal spilling.
- We personally liked the ones that later convert into a seat that fits onto the toilet (so your child doesn't have to balance or worry about falling in) and a little stepstool that helps your child climb up on the seat.
- It's sometimes a good idea to take your child to the store with you and let her pick out the seat of her choice.

Pull-Ups are a must when you're starting out, but only for bedtime and naptime (and for long trips in the car). They feel too much like a diaper and children will learn to pee and poop in them as soon as the newness wears off. You want your child to feel wet and uncomfortable in their regular underwear because it motivates them to use the potty.

You will need lots of extra pairs of underwear, and be sure to keep a pair and a change of clothes in your car too. Always be prepared for an accident because there will be plenty of them. (Include top and bottom because you never know where an accident is going to spread.) Keep a spare plastic or zip-top bag with you so you have a place to put soiled clothes to get them home.

Washable training pants can be helpful because they have a layer that is meant to absorb more urine than regular underwear, but they often still leak. Some moms really prefer training pants because the messes are a little less frequent.

Every Child Is Different

Some children will be bowel-trained before being bladder-trained and vice versa. It just depends on the child.

From Sara

I never used washable training pants on my children—Pull-Ups worked just fine for me. I realize I have probably contributed to the melting of a couple of icebergs through the years of use of disposable diapers and Pull-Ups, but I just didn't want to deal with washing poopy pants in my washing machine. However, as toddlers transition to underwear, accidents will still happen. We had a few underwear casualties during the potty-training months. Sometimes I just didn't think it was worth the disgusting hassle to save a pair of Cinderella underwear that probably cost a dollar. And let's face it, Cinderella underpants don't exactly have the same magic after they've been pooped in.

Patience! Patience! Patience!

Toilet training is a major process. Some experts feel that it is the first and biggest developmental step your child will take, generally taking several weeks to several months to complete.

Two Steps Forward, One Step Back

Don't be discouraged if you have a few good days followed by a few bad ones. This potty training thing takes time. Also keep in mind that times when your child is tired or upset are when most accidents or setbacks will occur.

A good way to get your child focusing on using the potty is to use a timer. Set it for every two hours. When the timer goes off, say, "It's time to go to the potty." Of course, if at other times he appears to need to go or says he wants to try, it's potty time. Make potty time something to look forward to. Keep your child company while he or she sits on the potty for a few minutes. You may want to have books and toys that are used only during potty time. Your undivided attention is a key ingredient.

If your child tries and nothing happens, praise him for trying. When accidents happen (and they will), don't scold your child. After a week or so of success, change potty time to "Head into the bathroom and sit on the potty—I'll be there with you in a minute!" When this is working well, progress to "Let me know when you're done—I'll check your bottom." Encourage his independence gradually.

"I Don't Want To!"

If your child resists your potty-training efforts, don't try to coerce him. Just wait a few weeks and try again. It's important for your child to be ready so he is willing to make the effort. You don't want it to become a power struggle or battle of wills. And don't tell him he is a baby and not a big boy to try to get him to go along with the process. Just be patient and tell him he can try when he is ready. Don't worry—all kids eventually do get out of diapers!

Rewards

Moms have all kinds of ideas for rewarding the use of the potty. Some keep a jar of M&M's in the bathroom and let the child take one each time he's successful. I've heard of one mom who used a movie ticket system. Her child chose a movie he wanted to see or buy. She made a movie ticket with the title of the movie. Every time her child used the potty, he got a hole punched in his ticket. When he got all 10 circles punched, they went to the movie.

Stickers or treats work well. When the child gets a certain number of stickers, she gets a prize. Be careful not to give big rewards for every potty use, or your child will learn to expect it. Then gradually phase out the rewards as using the potty becomes more routine. And keep in mind that rewards don't work for every child.

From Stephanie

Potty training sucks. It's gross, it's frustrating, and it's life-changing when you're going through it. What is so hard about going to the toilet when you have to pee or poop? My kids never had to go until we got into a store. There was something about the store that made my kids instantly have to go potty. And then even after they had the hang of it, they wanted to go visit the potty in each and every establishment we went to just so they could explore its particular bathroom. Apparently, bathrooms are like Disney World when you're three—there's so much to do to entertain yourself in there, with all those automatic hand dryers and those "magic" paper towel dispensers that shoot out a towel when you wave your hand in front of them. Public restrooms are a treasure trove of magical devices and unexplored lands.

I had a really hard time trying to remember to make them go potty before getting into the car to go somewhere. It was so chaotic getting two children into the car that the most important step was often forgotten. I finally put a Post-it note on my door that said "Go potty" to help me remember to take them to the bathroom before putting them into the car. Prevention is definitely the key to surviving potty training. If you get busy and forget to take them, they're going to have an accident. It's a very good idea to plan on staying at home during the first few days of potty training. Another good tactic is using your kitchen timer to help remind you. I set the timer for thirty minutes and every time the buzzer went off, my daughter knew it was time to go potty. We made it into a little game, and it worked pretty well and really helped her get the hang of it.

Bed-wetting

Once your child is potty trained, the next milestone is getting them to sleep through the night without wetting the bed. It may be a couple of years after your child has been successfully using the potty in the daytime. Parents are overly worried about this problem. And the reason they're overly worried is because it's a big pain in the patootie to keep washing sheets and mattresses. There is all kinds of equipment available, like alarms, pagers, even medications. The pagers and alarms fit into your child's PJs and alert your child at the first sign of wetness. In my opinion, these are a waste of money. By the time the thing is wet, so is your child and the sheets. Plus, what a cruel thing to be awakened in the middle of the night by an alarm when you're already uncomfortably wet.

Any seasoned mom will tell you that there are two things that make your kids sleep through the night without wetting:

1. Their bladder has to be mature enough. Until then, I don't think they have much control over it. When they are ready, they're ready. Sometimes they're not willing to try, but when they start having sleepovers and they have to put a Pull-Up on in front of their friends, they'll come home ready to try a little harder. In the meantime, my advice is to relax and keep buying Pull-Ups.
2. Don't give them anything to drink past 7:00 P.M., and make them go to the potty just before hopping into bed. Don't fall for the old "I just went a few minutes ago." Make them go immediately before getting into bed. When my kids are dying of thirst at 9:00 P.M., they can have a small sip of water, and then in return they have to use the potty a second time.

One of the best tips I've ever heard was to place a vinyl tablecloth or flat waterproof mattress pad on the mattress to protect it. Place a fitted sheet on the bed. Then put down the tablecloth and put another fitted sheet on top of that. If your child wets her bed in the nighttime, just pull off the top sheet and tablecloth and you're ready to have her climb back in and get back to sleep. Hopefully, she won't wet the bed more than once a night. If so, get another tablecloth and create another layer. This is a huge help at 3:00 A.M.

Tips on Training While Traveling

Now that you're potty training you're probably wondering how you will ever leave the house, much less go on a trip. Traveling can make potty training much more challenging. Here are some tips on training while on the go.

- **Go before you leave.** Don't forget to leave home with an empty bladder. Try to keep your first few outings brief.
- **Pack the potty.** If you're traveling in the car, bring your child's potty since little bladders need frequent pit stops. A plastic toddler potty seat that fits onto an adult toilet seat is useful for going in public restrooms. Carry extra tissue and wipes to use in bathrooms that are short on supplies.
- **Protect others' belongings.** Bring along a waterproof mattress pad, or even a small plastic tablecloth, to protect the mattresses of your family and friends. Hotel staff and future guests will also be appreciative.

- **Locate bathrooms immediately.** Kids always seem to wait till the last minute to tell us they have to go. As soon as you arrive at your destination, make sure you know where the restrooms are located as you will most likely have to rush your child to one of them!
- **Use caution.** Always accompany your child into public restrooms.
- **Use the handicap or family bathroom.** You'll have extra room if you use the stall for people with disabilities, but keep in mind that the seat may be higher than normal and your child will need more help. Many shopping malls and stores are now building unisex family bathrooms specifically designed for parents. These bathrooms are as large as handicap bathrooms, private, and can be stocked with needed toiletries like Kleenex and wipes.
- **Create a barrier against germs.** Teach children to line public toilets with strips of toilet paper as an added barrier of protection if toilet seat liners are not available. Or you can bring your own seat covers. Potty Topper is a disposable plastic cover you can place right over a public toilet seat to protect your child from germs. We sure know what a challenge it can be to keep little hands off the toilet when you're in a public bathroom. The Potty Topper has an adhesive backing so it stays in place, and wet spots from the toilet seat won't leak through. Available at www.tabletopper.com.
- **Don't expect perfection.** Remember that accidents will happen. Don't be surprised or upset if you child starts to have accidents. It's normal. If you need to temporarily go back to Pull-Ups it's okay; relax and enjoy your trip. Don't make your trip a battleground. Worry about training or retraining when you get back home.
- **Pay attention to your child's diet.** A change in diet during family vacations will often cause a change in bowel habits, either constipation or diarrhea, and likely delay your potty training progress. Again, you can wait until you get home to restart the training.

Clutter-Busting Resources

WEBSITES

www.drgreene.com
www.pottytrainingtips.com
www.keepkidshealthy.com

BOOKS

Once Upon a Potty
by Alona Frankel
(There is a book for boys and one for girls, so make sure to get the right one!)

DVDS

Bear in the Big Blue House: Potty Time with Bear
Disney

PRODUCTS

Potty Topper seat cover for traveling
www.tabletopper.com

Blue's Clues Soft Potty Training Seat (other cartoon themes available)
www.pottytrainingstuff.com

31

Dads and Daughters

It was important to both of us to include this chapter because we want moms and dads to know how vital the role of father is when it comes to daughters. Teenage girls who did not receive love, support, and attention from their fathers often go looking for love in all the wrong places. And although much of the information on this topic is more useful for the teenage years, we wanted to give you a glimpse into the future, so you can start working on the father-daughter relationship right now.

The father-daughter bond has become more important than ever, and the statistics are proving it:

- Promiscuity and pregnancy are frequently the outcome when daughters do not have a strong father-daughter relationship.
- A Vanderbilt University study showed that a young girl's relationship with her father may actually influence at what age she enters puberty. The study found that girls with close, supportive relationships with their parents tend to develop later, while girls with cold or distant relationships with their parents develop at an earlier age. Scientists hypothesize that girls who interact with their fathers on a regular basis have more exposure to their father's pheromones, which delays the onset of puberty.
- And believe it or not, girls who enter puberty later generally had fathers who were active participants in caregiving and were supportive of their wives. It is the father's involvement, rather than the mother's, that seems to be paramount here.

Stephanie is close to one family where the father was distant, selfish, and uninvolved and used fear as his main parenting style. Without knowing it, he was setting his daughter up to be the perfect prey for a sexual predator, and that's exactly what happened. At age eleven, this young girl was wooed by a much older neighbor. He convinced her how much he loved her, and by giving him what he wanted, she gained the male affection and support that she so badly craved from her own father. It's a classic case that happens over and over again. If not from a predator, she'll seek acceptance from a boyfriend.

"Every father and stepfather can make a huge difference in his daughter's life. A father is the first man his daughter knows. With that potent position of 'first man' comes the ability to set the norm of manliness for her—a norm that ultimately can be stronger than what anyone else tells her."

—Joe Kelly, author of *Dads and Daughters®*

Having a strong relationship with her father teaches a girl how it feels to be respected. She will expect boys to treat her with the same love and honor that she receives from her father. She won't be craving love and acceptance from a male because she'll already have it. This will help her to make good decisions and not just go with any male who shows an interest in her.

During our radio show, we interviewed a great dad, Joe Kelly, author of *Dads and Daughters®: How to Inspire, Support and Understand Your Daughter.* Joe is the father of twin daughters and a longtime advocate for girls and dads. He's encouraged thousands of fathers and stepfathers to make the country safe and fair for daughters.

There is a great dad quiz on Joe's website that will help dads recognize how involved they are in their daughter's life. It asks questions like:

Can I name my daughter's three best friends?

Can I tell my daughter what her strengths are?

Do I make dinner for my family?

Do I talk to my daughter about managing money?

Do I yell at my daughter's mother?

Do I initiate contact with my daughter at least five times a week?

These are just a few of the questions that will help fathers do some serious soul-searching. The website is also a great dad resource. It's written by dads for dads, so there are no insults. It's just great information for good dads.

Here are ten things all dads should do:

1. Respect your daughter's mother. Your wife is your daughter's most important role model. Your daughter will love and respect you more when you show respect to her mother. By being rude or demeaning to your wife, you are only creating distance between you and your daughter.

2. Don't be afraid to be affectionate. Hugs, kisses, and holding her hand are perfectly okay and very necessary. She needs to feel that you care.

3. Listen without offering advice. Girls are programmed to talk. They don't always want or need advice. They just want to air their thoughts and feelings. So listen without trying to solve her problems.

4. Start getting to know her friends, especially in the late elementary years and through high school. Friends are a huge influence on your child's life. Have a few parties or sleepovers so you can get to know them better.

5. Schedule father-daughter dates. Get out of the house and take her to lunch, to a movie, or bowling. Those few hours of one-on-one time can be very valuable in forming a bond with her.

6. Always be there for important dates. Never miss birthdays, recitals, first day of school, etc. These are the moments she'll always remember and you want to be a part of her memory.

7. Don't break promises. If you commit to do something with her, don't let anything get in the way. The quickest way to ruin trust is by disappointing her. Don't break a confidence.

8. Get involved in her interests. Go to her games and recitals, practice with her, ask her questions about her activities. Compliment her on her accomplishments. Notice her and let her know you've noticed.

9. Help with homework. It can be a great time to bond and solve problems together.

10. Respect her uniqueness; urge her to love her body and who she is. Show your daughter that you see her as a whole person, capable of anything. Treat her and those she loves with respect. Growing girls need to eat often and healthfully; encourage this and tell her she looks great.

Clutter-Busting Resources

WEBSITES

Dads and Daughters®
www.dadsanddaughters.org

Armin Brott, "America's most trusted dad"
www.mrdad.com

The National Center for Fathering
www.fathers.com

Fatherville
A resource for dads by dads
www.fatherville.com

The Center for Successful Fathering
www.fathering.org

BOOKS

Dads and Daughters®: How to Inspire, Understand, and Support Your Daughter
by Joe Kelly

Fatherneed: Why Father Care Is as Essential as Mother Care for Your Child
by Kyle Pruett, M.D.

The Dads and Daughters® Togetherness Guide: 54 Fun Activities to Help Build a Great Relationship
by Joe Kelly

200 Ways to Raise a Girl's Self-Esteem
by Will Glennon

32

Arming Your Kids Against Sexual Predators

We included this chapter in our book because we don't think that moms get enough information or training on how to protect our kids from sexual predators. Just look at these highly disturbing statistics:

- The National Alert Registry states that one out of every three to four girls and three out of seven boys has been sexually assaulted by the time they reach age eighteen, and one out of every six boys will be abused by age eighteen.
- About 551,000 sexual offenders have been *released* and are registered throughout America.
- Only 10 percent of sex offenders are ever caught or convicted.
- That means that over seven million offenders avoid detection and are seeking their next victim.
- Among rape victims, 44 percent are under eighteen years of age.
- Ninety percent of offenders have had some kind of relationship with the victim prior to the offense.
- The average child molester will molest fifty girls before being caught.
- A child molester who seeks out boys will molest 150 boys before being caught.
- Most sexual abuse happens between the ages of seven and thirteen.
- Eighty-five percent of the sexual assaults on children occur in the home of the victim or the attacker.

- Of the victims of registered attackers, 88 percent are girls, with half of those being between the ages of twelve and fourteen.

From Stephanie

Those numbers are hard to believe—but be afraid and take the necessary precautions to protect your children, even if it makes you sound crazy or paranoid. One in three girls means that your child has a very good chance of becoming a victim and you need to take this threat seriously. We've included this chapter because many kids are victimized by the time they reach kindergarten. It's never too early to start talking to your kids about appropriate and inappropriate touching.

There are more than 500,000 *registered* sex offenders in this country, and the laws are not tough enough to keep our kids safe. The word *registered* means that they have been convicted more than once for child sexual abuse. There's no telling how many more are lurking out there that just haven't been caught or have only been caught once. I have my own ideas about how to deal with sex offenders, and the Department of Justice hasn't contacted me yet, but I can promise you that if they used my methods, there would be a lot fewer freaks abusing innocent kids. And it's puzzling to me why Martha Stewart had to wear a monitor on her ankle keeping her under house arrest for a stock market scam, yet convicted sex offenders can walk around totally unmonitored. Until the laws catch up with the rate of abuse, it's up to us to protect our children. So read this chapter carefully, check out the websites we've referenced, and educate yourself on a crime that happens to too many of our kids. It's more prevalent than you think, so don't assume you're safe just because you live in an upscale neighborhood or your kids attend a private school. I once did marketing for a company who put on cheerleading competitions and events. They told me that they had at least one or two predators arrested at every competition. Predators see the advertising in the newspapers and local media and show up to prey on little girls. While I was at a cheer competition I saw a man being arrested for pulling his shorts up and exposing himself to a group of seven-year-olds. It's infuriating, and the laws just don't require a punishment harsh enough to deter the action.

There could be a sex offender living right next door to you. The federal law currently requires all fifty states to release information about sex offenders, but there are no requirements to actively notify members of a community that a sex offender has moved into the area. I am very close to a family whose daughter was a victim of a sexual predator for several years. Her family had no idea what was going on because the predator was their next-door neighbor and the victim's father's best friend. He was the local soccer coach, held an impressive title within his company, and was the guy that everyone thought they could trust—the kind of guy you'd want to be associated with, a guy who liked to buy ice cream for all the kids. I share this story with you to help convince you that it's good to be suspicious when it comes to your children. Be paranoid, be aware, do your homework when hiring nannies and babysitters, and don't be afraid to ask questions. Teach your children to judge people by their *behavior.* Since most victims know their attacker, just teaching them to beware of strangers isn't going to keep them safe.

The overwhelming majority of child sexual abusers are adult heterosexual males who are married and maintain normal adult responsibilities and relationships within their community. They are not homosexual (exclusively attracted to the same sex) or pedophiles (exclusively attracted to prepubescent children) and they are not mentally ill. They can be older children, a friend's brother, an uncle, a neighbor, a coach, or a babysitter's boyfriend.

Locating Offenders in Your Neighborhood

There are several websites that allow you to map the location of sexual offenders for your area. A great place to start is www.familywatchdog.us. This site will also allow you to register for e-mail updates in case an offender moves into your area. And it will give you a list of offenders who have moved to your area in the last seven days. It will also give you their photo and address. I challenge you to go to this site and see what you learn! The results will amaze you. Another site for locating predators is www.mapsexoffenders.com.

You should always be leery of unusually attentive adults. Sometimes predators will work hard to become friends with the parents, just so they can get to the child. And, trust your instincts! If a situation doesn't feel right, then it probably isn't. Screen sitters, child care providers, and anyone who is caring for your child. Be clear with babysitters about "no visitors" (since children have been molested by the friends and boyfriends of babysitters). Sadly, 60 percent of child molesters are the father or father figure in a child's life. Far too often the molester is the parent, grandparent, sibling, uncle, stepparent, cousin, neighbor, babysitter, coach, Scout leader, or spiritual leader, not a pedophile or a stranger.

Be sure to teach your kids the difference between "good touch" and "bad touch." A good rule of thumb is to teach them that no one should touch them in places that their bathing suit covers. And most of all, please teach them that it's okay to say no if someone is making them feel uncomfortable. It's also not a good idea to allow your children to play with older children. An older child may teach your children things they are not yet ready for. Older children may use their authority to persuade a younger child to try things that are inappropriate for your child's age.

Psychological Deceptions Most Often Used by Predators

Please . . . teach these to your kids! Or go to www.goodknight.org and order the DVD. They call them the "ABC's of Protection."

1. Authority figure. Some predators try to trick our children by dressing like security guards or police officers. Many predators are authority figures in our child's life like coaches or uncles. Warn your children that no matter how much authority a person has over them, nobody is allowed to make them feel uncomfortable. And they are allowed to say no when someone does.

2. Bribes. This is the oldest trick in the book (and still one of the most effective). Candy, a cute puppy, a toy, ice cream—a predator will try anything to lure a child closer. Make sure your child knows what to do in a situation like this. Instruct them never to go near cars or out of sight for any kind of reward.

3. Crisis. Predators will appeal to your child's helpful nature to trick them. For example, "Please help me! My puppy just ran into those woods and I can't find him." Or they'll stop to ask a child directions or ask them for help. Teach your child that a grown-up never has to ask for help from a child.

4. Danger. Predators will try to trick your child by saying, "Your mom and dad are at the hospital and they told me to pick you up and take you there!" This is why your family needs a secret code. Choose a word that they can remember. Whenever you ask a friend or neighbor to pick them up—they must know the password. If they don't know the password, your child doesn't get in the car. Practice this with your children and your friends. Make sure they never go with anyone who doesn't know the password.

These are just a few of the deceptions you'll find on this DVD. Talking about them with your child will help you, but the Good Knight network has done studies that prove that watching the video helps children to understand and retain the information far better than having it explained to them by a parent. The video uses actors to create the actual scenarios that help your child see and understand how predators trick their victims. Multisensory learning helps create that "uh-oh" feeling and helps them recall the strategies when they find themselves approached by a predator. And please view the video again and again as your child matures. As kids grow, they understand more and use different words, and you'll be able to explain more. The risks don't get any less as your child ages, so keep these lessons fresh in their minds.

Talking to Your Kids

The most important thing you can do to protect your children from predators is to teach them about it. Sometimes it's hard for moms to know what to say and what age is appropriate. Here is a great guideline from Mothers in Action to help you know when to talk to your children about sexual predators and what to tell them according to their age:

18 months	Teach your child the proper names for body parts. Predators use "cute" names to trick their victims.
3–5 years	Teach your child about "private parts" of the body and how to say no to people who are making him feel uncomfortable or making "bad touches." Give straightforward answers about sex. Teach your child modesty. Don't encourage nakedness and talk about what is appropriate in and out of the home.
5–8 years	Discuss safety away from home and the difference between being touched in private parts of the body (parts covered by a bathing suit) and other touching. Encourage your child to talk about scary experiences.
8–12 years	Stress personal safety and give examples of possible problem areas, such as video arcades, restrooms, malls, locker rooms, and out-of-the-way places outdoors. Start to discuss rules of sexual conduct that are accepted by the family.
13–18 years	Restress personal safety and potential problem areas. Discuss rape, date rape, sexually transmitted diseases, and unintended pregnancy.

Great Resources to Help Moms Talk to Kids

As we've said, one of our favorite resources can be found at www.goodknight.org. This organization offers a video that explains the ten psychological deceptions used by predators. It can be purchased with a $10 donation.

Another great video can be found at www.thesafeside.com. This video was created by Julie Clark, founder of the Baby Einstein Company, and John Walsh, host of *America's Most Wanted*. It gives parents simple, fun, and interesting ways to discuss difficult topics with their children. Following the Safe Side credo—"Smart. Cool. Safe"—children are empowered to make good decisions in potentially harmful situations. It costs about $15.

Signs of Sexual Abuse in Children

Be alert for these signs:

- Unusual interest in or avoidance of all things of a sexual nature. Watch for knowledge that is inappropriate for your child's developmental age.
- Sleep problems or nightmares, trouble sleeping alone or getting to sleep.
- Difficulty relaxing (irritable, panicky, jumpy, or clingy behavior).
- Depression or withdrawal from family or friends.
- Seductiveness or reenactments of molestation (usually in children under age six).

- Refusal to go to school or visit someone or somewhere that the child previously enjoyed. Watch for a child who pretends to be sick instead of going to church, school, athletic practices, etc.
- Aspects of sexual molestation in drawings, games, fantasies.
- Statements that their bodies are dirty or damaged, or a fear that there is something wrong with them in the genital area.
- Delinquency/conduct problems.
- Secretiveness.
- Unusual aggressiveness.
- Suicidal behavior.
- Regression in developmental stages—starting to wet the bed again or thumb sucking.

Sexual Abuse of Boys

The following information is from www.crisisconnectioninc.org.

> Boys can have a particularly tough time disclosing their abuse because our society tends to feminize victimization: to be a victim is to be powerless. The very adults the child needs to be able to trust and confide in (his parents) may be the very people who are perpetuating the myth that boys must be tough and that to be a man means to be strong. A boy is more likely to feel that he will not be believed if and when he does disclose abuse, because boys are often taught to keep their emotions hidden.
>
> Oftentimes the child victim is too young to recognize their victimization for what it is and/or to be able to put it into words. Know that the average age of a male child victim is only four. The fondling may feel good, similar to the warm feeling one derives from hugging and cuddling, and because of this the male victim must often later deal with confusion concerning his own sexual orientation,

"The sad, but simple truth is that we are not talking about sex, but the sexual abuse of a child: if I hit you over the head with a frying pan you probably wouldn't call it cooking. An adult male who abuses little girls is not engaging in heterosexual sexual behavior; he is sexually abusing little girls. The same is true when the victim is a little boy. The issues of anger, hostility, entitlement, and power are the same: the effects are equally harmful. The question, then, is not one of homosexuality or heterosexuality, but of the sexual abuse and its results on the child."

—www.crisisconnectioninc.org

not understanding or having been taught that molestation has nothing to do with the sexual orientation of either his perpetrator or himself.

Should the molester be a female, an older boy victim may meet with ridicule because he did not enjoy "scoring" on his initiation into "manhood." He is likely to be nauseated that his body was violated and used by a female he should have been able to respect and trust such as his mother, sister, grandmother, or teacher. Our society persists in teaching boys that men are the sexual aggressors. This archaic notion places a child victim of an older woman's sexual violation in a double bind. If it felt physically good then it couldn't have been abuse, but if it didn't feel good then the child must be a homosexual. The child is put in a no-win situation.

Sexual Abuse of Girls

Here's more from www.crisisconnectioninc.org:

> The statistics concerning the sexual abuse of girls are horrifying, yet the statistics don't even begin to tell the whole story. Girls are sexually abused at much higher rates than boys by family members, acquaintances, and strangers alike. There doesn't appear to be any difference what cultural heritage, economic level, or religious group the girl child comes from, the rates of abuse are staggering.
>
> The theory of "male entitlement" is believed to be particularly harmful for girls. Some men, including some fathers, feel entitled to use female children for their sexual enjoyment. The myth that some men use their daughters as replacements for indifferent wives has not been substantiated by research. Some men feel entitled to sexually use and abuse children simply because they choose to.
>
> Girls who are sexually abused tend to internalize their trauma as opposed to boys who tend to "act out" theirs. Girls oftentimes become withdrawn, depressed, develop eating disorders, self-mutilate, and engage in risky sexualized behaviors even at very young ages. Female victims will frequently begin viewing themselves as a value to others only as sexual objects, basing their self-worth solely upon being an object that will be abused by others. Their self-esteem can be totally destroyed because of the selfish and abusive choices of an adult. Girls commonly close off their feelings of terror, pain, and rage, intuitively understanding that they need to focus their energy on surviving. "Feeling" their true emotions can be a pain they may not be able to bear.
>
> If a girl perceives that she was not believed when she disclosed her abuse to adults, she may become very angry. Please remember that as a society we tend to be more comfortable with anger directed at females than at males. . . . Any feelings of disgust and nonviolent anger must be directed at the proper person,

the perpetrator, not at the victim. We teach our children to please adults, not to defy them: her abuser was an adult.

What to Do if You Suspect Abuse Has Occurred

So what's a mother to do when she does suspect that her child may have been sexually abused? Rule number one is to stay calm. Panicking is going to send the wrong message and may prevent your child from telling you the whole story. Also, you don't want to convey to your child that he or she is in trouble or has done something wrong. Freaking out is not going to help the situation. Ask your child open-ended questions (never plant ideas) and find out as much as you can as well as whether it's happened before. Don't call the authorities until you are sure something has happened.

If you are suspicious, contacting your child's pediatrician is probably the next best step. They are professionals who will know how to handle the situation and help you determine if there is cause for concern. They can provide support and counseling, and it can be easier for your child to talk about the situation with someone other than Mommy.

If you're having trouble deciding whether something did happen or not, or if your child is struggling to talk about it, we recommend the workbook that comes with the DVD we recommended from www.goodknight.org. There is a postevaluation test (which children take after viewing the video). This test is disguised as a fun activity book, but the answers your child provides will uncover the truth. Watching the video before completing the workbook will help your child understand the situation and help you make an accurate assessment.

If your child has been abused, don't be ashamed. You haven't done anything wrong—you and your child have both been victimized by a very bad person. Children should be able to live in this country without having to worry about sexual predators. It's infuriating that we have to even worry about something so sickening. Don't deny it because you are embarrassed. Face the issue and take charge of the situation. Report the abuse to your local child protection agency or to your local police. If you're just not sure what to do, call your local rape crisis center directly by calling the National Sexual Assault Hotline at 800-656-HOPE.

Your child needs you to stand up for her and make sure that it's not going to happen again. It's not going to go away by itself. And by keeping it to yourself, you are putting other children in danger too.

Online Predators

As they grow older, you need to think about how to keep your children safe on the Internet and phone.

How can you tell if your child is the target of an online predator?

It is possible that your child is being targeted by an online predator if:

- Your child or teen spends a great deal of time online. Most children who are victims of online predators spend a lot of time online, particularly in chat rooms. Children are especially vulnerable at night.
- You find pornography on the family computer. Predators often use pornography to sexually victimize children, supplying it to open sexual discussions with potential victims. Predators may use child pornography to convince a child that adults having sex with children is "normal." You should be aware that your child may hide pornographic files on disks or CDs, especially if other family members use the computer.
- Your child or teen receives phone calls from people you don't know, or makes calls (sometimes long-distance) to numbers you don't recognize. Online predators may try to contact young people to engage in "phone sex" or to try to set up a real-world meeting. If kids hesitate giving out their home phone number, online sex offenders will provide theirs. Some even have toll-free numbers so potential victims can call them without their parents' knowledge. Others will tell children to call collect, and then, with Caller ID, they can easily determine the phone number.
- Your child or teen receives mail, gifts, or packages from someone you don't know. It is common for offenders to send letters, photographs, and gifts to potential victims. Computer sex offenders even send airline tickets to entice a child or teen to meet them.
- Your child or teen withdraws from family and friends, or quickly turns the computer monitor off or changes the screen if an adult enters the room. Online predators work hard to drive wedges between kids and their families, often exaggerating minor problems at home. Sexually victimized children tend to become withdrawn and depressed.
- Your child is using someone else's online account. Even kids who don't have access to the Internet at home may meet an offender while online at a friend's house or the library. Predators sometimes provide victims with a computer account so they can communicate.

If You Suspect Your Child Is in Danger

- Regularly search the Internet history on every computer in your home, and don't be afraid to question the parents of other children your child may visit.
- Closely monitor chat rooms that your child may visit. Ninety percent of all initial contacts by sexual predators are made in Internet chat rooms. Monitor your child's access to all live electronic communications, instant messages, and e-mail.

- Do not allow your child to use a Web cam, digital camera, or video camera without your very close supervision.
- Monitor whom your child calls on the phone and who calls them. Often predators initiate phone contact after just a few Internet chats. Predators frequently send children prepaid phone cards to use so that calls cannot be detected on your phone bill or traced.
- Check your computer for pornographic files or any type of sexual communication. These are often warning signs.
- Never underestimate the persistence of a predator. These people are incredibly accommodating with potential victims and they are totally obsessed. If you are suspicious of any message your child receives, please don't hesitate to contact the Cyber Tipline at www.cybertipline.com. This site is operated by the not-for-profit National Center for Missing and Exploited Children. They will investigate your concern, report back to you, and contact the law enforcement agency in the appropriate jurisdiction. This is a free service!

Guidelines from the FBI: When to Contact Law Enforcement

Should any of the following situations arise in your household, you should immediately contact your local or state law enforcement agency, the FBI, and the National Center for Missing and Exploited Children.

- Your child or anyone in the household has received child pornography.
- Your child has been sexually solicited by someone who knows that your child is under eighteen years of age.
- Your child has received sexually explicit images from someone who knows your child is under the age of eighteen.

If one of these scenarios occurs, keep the computer turned off in order to preserve any evidence for future law enforcement use. Unless directed to do so by the law enforcement agency, you should not attempt to copy any of the images and/or text found on the computer. Internet predators are counting on your ignorance, so pay close attention and, again, be suspicious.

Kid-Safe Search Engines and Directories

A search engine is a site on the Internet that searches Web pages based on their titles, key words, or full text. Directories are similar to catalogs: sites are reviewed, selected, and categorized by age and interests and usually provide a range of other services. Many search engines and directories focus on kid-friendly information or filter out sites that are inappropriate for kids. Here is a list of some of the best on the Web. Encourage your kids to use these instead of the usual search engines. Make one of these your home page to make it easy for your kids to access.

Yahooligans!

http://yahooligans.yahoo.com

A kids' version of Yahoo!, this commercial directory only links to safe and appropriate kids' sites.

DibDabDoo

www.dibdabdoo.com

A noncommercial, fast search engine that only looks for adult-reviewed sites safe for children and teens. The site currently has about one million links in its database.

Ask Jeeves for Kids

www.ajkids.com

A unique commercial search engine that allows kids to search by using questions as well as key words.

Awesome Library

www.awesomelibrary.org

This noncommercial directory includes more than twenty thousand sites reviewed by educators. It has a translation service that lets visitors browse in several different languages.

Educational Software Directory

www.educational-software-directory.net

In this directory, volunteers have reviewed and organized more than twenty-three thousand sites into fourteen categories.

Great Websites for Kids

www.ala.org/Content/NavigationMenu/ALSC/Great_Web_Sites_for_Kids/Great_Web_Sites_for_Kids.htm

This American Library Association (ALA) directory includes links to online resources for fun and learning—all reviewed and organized by children's librarians.

KidsClick!

http://sunsite.berkeley.edu/KidsClick!

This noncommercial directory lists more than five thousand websites handpicked by librarians.

Canadian Kids Page

www.canadiankids.net/ck/default.jsp

Through this directory users can search hundreds of sites—particularly Canadian ones—by age and topic.

Clutter-Busting Resources

Center for Sex Offender Management
www.csom.org

Stop It Now
www.stopitnow.com

The Good Knight Child Empowerment Network
www.goodknight.org
With a small donation, you can order a video that teaches kids the ten psychological deceptions used by predators.

The Safe Side
www.thesafeside.com

Put in your zip code and see the predators who live near you:
www.familywatchdog.us
www.mapsexoffenders.com

National Center for Missing and Exploited Children
800-843-5678

Marriage

33

Husband Training

Get Him Involved Immediately

From Stephanie

We moms are so excited to finally bring baby home, we all fall into the trap of trying to do everything ourselves. This is one of those times when we women tend to be our own worst enemy. We're the ones doing the breast-feeding and the diaper changing and being the number one caregiver. So essentially, we train our husbands to stand back and watch us do the work. Any experienced mother will tell you that you simply must get your husband involved with caring for the baby from the minute you get home from the hospital. Let him do some of the bottle feedings, change diapers, and help with the laundry. There's no reason why a father shouldn't be helping with the nighttime feedings—lack of sleep is part of being a parent. Teach him or learn together. Dads need to be involved—it's good for them, it's good for the baby, and it's good for you too.

Sharing Your Brain

Sara and I often joke about a phrase we call "two people using your brain." This is because as soon as a baby enters your life, you will become the expert. Let me give you an example. One day my husband and I drove our kids to Florida on a trip. We stopped at a McDonald's drive-through for lunch. As soon as we got to the speaker, my husband turned to me and said, "What do they want?" (Like I'm supposed to read their minds?) I said, "I don't know. Can't you read the menu?" Of course that irritated him, but it's true. They were two and four at the time, which means they like something different every day. He's their father—can't *he* figure it out for a change?

Your brain will be used by every member of your family, whether you like it or not. And you'll respond to all their ridiculous questions, usually accurately, whether you like it or not. You'll know where everyone's shoes are (most of the time); where to find clean underwear; what condiments everyone prefers depending on the food that is being served; who is supposed to take what medicine, how much, and at what time; what little Johnny is supposed to bring for snack on Thursday; how many bowel movements baby's had since lunchtime; what time everyone is supposed to make it to ballet, karate, soccer, and baseball practice; the names of teachers, friends, and teammates . . . the list goes on and on. This is all information, however, that will completely elude your husband. In fact, he may not even remember that his son goes to preschool, and if you call your son's teacher or another child by her actual name, you'll have to follow that with "You know, Timmy's teacher" or "You know, Sara's friend we carpool with every day."

Your husband *can*, however, tell you useful things like who won the Super Bowl in 1992 and maybe even what the score was. I don't know why the world works this way—it just does. I can't fix it; I'm just telling you to expect it and accept it because you are powerless against it.

The rest of this chapter is designed for the man in your life to read by himself. We knew he'd be insulted and bored, so we added tips for having sex to keep him focused. Be sure to tell him that when you ask him to read this next section.

To the Fathers and Husbands of the World

Lesson 1: Don't Lose Interest

We women really don't want that much. We want you to appreciate us and tell us so. Show your appreciation by not walking away in the middle of our sentences. When we're telling you something, please look interested (even if you're not). When we were dating, you were interested in everything we had to say. You were interested in *us*. Don't lose interest.

Lesson 2: Touch Us When Sex Isn't the Goal

Touch us during the daytime when you're not thinking about sex. For you, sex is physical. For women, it's emotional. We don't *need* sex. You have to make us *want* sex. And when I say "touch" I don't mean grab, poke, pinch, or goose. I mean hug or kiss your wife. Kiss her like they do in the movies, with one hand on her face or her neck (we love that). Give her a squeeze and tell her how much you appreciate her or something she's done for you or the kids lately. Moms don't get performance appraisals or raises, so we love to hear that someone thinks we're doing a good job.

Lesson 3: Do Something Nice Regularly

Do something nice for us at least once a week. It doesn't have to cost money. Wash or vacuum our car; bring us a cup of our favorite coffee or a muffin from the local bakery for breakfast; if you went to a restaurant for lunch, bring us a nice dessert; put the kids to bed (without being asked); surprise us by bringing dinner home or cooking it yourself; write us a note or find a photo of when we were dating and remind us how much fun it was when it was just the two of us.

Women work so hard at home to keep things in order and keep kids healthy and happy. As a career woman, I had a nice title and a six-figure income, and I can tell you that I never worked as hard at my corporate job as I do now that I'm a mom. I can't explain it, but it's true. So honor your wife every chance you get because no one else will.

Lesson 4: How to Get Laid by Your Wife

Here are six surefire things you can do to get what you want:

1. "Honey, I know you've had a busy week. Here's twenty bucks—go get a pedicure while I watch the kids." (Oh yeah—that's hot.)
2. "You look tired, honey. Here, I printed out the movie listings from your favorite theater. Why don't you call one of your girlfriends and catch a movie tonight? I'll give the kids their baths and get them to bed." (Note: Do this *before* 2:00 P.M. so she has time to plan and scrape the Play-Doh from under her fingernails.)
3. "I know you love the kids and you're such a great mom, but I also know they can really be annoying. Why don't you go run some errands or go to the mall for a few hours? I'll take care of the kids so you can get a break."
4. "I'm taking you out to dinner tomorrow night, and I've already handled scheduling a babysitter. Be ready at seven." (Then help her get the kids ready that night so she can just have fun getting dressed for your night out.)
5. "I know you're tired. Why don't you sleep in tomorrow morning and I'll get the kids up and make breakfast?"
6. Say one or more of the below, in combination or on the same day. (Note: We've already taught your wife that you're too stupid to figure out what needs to be done on your own and that she has to *ask* you for help, so these should do the trick.)

- "Is there some laundry I can help you with?"
- "Is there anything you need me to do?"

- "I have my tool kit out. Is there anything you want me to fix?"
- "I'll cook dinner tonight. What do you think about grilled chicken?" (We love it when we don't have to plan or cook dinner.)
- "I took the trash out—from every room in the house."
- "I cleaned up the toy room for the kids. Boy, they make a mess. How do you deal with that every day?"
- "I had your car washed and vacuumed for you today, and the oil changed too."
- "Hey, let's take the kids to a restaurant tonight so you don't have to worry about dinner. You choose which one."

Lesson 5: For Fathers Who Travel

A "wise" man (ahem) once instructed me that I should always have sex with my husband the night he returns from a trip. This was a man who had no children, and his advice was very unrealistic. Do not come home expecting sex or anything else for that matter.

When you return from a trip, there's a 98 percent chance that your wife is probably on her last nerve. She hasn't had a lunch break or room service; in fact, every time she sat down to eat, someone interrupted her meal: "Mommy, I wanted ketchup" (or worse, "Mommy I *didn't* want ketchup!"), "Mommy, my food is too hot. Will you blow on it?" "Mommy, will you cut my meat?" or "Mommy, I want more!" (Before she's even taken her first bite.) No one has made her bed; in fact, she's made beds for herself and at least two other people every day this week, and probably changed and washed pee-stained sheets at least once. She hasn't had time to sit down even to eat lunch. And she's tired of people wanting things from her. So don't be one of those people.

When you return from a trip, realize that you have some catching up to do. Help with the kids or with some of the housework. Yes, you're tired from traveling and she's tired from being a single parent. It's not easy being outnumbered. Here are a few tips for making your homecoming more enjoyable for both of you:

- Tell her how nice the house looks (even if it doesn't).
- Telling her that you missed her isn't enough. Women need proof. We don't fall for the lines that worked on those college girls at the bar back in the day. We have experience—we're smarter now and we need more than words. *Show* her that you missed her. Bringing her something back from your trip tells her that you thought about her. It doesn't have to be expensive, or even cost money at all. A seashell, a note, something chocolate—just think: what does she appreciate?
- Come home with the intention of doing something nice for *her* (not for *you*). Too many dads come home thinking they deserve to have sex because they've

been out earning a living. Remember that she's been busy from morning till night protecting and maintaining and nurturing your most valuable assets, your family and your home.

I know you've heard the old adage "When Mama ain't happy, ain't nobody happy." Well, it's true. If you can consistently do some of the things we've mentioned, your wife will be happy and that happiness will trickle down to you and the kids. But it all starts with you, so don't waste another minute in letting her know how much you love and appreciate her. Marriage isn't that different from your job, except that on your job you don't get to have sex. Concentrate on your marriage, act to make it better and more enjoyable, and anticipate what's going to happen next. The more you put into it, the more you'll get back.

Clutter-Busting Resources

Porn for Women
by Susan Anderson
(Relax, it's a book about what women *really* want . . . and you will laugh your head off.)

34

Sex After Kids

Does It Exist?

Sleep or sex? It's funny how your priorities change after you become a mom. A lot of mothers experience a decrease in their desire for sex after having children. How many times have you heard one of your girlfriends say, "I've had people pulling and touching me all day long—I just want to be left alone"? Taking care of the kids all day, preparing meals, shuttling them to karate and ballet lessons, and negotiating all their disputes can take a lot out of a gal. Sometimes sex just feels like one more thing we have to do for someone else.

Stephanie and Her Bicycle

Here's the best way I can explain what happened to my sex drive after I became a mother. It's like when you're a little kid and you learn to ride a bike. All you want to do every day is ride your bike. You *love* riding your bike. When you're not riding your bike, you're thinking about riding your bike. And once you learn how to ride a bike, you never forget. But then you start a family. And now you don't really want to ride your bike anymore. You don't have the time or the energy to ride your bike. But it's still nice to know the bike is there waiting for you in the garage, just in case you need it.

Frankly, I get tired of hearing all the commercials for Viagra and Cialis. We don't need any more drugs that help men have sex. In fact, I've figured out a way to solve many of the world's problems: what we need is a drug that makes men want to have sex *less.* And then everything would be equal.

My question is, why are women almost always the ones to blame for not being interested in sex? Because here's the thing: our partner's actions and attitudes and levels of involvement have everything to do with whether we feel sexual or not. Before the children came along, they noticed us. We felt more connected to them, because they acted as if they understood how we were feeling. And now . . . Just the other day, I was trying to hang a picture over the stairs. I lost my balance and took a nasty tumble down a flight of stairs with the picture frame in hand. I wasn't hurt. But my husband found me lying at the bottom of the stairs covered in pieces of glass, asked me if I was okay, then proceeded to step over me and walk up the stairs to continue on with his business while I lay there covered in glass.

I think that fathers get distracted with the kids too, and they forget what their wives really want and need in order to feel close to them. And it's so ironic because, as their wives and as the mothers of their children, we're doing more for them now than we've ever done for anyone else before. Let's face it: at least in college I'd get a nice dinner and a few compliments first.

Sara: "Help Me Help You, Jerry"

Amen, sister. After two kids and thirteen years of marriage, my husband's idea of foreplay is turning off ESPN and rolling over. But as tempting as it might be, we moms can't blame our dwindling love lives completely on our guys not romancing us like they used to. (Don't worry—they'll *never* read this, so you don't have to be concerned about me cluing them in that they aren't responsible.) Some of this fatigue is just to be expected when a couple's been together for a long time. Just the other day, David told me that my legs "looked good from the knee down," and he truly thought he was giving me a compliment. He would have never said something like that while we were dating, but living together for years through the highs and lows and mostly in-betweens of everyday life has eroded any sort of formality that ever existed between us.

It takes effort and a lot of planning to keep things new and interesting, and who has the energy for that when they have a baby or small child at home? It's tough for both working moms and stay-at-home moms. Working moms want to spend every moment they can with their kids when they get home, plus take care of all that needs doing at home in the few hours they have. And they're really tired from work.

At-home moms have been with their kids all day. That means they probably haven't been able to eat, go to the bathroom, make a phone call, or accomplish even the smallest task without someone interrupting them, whining, crying, or fighting in the background. And they're really tired from all the work they've been doing.

So when the kids are in bed, the house is finally quiet, and you have a few precious moments before it's time to call it a night, what you want is some you time! You want to read the paper (finally), or watch the show you TiVo'd three weeks ago, or talk to your sister on the phone. Whatever you want to do, you really don't feel like taking care of someone else for another second, because this is the first minute you've had to yourself all day.

What we need here is some help. We need to drop the "I'm supermom and I can do it all" ideal and let (or force) Dad to pitch in. It's up to us to make them understand that if they help out and give us some time to ourselves to regain our sanity (and I'm not talking once a week here), they themselves will reap the rewards. Help me help you, Jerry.

But it's up to us to communicate this effectively. Without yelling. Because this is our marriage we're talking about. The kids will leave the nest eventually and we'll have to be a couple again. And I have to admit that when I am more accommodating to my husband's needs and he's not cranky, life in general is a lot easier. Though in reality I can talk a good game but I'm not always good at following through on the action part, if you know what I mean. In fact, my husband says I've perfected the Heisman Trophy move (you know, with the strong right-arm thrust)—in bed. The point is, we all have to keep making the effort. Me included.

You're Not Alone

About 80 percent of women experience a loss of libido in the first year after childbirth, and often it's difficult to ever fully get that desire back. Low sex drive affects one out of every three couples. It's the most common sexual problem among mothers.

Part of the problem is that while yours fluctuates, your partner's sex drive usually stays exactly the same. Your hormones have just made a shift from mating to nurturing. It's almost impossible for him to imagine how you're feeling. And the scenario usually goes a little something like this: The new mom is exhausted from taking care of the baby and her hormones have been on a roller-coaster ride, neither of which lends itself to feeling sexual. She may also begin to feel let down or distant from her partner because the children take so much of her time and energy. Unfortunately, the father is still just as interested in sex as ever. And while he misses the sex, the main problem is that he begins to feel that his partner doesn't care enough about him to approach him as a lover. He sees her going out of her way to please the children but doesn't understand why she no longer has the desire to meet his sexual needs. The woman begins to tense up every time her husband touches her because she's afraid it will lead to sex, so she begins to send signals that she doesn't want to be touched or kissed. Sound familiar?

The solution is to try not to take these changes personally. Having children changes everything about a relationship: the workload, the responsibility, the emotional environment, the financial risks, and more. Try to have empathy for each other. Make affection a part of

A Common Problem

Studies suggest that almost half of women in the United States suffer from some type of sexual dysfunction, with low libido (or sex drive) at the top of the list.

everyday life. Mention how much you appreciate what your partner is doing to contribute to the family. And men, be sure to touch her, affectionately and *nonsexually,* several times a day. (For the record, that doesn't mean pinching her in the butt when she bends over.)

So How Many Times per Week Is Normal?

This is a question that only you can answer. It's different for everyone. Most couples say it's one or two times per week; some say one or two times per month. You and your husband need to discuss what expectations each of you has and come to a conclusion. Establishing a number is a delicate thing. Your partner needs to understand that you aren't "required" to have sex that many times per week. If you feel pressured or required to have sex, you'll begin to resent it.

Men feel more intimate with and connected to their partners when they have sex. Women feel more like having sex when they feel emotionally connected. So it's a vicious cycle. As Billy Crystal said in *City Slickers,* "Women need a reason . . . men just need a place."

Why Do We Lose Our Libido?

Hormones play a critical role. Changes in hormones can be brought on by stress, lack of sleep, and just plain feeling overwhelmed. These changes mean lower testosterone levels (yes, in women) and less sex drive. It is perfectly normal for you to want less sex after becoming a mother.

Your age can be a factor because of the many changes that occur to your body during the aging process. Menopause and hormone deficiencies can cause a lack of interest in sex. Some women may have had a bad experience with sex in the past. And relationship problems and just plain boredom can also contribute.

In rare cases, there are medical reasons why women just aren't interested in sex. If your lack of libido is causing problems in your relationship, you should consult your doctor. Your doctor can help determine the root of the problem and prescribe the right treatment for you.

Antidepressants

No one's really talking about it, but we all know it. Lots of us moms are on antidepressants. And it's well documented that many of these drugs do have a negative effect on sex drive. If this is something you are concerned about, talk with your doctor. You may be able to change to a medication that doesn't impact your libido.

Four People Who Can Sabotage Your Sex Life

It's hard to believe, but there are a lot of things that change the way we feel about sex. Consider these four influences that might significantly impact your sexuality:

1. **Your parents.** Their attitudes toward sex will ultimately affect yours.
2. **Your ex.** Almost all of us have an ex looming in the back of our minds who made us feel bad about our sexuality or the way we look.
3. **Movie stars.** They portray sex in an unrealistic way, so the real thing rarely measures up to the perfection we see on the big screen.
4. **Your friends.** Listening to your friends talk about how wonderful their love life is can make you feel below par.

Keeping the Home Fires Burning

- Make sure your partner understands that you need help getting the chores done, so you're not so tired when you finally do get a chance to fool around. If he thinks it means there's a chance of a reward, he'll gladly help out. You will never feel sexual if you are too exhausted from trying to do everything yourself.
- Exercise can increase your sex drive by making you feel better about your appearance and by releasing hormones that give libido a lift.
- Most moms are reluctant to sacrifice sleep for sex. But try to focus on all the reasons you used to like sex, and give it a try. You'll like it again. Sex is calming, it helps you sleep more soundly, and it actually boosts your immune system. See? It's good for you . . . just like vegetables.
- A change in scenery can be a big help on the sexual front. Ship the kids off to Grandma's for a weekend and try to get away from your normal life. Check into a hotel, sleep naked, or try something different that you've always wanted to try.
- The chance that it's a physical reason is rare but always a possibility. So if you're trying and just not having any success, talk to your doctor. Sometimes the problems are hormonal. Birth control pills have been known to lessen libido. And your doctor may be able to help you identify what's really going on.

Clutter-Busting Resources

WEBSITES

Jennifer Berman, M.D., women's sexual health expert
www.bermansexualhealth.com

His and Her Health: Information About Sexuality, Prostate, Incontinence
www.hisandherhealth.com

Women to Women: Changing Women's Health Naturally
www.womentowomen.com

BOOKS

Reclaiming Desire: 4 Keys to Finding Your Lost Libido
by Andrew Goldstein, M.D., and Marianne Brandon, Ph.D.

I'm Not in the Mood: What Every Woman Should Know About Improving Her Libido
by Judith Reichman, M.D.

Secrets of the Sexually Satisfied Woman: Ten Keys to Unlocking Ultimate Pleasure
by Laura Berman, Ph.D., and Jennifer Berman, M.D.

35

Marriage 911

From Sara

When you become a parent, life is never the same again, and that includes your marriage. A baby means bye-bye freedom, hello responsibility. Gone are the days of spontaneously grabbing a bottle of wine and heading out for a picnic. Now a picnic has to be scheduled precisely in between naps and requires an hour of packing baby gear before you leave and an hour of unpacking after you get home. When a couple of years down the road you have a baby and a toddler, you doubt there is any possibility of the picnic being worth the effort and aggravation, so you stay at home. Life is less about the two of you and more about the kids. This is not necessarily bad; it's just how it is.

On the other hand, nothing cements your marriage like children. Even though your spouse may annoy you more than ever, the reasons for staying together are more important than ever too. I remember one night when David and I were driving to a restaurant with the kids and we were in a disagreement about something (I can't for the life of me remember what now). The kids were oblivious to our conversation, and out of the blue one of them said something hilarious—and it was the kind of humor from your kids that only you, as parents, get. David and I stopped talking and just looked at each other, somehow knowing that each of us was the only other person on the planet who would also think what our child just said was so funny. We both burst out laughing. We had been in the middle of a pretty heated debate, but that laughter reconnected us in an instant, reminding us both that even when we disagree, we have a bond that is always there.

Being parents connects you in a way nothing else can. But at the same time it exhausts you and sucks up every second of free time you once took for granted. We become so busy as parents that we no longer have the time (or the energy) to be a couple. It's easy to get in a rut and start taking each other and our marriage for granted. Very easy. Guilty as charged. David has even told me that I give *way* more to the kids than I do to him. Of course I do, I tell him. They're cuter and sweeter and they can't make their own meals and fold their own clothes. They need me more. Even still, I get the point. He needs me too.

When it comes to marriage, all the moms we've talked to and all the books we've read have shown us that we all have the same basic complaints. Do any of these sound familiar?

- How can we get them to help out more?
- He's a super dad but he's a rotten husband.
- My husband is a cheapskate.
- We have nothing in common anymore.
- He doesn't hear me when I talk.

It Takes Two to Tango (or Not)

Getting into a rut is never all one partner's fault. It takes two people to let things slide into a boring routine. Dads have to step up if they want their wives to have the time and energy for their relationship. Pick up the phone and call a sitter. Make a dinner reservation. Spend some one-on-one time with your wife. And Mom, your baby will be fine with a sitter for a few hours.

Guys, if you want your woman to have some energy left over at the end of the day, you'd better pitch in and start washing some dishes, making some dinner, and folding some laundry. And here's a novel idea for you men: *look around and see what needs to be done.* I know this concept is revolutionary to you, but you see, we women don't like having to tell you to do everything. We feel like we are nagging even though we are just stating the obvious.

But, alas, I am living in a fantasy world. We *have* to tell them. We always have to tell them. I don't know why but they don't see the room the way we see the room. We see the mess; they see the couch. One night not long ago, after putting the kids to bed and cleaning the kitchen, I walked into our bedroom to find David lying *on top of* the clean laundry (I had dumped it on the bed) watching a football game. I thought, *You have* got *to be kidding me.* Apparently there was a moment of divine intervention because I didn't say anything or even try to do him bodily harm. I simply started folding the laundry, which meant yanking it out from under him as he continued to watch football. Finally he got the hint. It was so ridiculous, he even laughed at himself. Not only was it too much effort to fold the laundry while watching the game, it was more than he could muster to actually move the clothes off the bed or even slide them over to the other side, so he just plopped down on top of them. Honestly, it's a miracle I have lived with this man for thirteen years without smothering him in his sleep. Since that night, I have gotten him to take over his own laundry duties. He now fully understands if you are lounging on top of clean unfolded laundry while watching TV, *nobody* is going to be doing the tango in this house. And I have learned that communication and humor, though they don't compare in terms of instant gratification, are in the long run more effective than violence.

Making Deals

Let's face it: men are never going to *want* to help us or be able to figure it out for themselves. He can't do his 50 percent all the time. So how do we ask without it becoming an argument? Carolyn Bushong says, "We have to make deals with them. They have to be deals that are extremely fair to us. Men like deals. For example: 'There's a batch of clothes that need to be folded. If you'll fold the clothes, I'll start dinner.' I will do this if you will do that."

The other problem women always mention is that things don't get done, even though we've asked and they've agreed. Carolyn says that we must have a plan that includes a timeline. Make a list of all the chores that have to be done and let him choose which ones he wants to do each week. Let him know that together, you'll reevaluate on Saturday mornings to make sure that everything gets done. (See Chapter 36 for more information on parenting as a team.)

If jobs aren't done, then there have to be consequences. It's not that you're disciplining your husband, but there has to be a consequence for not completing what he's agreed to. For example, "Will you fix the kitchen faucet by Wednesday? If you think you can't get it done by Wednesday, I'll call a plumber and we'll pay for it."

Why Don't They Hear Us?

There is new research that claims that women's voices are more difficult for men to listen to than the voices of other men. Because of the size and shape of a woman's vocal cords, the female voice is more complex than the male voice. A woman's voice has more sound frequencies, and processing it requires more brainpower. So maybe that could be part of the problem. Maybe.

There are also physiological differences in our brains that make men worse listeners. It's just biology—they can't help it. It all starts with testosterone soon after conception. About six weeks after conception, male embryos experience a "bath" of testosterone, which alters the male brain by damaging nerve fibers that join the left and right hemispheres of the brain. Men have fewer of these fibers, limiting the number of electrical transmissions that can flow from one side of the brain to the other. That's why men have trouble sorting out their feelings and why women are typically more articulate and more in touch with their thoughts and emotions.

But the real reason men don't hear us is simple—it's because we talk too much. We nag and talk and whine so much that men have learned to let it go in one ear and out the other and don't pay attention to us most of the time. Sometimes men whose mothers nagged and talked a lot are already programmed from childhood to tune us out.

Making Them Listen

From Stephanie

Sara gets frustrated because it seems David never remembers anything she's told him about their schedule. Author and relationship expert Carolyn Bushong advised her to follow up the comment with something that ensures that he's listening. For example, "John and Suzy are coming over Friday night. Do you want to put that in your calendar, or should I put a Post-it note on the fridge for you?" When you ask him to respond or act, it can help make the message stick. Too much of our conversation is in passing and just doesn't sink in. So make your conversations count. Try checking in with him first: "Honey, can you hear me?" Then tell him what you need him to know. I like to check in after my statement, like this: "I need you to pick Timmy up from school on Thursday because I have to go to a program at Sara's school. Are you okay with that?"

My husband has a really bad habit of walking away while I'm talking to him. Not only is it insulting, it's usually a sure sign that he didn't hear a word I said. So I ask him to please stand still and look at me. Eye contact seems to help get the message into their brains. (Yes, they have them too.)

Remember that couples have to work as a team, so instead of being disgusted about an ongoing problem, try to figure out what works for you and fix it. Maybe you have to do a little extra by writing a reminder note for him or sending him an e-mail. Those little extras can make a big difference in solving these communication problems.

Our family has a community calendar where we write everything and I mean *everything:* when bills are due, when paychecks are expected, appointments, flight schedules, ball games, practices, etc. The rule is that if it's not on the calendar, it doesn't count. If my husband forgets to write his trip or appointment down and I've already scheduled something for that night, then he's in charge of finding a babysitter.

My Husband Is a Cheapskate

The most common problem in marriage is money issues. Women have a different relationship with money than men (you can learn more about this in Chapter 37, "Moms and Money"). Money issues are often most challenging for moms who left their careers to raise children. When you were working, you could spend whatever you could afford of your own money, but now you're depending on someone else to supply the income, and you may get criticized for spending it. Women really get the shaft on this deal because we're the ones buying all the groceries, school supplies, medical services, birthday presents, and clothing to make sure that day-to-day life runs smoothly. Of course we are going to spend more on a daily basis than dads are!

"When my husband comes home, if the kids are still alive, I figure I've done my job."

—Roseanne Barr

Baby Is Not Just Mom's Job

If you choose to be a stay-at-home mom, it does not mean that the baby is your responsibility twenty-four hours a day.

Often, when husbands get home from work, moms are standing at the door waiting for him to relieve her on the baby front. The problem is that he's tired from working and commuting and is ready to relax. This often causes a fight. So try this solution. "Okay, honey. You know I'm at home with the baby all day long, and I know you need a half hour or so to unwind when you get home from work. After thirty minutes, I want you to take the baby, and two nights a week, I want you to take the baby for the whole evening so I can have some time alone." He needs to understand that your work is hard too—you're not at home eating bonbons all day. After work hours, the work has to be shared. That's what being a parent means.

Simple Ways to Keep the Love Alive

- **Give compliments.** Make sure you let your spouse know you still find him (or her) attractive. Show him that you still admire him and appreciate his hard work in supporting and protecting the family.
- **Spend ten minutes together daily.** You wouldn't think having ten minutes a day to talk to each other would be that difficult, but when you are busy parents, you need to make a point of setting this time aside to talk alone together each day. Make this a positive time to reconnect. Don't talk about problems or frustrations during this time. Talk about what you want to accomplish that day or what happened yesterday. Take a quick walk together if you can. Spend a few minutes together outside, having a glass of wine together after dinner.
- **Plan a regular date night.** Hire a sitter as often as you can (preferably once a week) and devote an evening to each other. If you can't hire a babysitter, consider taking turns babysitting with friends and neighbors.
- **Get away for a weekend.** Spend a weekend together with no kids, no TV, no Internet, no chores, and no work from the office to distract you from each other. Make this a time just for the two of you. Talk about good memories, future dreams, current concerns and fears. And have fun together!
- **Write an e-mail.** Talking about sensitive issues can be difficult. Some couples we know prefer working out these types of issues via e-mail. Writing down your

thoughts and emotions forces you to collect your thoughts before writing. You and your spouse will also have more time to comprehend what is bugging each of you because you are reading each other's thoughts. E-mailing can also keep a discussion from escalating into an argument. (Just don't type in all caps.)

- **Make plans for your future together.** Ask yourselves if you are living the way you want to live. If not, do some brainstorming about strategies to get yourselves to where you want to be—emotionally, financially, physically. What goals do you have for yourselves as individuals, as a couple, and as a family? Make specific plans for achieving those goals.
- **Do something new.** Try a new sport or hobby together. Take a cooking class or dance class together. Watch a television show or movie you haven't seen. Play a new card or board game. You'll likely learn something new about your partner and connect in a new way.
- **Maintain physical contact.** Always kiss and hug as much as possible. Not only is it vital for you, it's important that your kids see this physical evidence of your love for each other.
- **Communicate.** Try to make time every day to discuss what's happening in your lives. You may talk all the time, but do you really sit down and hear each other out on all the issues going on? Or do you let them build and blow up? Write love notes that are short and simple.
- **Nurture your individual interests.** Each partner needs time to enjoy hobbies or passions that are important to them. Time apart as well as together is vital. Balance the time you spend together with the time you spend as a family and the time you spend apart.
- **Don't nag.** If you have a problem or need something addressed right now, instead of nagging, try to communicate better. Ask him nicely to do something, instead of demanding that he do it.
- **Show respect.** Never berate your mate in public, in front of family, your children, or anyone else. If you have a problem, discuss it privately and rationally. Yelling and pointing out faults only drives a person away.
- **Pay attention to the little things.** It's all about the little things. They are what matter most. If you're the first one up in the morning, bring your spouse a hot cup of coffee in bed. Give your partner a card just to tell him you love him. Buy him tickets to the game when his favorite team is playing. Treat her to a pedicure. Take time to consider the little things that make your spouse happy and try to do those things.
- **Rekindle the romance.** Remember how it was before you had children? Make an

"Marriage is not just spiritual communion, it is also remembering to take out the trash."

—Dr. Joyce Brothers

effort to rekindle that feeling. Be attentive and romantic with each other. Light candles, put on romantic music, and dance in the living room. Give each other a massage. Show each other that your relationship is still just as worth the effort now as it was when you were dating.

What Husbands Want from Their Wives

Based on a plethora of unscientific research we conducted among our husbands and their friends, here is what the guys told us they *really* want from their wives. We found some of their answers quite surprising and bet you will, too.

- **Confidence.** Your attitude about his job, his success, and his failures plays a bigger role in how he feels about himself than you may realize. Our guys' egos are often more fragile than they let on. Let him know you believe in him and have confidence in him, even when he makes an occasional mistake.
- **Trust.** Guys need time with other guys. Let him know you trust him by giving him the freedom and space to have some male-bonding time. If you feel there are legitimate reasons you can't trust him, talk to a counselor, but don't spy on him or nag him.
- **A little peace and quiet.** Don't nag to get your husband's attention, or he'll just tune you out or get very irritated. Find another way to get through to him—a note, an e-mail. Try to wait for the right moment to talk (not when the game is on), and remember that guys simply don't need to chat as much as we women do.
- **Respect.** Don't make negative comments about him in front of others (this is one we both admit we need to work on!). Be considerate of his interests and understand that while owning ten fishing poles may seem silly to you, owning ten purses seems just as ridiculous to him.
- **Physical intimacy.** No surprise here. Where sex is a desire for women, for men it's a need. As Billy Crystal once said, "Women need a reason, men just need a place." Women can reconnect through talking and just being together, men feel connected to their wives through physical intimacy. It's one of the most important parts of the relationship for them, and it's hard for other components of your relationship to click if this part isn't working.
- **Don't Spend Money Carelessly.** Money is the thing most couples fight about more than anything else. The only solution is communication. Take the time to sit down together with bank statements and a calculator and create a budget that you both agree on. You will both have to make sacrifices, and you'll have to watch out for the little daily items that add up. Always discuss larger purchases and make it a point to talk about it daily. Try to be businesslike, not emotional,

when discussing money. And no matter how tight money is, reserve some to spend on your relationship.

- **Ask Nicely.** Stephanie's husband tells her to "Ask without making it sound like an insult." It's so easy to get into the habit of speaking to your husband like you do to your children: "I've asked you three times to please take out the trash, why is it still here?" Be respectful and use manners when speaking to your spouse. And by the way, if you're struggling over household chores, a good housekeeper costs a lot less than a marriage counselor and has saved just as many marriages.
- **Companionship.** Men want their wives to participate in activities with them, to share at least one or two hobbies. They want to be able to have fun with you doing the things they love doing because it's how they build friendship.
- **Appreciation and acknowledgment.** Men want and need to be appreciated for what they do for the family. We know, we know, we moms don't get appreciation and acknowledgment for a tenth of the things we do, but we manage to do okay without it. Men have a harder time. They need their wives to acknowledge their efforts in making money, helping out around the house—whatever they do to help make the household run.
- **Be a companion.** Your husband is not only your lover, but your friend. Staying friends and companions through the years requires that you find ways to make time together and to do things together.

Clutter-Busting Resources

WEBSITES

Carolyn Bushong, relationship expert
www.carolynsays.com

Marriage Builders
www.marriagebuilders.com

The Marriage Toolbox
www.marriagetools.com

Smart Marriages: The Coalition for Marriage, Family, and Couples Education
www.smartmarriages.com

BOOKS

Bring Back the Man You Fell in Love With
by Carolyn Bushong

Date Night in a Minivan: Revving Up Your Marriage After Kids Arrive
by Lorilee Craker

Babyproofing Your Marriage: How to Laugh More and Argue Less as Your Family Grows
by Stacie Cockrell

36

Parenting as a Team

From Sara

Parenting is no longer "women's work." Fathers play a larger role in their children's lives than ever. To me, there was no better evidence of this than recently when I watched Tiger Woods and his daughter after he won yet another major golf tournament. Tiger's wife came to congratulate him, their daughter, Sam, in her arms. But as soon as Sam spotted her daddy she stretched out her arms, leaning away from Mom and reaching for her father. That one little moment made it obvious that Tiger is a very involved dad. I thought about how times have changed. Here is one of the most well-known men on the planet, a perfect picture of male athletic ability (as one of my male friends says admiringly, "He's a bad-ass mofo"), who can't help but break into a goofy smile as he holds his little girl on national television. Oh, and by the way, dads: if Tiger Woods has time to be an involved dad, so do you.

As great as it is that dads are stepping up to the parenting plate now, it's created some issues for us moms. We all want the men in our lives to do their part with the child rearing, but that means letting them do it their way, which (c'mon, admit it) is hard. I've cringed when my husband took our then two-year-old daughter to a birthday party wearing a sweatshirt and jeans. (That was such a perfect opportunity to wear that cute little pink outfit with the matching hair bow!) He wrapped the gift and wrote the *To:* and *From:* right on the wrapping paper with permanent black marker. (But I have all those cute little "From Your Friend Anna" stickers!) There was no ribbon, just a roughly wrapped package with black marker writing on it. I started to protest, but he stopped me in my tracks and said, "Let me do it my way." He was right. Even though the sight of her leaving dressed that way, hair hanging bowless in her face, was downright painful, I took a few deep breaths and let it go.

Dads aren't moms. They aren't supposed to do everything like us. Kids learn different things from their fathers, and it's important that we moms don't get in the way of that. So what if the hair isn't exactly neat (a rat's nest), the clothes aren't perfectly clean (grape juice stain on the front), or they ate a less than nutritious breakfast (there are eggs in chocolate cake, after all). For us moms, this is a lesson in letting go of control. If we want our men to take part, we can't criticize their every move—unless of course they are putting our child in danger (which sometimes with my husband is not out of the realm of possibility). And we moms have to admit that we get a little superiority trip when Dad screws something up royally. We feel gratified with the evidence that we are better at this parenting stuff than they are. And it's so much fun to laugh about their ineptness with our mom friends. (Stephanie and I like to call our tales "Stupid Husband Stories"—and boy, do we have some humdingers between the two of us, or should I say, the two of *them.*)

Parenting together, or co-parenting, is an important concept in families now. Mom and Dad likely grew up with different styles of parenting, and we both bring our ideas to the table. Sometimes those ideas clash and we need to find a resolution. We also need to support each other and present a united front to the children. Otherwise, they will divide and conquer. When we can work together as parents, sharing the work and responsibility of raising kids, the children benefit and we the parents benefit because we can accomplish so much more than we could otherwise. Sharing the emotional and physical work of parenthood creates happier, healthier moms and dads.

Keep the Rules Consistent

Dad and Mom may do things differently, but the rules must stay the same. Dad can't allow the kids to watch a television show that Mom doesn't. Mom can't let the kids jump on the couch if Dad doesn't. Rules and boundaries must be agreed on between the parents and enforced equally.

Ideally, parents should agree on how you are going to discipline your kids ahead of time, before the situation arises. If parents argue about discipline in front of the child, the child will assume that one parent is taking his side and the other is not. Or he will simply ignore both of you, continue his bad behavior, and leave you to argue between yourselves.

Get Dad Involved from the Start

Encourage Dad to get involved from the moment the baby is born. If you are breastfeeding, pump occasionally so that Dad can also feed the baby. If you are bottle-feeding,

> "The typical dad spends 6.5 hours a week with his children, under an hour a day, and far less time than the typical mom spends. Still, that's more than double the 2.6 hours weekly that men devoted to their families 30 years ago."
>
> —*Parents* magazine, June 2008

ask Dad to do half of the feedings. Talk to him about schedules, encourage him to go to pediatrician visits, and ask him to be involved in each new part of baby's life, whether it's starting solid foods or adopting a new nap schedule. As soon as you are able, leave the baby alone with Dad for a few hours. He'll learn to do things his own way and gain confidence getting baby to eat and sleep. Don't take over all the responsibilities yourself because you assume you are better at it. Give Dad a chance to learn and bond with his child. You'll also be setting the foundation for shared child-raising responsibilities in the years to come.

See the Benefits

Shared parenting makes sense on many levels. If one parent is doing all the work, she will get burned out and become resentful. And the kids will only get the benefit of one parent's way of doing things and seeing the world. When parenting is a joint responsibility, dads become more involved in their kids' lives, which only helps the kids, and moms get a break and get to maintain a life of their own, whether it's working, volunteering, or spending time with friends or on a hobby. Everyone in the family will be happier and there will be less tension between the parents.

Make a List of Responsibilities

If you want the household duties to be shared equitably, you have to negotiate that between the two of you. Start by making a list of what needs to get done on a weekly, biweekly, and monthly basis. Make sure to list everything from cooking meals and driving carpool to watering the plants and walking the dog. Beside each task, write down how long that task will take. Divide tasks equally by the amount of time they take. In other words, although one partner's list may look longer, each list should add up to the same amount of time. Some tasks may need to be done by both parents, and some may be more enjoyable to one parent than the other. That's where the negotiation comes in. Sit down together after the kids have gone to bed and work out an arrangement of shared responsibilities that works for both of you. (Make sure you give your husband a couple of glasses of wine before sitting down to do this; he'll be a lot more agreeable that way.)

> "The number of men interested in coparenting is higher than it's ever been."
>
> —Kyle Pruett, M.D., clinical professor of child psychiatry at Yale University

Women Still Do More Housework

The most recent figures from the University of Wisconsin's National Survey of Families and Households show that the average wife does thirty-one hours of housework a week, while the average husband does fourteen—a ratio of slightly more than two to one. If you break out couples in which wives stay home and husbands are the sole earners, the number of hours goes up for women in this group, to thirty-eight hours of housework a week, and down a bit for men, to twelve, a ratio of more than three to one. Among couples in which both husband and wife have full-time paying jobs, the wife does twenty-eight hours of housework and the husband sixteen. That's just shy of a two-to-one ratio.

How Equal Do You Want to Be?

For some parents, splitting all the parenting duties right down the middle, including breadwinning and child rearing, works best for their family. Parents must both work part-time or flextime so that they both have equal opportunities to earn money for the family and spend time with the children. One major benefit of this arrangement is that it requires minimal or no outside child care. However, it can be difficult to work out, as many workplaces still do not embrace flextime or part-time work, particularly for higher-level positions. A great website for those interested in this type of parenting partnership is equallysharedparenting.com. Even if splitting everything fifty-fifty isn't the right solution for you, this website still provides great tips and tricks for those of you who want to share child rearing more equally with your spouses.

Don't Let the World (or Yourself) Get in the Way

From Sara

Societal tendencies can get in the way of shared parenting. When Anna was a baby I was amazed that even now, in the twenty-first century, every question—whether it was about her development, her schedule, her eating habits, it didn't matter—was directed to me. No one asked David any of these questions. If I knew the answer and he didn't, it was only because I had done the research and he hadn't. It wasn't because the process of giving birth somehow imbued me with the latest information in child raising that a father couldn't possibly know. It was just that I had read the books. So men, read the books. And women, don't expect Mom to be the only one who knows things about the baby.

Teachers may be more likely to e-mail mom, managers may be more comfortable giving mothers flextime employment than fathers, mothers are more likely than fathers (and it's more accepted by their employers) to leave early to pick up a sick child from day care. I'm still amazed at how David gets treated like a hero by other moms when he takes our kids to a birthday party. And he always comments that he gets questions from the other moms about where I am, as if I am AWOL from the job of motherhood. No one ever asks me where he is when I bring the kids to a birthday party. Don't get me wrong, the societal shift has begun—it's not like it's shocking to see a dad at ballet practice or pushing a stroller—but we've still got a way to go, and that is up to us.

I'm not immune to falling prey to societal expectations. I don't trust my husband to brush my daughter's hair properly, much less put it in an acceptable ponytail. He knows this, so he doesn't bother trying. I don't trust his vacuuming, cupcake making, or clothes folding either. And as a result, guess who gets to do all of that in our house? But I am trying, and so is David. He did attend breast-feeding classes with me when I was pregnant. He changed his fair share of diapers and always did his part on the middle-of-the-night feedings, whether he was going to work the next day or not. Having spent time alone with the baby, he knew that even though I wasn't going into an office the next day, I had just as heavy a workload ahead of me as he did. When he wanted to make the cake for our son's recent birthday party, I let him. It wasn't the cake I would have made (or bought)—we served it right from the pan—but it was adorable and the kids loved it. And it was one less thing I had to do, which meant I was a little less stressed and better able to enjoy my son's party. Isn't that the point, after all?

Fathers and Work

In a recent poll by Monster.com, a job-search website, fathers cited a flexible work schedule as the employee benefit they most appreciate, followed by telecommuting and on-site child care.

Do What Works for You and Your Family

The idea of equally splitting all the chores and responsibilities of child rearing between Mom and Dad may sound like the ideal situation to many of us, but the reality is that sometimes it's just not feasible or it just isn't right for your family. We should never demean the desire of those of us who choose to be home with our children full-time. That devalues the work of raising children, which is part of the problem in the first place. I've heard plenty of stay-at-home moms say that although they take care of all the child care and domestic duties while Dad is at work, when he gets home it becomes fifty-fifty. For many couples, one partner going to work, one partner being at home with the kids, and splitting the rest down the middle is a perfectly acceptable version of equally shared parenting. Just as with motherhood, there is no one-size-fits-all formula for sharing the parenting duties; families are unique and constantly shifting in their shape and dynamics as children grow and change. Find what works for you and your family and go with it. The point of all this is that we moms don't have to do it all anymore. And we shouldn't. When we try to be supermoms we become frazzled and spent, with little left to give to anyone. Dads can and should be involved and share the load. A mother who feels rested and has some time for herself can brighten the mood of the entire family. Because—say it with me—"When Mama ain't happy, ain't *nobody* happy."

Co-parenting Is Good for Kids

Here, saved for last, is the best argument of all for parenting together. Your children benefit from both parents being involved. There is science to back this up. Catherine Tamis-LeMonda, Ph.D., professor of applied psychology at New York University, has documented a link between the stimulating play style of both parents and improved language and cognitive skills in toddlers. Researchers at the University of Maryland determined that children who have fathers in their lives learn better, have higher self-esteem, and show fewer signs of depression than those without fathers. And according to Kyle Pruett, M.D., author of *Fatherneed: Why Father Care Is as Essential as Mother Care for Your Child*, studies of infants show that they seek comfort from their mothers but crave interaction with their dads. Dr. Pruett also states that children who are actively involved with their fathers from birth through adolescence develop more emotional balance, stronger curiosity, and greater self-assurance. Additional research shows that involved dads tend to raise children who experience more success in their careers later on. And those children are more likely to take an active role in raising their own families.

Kids also learn lessons from their dads that they don't learn from their moms. And this gets back to letting dads do things their way, even if it makes us cringe, because kids benefit from the "daddy difference." Whereas we moms tend to be protective of our kids, fathers are more likely to let the kids take risks. As Dr. Pruett says, "You can't learn to ice skate unless you fall down." Dads let the kids fall down; they understand the need to take risks in order to learn something new. They're also more likely to let a child fuss longer before reacting, something that drives many new moms batty. But again, this difference in parenting style is beneficial to the child. By not rushing in the moment a child is upset, dads are encouraging the child's own problem-solving abilities.

As we can both attest personally, men just don't read all the baby and child books like moms do. Even this can be a good thing! Dads tend to trust themselves more than the experts, while moms are more conscious of getting it right (probably because we're the ones who get blamed when something goes wrong). Fathers don't worry if their kids' clothes don't match—as long as the kids are appropriately dressed for the weather, they figure they've done their job. Moms, on the other hand, worry about their kids being a reflection on themselves, so they aim for perfection. Neither style is better than the other; the point is that kids benefit when they can experience both styles of parenting.

"Father involvement is associated with positive child characteristics such as empathy, self-esteem, self-control, psychological well-being, social competence, and life skills."

—Garret Evans and Kate Fogarty, University of Florida

From Sara

Researching this chapter has been a real eye-opener for me, as I tend to criticize David for not watching the kids closely enough when they play or laugh at the way he dresses them. Who knew they were actually learning valuable lessons from what I thought was his laxness? I sure didn't!

Clutter-Busting Resources

WEBSITES

Equally Shared Parenting
A couple shares how they divide working and raising children equally
http://equallysharedparenting.com

Third Path
Redesigning work and creating more time for life for parents
www.thirdpath.org

Alliance for Work-Life Progress
Helping parents balance work and family
www.awlp.org

Armin Brott, "America's most trusted dad"
www.mrdad.com

The National Center for Fathering
www.fathers.com

Fatherville
A resource for dads by dads
www.fatherville.com

The Center for Successful Fathering
www.fathering.org

BOOKS

Having It All: How Equally Shared Parenting Works
by Francine M. Deutsch

Love Between Equals: How Peer Marriage Really Works
by Pepper Schwartz

Family Man: Fatherhood, Housework, and Gender Equity
by Scott Coltrane

Fatherneed: Why Father Care Is as Essential as Mother Care for Your Child
by Kyle Pruett, M.D.

PRODUCTS

Fun, cool gear designed for dads
(We love the Diaper Vest, a wearable diaper bag for dads.)
www.dadgear.com

Work-Life Balance

37

Moms and Money

From Sara

When I left my job as a copywriter at an advertising agency to be at home with my first child full-time, I quickly became aware of what earning money meant to my self-worth, my marriage, and my independence. Ever since I was sixteen years old I'd earned a paycheck. Then, the day I left work at age thirty-one to become a stay-at-home mom, for the first time in my adult life I became financially dependent on another person. I didn't handle it well. Things got ugly fast. Every other job I'd had brought the reward of a paycheck and the knowledge that it was my money to do with as I wanted—after the rent and the car payment, of course. Money was a symbol of my power.

The job of mom is the most important one I've ever undertaken. It holds the most risks and the greatest cost of failure. Yet there is no paycheck, no performance review, no bonus, no certificate, no bigger title to go after. You're Mom. Even if you have twelve kids, you're still Mom. You're not a four-star mom or mom in chief or master mom. It's a tough transition to make, from independent working woman to dependent at-home mom. To many women, myself included, it feels like a huge loss of control. I've never regretted my decision to be at home with my kids when they were young, but it caused a major power struggle between my husband and me . . . one that I'm still not quite sure we've resolved.

Experts agree that money is the main issue most couples fight about. And it doesn't matter whether you have a little of it or a lot of it. Money is so much more than just paying the bills. It's our lifestyle, our status, our success. As women have gained more and more power in the workplace, money has become attached to our self-worth. Unfortunately, most of us don't do a very good job of managing it.

The average woman born between 1946 and 1964 will likely be in the workforce until she is seventy-four years old because of inadequate financial savings. One in every three women outearns her husband, but 60 percent of women say they prefer to spend as little time as possible managing their investments. Here's the really terrifying statistic, though: Between one-third and two-thirds of women now age thirty-five to fifty-five will be impoverished by age seventy.

That statistic was a wake-up call for me. The cold, hard reality is that we women take a financial hit when we become moms. We often scale back to working part-time or leave our careers altogether. If we do return to work, it's often after months or years of not saving for retirement. We moms need to stop and realize how important it is to start investing for ourselves. Most women outlive their husbands by several years, and we have to consider what our life is going to be like during that time.

We've fought hard to earn what we're worth, and though we've gotten better at earning money, we're still not good at holding on to it. Stephanie and I thought it was important to add this chapter to the book to remind mothers of the importance of paying attention to their finances and looking out for their own future.

From Stephanie

When saving for retirement, we often fail to consider how the cost of living is going to increase between now and the time we're actually going to need that money. What sounds like a lot of money now may not be very much at all when we're ready to retire. I lost my grandfather a few years ago. And as he got older, my mother (his daughter) would ask him, "Daddy, do you have a life insurance policy?" And he would always say yes, and we just assumed that it was substantial. After his death, when we were going through the papers, we found the policy and were shocked to find out that it was only worth $800. Back in the 1950s, when he bought it, it was a decent amount of money. But he never updated it and never considered that it would take a lot more than $800 to make his wife comfortable after his death. My point is, ladies, it's important to look out for yourself.

You know, whether we realize it or not, women have a strange relationship with money. Think about it: we know more about our friends' sex lives than their financial lives. Does that sound rational? We've been conditioned for generations not to talk about money, but it's a subject we must stop sweeping under the rug. Bankruptcy rates are higher among single mothers than any other population group. And how about this statistic: according to Amelia Warren Tyagi, author of *The Two-Income Trap,* having a child is, for women, now the single best indicator of financial collapse. For us moms, particularly those of us who have left our careers to care for our children full-time, that's one frightening piece of information. Read on to find out how you can ensure that your financial future is secure.

The Price of Motherhood

When women become mothers, their earning power suffers. It's a sad commentary on the way our society views motherhood, but according to sociology professor Jane Waldfogel of Columbia University, in 1998 non-mothers made 90 cents to a man's dollar, while mothers made only 73 cents. For single mothers the news is even worse: they made 60 cents to a man's dollar.

For many women, this wage penalty occurs when they "off-ramp," or put their careers on hold for a while to be at home with their children. Degreed professional women who spent less than one year out of the workforce saw their salary set back 11 percent, while an absence of three or more years set it back 37 percent, according to the Center for Work-Life Policy in a 2004 report. Those figures don't take into consideration the loss of retirement funding through company-sponsored plans and the fact that mothers who don't work have less money to invest, don't contribute to social security, and therefore will have less to draw from when they are old enough. It can take many years for a woman to rebound from that kind of earnings and savings penalty.

Once a mother is out of the workforce, getting back in can come at a price too. A Cornell University study testing two professional profiles—of mothers and of non-mothers—demonstrated the mothers were 44 percent less likely to be hired. The same study showed that mothers were offered $11,000 less in starting salary on average.

Know Your Worth

If you're a stay-at-home mom, don't think that you're not contributing to your family's bottom line because you aren't bringing home a paycheck. You are. By taking over the majority of the to-do list at home, you're freeing up your husband to focus more of his time and energy on his job, meaning he has the potential to earn more. And he wouldn't be able to devote himself to his job without your support at home.

If you're still not convinced of your worth to your family, the website www.salary.com estimates that if the average stay-at-home mom was paid for all the services she provides, she'd make over $138,000 a year. The point is that, paycheck or not, your role as mom is just as valuable to your family as your husband's job, and you should have an equal say in family financial decisions.

Curbing the Spending Habit

Women account for 80–90 percent of the total consumer spending in the United States. We control $6 trillion in annual buying power, and we make 88 percent of all retail purchases. America is a nation of consumers. Products and services that were once considered luxuries are now considered needs. Average credit card debit is around $8,000. And Americans only save around 1 percent of their wages, which is a much lower percentage than in any other industrialized nation.

The saying "born to shop" is largely accurate when it comes to women. We are the collectors of stuff. According to a study by Iowa State University, women's sense of self is closely connected with our spending habits. Women are far more likely than men to buy something they don't need, buy something because it's on sale, shop impulsively, and shop to celebrate. Yet less than half of the women surveyed said they were satisfied with their bank accounts, compared with 60 percent of men.

Shopping is far from a harmless habit. Ruth Hayden, author of *For Richer, Not Poorer: The Money Book for Couples,* says shopping deprives women of the opportunity to grow money through investing. "In their twenties and thirties, when their male counterparts are buying homes and investing in mutual funds, many women are spending on clothes, cars, and decorating the apartment."

The good news is that there are lots of ways we moms can spend less and keep more money in our accounts to invest. Let's start with the grocery store because that's where many of us get in trouble buying things that we don't need that go to waste. Efficient grocery shopping is all about planning. Make a habit of sitting down with your favorite cookbooks and planning a menu for the week. Write down your shopping list along with the menu. Be sure to include the page number for the recipe so you don't forget. Then stick to your shopping list and only allow yourself a set number of impulse buys each trip. And remember, the fewer people you bring on your trip, the less money you will spend. Try to shop when the kids are in school or when Dad's at home. You'll have a much less stressful and less expensive trip to the store.

Did you know that groceries on the Internet cost around the same as at your local grocery store? Shopping on the Internet will also help prevent impulse buying and it's easier to find sale items because they pop right up on the screen while you're shopping. You'll save gas money too, but keep in mind that most online grocers charge delivery fees and you have to be home when they arrive. Some grocers offer online shopping and have the items ready for you to pick up curbside at the store for a much smaller fee. Some online grocery stores are NetGrocer, Amazon Grocery, Peapod, and Albertsons (see "Clutter-Busting Resources" at the end of this chapter for contact information).

Never be afraid to ask for a rain check if the store is out of a sale-priced item. Stores are happy to give them to you. Check your store to see if there are any special programs. Most supermarkets have special programs for frequent shoppers, a baby club, and even senior or college discounts. There is usually a special

Keep Money in Your Name

Financial experts say it's important to establish credit by having at least one major credit card in your own name. Make sure to use it and pay the balance on time. Likewise, your house, likely your biggest asset, should be in both your name and your husband's.

program for everyone. And go over your grocery list and try to buy more store-brand products. Most of the ones we've tried are just as good as their more expensive counterparts.

Little Ways to Save Money Every Day

- Try to make tea and lemonade at home, and drink water instead of spending money on numerous cans of soft drinks. They're all cheaper and healthier. You really can change your family's drinking habits and get them used to something new.
- Check out movies from the library instead of renting them. The same with books: borrow instead of buy. (Except of course, *The Must-Have Mom Manual*! Every mom should have a copy of this book on her shelf.) Set up a toy and book trade with some of your neighbors or your play group. Put your name on everything or make an inventory list and put it in a storage container with all the stuff and rotate it every week at play group. It's like getting new toys and books every week without spending a dime!
- Try going on a picnic instead of going to a restaurant. It is more fun and much cheaper!
- Instead of hitting the fast-food drive-through line, pack sandwiches for you and the kids when you're out running errands. Toss some juice or water into a small cooler to bring in the car. A peanut butter and jelly sandwich doesn't take long to make and it will save you money. It's also a lot healthier than a double cheeseburger.
- Take your loose change seriously. Collect loose change around the house and put it in one central location. At the end of each day have everyone in your household turn in his or her loose change. Many grocery stores offer machines that will count your change for a small fee. They'll give you cash or a store credit for your coins.
- It's the little things that count. People who are really good at saving money consider every precious penny. Cutting back on your daily $4 fancy coffee drink adds up to $80 a month. Review luxuries you take for granted; spending only a little here and there adds up quickly!
- We have a love/hate relationship with coupons. We hate cutting and organizing them—they're such a pain—but they do work. They can also backfire, so the key is to cut only the coupons for the products you actually use. Don't let them entice you to buy something you normally wouldn't buy.
- Here's some great advice from the authors of *Dress Me Now* (www.dressmenow.com): when buying an item of clothing, the question you must ask yourself before putting down your hard-earned plastic for a bargain is, "Why am I

buying this?" If it doesn't go with two things in your closet, put it back! It is a waste of money. Either you will never wear it or you will have to buy more things to go with it.

- Utilize the barter system. Never be afraid to ask to trade your skills or services for something you want. Stephanie met another mom who owned a great furniture store. She needed some help with marketing her store, and Stephanie wanted a new bunk bed for her son's room. So they wrote up an agreement of how many hours Stephanie would spend and what she would accomplish in return for a new bunk bed that Stephanie selected. The agreement was based upon the value of the bunk bed versus Stephanie's hourly rate. Both moms got just what they wanted.
- Keeping your car tuned and your tires properly inflated will save money on gas.
- If you have credit card debt, ask your credit card company for a lower interest rate. They may say yes rather than lose your business!
- Sell items you no longer need or use on eBay.
- Just turning your thermostat down a couple of degrees at night and throwing on an extra blanket will save on your heating bill.
- Don't pay for more than one movie channel on your cable or satellite service. Most of the movies rotate through them all anyway.
- Do your laundry at night. The energy rates are much cheaper.
- Give your clothes an extra spin in the washing machine to get all the water out, because it costs less to run a washer than the dryer.
- Buy clothes and shoes for you and the kids from the clearance racks. And really think about how many outfits your kids actually need. Let's face it, they ruin most of them anyway.

Mars and Venus: How Men and Women See Money

From birth, women and men are raised to view and spend money quite differently. It's no surprise that money disagreements are the leading cause of divorce nationwide. Jay MacDonald at Bankrate.com says we tend to model our financial behavior after that of our same-sex parent. Most women are trained to nurture and seek acceptance, so we tend to spend on things we think will make us liked and accepted. We view money as a means to create a lifestyle. We spend on things that enhance day-to-day living. We generally have a "now" money orientation. That desire to enhance our lives now becomes even greater when we have children.

Men, on the other hand, are trained to fix and provide. So they view money as a means to capture and accumulate value. Men don't spend; they invest. Men don't want something; they need it. Theirs is a future-money orientation.

Even our approach to shopping differs greatly. We take a trip to the mall and dive into the clothing racks to find an outfit that expresses our own personal style that's fashionable. Our husbands make a beeline to the first shirt that works.

The one thing both sexes have in common is that we don't talk about finances. Both parties come to the relationship with our own views on money based on what our parents did, and we assume that is the right way to handle it. Instead, we should be deciding how we will handle money as a couple and a family.

Money and Your Marriage

Jean Chatzky, financial editor for the *Today* show, says that when couples fight about money, it's not actual dollars and cents that they're fighting about. Money fights are about who wields the power in the family. They're about controlling the actions of your partner or spouse. If assets are unequally divided (as is the case if only one partner is earning an income), they're about self-esteem. Chatzky says that for some people, spending money is a direct expression of love. It's really important that you try to understand what's driving your anger toward your partner. That'll go a long way toward helping resolve money issues in your marriage.

Keep Money Issues from Plaguing Your Relationship

Here are some tips from the experts (and we don't mean us):

- **Call a money meeting.** Steven Pybrum, a CPA, couples therapist, and author of *Money and Marriage: Making It Work Together,* suggests holding weekly meetings and starting with a ten-minute time limit. Set an agenda, stick to it, and stop when the time is up, he recommends. And remember: no blaming.
- **Put it in writing.** At your meetings, draft a budget and cash flow statement. "It's like going on a diet," says Victoria Collins, a financial planner, psychologist, and author of *Couples and Money.* "You hate to step on the scale, but if you come up with a concrete action plan, it's easier to follow through." Try creating a budget of what you *should* be spending, and then compare it to what you actually spent last month. It's an eye-opening experience. Having it in writing makes it clear for both parties.
- **Work together.** The most important thing a couple can do is to stop thinking like two and start thinking and acting like one. To do that you need to agree on a set of shared goals. Make a point of sitting down together on a regular basis to hash out what your financial priorities are and evaluate your progress toward your aspirations. Having a shared plan and talking about it regularly provides accountability when one of you wants to splurge on a large impulse buy.

- **Set up separate accounts.** Even if you pool all your resources, each partner should have his or her own checking account and credit card—not to hide assets and spending, but to establish an independent credit history. If anything ever happens to your husband, you'll be better prepared to support your family.
- **You should both have your own money.** When you do your budget, give both yourself and your spouse a discretionary allowance. You each get an equal amount to spend on whatever you want—no explanations required. It will give you a little freedom to spend your money on items you want. It's important for both of you to feel like you don't have to answer to someone else for every purchase you make.
- **Agree to discuss large purchases.** Jean Chatzky says if you're trying to stick to a budget, it's a good idea to discuss big expenses with your spouse before you buy. Pick a number that makes sense given your financial situation—$300, $500, $1,000—and agree with your partner that you're not going to spend more than that without talking about it first. That doesn't mean that he can't buy that great new digital camera or that she can't buy that incredible new suit. It just means that you have to talk about it first to make sure it's not going to throw some sort of monkey wrench into the rest of your finances for that month or that year.
- **Don't make secret purchases.** Financial deceit has become the new kind of infidelity. A poll conducted by *Redbook* magazine found that nearly 29 percent of U.S. adults ages twenty-five to fifty-five in a committed relationship say they have been dishonest with their partner about spending habits. Another study showed that one in four women lie to their partners about spending on discretionary items like clothing or shoes. Women are more likely to be the ones keeping information from their partners because it is easier for women to hide those extra purchases or overdue bills in the household budget.

  Don't hide your spending because chances are he'll find out anyway. If he does, even if the purchase is justifiable, he will probably be upset that you kept it from him.
- **Understand your own attitudes toward money.** For example, do you think you deserve to spend extra money on little luxuries? Or do you never buy anything for yourself because you feel like there's never enough money? Where are your spending weaknesses? Fill in this sentence: "My debt is largely due to ___." When you understand your own issues with money, you can do something about them. The power is shifted back to you, and you can choose whether or not to change your current situation. Identifying and talking about your attitudes toward money with your spouse will help you understand more and argue less. When you get to the heart of the problem and begin to solve it, your spending issues tend to take care of themselves.

- **Stop blaming.** If you don't stop blaming, you won't stop fighting. You each have to take equal responsibility for your financial situation and work as a team. But what if it's your husband who ran up the credit card bills? It doesn't matter—stop pointing fingers. Blaming does nothing to get you out of the situation you're in. Accept the reality and make a plan to fix it. Focus on what action you need to take, not who is more responsible.
- **Don't let it fester.** Don't wait for the issue that's bugging you to become a fight. The fact is, most of us start out a little irritated—and that's the time to bring it up, instead of waiting for it to fester and become worse.
- **Fight fair over money.** When a fight over money is starting to brew, remember to stick to the subject. Discuss money and nothing else. Don't get off track by bringing up other issues. Fight *for* each other and not against each other. Try to remember that you are a financial team instead of letting money arguments polarize your positions. Creating shared goals and combining your strengths can help you see eye to eye in your financial life. Working together to solve financial problems can enhance your teamwork as a couple in other areas of your life as well.

Retirement Planning for Moms

The job of stay-at-home mom doesn't come with a benefits package. There is no company-matched 401(k) savings plan or company pension. You're also not contributing to social security, which means your benefits will be lower when you are old enough to receive benefits. When you step out of the workforce, it's easy to forget about saving for retirement. Even moms who work part-time often don't receive retirement benefits. But the years spent not contributing have a huge impact on your retirement savings, so regardless of your employment status, it's important to plan now.

When we become mothers, women often turn over the retirement planning decisions to their husbands, but experts say it's important for each partner to be fully informed about how the money is being invested. Women should know the status not only of the retirement accounts but also of college savings funds as well as the mortgage and other debt.

Fortunately, there are things you can do to prepare for your own retirement. Of course, if you aren't making an income, you'll have to make some sacrifices in order to have some money to put aside. But it's more than worth it in the long run.

Setting a retirement savings goal is a simple first step to get you started. Most experts agree that you can estimate your expenses during retirement to be approximately 80 percent of what they are now. This doesn't include inflation, investment decisions, and lifestyle choices that will make a difference in the amount of money you'll need. But it's a simple estimate that can get you started. Here's an example: If you're currently spending $40,000 a year on living expenses, figure you'll need 80 percent of this, or $32,000 a year, to cover your expenses in retirement.

Consider contributing to an IRA (individual retirement account). There are several types, including traditional IRAs, Roth IRAs, and spousal IRAs. Whatever account you decide is best for you, make sure it's in your name. Visit www.irs.gov/publications/p590/index.html for more information on IRAs.

Determine a monthly amount that you can contribute and set up an automatic draft from your checking account into the retirement account. This way the money is automatically deposited into the retirement account each month. You don't have to remember to write a check and you're more likely to stick to your budget when you know the money is automatically going out of your account.

If you don't have an income to invest with, think of ways you can cut spending to find money to invest. Financial guru David Bach coined the term *latte factor* for all the excess spending we do throughout the day. Can you cut back on pricey coffees, trips to the mall, magazine subscriptions, pedicures? Look closely at your spending to see if you can find $50 or even $100 a month to put into a retirement account. Stick with it and it will add up faster than you think.

Working part-time may be an option as well. More and more companies are offering part-time positions to moms. Organizations like Mom Corps match moms looking for part-time and flexible schedules with companies' employment needs. Work-at-home positions are often available on their job board postings (see "Clutter-Busting Resources" at the end of this chapter). Working does have real advantages in terms of your retirement. It assures you that some money is going toward social security, and it gives you a little extra money to invest in your retirement account.

More and more moms are starting businesses in their homes. Home businesses often involve very little start-up cost and give moms the control over their schedules they want. Lots of moms we know make and sell jewelry, do medical transcription, give piano lessons, sell clothing, run websites, and design and sell stationery right in their home offices.

Consider joining or forming an investment club with other moms. These can be fun and profitable. You can make it a social gathering where you all share tips on investing and saving. Members often take turns reading books on stocks and mutual funds and sharing what they've learned. In some clubs, members

Stay-at-Home Moms Staying Marketable

Even if going back to work is the farthest thing from your mind today, that may change out of need or want down the road. Stay connected to former coworkers by e-mailing, calling, and getting together for lunch occasionally. Stay in the loop by attending conferences and reading professional publications in your field.

Are You Insured?

One of the biggest mistakes moms make is not having enough insurance. If something happened to you, your husband would have to hire someone to cook, clean, shop, and take care of the children while he worked. Most financial experts say you should have a policy worth at least $500,000.

contribute a small amount of money ($25–$50) and pool that money to invest in funds they've researched and discussed as a group.

The bottom line is to start doing something. Just contributing a small amount of money each month can really add up years from now, when you are ready to retire. The sooner you start the better, because the more years your money has to grow, the bigger your nest egg will become.

Clutter-Busting Resources

MONEY-RELATED WEBSITES

Club Mom on retirement planning
www.clubmom.com/display/249906

Not Made of Money
Money management and saving tips
www.notmadeofmoney.com

Individual retirement accounts
www.irs.gov/publications/p590/index.html

Moms Rising
Working together to build a family-friendly America
www.momsrising.org

Mom Corps
A matchmaker for corporations and moms looking for flexible schedules
www.momcorps.com

Jean Chatzky
Financial expert
www.jeanchatzky.com

David Bach
Financial expert
www.finishrich.com

Victoria Collins
Financial expert
www.victoriacollins.com

Morningstar
News and information for investors
www.morningstar.com

The Motley Fool
Investment experts
www.fool.com

Suze Orman
Acclaimed personal finance expert
www.suzeorman.com

ONLINE GROCERS

NetGrocer
A national Internet grocer
www.netgrocer.com

Amazon Grocery
Available nationally
www.amazon.com

Peapod
Internet shopping available in the East and Midwest regions of the United States
www.peapod.com

Albertsons
Available in the western states
www.albertsons.com

BOOKS

Women's Guide to Financial Self-Defense
by June Mays

Couples and Money: A Couples' Guide Updated for the New Millennium
by Victoria Collins with Suzanne Blair Brown

For Richer, Not Poorer: The Money Book for Couples
by Ruth Hayden

Smart Women Finish Rich
by David Bach

All Your Worth: The Ultimate Lifetime Money Plan
by Elizabeth Warren and Amelia Warren Tyagi

38

Reentering the Workforce

From Sara

There's been a shift in women's attitudes toward career and motherhood. According to the Center for Work-Life Policy, more than half of women in the United States will take time out of their careers. Sometimes they leave to take care of a sick or elderly parent, but more often they leave after the birth of a child. Since women are now having babies later in life, they are leaving high-paying jobs where they had a decade or more of experience.

The problem is, it's not always easy getting back in the game. It can be difficult to get hired, and when you do, the salary may be substantially less than you expected. (One recent study showed that businesswomen who left the workforce to care for their children earned 20 percent less than those who never left.) When moms start to consider the roadblocks in their path, they can quickly lose confidence about their ability to perform at work.

But who says just because you've been at home, you haven't been acquiring skills? Actually, you've probably gained new talents that are valuable to your résumé and can help you land a job. In fact, motherhood can make you a better employee, and more marketable.

Are You Ready to Reenter the Job Market?

Tory Johnson of WomenforHire.com says that you should be able to answer the following questions before embarking on a job search:

- Are you really ready to reenter the job market?
- Have you kept up with the trends and issues impacting your industry?
- Are your skills current and up to date?
- Do you have realistic expectations of today's workplace?
- Can you articulate how your time off will benefit your future career endeavors?

Before You Start to Look

Building a Functional Résumé

Don't agonize over the time gap in your résumé. Instead of a chronological résumé, create a functional one. Focus on your key skills and life accomplishments. What contributions have you made to your community? Did you chair the volunteer committee at your child's school? Manage a successful fund-raiser for your church? Just because you weren't paid for something doesn't mean it's not valuable. Creating a functional résumé allows you to focus on your abilities and achievements instead of a timeline. You can find templates for functional résumés at www.womenforhire.com.

Do You Need a Refresher Course?

You may need to brush up on your job skills. People who have become "outdated" can become marketable again by taking classes, doing volunteer work, asking for assistance and coaching. Tell potential employers about your recent training to alleviate any worries they may have about your skill level.

Hone Your Interview Skills

You'll also need to start preparing for the standard interview questions. Here are a few you'll likely get: "What are your best qualities? Why do you want to work for this company? Why should we hire you?"

But don't just stick to answering their questions. Practice selling yourself before you go to the interview. Getting a job is only partly about your experience level and education. The right personality that fits well with the corporate culture is just as important.

Searching for Opportunities

Network

We hope you've kept your foot in the workplace door by staying connected with former co-workers and professional associations. Let your work friends know you're interested in getting back in the game. Make a list of people you know in your field or the industry you're interested in and meet with them. Ask for their recommendations and if they know of anyone you should talk to.

Tory Johnson encourages moms to start by connecting with their own network. Consider friends and neighbors who have seen you function successfully as a mom. Maybe they've watched you hustle to raise money for the soccer team or seen you organize a PTA fund-raiser. There are countless people to turn to for advice and assistance. Get the word out that you are looking. Make a list of the personal contacts you can approach.

Mom Corps (www.momcorps.com) offers Coffee Clubs in various cities around the country where moms get together to network, discuss flexible career opportunities, and get tips for reentering the workforce.

The Internet is the fastest and most efficient way to build and maintain personal and business connections. One of the fastest-growing professional networking tools is LinkedIn (www.linkedin.com). LinkedIn has more than twenty-five million members and is adding well over a million new users per month. All five hundred of the Fortune 500 companies are represented on LinkedIn. You can build your network when you invite people in your friends' networks to become connections of your own. And you can look for available jobs on LinkedIn.

Social networking sites like Facebook are also a great way to reconnect with high school and college classmates, and keep in touch with current friends—and to let them know the latest news in your life (i.e., I'm looking for a job! or Buy my new book!). You can build your network here in much the same way you can on LinkedIn. Just remember that what you post online may be seen by lots of users.

Attend a Career Conference

Women for Hire and Mom Corps both offer career conferences and seminars for moms looking to reenter the workforce. You'll be able to meet recruiters and hiring managers as well as get advice on job searching and career development. Visit www.momcorps.com and www.womenforhire.com for more information.

Consider a Staffing Agency

A staffing agency is a service that matches the labor needs of its corporate clients with individuals who have the skills to meet those needs. According to Richard Wahlquist of the American Staffing Association, temporary staffing firms are an excellent first place to start for mothers who have been out of the workforce raising their children. Staffing agencies often provide the flexibility moms need to continue caring for their family. They're also a good way to find out if you really want to go back to work before making a long-term commitment. Most staffing companies also offer health insurance and retirement plans as well as vacation and holiday pay. Some provide free training. Wahlquist suggests finding a staffing firm that will help you do a skills inventory checklist. Visit www.staffingtoday.net for a list of staffing firms in your area.

Post Your Résumé Online

Send your résumé to MomCorps.com. Mom Corps matches your skills to companies' needs with an emphasis on flexible working arrangements. You can also post your résumé on LinkedIn.com. Why didn't someone think of this sooner? (See "Clutter-Busting Resources.")

Be Positive and Enthusiastic

Yes, there are obstacles, but it's important to focus on the advantages. Moms reentering the workforce often have experience, skills, and knowledge that make them more desirable candidates than those entering the workforce for the first time. Focus on those strengths and be confident about what you can offer an employer.

Leave your personal frustrations at home. If you're looking for work because you're divorced and finances are tough, keep that information private. You don't want sympathy—you want a job.

Be Realistic

Remember that significant changes may have occurred while you weren't working—changes in you, in the career field, in the competition. It may be unrealistic to think a career that has been put on hold can now be resumed without taking a step back on the career ladder.

Even with a stellar résumé, job searching takes time. Nothing happens overnight, so cut yourself some slack. Don't expect immediate results.

Clutter-Busting Resources

WEBSITES

Mom Corps
www.momcorps.com

Women for Hire
www.womenforhire.com

Moms Back to Work
www.momsbacktowork.com

The American Staffing Association
www.americanstaffing.net

Mommy Track'd
www.mommytrackd.com

LinkedIn
www.linkedin.com

Facebook
www.facebook.com

BOOKS

Going Back to Work: A Survival Guide for Comeback Moms
by Mary Quigley

39

Working from Home

We're known as mompreneurs or WAHMs (work-at-home moms), and we represent an increasingly attractive labor pool for employers, allowing companies to outsource domestically.

It's the best of both worlds—you get to earn a living and still be home with your family, right? Well, sort of. It can also be extremely frustrating because of all the interruptions, and lonely because there are no co-workers. It can also be a hard adjustment for your family.

Here are some great facts from www.MommaSaid.net:

- On May 10, 2007, the *CBS Evening News* reported that fewer women are returning to their high-powered jobs after becoming mothers.
- The Bureau of Labor Statistics reports that the number of working mothers has decreased to three million from four million in 1997. Between 1997 and 2005, the number of working married women with college degrees and children under one dropped by almost 8 percent, from 70.6 percent to 62.9 percent.
- According to the Census Bureau, there are about 6.8 million full-time stay-at-home mothers nationwide. There are nearly 1 million at-home fathers. The same report shows that 88 percent of at-home mothers are staying home to care for their homes and families. That figure was 15 percent for stay-at-home fathers.
- Forty-two percent of at-home mothers had children under three in their households.

- The U.S. government considers stay-at-home mothers "unemployed" and therefore ineligible to accumulate social security credits. Yet stay-at-home mothers work an average of fourteen hours a day, and they're on call all night—far longer than most government employees work. Plus, they're responsible for most management, human resources, labor relations, transportation, purchasing, logistics, health care, and waste disposal functions for the facilities they run.

"Mommy!"

The average preschooler requires his mother's attention *every four minutes,* or 210 times a day—about fifty times more often than he'll call Mom *in a year* after he's grown up and moved away.

Tips for Working at Home

From Stephanie

The two biggest keys to working at home are scheduling and self-discipline. There are plenty of mornings when I know I have to ignore the mail piled on the counter and the dishes in the sink and go straight to my home office. The other stuff can be done while the kids are doing homework, but I know I have to use those few quiet hours to concentrate on my work.

Scheduling also means knowing when to leave the computer and spend some time with your house and kids. There are things that have to be done daily, and they can't be ignored. And your kids need one-on-one time with you every day. In fact, you may have the most success when you spend some time with them first and then go back to your work. They'll interrupt you a lot less.

Self-discipline is the other key. If you only have a few precious hours of office time each day, then make them count. When friends call, politely tell them that you can't talk until after 1:00 P.M. Don't answer personal e-mails or shop online when you're supposed to be working. Turn off the TV and keep distractions to a minimum.

More tips:

- Get dressed and go to your workspace, just like you were going to an office.
- Open a separate bank account and get a separate phone line for your home-based business.
- Ask friends not to drop by during your workday.
- Make sure that when you leave your workspace at the end of the day, you leave your work behind. This is the time to con-

Patricia Cobe and Ellen H. Parlapiano, co-authors of *Mompreneurs Online,* offer this advice: if you don't treat your business like a business, no one else will.

centrate on your home and family. You do not need to answer e-mails twenty-four hours a day, so don't get addicted.

- Hire a mother's helper or babysitter to keep the kids busy when you are working. There is nothing more frustrating than trying to concentrate with kids at home competing for your attention. They start yelling and fighting when you're on a phone call, or they constantly interrupt you and you can't even finish a thought. A mother's helper is a young person who isn't old enough to babysit alone but is great at keeping kids busy and safe—and is less expensive than a qualified babysitter.
- Don't volunteer too much. Being at home does not necessarily give you more time to volunteer in your community or your child's school. Be realistic about how much free time you really have, and become an expert at saying no.
- Help your child make a child-readable sign for the office door so that he will know when it is and isn't acceptable to burst into the office.
- Identify time wasters in your day. It's a different thing for everyone. Maybe it's the TV; maybe it's friends calling to chat in the middle of the day; maybe it's activities that seem necessary but really aren't productive, like posting a lot in message forums. Whatever it is, identify it and eliminate it if possible, or at least manage it. Let phone calls go to your voice mail so you can call people back when it's a better time for you.
- A kitchen timer can be a huge help. You can set it to tell your children when you'll be available for them. Young children have difficulty comprehending time, and the timer will set them at ease so they won't bug you for that entire period. It also keeps you on track and helps you finish up tasks more quickly. Use it when you're reading e-mail, cleaning house, or doing something else you want to accomplish fast.
- One of the benefits to working at home is that you can multitask. I often throw a load of laundry into the washing machine on my way to my home office (which is right next door to the laundry room). The downside to this is that instead of folding the clothes, I put them in a laundry basket until the end of the day, when I can sit and fold them in front of the TV. They get a little wrinkled, but everyone has clean underwear, and I've been very productive. Always try to think of things you can get done while you're working.

Advantages and Disadvantages of Working from Home

Here's a great list we found from the National Federation of Independent Businesses (www.nfib.com) that highlights some of the benefits of working at home, and some of the drawbacks. This is great information to consider if you're thinking of setting up a home office.

Advantages

- Working from home can actually save you a lot of money and increase your tax write-offs. Of course you can declare your workspace and supplies, but there are other financial advantages too.
- You don't have to spend money on your clothing. We all spend too much money on fashion when we're competing in an office environment. Clothing can cost thousands each year, not to mention the dry cleaning bill. Working at home allows you to dress casually and less expensively.
- Meals are quicker and less expensive and even healthier when you're eating at home instead of those fancy corporate lunches. Plus you save on gas traveling to restaurants and doing personal errands. Now you can spend your lunch hour taking a relaxing walk in your neighborhood.
- When you work from home you save tons of money on car expenses: gas, maintenance, repairs, tires, and general wear and tear. Plus you'll have much less stress because you're not sitting in rush-hour traffic.
- Parents who work at home save money on child care. Even if you hire a mother's helper or a sitter, it will be cheaper than what you pay a professional day care facility.
- You can be home with your child after school. This is huge. Having a parent there in the afternoon has tremendous advantages for your child and for you. Studies show that when parents are involved in homework, kids get better grades and enjoy school much more.
- Theoretically, you should be able to get more done in the course of a day than you would in an office setting. You're not spending time commuting or dealing with office politics or interruptions from co-workers. This may translate into a higher income and more career satisfaction.

Disadvantages

- It can be tough to separate home and work life. You really have to know how to solidly end your workday and turn your attention to your home and family.
- Initial setup of a home office can be a little difficult at first. And not having a computer services or IT department can eat up a lot of your time when computer problems occur.
- Domestic distractions and interruptions can be a huge frustration and a deterrent to your productivity.

- Expect to be a little lonely. Try to schedule lunch dates with friends or other working moms in your neighborhood. Or go to the school and have lunch with your kids.
- Your family may have a hard time adjusting to your new work-at-home status. They're used to having your attention whenever they want it, and there will be a transition period while you train them how to deal with you working from home. For example, they must know to be quiet when you are on the phone—you can develop a signal to let them know, or create a sign that you can display when you need them to be quiet. You are going to have to set and enforce some new rules.

Excerpts used with permission from the National Federation of Independent Business. NFIB is the leading advocacy organization representing small and independent businesses. A nonprofit, nonpartisan organization founded in 1943, NFIB represents the consensus views of its members in Washington, D.C., and all fifty state capitals. Visit www.NFIB.com to learn more.

Clutter-Busting Resources

WEBSITES

Home-Based Working Moms
www.hbwm.com

Freelance Mom
www.freelancemom.com

Home Office Women
Online community for women who work from home
www.homeofficewomen.com

Smart Momma
www.smartmomma.com

Mompreneurs Online
www.mompreneursonline.com

Hire My Mom
Outsources jobs and projects to professional women working at home
www.hiremymom.com

The National Federation of Independent Businesses
www.nfib.com

BOOKS

The Stay-at-Home Mom's Guide to Making Money from Home: Choosing the Business That's Right for You Using the Skills and Interests You Already Have
by Liz Folger

Will Work from Home: Earn the Cash—Without the Commute
by Tory Johnson and Robyn Freedman Spizman

Mompreneurs: A Mother's Practical Step-by-Step Guide to Work-at-Home Success
by Patricia Cobe and Ellen H. Parlapiano

Mompreneurs Online: Using the Internet for Work at Home Success
by Patricia Cobe and Ellen H. Parlapiano

40

Tips for Busy Moms

From Stephanie

One day I went to meet the governor of Georgia wearing two entirely different shoes. One had fluffy black and white flowers across the toes while the other had a small black buckle, and even the heel heights were different by at least one-eighth inch. I didn't do it on purpose—I'm a mom. It's not often I get the chance to wear nice clothes, or even clothes that coordinate for that matter. But on this day, when my daughter's highly awarded cheerleading squad was bestowed the honor of an audience with the governor, I unsuspectingly boarded the police-escorted charter bus with my wardrobe a little less put together than I would have liked.

It all started when I was trying on two different shoes to decide which one looked best with my outfit. I was standing in front of the mirror, trying to make a decision, when my son and daughter began fighting, and it quickly turned into a full-fledged meltdown. By the time I got that solved, I had totally forgotten that I had not made a shoe decision. Once everyone found their respective shoes and coats and backpacks and homework and we'd rushed to drop my son off at preschool, my shoes were the furthest thing from my mind. I was sitting on the bus with my daughter when I reached down under the seat for my purse, saw my feet, and realized that I was wearing two entirely different shoes! I was mortified! But I was on a charter bus with fifty kids, so there wasn't much I could do other than laugh about it.

I was standing in the capitol building waiting for Governor Sonny Perdue to come and greet us when one mom (who didn't know about my error) came up to another friend of mine and said, "I love her shoes!" My friend laughingly replied, "Which one?"

And we laughed some more. Just for the record, the governor didn't notice and I stood in the back for the photos.

These are the things that happen to mothers because we're constantly being rushed, interrupted, spilled upon, telephoned, and volunteered. How many times have you packed a suitcase for your kids and remembered everything for them but forgotten some of your most obvious necessities? It's okay, even normal. We're moms and we're busy . . . very, very busy.

Are We Busier Than Our Moms Were, or Just Bigger Whiners?

From Stephanie

This is a question that Sara and I have often pondered. Did our moms actually complain as much as we do? Maybe they did and we were just too young to remember. Were they just fitting into the "Stepford wives" role because they didn't have as many choices as we do? Is it a fact that today's moms are busier, are more stressed out, and have more demands on them than any generation before? How can that be when previous generations didn't have microwaves or dishwashers or all the other modern conveniences we have?

Recently, my husband said to me, "Why do you complain so much? You live a charmed life, Stephanie." Right after I punched him in the neck, I realized he did have a point. I have two gorgeous, perfect children and a nice house, and I'm privileged enough to be a stay-at-home mom. What more could a girl want? So why *do* I complain so much? When I was contemplating leaving my career to become a full-time mom, I had all these fantasies about how much time I would have on my hands: how I would be able to do crafts with my kids, read and play with them for hours on end, have a clean, organized house, bake cookies, and all that *Leave It to Beaver*–type mom stuff. The fact that I feel so stressed out and rushed all the time and that I have even less time than when I worked full-time completely baffles me.

So are we busier than our moms were despite all our modern conveniences? The answer is yes. There are many more demands on today's moms. Society (I blame Martha Stewart) bombards moms with completely unrealistic expectations.

Home Maintenance

Today's moms have bigger houses and more stuff to maintain. There are entire cable networks that tell us how to decorate, organize, clean, sew, cook, and be perfect in every way. The media thrives on portraying moms as perfect: waiting in perfectly clean houses with our perfectly applied makeup to greet our perfect husbands at the door with the perfect meal on the table. Blah, blah, blah. Never mind the fact that it took an entire *crew* to create that television scene. But for some reason, we think that's what is expected of us. It's deeply implanted in our heads that this is what we want to be like. Then we've got Oprah telling us to vacuum our mattresses and wash our sheets in hot water every couple of days to kill the dust mites that are living in our beds and feeding on our dead skin cells (I didn't sleep for a week after that show). And Martha Stewart has some impossible project every day that I get all excited about, and then I realize, "But I can buy a nice candle for $1.79 at Wal-Mart—why in the hell would I make my own?"

We're supposed to clean our toilets at least twice a week with disposable thingies. Did you know that? Did our mothers know that? And apparently there are deadly bacteria living all over my kitchen, but the chemicals that I'm supposed to use to kill the bacteria can be harmful for my kids to breathe. And if I see one more commercial where some bald guy stops by to clean my toilet bowl, I'm going to scream! I have three toilets, and no bald guy has ever shown up to clean them.

I remember when my grandparents came to visit us in our first house right after we were married. It was 2,400 square feet with four bedrooms, and we had no kids yet. They laughed and laughed at us. They thought we were ridiculous. They asked, "What are you going to do with all this space?" Sara's mom and dad told her that when they were first married, they had one chair and an ottoman in the living room and they took turns sitting on the ottoman. Let's face it—the more house you've got, the more house you've got to clean. Everything today is bigger and more complicated.

Education

From Stephanie

Today's moms are much more involved in our children's educations. We are held accountable for our child's academic progress. (My parents were not required to be as involved in my education—that was up to the teacher.) And schools operate differently nowadays. Just this week, my four-year-old son had Bike Day on Tuesday, and had to bring in things that started with the letter *Z* by Thursday. My daughter had to be prepped for class photos on Thursday, had homework due Friday, and went on a field trip to a dairy (which I chaperoned). Things are much more complicated, and I haven't even told you about the extracurricular activities cluttering our calendar, including baseball, cheerleading, and ballet. Then there were the dishwasher repairman, picking Daddy up from the airport, my tennis match, paying the water and electricity bills, making sure there was money in the school lunch account, and trying to find Mother's Day gifts for all the grandmas. Need I continue? (Yes, there's more.) In fact, I just recently began keeping the pages from our family calendar so we'll be able to look back and laugh at how full and chaotic our lives were during this time. I'm sure it will be funny one day; right now it makes me committed to filling my Lexapro prescription monthly without fail.

The Internet

Some modern technology works against us. Sure, the Internet is an amazing tool for moms. I use it daily. It gives us a chance to communicate with each other, and it's a great resource for finding out if that rash on Junior's bottom is poison ivy or a food allergy. But it also eats up a great deal of time. Mothers today are much more knowledgeable and informed, and that takes time. I always use this example: Before you go to the zoo with your kids, you get on the zoo's website and find out what time you should arrive depending on the special exhibits for that day. You get directions, print out coupons, and find out what time they feed the elephants, and if you're an experienced mom, you print out a map of all the bathrooms and snack bars. Our moms never did that—they threw us in the car (with no seat belts or car seats, by the way) and hoped for the best. If the damn zoo was closed, we had a picnic, and we were okay with that. Today's parents feel a lot more pressure to create learning experiences for our kids.

Modern Conveniences

One thing that people don't realize is how much time it takes us to clean and maintain all the new equipment technology has brought into our households. Sure, the microwave is great for heating up a bowl of soup in two minutes—but you also have to scrape all the dried SpaghettiOs off the insides, clean all the crumbs out of it, disinfect the keypad, and wash the glass turntable that goes inside it. And the computer can destroy your schedule as soon as something goes wrong, like a virus—you have to spend all afternoon on the phone with tech support. Plus it has to be maintained regularly too (my keyboard looks like the inside of a toaster right now). I have three different kinds of vacuums and I love them all, but why? And all these "time-saving" devices mean that people expect you to get even more done in a day.

Demands on Kids

The expectations for our kids are higher than ever before too, which translates into more demands on us. Everything is more competitive, and kids are playing sports and participating in activities at earlier ages. Which means we're driving them to practices and meetings and events. We're trying to be good parents and get involved in their activities by volunteering for the booster club and working the concession stand. That takes a lot of time and effort. Academic demands are higher too, which translates into more work for parents. (Not to mention overseeing grades and savings accounts for college.)

Unsafe World

When we were kids, we used to go outside and play for hours. Our mothers didn't have to worry about pedophiles or bad guys snatching us out of our front yard. We could go out at lunchtime and not show up again until dinnertime. Moms today have to watch their kids, even in their own backyards.

And what about going shopping? I remember my sister and me shopping with our mom. If we were misbehaving in the store, she would send us to the car to wait for her. Nowadays it's illegal to leave your kids unattended in the car. And mothers are terrified to do it anyway—there's no telling what might happen. Moms today have to spend a lot more time watching over their kids.

We Are the Enemy

We are usually our own worst enemy. We make everything more complicated than it has to be. We don't say no enough. We come up with these hare-brained schemes that we've seen in a magazine and decide to imitate. We are overly ambitious in planning what we can achieve in a day's time. And we think we can do it all with no help.

I have to share a story about one of my best friends who was preparing for a trip to Disney World with her husband and two young daughters. The reason for the trip was to celebrate her daughters' birthdays. About four days before they left, I went with her to Target to pick up some last-minute vacation supplies. My dear friend worked herself into quite a frenzy when she got it in her head that it would be fun to give each daughter a little birthday gift each morning of their vacation. That's five days multiplied by two girls—ten gifts that she would have to wrap, pack, and pay for, even though her husband had asked her to limit spending to save money for their trip. Then we proceeded to the little girls' department, where she found matching tank tops for her girls and planned to glue crystals on the front of each to form cute princess-themed sayings. One shirt each would have been reasonable, but she decided to make three shirts each. Now, this was all happening just hours after she had told me how she was still in the middle of doing laundry and packing and feeling behind schedule. I couldn't convince her in the store that the kids were going to see Mickey Mouse every day and those little presents were going to be forgotten, or that she was going to make herself miserable sitting up till 2:00 A.M. gluing rhinestones onto shirts. She didn't come to her senses until after we checked out, and then we ended up returning some of the items and laughing about how we women get ourselves all worked up over an idea and can't stop ourselves.

I share this story not to belittle my friend but because I think it's a fitting example of how we get some perfect picture in our minds and then end up putting too much pressure on ourselves. We need to make better choices about what matters most to our children (which is usually the chance to spend more time with us) and how we choose to spend our precious time. I've made a conscientious effort to say no more often, and even though I still don't say it enough, it does give me more time to relax and breathe. I know some of you are making excuses for overcommitting, so here's some ammunition to help you. If you're thinking, "But if I don't do it, it won't get done," I promise you, it will. Just take a step back and give someone else a chance to step up. Or what about "I can do it better"? Please understand that whoever is doing it, it will work out fine, even if you think your way was better.

Suggestions for Giving Yourself More Time

Make a Schedule and Stick to It

Choose a day or night to do your grocery shopping and errand running each week and stick to it. Choose which days you are going to spend cleaning your house. I try to clean one room each morning or evening. Stick to your schedule and then you won't worry about these chores all week.

Finish What You Start

When you start a project, finish it, even if you get interrupted. Schedule enough time to make this possible. Leaving projects unfinished just creates anxiety, and you're not accomplishing anything.

Write Things Down

Keep a small notepad on hand. Write down your to-do lists, your phone messages, and anything else you want to do or remember. Carry it with you. This will save you lots of time looking for lost Post-it notes with phone numbers, and it will give you some peace of mind when you see your list on paper. Your to-do list seems much more overwhelming when it's all swimming around in your head. When you see it on paper, you'll feel much better—plus you won't forget anything.

Make a File System

An organizer once taught me to make a file box for all the things that pile up on the counter. The reason they pile up is because you don't know where to put them. She said to make folders for things like photos (the ones you need to give to your friends but haven't yet), cool things you want to share with your husband, coupons, and things that are "waiting"—like upcoming parties or confirmations for online orders that haven't arrived yet. You'll know where to put those papers, and later you'll save time looking for them.

Do It Now

From Stephanie

I'm the messy one. Sara is neat and organized and takes time to place things where they belong. I throw things into a pile and move on to the next thing. The problem I struggle most with is whether I should do it right now or whether it can wait. I believe that I am so busy and things are so hectic that I don't always have the time to put something away immediately. I leave breakfast dishes on the table when we're running a little late. I hardly ever make my bed because I think it's a big waste of time. (Oprah said an unmade bed gives the dust mites a chance to escape, so that's my justification—it's just not healthy to make your bed every day, I reassure myself.) I do some housework every day, but you usually have to look under the layer of toys, mail, pulverized Cheetos, and shoes to see that the floor is spotless. The professional organizer who gave me the gift of the mom-style file box also gave me this bit of advice: "If it takes less than thirty seconds, do it now." It really clarified things for me. It helps me make the decision about what I should do right now and what I can get back to later.

Prioritize

When you make your to-do list for the day, put a little *1* by the things that are most important, a *2* next to the things that are sort of important but can wait till tomorrow if necessary, and so on. When kids are involved, things happen that you weren't expecting. By prioritizing, you know what you can bump off today's list and do later in the week. Don't get run down by overscheduling yourself. Remember that you are only one person and there's only so much you can do in a day.

Delegate

Moms need to be experts at delegating. Ask for help! Ask your husband and other family members, and don't forget to get your kids helping out around the house as early as possible. And don't underestimate what your children are capable of. This week I learned that my seven-year-old is a champ at washing dishes! And my six-year-old thinks it's fun to run the Swiffer vacuum. I am taking advantage of their newly found skills. It's *so* important to teach your kids what's involved in making their world turn. Life is not all SpongeBob reruns and people serving your every need. It's their home too, and they need to be a part of making the household run smoothly.

Dads need to be asked to help around the house more too. And ask nicely—don't state your request in the form of an insult (I'm really good at that). They will never look around the room and see all the things that need to be done like you do, so just ask. If it doesn't get done in a timely fashion, hire help. Once he sees the bill, he'll pay more attention the next time you ask him to do something. It makes a strong, memorable point without the yelling.

Maximize Your Trips

On your way to work, are there errands you can run so you don't have to do them at night or on the weekends? Can your husband pick up a prescription at the pharmacy on his way home? Try to take care of as many things on your to-do list as you can in one trip. You'll save money on gas and time.

Be Present in the Moment

From Sara

We moms are constantly bringing future worries into the present. Richard Carlson, Ph.D., author of *Don't Sweat the Small Stuff,* called this "anticipatory thinking." Tap into your Zen-self and focus on the present moment. Eckhart Tolle, author of the *Power of Now,* suggests getting back to the "now" by taking a few seconds to focus on your breathing or by spending time in nature simply watching the trees sway in the breeze or listening to the birds in your backyard. Being present in the moment physically reduces stress and brings us back to what is important. Being present for our kids lessens our stress about whether we are spending enough quality time with them and makes them and us happier.

Don't Brag About Being Busy

Avoid the trap of comparing notes with other parents about how busy you are. Having a packed schedule is not a sign of being a great mom or having happy kids. In fact, it may be just the opposite.

Happiness Can Be Just a Thought Away

From Sara

Be conscious of your self-talk throughout the day. Are you elevating inconveniences into disasters in your mind? Self-talk can help us control our emotions and our stress level. When things go wrong, remind yourself that it's not the end of the world. When I recently got a speeding ticket on the way to a beach vacation, my first reaction was frustration and aggravation. The fine, the inconvenience of traveling to traffic court out of town . . . But then I stopped myself and reminded myself that my children were safe in the car, no one else was hurt, and I had just gotten a very good reminder to pay more attention and be safer behind the wheel. And I got that reminder without having to have an accident. As fast as I was driving, we would likely all have been seriously hurt. Suddenly my perspective changed, and I was thankful that I had only gotten a ticket!

Become an Early Riser

Wake up fifteen to thirty minutes before the kids and enjoy a cup of coffee and the morning paper or *Today* show in peace. Pop in a yoga DVD or do a few stretches, or read something inspiring. Take a few minutes to plan your day and prioritize the three most important tasks that need to get done. You'll start the day focused and fresh.

Find the Source of the Problem

From Stephanie

Sara the Organized once told me moms spend several hours each week looking for lost items. I thought she was full of poppycock until I found myself feverishly digging through my sock drawer three days in a row. And with my arm elbow-deep in a drawer of approximately two hundred socks, none of which appeared to have a mate, I thought of her comment and began laughing out loud. The next day, I dumped out my sock drawer, found whatever matches I could, and threw out the rest. I also put a small basket in my closet for all those socks that come out of the dryer "divorced" from their mate. Now I have a place to keep these lost singles so I don't clutter up people's sock drawers. I know it sounds silly, but I'm telling you I probably save thirty minutes per week. Find the source of the confusion and fix it. If you spend time each day looking for keys, put a hook by the door. If kids' shoes are a problem, put a big basket by the back door and don't let them into the house until they've placed their shoes in the basket. Be conscious about where you waste time and try to fix it.

By the way, a great tip for keeping socks from getting lost in the wash is to put your socks into one of those mesh lingerie bags as soon as you take them off! Washing them in the bag will keep them from disappearing in your laundry. Just don't overfill the bag and they get clean without getting lost. Try it!

Prepare the Night Before

You'll feel much less stressed and be much more prepared if you get ready the night before. Don't wait until morning to pack lunches, backpacks, coolers, etc.

Photos

Are you haunted by envelopes of photos that you just can't seem to get into an album? Go to www.togetherbook.com. You can send them twenty-five to one hundred of your photos and they will organize them and put them into beautiful linen albums for about $30. You can select the color of the album and add tasteful embellishments. It might just help you get caught up.

Phone Numbers

Program all-important phone numbers into your cell phone. Include your favorite restaurants, the school, the dry cleaner, the babysitter, the doctor, the pharmacy, etc. Or you can carry a phone book around in your car. This will help save money on those 411 information calls and it will save lots of time too.

Mother's Helpers

From Stephanie

Depending on the state you live in and your own standards, most babysitters have to be at least thirteen years of age to be left alone with your kids. But I've had great success using girls around eight to ten years old who are looking for babysitting experience while I'm at home. These "mother's helpers" are an awesome resource for new moms. They keep your kids happy and out of your hair while you get a little work done in the office, prepare dinner, pay bills, or do whatever else you need to do without interruptions. They make about half of what a regular babysitter makes and they can be a huge help. (How do you think I had time to write this book? Thank you, Chandler, Mackenzie, and Lauren!)

Clutter-Busting Resources

WEBSITES

Time-saving tips from real moms
www.babyzone.com/momtomom/default.asp
www.momsintheknow.com

Together Book
www.togetherbook.com

BOOKS

Don't Sweat the Small Stuff with Your Family
by Richard Carlson, Ph.D.

Everyday Blessings: The Inner Work of Mindful Parenting
by Myla Kabat-Zinn and Jon Kabat-Zinn

The Power of Now
by Eckhart Tolle

41

Time for Yourself

From Stephanie

Isn't it truly amazing that as a mom, you can go through an entire twelve-hour day and not get even ten minutes to yourself? It's typical for me to go all day, and the only time I sit down is to answer my e-mail. Isn't that nuts? I have a beautiful covered deck on the back of my house overlooking a creek and a golf course. Every spring I spend a great deal of effort hanging bright red decorative curtains in the corners and scrubbing the pollen and winter dirt off the railings. I plant pots with colorful flowers and have two comfy Adirondack chairs that Sara's dad made for me that I painted a deep red. There's a colorful striped rug and pillows and candles and a palm tree, and I work so hard to make it a perfect spot to have a little mini-vacation whenever we want to. But do you think I *ever* get a chance to sit down out there? No. Out of the entire summer last year, I probably spent a total of two hours sitting on my lovely porch. And the minute I do sit down and put my feet up, somebody immediately starts demanding something or falls down or starts fighting. So what's a mother to do?

The thing you have to understand is that the fact that I don't sit on my porch is nobody's fault but my own. If you go all day and don't sit down or make a few minutes for yourself, it's your own fault. And you're not doing anybody any favors, including your kids.

Moms need some down time. We're all drowning in our own self-imposed guilt, and we're overwhelmed by the amount of work that needs to be done to keep the kids, the husband, and the household going. We just whip from one task to the next and never stop to think about a little time for ourselves.

Let me assure you that you will be a better mother and wife if you take a little time for yourself *every day.* One inspirational book I read said, "Do something every day that makes your heart happy." If you're not happy, how can you pass happiness on to your kids? They don't care if the kitchen floor is clean (there's dried-up ice cream on mine right now—they put it there and they don't care). They want a mommy who is happy and silly and available to spend time with them.

Aren't there days when you look back and think, "All I did today was yell at them and order them around all day long"? I hate when that happens. Make it a priority to schedule time for yourself and downtime to spend with your children every day. When they become adults, they won't remember how clean the house was, but they will remember that you had water balloon fights with them in the backyard.

We all walk around talking about how stressed-out we are. One mom told us that she's careful about how she chooses her words. She tries to say "I'm so busy" instead of "I'm so stressed." Think about it. Our jobs as moms consist of housework, schoolwork, running errands, and chauffeuring the kids around. But we get to be with our kids, we don't have bosses or jobs or co-workers to deal with, and we get to make our own schedule and do what we want with our days. So, is saying we're stressed really accurate?

The Power Nap

I've heard so many moms talk about taking power naps and how much it helps them. But for me to recommend it in our book, I just had to try it out for myself. I have to admit, I'm not a good napper. I set the timer on the microwave for twelve minutes and lay down on the couch. The kids were at school, and I unplugged the phone and shut my eyes. It felt nice to be horizontal. But even though I kept my eyes shut, my mind started wandering: "Did anybody feed the turtle today? I have to bring snacks to baseball tomorrow—I have to remember to pick something up from the store . . . cheese, maybe cheese. This feels nice. I love this couch. [Sound of a lawn mower] I wonder who's mowing their lawn on a Thursday? When I get up from here, I think I'm going to have to poop. [That made me giggle; then I thought about writing that in this chapter to share with you, and that made me giggle even more.] I wonder if I could type faster if I took a diet pill with a Coke. What is wrong with my mind? I have to relax. Relax now. Sleep now." About the time I drifted off, the timer went off, and then I was just groggy. But I have to say that even though I didn't get to sleep, I do think it gave me a little boost of energy. And if nothing else, it gave me a little clarity and peacefulness to be alone with my thoughts for a few minutes. By the way, before you lie down, better go to the bathroom first.

Short-Term Stress Relief

I found the following tips on a website (http://life.familyeducation.com/stress/home management). They were excerpts from a book called *Mother Nurture: A Mother's Guide to Health in Body, Mind, and Intimate Relationships* by Rick Hanson, Jan Hanson, and Ricki Pollycove. These are such wonderful suggestions that I wanted to share them word for word with you. Some of them are things you probably already do, but never realized how healthy they are for you. Little things during the course of a busy day can make a huge difference in your stress level. Stress is something all women need to be aware of. It puts terrible wear and tear on your body, causes premature aging (I'm talking wrinkles here, ladies), and it's just no fun to live with. The following small exercises done several times a day will help you get control of your stress level and make you feel better all over.

One-Minute Soothers

- Take four long, slow breaths, and as you exhale, imagine that a gray cloud of stress, worries, or troubles is leaving your life, and as you inhale, imagine that peace and love and wisdom are filling you up.
- Take your shoes off, rub the bottoms of your feet with your knuckles, and massage the joints and tips of your toes.
- Smell something nice, like an orange or your child's hair, or put on a dab of perfume.
- Roll your head around to loosen your neck.
- Splash water on your face.
- While standing, bend over to touch the floor, shake your arms loosely, and straighten up slowly as you take in a big breath.
- Look at something pretty.
- Knead your neck and shoulders.
- Nibble something good.
- Rub your eyes and the bones around them gently.
- Hug your child or partner for one whole minute.
- Stretch your mouth open as wide as you can, like a lion roaring, and then let your face relax.
- Remember a good joke.
- Repeat a favorite saying or prayer to yourself.

Five-Minute Soothers

- Make yourself a cup of tea.
- Lie down, close your eyes, and imagine a warm, golden balm settling over you, softening the edges of your feelings, and gently carrying away any distress.
- Listen to your favorite music, from Bach to the B-52s.
- Ask someone for a sincere compliment.

- Step outside and watch the play of sunlight dancing on leaves, or the moon and the stars.
- Do a few minutes of stretching or yoga.

Fifteen-Minute Soothers

- Take a long shower.
- Read a magazine.
- Go for a short walk and look for beauty.
- Arrange flowers in a vase.
- Cuddle up with your children or your partner.
- Call a friend for a quick chat.
- Be especially loving with someone.
- Lie down for a brief nap.
- Meditate for fifteen minutes.
- Exercise, dance, stretch, or do yoga.

Thirty-Minute Soothers

- Read a good book.
- Take a bath—maybe with bubbles.
- Watch a TV show.
- Go for a walk.
- Treat yourself to a good nap.
- Trade a neck rub or foot massage with your partner.
- Do some art or a craft.
- Play a musical instrument.
- Put some flowers in every room in the house.
- Call a friend and really talk.
- Make love with your partner.

One-Hour Soothers

- Go for a run, swim, or bike ride, even if you have to arrange special child care to get an hour to yourself.
- Get a manicure.
- Go out to lunch with your partner, a friend, or a good book.
- Visit your church or temple.

- Browse through a bookstore.
- Provide a simple charitable service to someone in greater need than you.
- Go for a walk in a park.
- Prepare a really nice meal just for you, or treat yourself to a special lunch.

Excerpted from *Mother Nurture: A Mother's Guide to Health in Body, Mind, and Intimate Relationships* by Rick Hanson, Jan Hanson, and Ricki Pollycove.

Clutter-Busting Resources

WEBSITES

Mom De-Frazzler
www.mom-defrazzler.com

Busy Moms, Healthy Moms
http://busymomshealthymoms.com

A Matter of Time—Time Management for Moms
www.a-matter-of-time.com

BOOKS

Mother Nurture: A Mother's Guide to Health in Body, Mind, and Intimate Relationships
Rick Hanson, Jan Hanson, and Ricki Pollycove

Your Expanding Family

42

Birth Order Psychology

From Stephanie

Well, like Sara and me, you've probably wondered how your children, whom you are parenting virtually the same way, can have such dramatically different personalities. Of course children are born different; it's in their genes. But many psychologists believe that a large part of our personalities is determined by birth order, because each child is essentially born into a different social environment. The firstborn comes into a family being the only child to novice parents who take thousands of pictures and try to set definite guidelines. They've read all the books and approach parenting very scientifically. Then comes the second child, who "dethrones" the first and who may not get to experience life as an only child until he becomes a teenager. If there are three or more children in the family, you have the middle child, stuck in between, who will never get to experience life as the only child. As parents, we raise our children differently depending on how many we have and the things happening in our lives at the time. We don't do it on purpose; it's just human nature or in some cases survival! So when you think about it, how can birth order *not* affect who we become?

Those relationships within the family that we learn from birth set a pattern for how we react to and relate with friends, teachers, competitors, co-workers, our spouses, and even our own children. Alfred Adler was one of the first psychologists to assert that birth order is a major determinant of personality. Adler said that each child is in effect born into a different family, depending on their birth order. He theorized that each child is striving for superiority and struggling to find attention and affection from his parents. As they compete for attention, sibling rivalry emerges and they develop different personality traits based on striving for this power and attention. This may sound primitive and selfish, but most of the time it proves very accurate.

The bottom line is that we're totally different parents the first time around. Any pediatric health care provider can tell you about the dreaded "first-time parents." We're inexperienced, terrified, and certifiably insane. I am embarrassed to tell you how many times we took our firstborn to the emergency room at the special children's hospital in Atlanta. There was one day in particular that baby Sara had her regularly scheduled well-baby checkup. Everything checked out fine, except she was suffering some upper respiratory congestion due to the latest virus she had picked up at day care. Later that evening, the virus seemed to worsen and she developed a fever. So my husband and I took her to the after-hours care clinic. They gave her a dose of Tylenol and sent us home. We both thought the dose of Tylenol seemed rather large (we didn't realize at the time that they gave her children's Tylenol, which is more diluted than infants' Tylenol, so she needed a slightly larger dose).

At about 11:00 P.M., we were convinced that her breathing and heart rate were extremely elevated, and we decided the nurse had given her an overdose. When we called the clinic, my husband explained the problem and was extremely insulted when the nurse asked him, "Is this your first child?" I remember him shouting into the phone, "I used to be a physical trainer, I know how to take a heart rate!" When he hung up he was livid. They'd instructed us to take her to the ER if we thought there was a problem. (They probably figured if we were stupid enough to believe that they would overdose our child on Tylenol, we deserved to sit in the waiting room until 3:00 A.M.) When we walked out of the ER sometime past midnight, Tim said, "You know, we've covered every co-payment on the insurance card today: the scheduled visit [$15], the after-hours care

Does Birth Order Affect Job Choice?

A recent study conducted by Professor John Leong of Ohio State University shows that birth order may play a role in the occupations that are chosen as an adult. "One of the strongest findings was the fact that only children and firstborn children tended to have more cognitive and analytical interests, while later-borns were more artistic and oriented to the outdoors," Dr. Leong says. "Parents typically place different demands and have different expectations of children depending on their birth order. For example, parents may be extremely protective of only children and worry about their physical safety. That may be why only children are more likely to show interest in academic pursuits rather than physical or outdoor activities.

"As they have more children, parents tend to become more open and relaxed, and that may allow younger children to be more risk-taking. If the firstborn or only child wants to be a poet, that may concern parents. But by the fourth child, parents may not mind as much."

[$25], and the emergency care [$50]. That's impressive." As it turned out, Sara was fine. Tim and I were exhausted at work the next day, and it was probably all for nothing. But that's what first-time parents do. We're paranoid. We can't help it. Keeping another human being alive is a huge responsibility.

Think about birth order in terms of baby bottles.

First child: You have to boil everything that comes in contact with your baby's mouth. All the baby bottles are color-coded and neatly lined up in your bottle holder.

Second child: You buy a convenient plastic rack to hold baby bottle lids and nipples, and the dishwasher becomes your main source of sterilizing.

Third child: You rinse it out under the faucet and keep going.

And then there are the baby books:

First child: You record every coo, save their hair, and fill out every line, pasting photos in all the appropriate pages.

Second child: You keep your baby book in a big storage box along with all of the important notes, scraps, and photos in hopes of one day finding time to record all the memorable moments.

Third child: Memorabilia gets hung on the refrigerator with a magnet.

It's sad but true. The more babies there are, the busier moms get and the more relaxed we get as parents. Don't even get Sara (who is a middle child) started about the fact that there are no photos of her when she was Cinderella in the sixth-grade play or her high school graduation. She is convinced that middle children have it worst of all.

So let's talk about the characteristics found in each child according to birth order.

The Firstborn Child

"Most scientists believe that there are two types of firstborns. Both desire control, but they use different methods to attain it. The first type is a compliant nurturer or caregiver. The second type is an aggressive mover and shaker.

Firstborn Traits

- Natural leader—majority of politicians, directors, and spokespersons are firstborns
- High achiever—sets goals and reaches them

- Picky and precise—pays attention to detail and expects perfection
- Organized and competent
- Punctual
- Likes to be in control and doesn't like surprises
- Can be moody and lack sensitivity
- Can be intimidating and refuse to take no for an answer
- Sometimes can be a know-it-all
- Often bossy and feel that they are right
- Responsible and tries to keep the rules; will misbehave if rejected
- Tries to please others, especially adults; may not say no or disagree because they don't want to cause problems
- Poor at delegating because they want to make sure it's done right

"Children who are a first daughter or son with an older sibling of the opposite sex might exhibit firstborn traits. Children born with more than five years between them can often exhibit only-child or firstborn traits as well."

Parenting the Firstborn Child

- **Don't pressure him for perfection.** The firstborn child puts a lot of pressure on herself naturally, so don't push too hard. In fact, talk to your child about what your expectations are. Firstborns are usually never satisfied with their own accomplishments and probably assume that your expectations are higher.
- **Give lots and lots of praise.** Firstborns love to get your approval.
- **Don't demand too much.** Teresa McIntire from families.com says that older children often do more work than their younger siblings. Divide the workload as soon as the younger child is capable. Don't expect your firstborn to be an instant babysitter. Check with his schedule and pay him when appropriate.
- **Don't put too many responsibilities on your child.** You can't expect a six-year-old to watch her younger siblings and then be responsible if something happens. Let her know that it is not her fault and praise her for telling you about the incident.
- **Teach patience.** Eldest children are often bossy, says McIntire. They can do more than their younger siblings, so they feel like they are better. "Remind them that they were young once and to have patience," she points out. Help your child work through their frustrations with their younger siblings. "It is their job to teach their siblings, not rule over them."
- **Spend some special time with your oldest child.** Firstborns often feel overlooked because so much attention has to be spent on younger siblings.

Facts About Firstborns

- Fifty-two percent of U.S. presidents have been firstborn children, and most of the others were firstborn sons.
- Many newscasters and TV and radio talk show hosts are firstborns: Walter Cronkite, Peter Jennings, Dan Rather, Ted Koppel, Oprah Winfrey, Phil Donahue, Geraldo Rivera, Arsenio Hall, and Rush Limbaugh.
- Most astronauts sent into space were firstborns.
- Famous firstborn women include Hillary Rodham Clinton, Jacqueline Kennedy Onassis, Bette Davis, Sally Ride, and Joan Collins.

The Middle Child

Middle children typically get more independence. That's why they are usually more adventuresome, fun-loving, and outgoing.

They can also be rebellious, envious, and insecure. Many middle children feel parental neglect. They tend to feel inferior and crave affection. It's almost impossible for a middle child to establish power within the family. Many feel inadequate when compared to an older sibling.

Parenting the Middle Child

Here are some tips from Dr. Kevin Leman, author of *The Birth Order Book: Why You Are the Way You Are:*

- **Recognize that many middle children avoid sharing how they really feel about things.** If your middle child is an avoider, set aside times for just the two of you to talk. It's important to give this kind of time to every child, but a middle child is least likely to insist on his fair share. Be sure he or she gets it.
- **Take extra care to make your middle child feel special.** Typically the middle child feels squeezed by brothers or sisters above and below. The middle child needs those moments when you ask for his opinion or allow her to make choices.
- **Set up some regular privileges for the middle child.** Perhaps it is something as simple as watching a certain TV program with no interference from others in the family. Maybe it's going to a certain restaurant. The point is, this is the middle child's exclusive territory. When was the last time you made a special effort to give your child a new item of clothing rather than a hand-me-down? In some families, income is sufficient so that this is not a problem, but in other homes

economics make hand-me-downs a regular part of growing up. An occasional hand-me-down is fine, but your middle child may be particularly appreciative of something new, especially a key item, like a coat or jacket.

- **Listen carefully.** Pay attention to your middle child's answers or explanations for what is going on or what he or she thinks of certain situations. His or her desire to avoid conflict and not make waves may get in the way of the real facts. You may have to say, "C'mon now, let's have the whole story. You aren't going to get in trouble. I want to know how you really feel."
- **Be sure the family photo album has its share of pictures of your middle child.** Don't let him or her fall victim to the stereotyped fate of seeing thousands of pictures of the older brother or sister and only a few of him or her! And be sure you take some of your middle-born alone, not always with big brother or sister.

Middle-Born Traits

- Flexible
- Easygoing
- Peacemaker—can see all sides of a situation
- Social—may not feel that they have a special place in the family, so friends become more important
- Generous—they are used to sharing
- Secretive—don't openly share their feelings
- Avoids conflict—tries to keep life smooth
- May feel life is unfair
- May become a problem child if discouraged
- Independent
- Inventive—more likely to be an entrepreneur than a CEO
- May become co-dependent as they try to please everybody
- May feel unloved
- Strong negotiator

Facts About Middle Children

Some famous middle-borns include George Washington, Madonna, David Letterman, and John F. Kennedy. One birth order expert says that CEOs may tend to be firstborns, but the entrepreneurs, the "mavericks" who go out and do things on their own, are middle children. Bill Gates is a middle child.

The Last-Born Child

Last-borns have the fewest rules. By the time they come along, the parents are relaxed. The youngest is typically given very little responsibility around the house and has lots of people taking care of him. He tends to be the most spoiled. This is the child that gets coddled because parents recognize and appreciate that this is their last chance and they want to baby their child as long as possible. Because of this, youngest children are usually very happy. They are confident and secure, likeable and free-spirited. The youngest child almost always has someone to play with and grows up to be very social. And since the older siblings are responsible for most of the household chores, last-borns get more of a chance to develop their personalities and be silly.

Last-Born Traits

- Risk taker
- Outgoing
- Creative—idea person
- Strong people skills—love to talk to others
- Extrovert
- Competitive—pushes themselves to keep up with older siblings
- Financially irresponsible
- May be spoiled and self-centered
- Strong fear of rejection
- Feels small and weaker
- Sense of humor—likes to make others laugh
- Short attention span and gets bored quickly
- Expects others to do things for them
- Gets their own way
- May be jealous of older siblings
- May use manipulation to get his way
- May be the class clown

Parenting the Last-Born Child

Dr. Kevin Leman, author of *The Birth Order Book: Why You Are The Way You Are,* taught us this about parenting your last-born:

- **Enforce the rules.** It's a fact that last-born children get away with more and receive the least amount of discipline. Maybe that's why they are known risk takers. Try your best to enforce the same rules that you did for your other children.
- **Teach responsibility.** The youngest child is often seen as too small and helpless to help. Dr. Leman writes, "You want to raise a confident, self-reliant child so don't promote this helpless image."
- **Applaud accomplishments.** Leman says that last-borns often feel that nothing they do is good enough. So make a big deal out of their accomplishments. You may have seen your older children tie their shoes, but for your youngest this is her first time.
- **Don't baby them.** We can't help it—after all, they are our babies and it's so cute when they still pronounce a word wrong or do cute, babyish things. Leman says, "The last born is the one who will probably still have a pet name although he's 29 and has a master's degree." Doing things for your child that he can do for himself will become a habit that will grow with them. Teach your child to do things for himself and become self-sufficient.

Facts About Last-Borns

Many writers, artists, and musicians are youngest children. Many actors and comedians are the youngest children in their families: Drew Carey, Jim Carrey, Steve Martin, Billy Crystal, Eddie Murphy, Goldie Hawn, Jay Leno, Chevy Chase, Danny DeVito, and Whoopi Goldberg.

Does Birth Order Affect Intelligence?

Many studies over the years have shown a relationship between birth order and intelligence, reporting slightly higher intelligence among older siblings. However a recent study by Ohio State University provides evidence that birth order doesn't have an affect on intelligence.

The study suggests a critical flaw in previous research. Those studies compared children from different families, meaning the differences they found were due to the size of the families, not birth order. According to Aaron Wichman, lead author of the study at Ohio State, children from larger families have disadvantages that impact their intelligence. Wichman says in reality the fourth-born child is just as intelligent as the first-born, but they don't do as well as children from smaller families.

In addition, the younger a mother at the birth of her first child, the lower intelligence scores were within a family. Younger mothers tend to have less education, more children, lower income, and other factors that negatively affect the intelligence of their children.

What that tells us is that the time we spend around the kitchen table helping our kids with homework is what really makes the difference in their education and their intelligence.

The Only Child

Only children have many of the same characteristics as firstborn children, only multiplied. They tend to be even more responsible and greater perfectionists. They spend most of their time with adults, so they are very comfortable with adults and with older friends.

Only-Child Traits

- Close relationship to parents
- Good self-control
- Leadership skills
- Mature
- Dependable
- Unforgiving
- Demanding
- Sensitive—feelings easily hurt
- Difficulty sharing
- Overly critical of others
- Private
- May feel under pressure to succeed

Parenting the Only Child

- **Let them be children.** Usually, only children are very mature for their age and it is easy for parents to find themselves treating their child as an adult or expecting too much from them. Don't forget that he or she is a child.
- **Involve them in peer-group situations.** Give your only child plenty of opportunities to play with and spend time with other children. One of the biggest challenges is learning how to share. This is a learned skill and it takes lots of practice.
- **Don't expect perfection.** Much like firstborn children, only children feel pressure from their parents to be perfect. Make sure your child knows that it's okay to make mistakes. Make sure your expectations are realistic.

Famous Only Children

Athletes: Joe Montana and Tiger Woods. Actors: Cary Grant, Frank Sinatra, Robin Williams, Elizabeth Taylor, Tommy Lee Jones, Robert De Niro, Natalie Portman, Charlize

Theron, Sarah Michelle Gellar. Politicians: Franklin Delano Roosevelt, Winston Churchill, Alan Greenspan. Other only children include Elvis Presley, Robert Louis Stevenson, and Leonardo da Vinci.

Clutter-Busting Resources

WEBSITES

www.families.com
Much of the information from this chapter came from this great website, by mother of four Teresa McIntire.

BOOKS

The Birth Order Book: Why You Are the Way You Are
by Dr. Kevin Leman

43

Getting Ready for Number Two

From Stephanie

As usual, I'm just going to put it out there right away: having two children is a lot harder than having just one. I am convinced (and I've had a doctor back me up on this) that your second pregnancy is harder than your first. Pregnancy takes a lot out of your body, and it takes years to recover (if you do ever recover fully). The latest advice says that it takes your body at least eighteen months to recover from pregnancy and delivery. If you have your children close together like I did, it's exhausting. It pays off later on because they have a perpetual playmate, but those first few years take a lot out of a mom, physically and emotionally.

My second child was a complete surprise. In all the books I had read and all the research I had absorbed, somehow I missed that whole thing about how you can become fertile while you are still breast-feeding. In fact, I was down to breast-feeding only about one time each night when I realized I was pregnant with my second child. My baby was only eight months old when number two became a reality. I was pregnant for almost two months before I even realized I *could* be pregnant. I had returned to work from maternity leave only four months prior. And while I *know* how it happens, I'm still not sure *how* it happened. I can't even remember having sex. I was breast-feeding and bottle-feeding, up a few times each night, and utterly exhausted because I was juggling a full-time career, day care, a house, and a husband who traveled all the time.

I was casually complaining over the phone one day to my friend Laura (a mother of four) that I was tired, didn't feel good before I ate, and didn't feel good after I ate, and I thought I should see a doctor because maybe I had caught the latest virus going around the day care. Suddenly I heard laughter coming from the phone. "Stephanie, you're pregnant!" she said. I explained to her that that was physically impossible—you have to have sex to get pregnant, Tim had been out of town most of the month, and the one week that he had been in town, I'd had the flu. But she got me thinking, and I happened to have a pregnancy test in the cabinet, so I decided to pee on the stick. Sure enough, it turned pink.

I was in total shock and disbelief! I had only been back from maternity leave for four short months! How was I going to tell my boss? My husband was going to think it was the second immaculate conception. How could anyone be this fertile?

Ironically, my boss found out before my own husband! It was early morning when I completed the positive test, and my husband had already left for work. I didn't want to tell him over the phone, so I decided to wait until that night. At lunch that day, I was with my boss and co-workers at a gourmet Mexican restaurant in Buckhead when I suddenly felt very sick. I was sitting at the linen-draped table gulping as much ice water as I could in an effort to keep things going in the down direction. When it came time to order, I couldn't. I couldn't stand the smell of food at that moment, let alone Mexican food. I rushed to the restroom and hid in a stall. I was sitting on the floor (which proves just how sick I was, because I normally don't even like *standing* on the floor of a public restroom) and decided to call my husband. Surely he'd be my hero and pick me up so I wouldn't have to ruin the party by having someone drive me home.

Of course he was anything but understanding. He had his own set of business-related circumstances and reminded me that I was only four blocks from my office—I could stick it out or have someone drive me back. Then he asked if I was pregnant. I denied it, and I think I called him a name and hung up. I dragged myself back to the table. Everyone could see that something was wrong. Someone commented about how pale I was. And my boss chimed in with, "You're pregnant!" I denied it again. Someone suggested that we stop and buy a pregnancy test on the way back to work, but I firmly informed them that I was not about to pee on a stick for the entertainment of the office. "We're close, but we're not that close."

The interesting thing about this surprise pregnancy was the mental torture I put myself through over the fact that I was having another baby too soon after the birth of my first. I was devastatingly guilt-ridden and thought that I was cheating my daughter out of her babyhood by bringing another baby into our family too quickly. I really struggled with this, right up to the night before I was scheduled to be induced. I was sitting in the bathtub crying and lamenting the loss of my firstborn's babyhood. If you have feelings like this, I assure you that you are entirely incorrect and that it's probably a result of hormones.

The minute my daughter saw her baby brother, she knew he was *hers*. We have the most remarkable photos of her meeting him for the first time, with her wholly and utterly thrilled. She was immediately in love, and in fact, when the nurses came to take her baby brother for his first bath, she screamed her head off. From that time on, all doctors and nurses were required to do what they had to do to her baby brother within his sister's line of sight. She was terrified that someone was going to take him. It didn't take me long to realize that I had actually given her the greatest gift anyone ever could—a brother and a live-in playmate. They are just seventeen months apart. Neither has ever known life without the other. It has given them a very close and special relationship that I pray they will cherish for the rest of their lives, long after their parents are gone.

From Sara

My mother is an only child and she never quite understood why my two sisters and I insisted on fighting all the time. "Why do you have to fight?" she'd say. "You're so lucky to have each other." You can imagine whether that made us stop in our tracks, reconsider our disputes, and pledge our undying sisterly love to one another. But as anyone with siblings knows, no matter how many fights you had growing up, you actually do have that undying love for each other. That's the beauty of having a second child, if you decide to.

The other plus is that you have a much, much shorter learning curve the second time around. You have the confidence of knowing you've managed all right so far with the first child, so you can probably pull it off again. And you're much more laid back with the second child. My older sister always jokes about how she was grounded when she got her first B in school. By the time I came along, B's were just fine!

However, bringing a second child into the family can be a big adjustment for some other folks in your house: your first child and your husband. Your older child will undoubtedly go through an adjustment period, and some of it might not be pretty. And if your husband is like mine, he may have a tougher time adjusting to the second child than the first. I always tease David that I went through postpartum depression when Anna was born and he went through it when Cade was born. Having a second baby means "all hands on deck." Dads have to take on more than ever, generally taking care of the older child while Mom takes care of the new baby. The free time they enjoyed before is suddenly gone. It's kind of hard to muster any sympathy for them, though—hey, at least they know how we feel now!

Of course, all the extra work and effort of having a second child are so worth it. If you ever wondered if you could love another child as much as your first, you now know that your heart expands with each child. When Cade was born I felt that same overwhelming, overpowering love (the kind that lets you know you'd throw yourself in front of a truck for this little person) that I had when Anna was born. We marveled (and still marvel) at his uniqueness—how can two children from the same parents be so utterly different?

I'll never forget how Anna reacted when Cade was born. She was two and a half and she kept telling everyone in the hospital, "My baby brudder's here, my baby brudder's here!" With the birth of a second or third (or fourth . . .) child, you've given your children friends like no other—the kind they will always be able to count on no matter what. Try to remember that, because it won't be long before you'll feel like you need a referee's whistle.

Your Pregnancy

From Stephanie

Evaluate your first birth experience and talk to your doctor about it. What went well, and what would you change this time around? No birth is the same, so you have to prepare and educate yourself all over again. My second birth resulted in a C-section (my son's head was in the 90th percentile in size and I had to be induced a little early, but still ended up in surgery). Plus, medical techniques get changed and updated quickly, so don't assume you know all there is to know. You'll also be surprised at how much you've forgotten. When your mind is concentrating on the latest stage of development of the child you already have, your attention won't be on what happens during pregnancy and childbirth. The same goes for breast-feeding. Just because it didn't work for you the first time doesn't mean it won't work better for baby number two.

Try to take time to appreciate and enjoy your pregnancy. You won't have as much time as you did with number one because you're already a mom. You'll probably feel both much more tired and much more relaxed during your second pregnancy. You'll know what things feel like and what to expect. Take the time to document your progress and appreciate the moment. Pregnancy is such a brief period in our lives, and it's such a privilege to share your body with that new little person.

Loving Another

Almost every parent wonders how they will love a second child as much as they love the first. From my own experience, I can tell you that you have enough love for both. There will be times when you prefer one more than the other (depending on ages, activities, and who recently pissed you off the most). You will love them differently, but the intensity of your love will be the same for both. Don't worry about it—it will just happen. And your firstborn will not suffer because of it.

Prepare Your Home

Remember that just because your house is kid-friendly doesn't mean that it's babyproof. Big sisters and brothers have toys with lots of pieces that can be a real threat to a new baby. So be sure to put childproofing on your to-do list. And teach your older child how to keep toys with small pieces out of baby's reach.

Breaking the News to the Older Child

When?

From Stephanie

Some psychologists believe that it's better to wait to tell younger children during the second trimester, when the pregnancy is more stable and children are able to better understand because they can see the physical changes in mommy.

Personally, I prefer the school of thought that says you should let siblings in on the big news as soon as possible. I don't like keeping such a big secret from my kids; it's too hard to hide. And I think it makes it more special when siblings are included in doctor visits and sonograms and planning.

Let your older child help with making preparations for the nursery and baby equipment. Let him pick out a toy for his new baby brother or sister. These things help build the anticipation, and they concentrate on the positives rather than feelings of being "replaced."

Also, if your child is a toddler, be sure to make any big changes *before* the arrival of the new baby. For example, potty training and learning to sleep in her own bed are the kinds of things that will go much easier when the changes can't be blamed on the arrival of the new baby. It will also be easier on you—potty training is no small task. If your child is still sleeping in a crib or with you when you get pregnant, be sure to transition them to their own bed as soon as possible so your older child won't feel as if he's been pushed out to make room for the new baby. Some psychologists even recommend taking his old crib down, and putting it back up only right before your second child is born.

How?

Make sure you phrase it as "We are going to have a baby," not "I am having a baby." This big event is happening to the whole family, and you want them to feel that they're a part of it too.

Dr. Andrea McCoy, assistant professor of clinical pediatrics at Pennsylvania State University and the Penn State Geisinger Health System, suggests arranging an area for your toddler to set up a crib and other things for a baby doll. "Older toddlers are great imitators," she says. "They can mimic preparations going on around the home. Talking and imitating help the toddler feel involved and less frightened of the unknown." Let your child practice baby care with the doll. Talk to him about supporting a baby's head and explain that babies need to be handled very gently and slowly.

Talk to your older child about what to expect when baby arrives. Look at the scrapbook/photos and video of your older child's birth and babyhood. Talk to them about what it was like and how everyone wanted to see and hold them. Explain how tired you will be and that the baby will take a lot of time and care. Emphasize that the baby will not be a playmate for a while, that new babies don't do much except eat, sleep, cry, and poop. Reassure your older child that you will still love her just as much—even when you're paying more attention to the new baby.

If you have friends with a new baby, visit them. Point out their baby's hair and wrinkly skin and how she doesn't have teeth yet. Help your child learn to appreciate why babies are special.

Read books about babies and siblings to reinforce what's expected and how life will change with the new baby's arrival. We like *I'm a Big Sister* and *I'm a Big Brother* by Joanna Cole. Be careful, though, because some big brother/big sister books describe negative behaviors. And give your child plenty of opportunities to ask questions and express her own feelings.

A Gift from Baby

From Sara

One great idea that I and many other moms have used is to provide a gift from baby to your older sibling on the day that you come home from the hospital. There is so much attention focused on the new baby that feelings of resentment can often creep in quickly. A little gift from the new baby to big brother or sister can help make the day special for them too.

A Big Brother or Big Sister T-Shirt

Buy or borrow a T-shirt for your child that says "I'm a Big Sister" or "I'm a Big Brother" for your child to wear to the hospital to see the new baby. Make a big deal about the importance of your child's new role in the family.

When Baby Comes Home

Most of us worry about our first child being jealous of the new baby. And once they realize that the baby isn't going back to the hospital, this is a very real problem. Seeing Mommy holding and caring for the new baby is the hardest part for young siblings. Many toddlers will regress—which means they will start talking like a baby, wetting their pants, or behaving badly in an effort to get your attention. Here are a few tips to help you deal with and/or prevent sibling rivalry:

- Ask your friends and family members to bring "big brother" or "big sister" gifts instead of baby gifts so your older child won't feel left out.

- Spend some one-on-one time with your older child. Both parents should schedule some time every day. Just spend a few minutes with your older child in your lap, listening to him tell you about his day, reading to him, or playing a game. A few minutes can go a long way.
- Be a great listener. Let your older child talk about how he or she feels about the new baby. Don't belittle her opinion. If she expresses some negative feelings, help her work through them. Point out things that are special about her and use positive talk to refocus her perceptions.
- Take every opportunity to point out the benefits of being the oldest: not having to eat disgusting baby food, riding a bike, playing at a friend's house, etc.
- Make sure your child understands that hurting the baby is never allowed. Give your child other ways to express angry feelings they may have toward the baby. For example, they could draw a picture or roar like a lion.
- If they need to be "babied," then do it. Parents tend to expect more from their older child the minute the younger child enters the home.
- When visitors stop by, bring your older child into the conversation as much as possible. It's so easy to overlook the older sibling when there's an adorable new baby around. Talk about ways your older child has helped you or how the baby has reacted to his big brother.
- In the beginning, big brothers and sisters need some space to call their own. Don't make them share every toy. Some things are special and are just for them.
- Give your child special chores to do to help with caring for baby. Make him take some ownership and pride in caring for his baby brother or sister. He can help with pushing the stroller, bathing, or even changing diapers.

What About You?

Having a second child is no small challenge. Exhaustion and anxiety are very common. During the first few months of your baby's life, you will have little to no time for yourself. Schedule time for yourself *every* day, even if it's just thirty minutes to flip through a favorite magazine or take a quick power nap. Just a few minutes of recharging will make you a better, healthier, happier mom.

Adding another child to your family will also cause a strain on your marriage. You'll have less alone time with your spouse, you'll almost never be able to finish a conversation without being interrupted, you'll fight about the division of labor, and sex will pretty much become a thing of the past. Your husband will have to become an active participant in the care of your children and your house. Make him understand that a second child means more work for everyone. You both need to make a list of things that have to be done and negotiate what responsibilities he will need to take on. He will really need to focus on getting involved with your firstborn child during the first few months of your new baby's life. Your older child will need the extra attention because the majority of your time will be spent on the new baby and healing yourself. So let go of some of the chores you do and be happy with the way he does them, even if it's different from the way you do them. This isn't about perfection—it's about survival.

Get a Double Stroller

It is impossible to go anywhere with two young children unless you can confine them in a stroller. It will make your life easier, and it will make their life easier. Trust us, your older child is going to throw a fit if you make him walk and put the baby in a stroller. And most mothers agree that the best double strollers have one baby in front and one in back. The side-by-side double strollers are too wide to navigate through doorways and clothing racks. Plus, when they're side by side, they tend to fight more. Another great rule to keep is "We stay in the stroller [or shopping cart] when we're in a store." Never break this rule—even if it means you have to make a scene a couple of times to make the rule stick—and you'll never have to have a power struggle with kids who want to run around the mall or store while you're trying to get your shopping done. It will give you hours of peaceful shopping for a few years.

Get Organized

From Stephanie

I know this is a shocker coming from me, but moms are responsible for a lot of stuff and you have to have a system to survive. I found one website that said, "One child is a relationship. Two is a small business." This is so true. Make sure you get a good system for organizing your family. Two kids means everything doubles. You have to keep up with two sets of homework, two sets of doctor appointments, two sets of friends, two sets of sporting events, two sets of social engagements, sometimes even two different schools.

I currently have a second grader and a first grader at the same school. I am constantly sending the wrong supplies to the wrong teacher. When they were doing a school fundraiser, we were creating raffle baskets. One teacher's theme was a cat lover's basket and the other teacher's theme was family fun. Of course, I sent a cat toy to the family fun classroom. The teacher looked into the bag, gave me the funniest look, and asked, "What's this for?" I realized my mistake. Thank goodness she didn't have a cat and think I was just bringing her a gift; otherwise I would have had to go out and find another donation!

My friend Chrise actually dressed her four-year-old up and took her to the teacher meet and greet on the wrong day—*twice.* Her daughter had to start preschool without meeting her teacher prior to the first day of school (and it wasn't pretty). She's not an idiot—she's a busy mom with three kids. It's not easy to keep up with everything, so you have to have a system! We use a huge calendar that hangs in an entryway in our kitchen. *Everything* for everyone in the family (including Dad) is recorded there: bills, social dates, reminders, deadlines, travel plans, sports practices, work schedules, you name it. I would not survive without it.

If there are closets you want to clean out or rooms you want to paint, etc., do it all now. When you have two children, you'll have very little time to accomplish anything again until they're old enough to go outside and play by themselves.

Preschool or "Mom's Morning Out" Programs Are a Huge Help

From Sara

Put your older child in a preschool program for a couple of hours each day. Many churches have these programs available and they're great. It gives you a few hours of bonding time with the new baby, and it gives your older child a chance to do something on his own, make friends, and stay stimulated.

Fashionable Purses Are Optional

From Stephanie

Forget the chic, expensive designer bags. When you're a mom of two or more, the more pockets and zippers you have, the better. Sara (who has a major purse fetish) won't agree with me on this, because sure, there are a few designer bags out there that are functional, but sorry, those never fit into my budget. And besides, kids' stuff destroys your purse. I can't tell you how nasty the bottom of my mommy purse is. It's full of crumbs, balled-up tissues, half-eaten lollipops, pieces of broken toys, socks . . . I could go on and on. It's not because I'm gross—it's because I'm a mom on the go, with kids in tow. It just happens. Sara's even had a child vomit into her purse. My point is, get a functional bag that can hold baby stuff, kid stuff, mommy stuff, and lots of extra wipes. While your kids are young, fashion is not the most important thing.

Relax

The good news is that newborns sleep a lot and they can't fight with their siblings until they learn to sit up. So savor those early days. Take naps or spend one-on-one time with your firstborn.

It's All About Me

I've read more and more websites that recommend asking for a gift for yourself. You get the big baby shower the first time around, so you probably have everything you need for baby. Request a nice robe, jewelry, or something else for the hardworking mom. And by the way, if you have babies several years apart or are having a different gender this time, it's perfectly acceptable to have a baby shower for baby number two—*if* you can stand to listen to all the horror stories as your friends share their birth experiences. Chances are they've had their first baby by now too, and moms love to tell their stories—so think about that before you commit to a big get-together.

Clutter-Busting Resources

WEBSITES

www.growingafamily.com/preparing.htm

BOOKS

I'm a Big Sister
by Joanna Cole

I'm a Big Brother
by Joanna Cole

44

Pets and the Family

From Sara

"Those who love me, love my dogs." I have a bone-shaped paperweight engraved with that saying on my desk. And it's true. In fact, for ten years we had two big ones. Actually, one big one and one gigantic one—the latter weighed 125 pounds. Their heads hit most people right at crotch level, which was really convenient for the dogs but not so much for the humans. When guests were invited to dine at my house there'd usually be a dog or two lying under the dining room table. Accepting that invitation meant understanding that while you were cutting your steak, you might also be getting licked on the ankle. Personally, I considered that a bonus.

My husband and I often joked that our dogs cost more than our kids. Our dogs didn't have health insurance, so trips to the vet cost full price. They required a lot of food, a big yard and a fence, a large vehicle, dog sitters, and trips to the groomer. The only point they had in their financial favor was that they wouldn't go to college. They were big, expensive, furry creatures who shed a lot and constantly got my carpet dirty. There were scratches on every door in the house and nose prints on every window. But I wouldn't have had it any other way. No one in my family would, not even my husband, David, who feared he might be allergic to our second dog the night we brought him home with us. "I hope not," I told him. "I'd hate for you to have to leave."

I realize not everyone is as big a dog lover as me. But the subject of pets and family is important, because if you're a mom, at some point your child will ask you for a pet. It may not be a dog or a cat—it may be a turtle or a fish or a hermit crab—but believe me, you *will* get asked the question. And when it comes, you'd better know how to answer.

Should You Get a Pet?

The idea of getting a pet goes through every parent's head at some point. Generally this happens after your child has asked you for the hundredth time. The decision to bring a pet into your home, particularly a dog or cat (they require the most care), should not be taken lightly. Animals are not disposable. They are living, breathing, feeling creatures who require significant care, time, and money.

From Stephanie

Caring for puppies is much like caring for a newborn! They cry in the night, they pee and poop all over the place, and they require huge amounts of attention and care. Tim and I actually used to look at each other when we were on our way to a spontaneous dinner (before kids) and say, "I'm so glad we don't have a dog."

From Sara

Even though pets undoubtedly add work to your life, they also add equal amounts of joy. Pets have real benefits for both kids and adults. According to the Humane Society, children raised with animals have stronger immune systems and are better socialized and more empathetic. Animals tend to stimulate compassion and good behavior, and they are great stress relievers, which also helps the immune system. You've probably heard that petting a dog or a cat has been shown to reduce blood pressure. Children who live with animals are also less likely to have allergies because their bodies learn to fend off the pet's allergens. Children who care for pets learn at a young age about responsibility for another living creature. Pets widen our experience of life, taking us outside of ourselves, helping us to explore and appreciate the natural world that we are a part of. Pets are a reminder of our connection to nature and the impact our actions have on it.

But it's important to have realistic expectations. Pets are expensive and a lot of work—which usually falls to the parents. It's unrealistic to expect a child to be completely responsible for an animal. Older children can help with feeding and bathing, but ultimately the dog is the parents' responsibility. You can teach your kids about responsibility by example.

Remember that your children will need training, too. Children must understand how to interact with animals safely. No putting their hands into food bowls, taking away treats, and so on. Most accidents are the result of inappropriate behavior such as this. Your pet may be a full member of your family, but it's crucial to remember that he is an animal and not a human.

Dogs

Since they are generally at the top of the wish list and require the most care and attention, let's first talk about dogs. No animals possess a greater ability to love and bond with human beings than dogs. They are always happy to see us when we come home, they forgive us when we accidentally step on their tails, and they love to be with us, even when we don't look or feel our best.

However, people who adopt dogs often don't know what they are getting into. That's why there are so many dogs abandoned by their owners or, even worse, mistreated and abused by the ones who chose them in the first place. Adopting a dog is a big decision. Dogs require our time, care, attention, patience, and love throughout their lives. A dog is a living, breathing being, not a possession to be discarded when it becomes inconvenient. When you are looking at that cute little puppy, remember that you are looking at a twelve-to-fifteen-year commitment. Adopting a dog means making a promise. If you are ready to make that promise, then you are ready to adopt a dog.

There are many factors to consider when deciding to adopt a dog. Where you live, your lifestyle, other family members, other pets, and your financial situation should all be considered when making the decision to adopt a dog.

Dogs require daily exercise and trips outside, even when it's cold and raining. They greatly benefit from organized obedience classes as well as training at home. Unlike many other pets, dogs need proper arrangements for their care when you go on vacation. They need ample room to run and play and shelter from the cold and heat. Dogs are social animals and thrive when they are made full members of your family with plenty of social interaction and love.

PetEducation.com from Drs. Foster and Smith established a Pet's Bill of Rights. If you provide your dog with the basic "rights" as they are outlined here, you will be rewarded with a relationship with your dog that will exceed even your highest expectations.

The Pet's Bill of Rights

1. We have the right to be **full members of your family.** We thrive on social interaction, praise, and love.

2. We have the right to **stimulation.** We need new games, new toys, new experiences, and new smells to be happy.

3. We have the right to **regular exercise.** Without it, we could become hyper, sluggish, or fat.

4. We have the right to have **fun.** We enjoy acting like clowns now and then; don't expect us to be predictable all the time.

5. We have the right to **quality health care.** Please stay good friends with our vet!

6. We have the right to a **good diet.** Like some people, we don't know what's best for us. We depend on you.

7. We have the right **not to be rejected** because of your expectations that we be great show dogs, watch dogs, hunters, or babysitters.

8. We have the right to receive **proper training.** Otherwise, our good relationship could be marred by confusion and strife—and we could become dangerous to ourselves and others.

9. We have the right to **guidance and correction** based on understanding and compassion, rather than abuse.

10. We have the right to **live with dignity** and to die with dignity when the time comes.

Things to Consider

Do You Have Time for a Dog?

Dogs require considerable time from their owners. Certainly you have demands on your time already. Do you have the time to take your dog for a walk every day and take him to the vet for regular checkups and when he is sick? Do you frequently spend time away from home working or on vacation? A dog doesn't need for you to be with him every minute, but he will need a place in your daily schedule. Take a realistic look at your life and decide if you have the time a dog requires.

Do You Have Room for a Dog?

Do you live in an apartment or a house? Many dogs can adapt well to apartment living, but it takes a special commitment from the owner. Small dogs are usually best suited to apartments; larger dogs need more room and a yard where they can run and play. And if you want a larger dog, you'll need a fence too. Make sure the fence is properly built and high enough so that your dog can't get out to roam unattended.

Can You Afford a Dog?

You've probably realized by now that owning a dog is also a financial commitment. Do you have the resources to provide the veterinary care (including spaying or neutering), shelter, fencing, training, food, and other supplies your dog will need?

Are You Allowed to Have a Dog?

Some apartment communities do not allow pets or charge extra if you own a cat or a dog. They may also put a limit on the number of pets you can own. Make sure you check your lease before you take home any pet.

Do You Have Other Pets?

Four-footed members of your family will have to get used to a new dog, too. Dogs are pack animals, so they usually enjoy company, but just like humans, they can become jealous. After a while, this will probably go away, but you may feel like a referee in the beginning. Cats and dogs usually live together well. Even if they don't become best buddies, they typically learn to peacefully live in the same space.

Puppy or Adult Dog?

Puppies and adult dogs each offer specific advantages, depending on your lifestyle. There is no right or wrong answer to this question, it is simply a matter of determining what is best for you and your future pet.

The greatest advantage of adopting a puppy is that she will be able to grow up with you. You'll be able to train her and teach her your rules before she's had a chance to learn many other bad habits. However, puppies require lots of time and patience from their new owners. You'll need to housetrain your new pup and puppyproof your home to keep her from chewing up anything you treasure. Puppies need to chew, so you'll want to provide your pup with plenty of safe chew toys. It's probably not a good idea to get a puppy if you are going to have to leave her alone all day. Adult dogs can spend eight hours by themselves without too much trouble, but a pup needs people around to take care of her needs. Housetraining will be much easier if you don't leave your pup alone for long periods of time.

Adult dogs, on the other hand, are often already housetrained and over their puppy chewing stage. It's important to remember that shelter dogs have probably had pasts that strongly influence their personality. Some have been abused or neglected in their previous homes. Some have never lived with people. When you adopt an adult dog, you are adopting her previous experiences, too. She'll need your understanding and patience as she adjusts to her new life. Don't worry, she won't blame you for things done to her in the past. She'll be more than willing to give you the chance to earn her trust, and she'll adore you as if you've been the only person or family she's ever had.

Which Kind of Dog Is Right for You?

If you've spent much time around dogs, you know they really do have distinct personalities. Some are active and love to fetch a ball all day. Others could care less about a ball and would rather snuggle with a teddy bear. Some like to be in constant contact with humans, while others like more time to themselves. Some dogs have dominant, assertive personalities, while others tend to be more submissive and passive. Assertive dogs will require lots of training and proper leadership from you. More submissive dogs may need extra care, as they might get upset when you correct them too firmly. Dominant dogs are more likely to be protective than passive ones. But never get a dog simply to be an alarm system for your house.

This is another important reason to consider your lifestyle. Are you an active, outdoorsy person and want a dog who will enjoy nature as much as you? Or do you want a dog who will enjoy curling up with you by the fire? Do you have the time to spend on extra training for an active dog? Do you have the room for an active dog to play and run? Confining an active, athletic dog to a small area is a sure recipe for destructive behavior. Try to find a dog with a personality that complements your lifestyle.

Before you adopt a dog, do your homework! If you know what breed of dog you would like to own, find out as much as you can about that breed so you'll know what to expect. There are books published on virtually every breed in existence. You can find them at your local bookstore or pet store.

Male or Female?

You've probably heard a lot of different opinions about the specific traits of male and female dogs. Most of the stereotypes are not true, but a few are. Female dogs do tend to be smaller than their male counterparts of the same breed. And males typically are more territorial than females—they mark and defend their property, although neutering helps alleviate that urge.

Where to Find a Dog

Once you've made the decision to adopt a dog and decided on the breed, gender, and age you would like, where do you go to find your pet? For puppies, it's best to go to a reputable breeder or animal shelter. The Humane Society advises against buying a puppy from a pet store. Often the puppies in these stores come from "puppy mills," mass breeding facilities that typically keep dogs in cruel and inhumane conditions. Puppies from puppy mills often have multiple and serious health problems.

Make sure to research your breeder thoroughly. Be wary of newspaper and website ads. Any good breeder should care where their puppies are going and should carefully interview you as well.

If you are interested in an adult dog, purebred rescue groups are a great place to find a dog to adopt. These rescue groups are generally run by people who have an in-depth knowledge of the breed. They foster dogs until they are adopted, so they can usually tell you a lot about the personality and temperament of the dog you are interested in adopting. To find a rescue organization near you, call the U.S. Humane Society at 202-452-1100 and ask for the companion animals section.

Petfinder.com features adoptable pets from thousands of rescue organizations across the United States. You can search by breed, age, gender, size, and location.

Introducing Your New Baby to the Family Pet

If you already had four-legged children before your human babies entered the family, you've probably wondered about the best way to introduce your pets to the new baby so that everyone makes as smooth a transition as possible (i.e., no one starts destroying furniture or pooping on the rug). You can help your pet cope with this big change the same way parents help children understand that a new brother or sister will be joining the family. By following these tips from the Humane Society, you can ease your pet's stress, help her welcome your new baby, and prevent any problems.

Before the Baby Comes

- Take your pet to the veterinarian for a routine health exam and necessary vaccinations.
- Spay or neuter your pet. Not only do sterilized pets typically have fewer health problems associated with their reproductive systems, but they are also calmer and less likely to bite.
- Consult with a veterinarian and pediatrician if the thought of your newborn interacting with the family pet makes you uncomfortable. By working with these experts before your baby is born, you can resolve problems early and put your mind at ease.
- Address any pet training and behavior problems. If your pet exhibits fear and anxiety, now is the time to get help from an animal behavior specialist.
- If your pet's behavior includes gentle nibbling, pouncing, or swatting at you and others, redirect that behavior to appropriate objects.
- Get your pet used to nail trims.
- Train your pet to remain calmly on the floor beside you until you invite him on your lap, which will soon cradle a newborn.
- Consider enrolling in a training class with your dog, and practice training techniques. Training allows you to safely and humanely control your dog's behavior and enhances the bond between you and your pet.
- Encourage friends with infants to visit your home to accustom your pet to babies. Closely supervise all pet-infant interactions!

- Accustom your pet to baby-related noises months before the baby is expected. For example, play recordings of a baby crying, turn on the mechanical infant swing, and use the rocking chair. Make these positive experiences for your pet by offering a treat or playtime.
- To discourage your pet from jumping on the baby's crib and changing table, apply double-sided tape to the furniture.
- If the baby's room will be off-limits to your pet, install a sturdy barrier such as a removable gate (available at pet or baby supply stores) or, for jumpers, even a screen door. Because these barriers still allow your pet to see and hear what's happening in the room, he'll feel less isolated from the family and more comfortable with the new baby noises.
- Use a baby doll to help your pet get used to the real thing. Carry around a swaddled baby doll, take the doll in the stroller when you walk your dog, and use the doll to get your pet used to routine baby activities, such as bathing and diaper changing.
- Talk to your pet about the baby, using the baby's name if you've selected one.
- Sprinkle baby powder or baby oil on your skin so your pet becomes familiar with the new smells.
- Finally, plan ahead to make sure your pet gets proper care while you're away having your baby.

After the Baby Is Born

- Before you bring your baby home from the hospital, have your partner or a friend take home something with the baby's scent (such as a blanket) for your pet to investigate.
- When you come home from the hospital, have someone else take the baby into another room while you give your pet a warm but calm welcome.
- After the initial greeting, you can bring your pet with you to sit next to the baby. Reward your pet with treats for appropriate behavior. Remember, you want your pet to view associating with the baby as a positive experience. To prevent anxiety or injury, never force your pet to get near the baby, and always supervise any interaction.
- Try to maintain regular routines as much as possible to help your pet adjust. And be sure to spend one-on-one quality time with your pet each day—it may help relax you, too. With proper training, supervision, and adjustments, you, your new baby, and your pet should be able to live together safely and happily as one (now larger) family.

Keeping Kids and Pets Safe

Here are some helpful tips from *Parenting* magazine on protecting your child and your animal from each other.

Dogs

Every year about four hundred thousand kids need medical help for dog bites, and about 80 percent of canine bites are from animals that children know well. "Dogs may bite because they're frightened—especially if they're being teased—or because they're protecting their bed, a toy, or their food," says Stephanie Shain, director of outreach for the Humane Society of the United States.

- Teach your child to "be a tree"—to stand still with her hands at her sides and let a dog she doesn't know sniff her. Explain that if she runs away, the dog may think she's playing and chase her. Tell her to curl up into a ball to protect her face and hands if a dog knocks her down.
- Enroll your dog in an obedience class (you can do it as early as twelve weeks) so he learns not to jump on people and to follow some simple commands, which can help keep him under control around kids.
- Use baby gates to keep your dog in a room away from your child when necessary. A crate, which provides a safe haven for him and protection for your child, can be a very good idea.
- Teach your child to avoid dogs that are growling or baring their teeth or whose fur is standing on end.
- Instruct her never to stare into a dog's eyes, which can antagonize it.
- Show her how to stroke a dog's back and sides instead of reaching over his head.
- Never play tug-of-war or wrestle with a dog; roughhousing can trigger a bite.
- To prevent diseases caused by parasites, leave poop scooping to adults, and take your pooch for regular veterinary checkups.
- Have your dog spayed or neutered (at around five months), which can calm him.

Cats

"Unlike dogs, cats typically run away when bothered by a child. A cat will rarely chase anyone who runs away from it," says Shain. "But if a child chases a cat or corners it, the animal may lash out. Your child should learn to just let it go."

Special Considerations for Pregnant Moms and Cats

Avoid contact with cats because they can carry toxoplasmosis, a disease that may increase the risk of miscarriage or fetal deformities. To reduce your risk:

- Keep your cat indoors, where he's less likely to hunt mice or other small animals. (Cats get the parasite from eating raw meat.)
- Feed your feline only commercial cat food—never undercooked meat.
- Have your spouse clean the litter box daily. If you have to do it yourself, wear rubber gloves and wash both your hands and the gloves thoroughly when finished.
- Avoid stray or outdoor cats; you don't know what they may be carrying.

- Teach your child that if a kitty flips its tail back and forth quickly, it's more likely to scratch or bite, so avoid it.
- If your child is scratched or bitten by a cat, wash the area well with soap and water, and rinse for at least thirty seconds. If the bite punctured the skin, call your doctor. After a scratch, watch for swollen glands or lingering tenderness at the site over the next two weeks—signs that your child may need antibiotics.
- If your cat tends to scratch people, ask your vet about declawing—but only as a last resort, and only if your cat never goes outdoors.
- Keep your cat indoors to minimize exposure to ticks and fleas and to keep her safe.
- Teach your child not to pick up a cat, but just to pet it gently on the back or behind its ears, and never to bother one that's sleeping or eating.
- Don't let your child handle the litter box.

Birds

- Choose a small, domestic bird, like a cockatiel, parakeet, or canary, which won't hurt your child if it bites him (which is unlikely). These birds are fairly easy to care for and are less likely to spread parasites or bacteria than larger, imported ones.
- Don't let your child hold the bird; if he wants to pet it, you hold it and let him stroke its back.
- The cage should be cleaned daily by an adult. Wear rubber gloves, then wash them and your hands thoroughly afterward.
- Teach your child never to tap on the cage or stick any objects into it.

Fish

Tropical fish are among the safest, most colorful, and low-maintenance pets, but even they can present problems.

- Tell your child never to put his hands in the tank. The water may contain salmonella or other harmful bacteria.
- Don't buy predator fish, such as piranhas.
- As with all pet foods (and medicines), store fish food and any chemicals for the tank out of your child's reach. Teach your child not to overfeed fish.

Reptiles

About 3 percent of U.S. homes have a turtle, snake, or lizard, and more than seventy thousand people contract salmonella each year from contact with these pets. "Don't believe pet-store certificates that claim an animal is salmonella-free," says Gary Smith, M.D., director of the Center for Injury Research and Policy at Children's Hospital in Columbus, Ohio. "A reptile can test negative for salmonella one day and the next day it may show up in its feces." Because salmonella can be especially severe in young children, the Centers for Disease Control and Prevention recommends you keep reptiles out of homes with children under five. If you do have a reptile, keep the animal and its cage away from the kitchen and food.

Hamsters and Other Small Mammals

Little critters like hamsters, guinea pigs, and rabbits are gentle—and easier because the mess is contained in an enclosed space. To keep risks to a minimum:

- Choose your pet carefully. Hamsters, guinea pigs, and rabbits, for example, enjoy being handled more than gerbils and mice.
- Before you bring an animal home, make sure it has no signs of "wet tail" (wetness near its bottom) or labored breathing; either could mean it has a bacterial infection.
- Handle the animal with your child for at least fifteen minutes a day. "Your pet is less likely to bite or scratch when they are used to being handled frequently."
- Teach your child to hold his pet securely but very gently. "Kids can easily drop or squish a small pet, or pull its fur," says Bonnie Beaver, a veterinarian and professor in the department of small animal clinical sciences at Texas A&M University in College Station. When the pet is being held, offer it a treat—like a baby carrot or a blueberry—so it's a pleasant experience.

- Keep the cage in a place where you can supervise the animal—and your child.
- Avoid ferrets or wild "pets," such as raccoons, chinchillas, and hedgehogs. "Ferrets have been known to attack children," cautions Beaver.

From Stephanie

As of this writing, I share my home with two gerbils (they are both female; however, my son insists that his is a boy), a male rabbit (which my daughter named Amber, insisting that she was a girl), a turtle (a red-eared slider whose gender is acceptable to everyone—even though we're not sure *what* gender it is), two lizards that my son captured in the backyard, a Shetland sheepdog, and an American bullfrog that my son found at the neighborhood pool. Oh, and I almost forgot to mention the mutant frog that Aunt Julie gifted us with for Timmy's last birthday. It looks like a cross between a frog and a catfish. They're hardy little tadpoles that arrive via the U.S. Postal Service just in time for us to watch the miraculous metamorphosis from tadpole to frog. The first two arrived dead—one died from heat exhaustion, while the other was in pieces, as if the postman dropped it in the blender before placing it in our mailbox. After the tears and gnashing of teeth, we called the company and arranged for a new one free of charge (although I could probably sue them for the emotional distress). I will also admit that there are at least two hamsters and one gerbil carcass currently rotting somewhere in the walls of my house, or in a box labeled "Christmas" that will be surely be revealed this year during the decorating process (I blame defective cages coupled with the underdeveloped motor skills of six-year-olds).

I admit it—I'm an animal lover. We call Timmy "the crocodile hunter" because he catches any kind of animal he sees. I love his interest in animals and what makes things tick, so I'm always willing to set up a new environment for our newly acquired friends and make an extra trip to the pet store for a few feeder crickets and minnows. It's been fun to watch and learn about the animals that we share our yard with. It's also a great chance to teach compassion and respect for the creatures around us.

And while I agree with Sara's guidelines about how much commitment pets are, I also encourage you to take the plunge and say yes when your kids ask that age-old question, "Mommy, can we keep it? Please?" Sometimes we end up letting our catches go after a week or two—back to the home where they originated.

The Internet is a mom's best friend when it comes to learning what creatures eat and what provisions they need to survive. For example, did you know that tadpoles can live on boiled lettuce? And turtles, along with their convenient processed food from the pet store, also thrive on a diet of feeder minnows and crickets? Turtles and lizards need a heat lamp to warm themselves, but frogs do not. And pets of the rodent variety like fresh fruits and veggies and have to have a wheel to run in for exercise (which they will do all night long, so don't house them in your child's bedroom). Despite popular belief, baby bunnies cannot digest carrots. You really have to do your homework when you decide to keep a pet (even a temporary one). But it's usually not as much work as you'd expect.

There is a pet store located next door to the market that I frequent, and I can't tell you how many times I've done my shopping with a bag of live crickets inside my purse. (They can't withstand the temperature in the car, so what choice did I have?) I often laughed about what people would think who happened to glance into my purse at the checkout counter and see all those little bugs crawling around next to my lipstick and car keys. Things like that entertain me for some reason. I already rehearsed my answer in case anyone had the guts to ask me: "Oh, they sell them in the deli now—they're loaded with protein. My kids love them on their ham sandwiches." My point is, it's very easy to feed most of the frogs, lizards, turtles, and other creatures that your kids unearth. Sure, we've had a few casualties along the way, but nothing that a hawk or cat wouldn't have made a meal out of anyway—so no great loss.

And the family bonding that our pets and prisoners have brought into our home far outweighs the workload. The day Timmy caught that huge bullfrog at the pool, he was thrilled! It was better than the Christmas morning when Santa brought his motorized Batmobile. All the kids, lifeguards, and parents were crowding around him asking about his newly acquired frog. He was a hero that day—at least in kid world. Together, we picked out an aquarium and rocks from Wal-Mart and researched what a bullfrog would need to live comfortably inside a four-bedroom home in the Atlanta suburbs. He told me it was "the best day ever." We put the tank on a table in our family room, and we've all enjoyed watching and learning what frogs eat, how webbed their feet are, how well they float, and what sounds they make. The entire family has gotten involved and learned a lot from one slimy, half-drowned frog that was fished out of the swimming pool by a small boy in SpongeBob swim trunks. And actually, if you look closely, he's kinda pretty (the frog—but the boy's cute too).

Our favorite pet by far is our dog, Lulu. We adopted her at age five from a wonderful breeder in South Carolina who had too many dogs and felt that Lulu would be happier in a home where she was the only (dog) child. From my experience with Lulu, I would have to say that adopting an older dog is definitely the way to go. She came into our home already trained and well-mannered, and fit right into our lives. She's so easy to be with, we haven't had any complaints at all. She is a sheltie (Shetland sheepdog), so she's the perfect size for our house and yard and kids, and is the perfect mixture of playful and calm, playing with the kids in the afternoon and lying by my feet in the office while I work. Learning about the characteristics of breeds is absolutely key in choosing your dog. I worked at a veterinary hospital for several years when I first graduated from college, and I can assure you that different breeds have different personalities. Sure, there are a few that prove to be an exception to the rule, but for the most part, breeds of dogs usually have specific traits. For example, shelties don't do well with toddlers. I don't know if it's because they were bred to herd sheep and toddlers tend to be the same size as a sheep, but Lulu hates toddlers. My sister began calling her "Cujo" (after the monster dog from the movie) after our sweet Lulu nipped at her two-year-old. She's always been great around older kids and adults, but for some reason she is not a fan of the chaos that a toddler brings. And all the sheltie websites warn "no toddlers" in their adoption ads, so it must be a breed thing. Some dogs are more active than others; some bark a lot, while others tend to be quieter; some breeds shed more than others; some need more exercise; some are better with kids. There are plenty of websites and books that will help you decide which breed best matches your family and lifestyle. And if you want a successful relationship with a dog, you've got to do your homework. Take your time, ask questions, ask breeders and veterinary hospitals, and don't rush into the decision lightly or out of sympathy. Even the best-behaved dogs are a huge commitment. In the meantime, repeat after me, "Yes, honey, you can keep it."

When a Pet Dies

From Sara

The two huge golden retrievers I wrote about at the start of this chapter both died within a short period. The younger one died very suddenly of cancer, which was a heartbreaking shock to our entire family. Our older dog grieved too. He would stare at me for the longest time and then let out a mournful moan. Then, two months later, he was gone as well. We happened to be in Atlanta visiting the Tripletts when all of a sudden Sam wouldn't get up, eat, or take a drink of water. Although I already know what a true friend I have in Stephanie, she showed me once again how lucky I am to have her in my corner. She went with me to the emergency animal hospital and stayed with me (and Sam) for four hours on a Saturday night. When they wouldn't let me go back to the treatment area with Sam, Stephanie went to the front desk and told them I had just gotten through chemotherapy and just lost my other dog and that I was a special case, damn it! I was an emotional wreck, unable to do much more than wipe my tears and runny nose. But Stephanie had my back.

The next day Sam only continued to get worse, declining into such a pitiful state of vomiting, diarrhea, labored breathing, and sunken eyes that David and I knew we couldn't let him go on that way. We desperately wanted to get him home, but the veterinarian doubted he would survive the drive back to Charlotte. So we made the decision to euthanize him. He had been too good and too dear to us to let him suffer like that. Fortunately, the veterinarian, who was a complete stranger to us because all this was happening in Atlanta, was wonderfully compassionate. Sam's passing was peaceful. His labored breathing slowed, then stopped, and the light went out of his eyes. We hugged him and I kissed his big velvety cheek one last time. The kids were waiting in the lobby and we went and got them and told them he was gone. They wanted to see him again and we let them. I think it was reassuring to them to see him—to know that he still looked the same—especially since our younger dog, Luke, had passed away during surgery and we never got to see him again.

It was a long, lonesome trip back to Charlotte. Our house never felt as empty as it did that day when we came home—for the first time in over ten years without a dog greeting us or walking in the door with us.

Many months have passed since our dogs died, but writing this unlocks the grief that is still inside me, and as I type the tears are rolling down my cheeks. I share this with you because losing a pet is not a brief, passing pain, as some people think it is or expect it to be. Psychologists have recently pointed out that losing a pet can be just as devastating as losing a family member. Since pets generally have much shorter life spans than we do, when you get a pet, realize that eventually losing him or her will be part of the process. Not to say it isn't worth it. It is. It so, so is.

Anna and Cade grieved differently than I did. They seemed to be better in a few days, but then their hurt would come out in an overreaction to something. A few days after Sam died Anna wanted to have a friend over, but I just wasn't up to it yet. When I said no, she threw herself down on the couch in tears and said, "I have no dogs and no friends!"

A dear neighbor gave us a book called *Dog Heaven* that really helped the kids feel peaceful about our dogs being gone. The Humane Society and the ASPCA websites also have helpful resources for people who have lost a pet. It wasn't long before our kids started asking to get another dog. But I was afraid we were doing it too soon. Those resources, and some other dog lover friends, helped us all decide when it was the right time. Now we have a new dog named River. We got him as a puppy because the kids said they wanted a puppy, not an older dog, so we could have him as long as possible. I knew the mess and work I was getting into with a puppy, but I couldn't resist. For me there was really only one reason to get a puppy, but it was the most important one: it's nearly impossible to be sad with a puppy licking your face.

When we brought our new little fur ball home, I couldn't help feeling a little bit of sadness and guilt. No one could ever take the place of our Sam and Luke. As ridiculous as it is, I couldn't bear the idea that they might somehow sense they were being replaced or forgotten. As we were cuddling River, I asked Anna what she thought Sam and Luke would think about our new dog. In that old-soul way of hers she said, "I think they'd say, 'Look! We've got a new little brother.' " Sometimes kids are wiser than we give them credit for being. Those were the most healing words I could have heard. And with those words, I accepted our new little family member with a wounded but open heart.

Talking About Euthanasia

Many animal experts stress the importance of not using the phrase "put to sleep" when you talk about euthanizing a pet to your children. Younger children may not be able to distinguish between their pet going to sleep and dying at first, and may become fearful of going to sleep themselves.

Helping Your Kids Deal with the Loss of a Pet

From Stephanie

First, it's always best to be honest with your kids. Telling them that their pet ran away can cause them to feel depression, guilt, or anxiety. It's better to tell them the truth and let them learn about the grieving process. Most times, younger kids won't really understand the permanence of death, and they'll keep asking questions that have to do with when their pet is coming back. Sometimes kids don't take it as hard as you think they will. After our first bunny died, my kids immediately responded with, "Let's go get a new one!" I had to sort of guide them through the grieving process and try to teach them the value of a life. The American Academy of Child and Adolescent Psychiatry (AACAP) notes that children under five years old will tend to see death as temporary and potentially reversible. From age six to around age eight, kids begin to understand the permanency of death and its consequences. The AACAP recommends that you explain to very young children that when a pet dies, it stops moving, doesn't see or hear anymore, and won't wake up again.

Younger children may have a harder time expressing their grief, so ask them to draw a picture or sing a song about how they feel. The best thing you can do is to be there for them: listen, validate their feelings, and comfort them. Never try to minimize their loss or talk your children out of their feelings.

Most experts recommend that you not let children under the age of eleven witness the euthanasia of your family pet. It can be extremely traumatic—even adults report having nightmares and flashbacks for weeks afterward. I think Sara was correct in bringing her children into the room to see Sam after the euthanasia process was over. It's good for them to be able to say good-bye and have some closure and understanding. It's also a great idea to create a memorial garden or have a little ceremony for your pet. Share favorite memories or create a photo album. The AACAP recommends not getting a new pet right away. Children need time to grieve, to understand the nature of loss, and to get over their grief before they are ready to love and welcome a new pet into the family.

Ginger Went to the Light . . . Finally

From Stephanie

Our cat Ginger died recently. Ginger had been with me for over eighteen years, and although she had been a gorgeous long-haired calico in her younger years, her advanced age caused her to look as though she had already begun to decay long before her death. The kids petted her once in a while, but I'd become highly allergic to her, so I couldn't brush her or even touch her. I used to walk by her and say, "Ginger, we love you, but if you see the light, go to it." It was time. When she finally passed on, my kids were devastated—

wailing and crying and carrying on. For a while, I tried to be a good mommy, but after about an hour of the drama, I snapped. "I don't understand why you are so upset! This is the animal that I asked you to feed and all you would do is complain. If I asked you to give her water or bring her a blanket, you had a fit! And now that she's dead you're upset? Maybe we should use this as a lesson to remind us to take better care of the pets we have that are *alive*!" (There goes the ol' Mother of the Year Award . . . again.) We did have a lovely funeral for Ginger. We buried her near the creek in our backyard. My friend Laura was here visiting with her children, and my friend Chrise showed up with my daughter's best friend and a few other little girls, all dressed in black dresses, white pearls, high heels, gloves, and hats, and we had quite an impressive funeral. My husband, Tim, presided over the ceremony with sarcastic humor about the life of our cat (that was over the kids' heads) and Ginger got quite the send-off. A few days later (on Father's Day), we got the news that my father-in-law had passed away. My husband and I were sitting around the breakfast table with the kids, feeling pretty bad, when my son (age six) weighed in on the scene: "Man, Daddy, first the cat, and now your dad!" As our eyes met across the kitchen table, all we could do was crack up. Kids are clueless about death, but they sure can lighten the mood.

Clutter-Busting Resources

WEBSITES

The Humane Society of the United States
www.hsus.org

American Society for the Prevention of Cruelty to Animals (ASPCA)
www.aspca.org

Dogs and Storks
Introducing your dog to your baby
http://dogsandstorks.com

Care Guides for Pets from PetSmart
www.petsmart.com/uc/careguides.jsp

The American Academy of Child and Adolescent Psychiatry
www.aacap.org

BOOKS

The Adoption Option
by Eliza Rubenstein and Shari Kalina

The Art of Raising a Puppy
by the Monks of New Skete

Dog Adoption
by Joan Hustace Walker

How to Be Your Dog's Best Friend
by the Monks of New Skete
www.dogsbestfriend.com

Puppy Care and Training
by Bardi McLennan

Dog Heaven
by Cynthia Rylant

Cat Heaven
by Cynthia Rylant

The Scoop on Schools

45

The Real Truth Behind Our Kids' Education

From Stephanie

Parents today have more choices than ever about our children's education. In addition to public schools, private schools, charter schools, and even homeschooling are increasingly available alternatives. And it's not an easy decision to make. Questions about curriculum, teacher qualifications, test scores, and quality are very common topics in every parent's daily conversations.

I would warn you to make sure you have solid facts and not just inaccurate biases when you make your choice. Many parents are surprised to find out that private schools aren't necessarily better than public schools. Sure, the parents who are paying in excess of $10,000 per year for their kids to attend these schools are convinced otherwise, but public schools have learned that they are competing with private schools and have made great strides. The latest studies show that public schools are matching and in some cases even surpassing the achievements of private schools all across the country. So don't be too hard on yourself if you can't afford to send Junior to the ritzy private school around the corner. Of course, I have to add that these comparisons depend totally on your particular area, so I encourage you to do your research.

Many parents are choosing to homeschool their children. I love being with my children, and I cried my heart out when they started kindergarten, but I'm also realistic enough to know that homeschooling just wouldn't work for me. I don't have the discipline or the patience it would take to give my kids a solid education, and it would take a supply of Lexapro that the U.S. pharmaceutical manufacturers are not prepared to meet. But many parents do have what it takes to homeschool and there are many, many benefits to it. All homeschooling parents tell me that the best part about it is that they're usually done with their schoolwork by lunchtime. Not having to wait in lines or deal with a classroom of kids makes education much more efficient, and so they finish their daily curriculum in half the time.

And now there's even something called charter schools. These schools are started by a community or group of parents and teachers who want to create a school tailored to their own beliefs and standards.

By giving you the pros and cons of each kind of school, we'll try to make it easier for you to choose the right option for your family. You may be surprised by some of the facts you'll find here. And we remind you that you must get to know the schools in your own community before you can make the best decision for your own child. Each child is different, just as each school and community is different.

There are several ways to get the scoop on your local school system. The best way is to talk to the other moms in your neighborhood, especially the ones who spend a lot of time volunteering at the school. Try to go to a neighborhood event to meet them, and if that's not possible, then simply call them or bring them a pie. They'll be ready and willing to gush about their school and give you the lowdown. Also, call the school and make an appointment to talk with the principal. This is not weird or abnormal—lots of parents do it and the school is prepared for it. I did this the spring before my daughter started kindergarten and it was very enlightening as well as comforting. The principal gave me a tour of the school and talked to me about what their goals were, what they did well, and what they still needed to work on. During our walk, I got to see her interacting with students and teachers, and I was so impressed that she knew so many students by name. When she opened a door into a classroom, the students would turn to see who it was, and then turn their attention back to their teacher as if seeing the principal enter the room was a regular occurrence. She spoke to me about test scores and plans for the future, as well as what my kindergartner could expect. I immediately knew that my daughter would be in good hands and I felt so much better. I think it also sent the message that I was going to be an involved parent.

The other way to learn about the schools in your area is the Internet. Do a search for your district and you'll be able to find statistics, test scores, rankings, and more. This can be a big help in making your decision. If you can't get access to a computer, try your local library. Another idea is to talk to a Realtor—they are usually a wonderful resource regarding the schools in their area because it's normally a huge selling point.

Public Schools

The Good

- **Public school teachers have more qualifications.** I know you poor parents paying those big bucks don't believe it, but it's true. According to a major study from the National Center for Education Statistics, public school teachers tend to be more qualified in terms of both education and experience. Public schools often can pay higher salaries and have better benefits, so they tend to attract the most qualified teachers. Private schools have no personnel standards other than their own.

- **Public schools offer more choices and more activities.** Public schools have larger facilities and more resources when it comes to extracurricular sports and clubs. Most public schools are larger than private schools and have enough students and supplies to support a variety of clubs and activities. And federal and state laws require public schools to provide diagnostic and disability services too.
- **Public schools have a diverse student body.** If you want your child to get to know children from all walks of life, public schools will introduce your child to students from other races, socioeconomic backgrounds, and religions (just like real life).
- **Public schools have regulated standards.** In a public school, you will know what to expect in terms of curriculum and philosophy. All public schools adhere to state and federal regulatory standards and the curriculum and grading are standardized.
- **Students spend more time studying fundamental subjects.** According to a major study from the National Center for Education Statistics, public school students study fundamental subjects like English, math, science, and social studies three more hours per week than private schools.

The Bad

- **More dropouts and violence.** Dropout and violence rates are generally higher in public schools, but such statistics do not apply to all schools. Research your local school system and find out how your schools rank statewide and nationally.
- **Gifted students may suffer due to class majority.** Although most public school systems have programs for "gifted" students, often the best students cannot be challenged to their fullest potential because teachers have to operate according to the class majority.
- **Less personal attention.** Class sizes tend to be larger in public schools than in private ones, so your child may receive less personalized attention.

Private Schools

The Good

- **Better standardized test scores.** In a June 2002 report, the National Center for Education Statistics found that private school students scored higher on standardized tests, had more demanding graduation requirements, and sent more graduates to college than public schools. The report said that students who had completed at least the eighth grade in a private school were twice as likely as other students to graduate from college as a young adult.

- **Smaller classes.** Most private schools offer smaller class sizes. This usually means more individualized attention.
- **Less bureaucracy.** Since private schools don't have to abide by state regulations, they spend less time concentrating on mandatory paperwork. Teachers usually have more creative control over the classroom.
- **Strong parent involvement.** The parents of private school students tend to be much more involved in their child's education.

The Bad

- **The expense.** Private schools can be very expensive. While public schools are prohibited from charging state residents any form of tuition or other fees for materials, supplies, textbooks, or transportation, many private schools charge tuition plus fees for supplies, uniforms, transportation, and other items.
- **Not necessarily better teaching.** Overall, private school students tend to do markedly better on standardized tests. But most studies suggest the reason for this is because they draw students from wealthier and more educated families, not because they're better at teaching students.
- **Status symbols.** Too often kids are put into private schools because it's a status symbol for their parents.
- **Problem kids have nowhere else to go.** Often the "problem kids" who got kicked out of public school are found attending private schools, so parents who choose a private school for the benefit of surrounding their child with better students may be disappointed.
- **No personnel requirements.** Unlike public schools, private schools have no faculty or staff requirements other than their own. Some don't even require a college degree for their teachers.
- **Not governed by state requirements.** Public school students must meet state graduation requirements that include a standard number of credits, a 2.0 high school grade point average, and a passing score on a state-prescribed test. Graduation requirements for private schools are left to the determination of each school and are not subject to any state requirements.

Charter Schools

A charter school is basically a school that is created by a group of parents and teachers, a school district, a municipality, or even a company, with specific goals for the children's education. Charter schools have more freedom and choices and do not adhere to many of the state regulations that apply to traditional public schools. A "charter" is basically a contract that outlines the school's goals, curriculum, and how it will measure success. Charters are usually granted for a period of three to five years, and at the end of that time the entity granting the charter (usually a state or local school board, but sometimes a state university or community college) may renew the school's contract.

Charter schools are funded based on their enrollment, and just like public schools, charter schools are not permitted to charge tuition. In some states, such as Alaska, Colorado, Minnesota, and New Jersey, they receive less funding than local public schools. In other states, like California, additional funds or loans are made available to them. In most states, charters do not receive capital funds for facilities. They are entitled to federal funding for which their students are eligible, such as Title I and special education monies. Federal legislation provides grants to help charter schools with start-up costs. Through the Public Charter Schools Program, the U.S. Department of Education offers grants to states, which then award subgrants to assist in the planning, design, and initial implementation of new charter schools.

To find a charter school in your area or start a charter school, you can visit www.uscharterschools.org. There, you will find contact information and links to the websites of your local charter school resource center and state department of education. They will have a complete list of authorized charter schools in your state.

The Good

- **Choice.** The main advantage of charter schools is choice. Parents have an option other than public schools that doesn't involve the high cost of private schools or the high commitment of homeschooling.
- **Flexibility.** Certain regulations are eased for charter schools, giving teachers more freedom to develop and implement new learning strategies. Many believe that charter schools function as laboratories for educational experimentation and innovation.
- **Motivation to perform.** Charter schools must perform well or face closure. This increased accountability impacts the teaching environment, motivating teachers to find new ways to enable kids to learn.

The Bad

- **Limited resources.** Because charter schools often do not receive as much funding as traditional public schools, they may not be able to serve students with disabilities or limited English proficiency as fully. Classrooms may be missing valuable resources such as computers, software, interactive white boards, etc. Because charter schools are often housed in older school buildings or facilities originally intended for other purposes, they may not have a traditional cafeteria or gym. Extracurricular activities may also be limited. And you will likely have to drive your child to a central location to catch a bus instead of walking to the bus stop on your street.

- **Economics.** Critics of charter schools say they are too vulnerable to economic forces, which can force them to deprive students of valuable programs or to even close and disrupt children's education mid-term.

Homeschooling

Homeschooling has been around for a long, long time, and in the past few years it's made a comeback. The U.S. Census estimates that as many as two million children are being homeschooled in the United States, and the numbers are increasing all the time. The number one reason parents choose this option is religious convictions, but some choose to homeschool because they are not happy with their local schools, and some want to have more control over the type of kids (and families) their kids are exposed to. Homeschooling is legal in all states, but laws do vary from state to state. For instance, as of this writing, parents in California cannot homeschool their children without acquiring a professional teaching credential. We've listed how to find out what the laws are in your state under "How to Get Started."

There are many different methods of teaching at home—it's not limited to just sitting around the kitchen table. For example, there is a "unit studies" approach that integrates subjects together into themes, and the Charlotte Mason method encourages the use of "living books" (as opposed to textbooks) and requires students to listen to short narrative stories and then orally report on what they've been taught as well as do copy work (learning by copying directly from a book). Thanks to the Internet, a variety of curricula are easy to find and are typically affordable.

How to Get Started

First, talk to other moms who homeschool their kids. You can usually find them at afterschool activities, so just ask around. You may also search for other homeschooling parents on local mom-oriented community websites.

Next, find out about the homeschooling laws for your state. You can visit www.homeedmag.com/lawregs/lawregs.html or www.homeschoolcentral.com for information on each state's laws and contact information. Some states have testing requirements. Some have specific curriculum requirements. State support groups generally have a summary of their state laws. It's easy to find a support group by doing an online search, then find a support group in your area. The links that we have provided offer websites that can connect you with homeschooling resources near you. It's important to stay active in these groups so that you can be aware of changes in laws and standards, and also because they will help you find ways to provide socialization outlets for your children. Plus, as with anything else, you'll learn a lot by talking with your fellow moms.

It Doesn't Have to Be Forever

Remember that choosing to homeschool your child doesn't mean a lifetime commitment. Most families take it a year at a time.

The Good

- **Finish in half the time.** Teachers spend about six hours a day teaching twenty children. If you're only teaching a couple of children, you'll be able to accomplish as much in about two or three hours a day.
- **More control over lessons and influences.** You are able to tailor the lessons to your child's interests or your own family's religious or ethnic background.
- **Flexible schedules.** You have the ability to come and go as you please—you create your own schedule. This helps when scheduling vacations and after-school activities.

The Bad

- **Time commitment.** Sure, you might not spend that much time teaching—but the preparation time can be overwhelming. It's not just the lesson plans; it's the progress-tracking, filing, grading, keeping up with supplies for experiments, etc.
- **Time for you.** Homeschooling parents have to be careful to make time for themselves. It's a huge commitment, and moms have to be careful not to get burned out.
- **Family agreement.** Make sure that your child and your spouse are both willing to make this commitment. You'll have a battle on your hands if you don't have the support of your family.
- **Financial sacrifice.** If your family is used to a dual income, you might be sacrificing earning power by choosing this route. Homeschooling can get expensive depending on the cost of the curriculum you choose. Some curricula can cost as much as $3,000 per year. In addition, some homeschooling moms also enroll their kids in additional tutoring, which is another financial commitment. And in some states, you'll still be paying taxes to the local school district with no tax benefit. Of course, purchasing curricula and extra classes is a personal choice; it is not required.
- **Household chores.** If you like a spotless house, forget it. Having children in the house all day means your house suffers. Homeschooling usually creates plenty of

clutter. And you'll have to learn to let go a little when it comes to daily household chores so you can focus on getting your schoolwork done.

- **Socializing.** You'll have to make it a point to schedule play dates and give your children other opportunities to play with other children. Most homeschooling support groups have clubs and meetings to help you accomplish this.

Frequently Asked Questions About Homeschooling

Are there standards?

Yes. Some states require annual "proof of progress" or periodic testing. Regulations vary, so refer to your state laws. Your state may offer to test children at no charge, may test for a fee, may require that children be tested independently, or will expect parents to test at home. Acceptable tests can vary by state or even county. Check your state law and ask questions of your local group or network.

How do you find a curriculum?

Thanks to the Internet, it's very easy to find an appropriate curriculum for your student. The Web abounds with homeschooling sites loaded with advice, free printouts, themes, and curricula. The first step is to find out your child's learning style and what approach you are planning to use; then you can search for your curriculum. Some of the books used in homeschooling are written for parents, to help them become better homeschool teachers, while others are aimed at instruction. Some curricula are Web-based. Teacher supply stores can also be a great resource for thematic units and tools. Also, you can talk to the librarians, reading specialists, and faculty members in your public school system. Often they are happy to work with you to provide textbooks and give you guidance.

Another source of information about curricula are homeschooling conventions. You can do an Internet search to find one in your area. And some curricula have online resources for helping homeschool teachers. For example, A Beka's website (www.abeka.org) provides three different homeschooling options—you can actually look at the materials and speak with their representatives before making the purchase.

What can you do if you are weak in a subject that you have to teach to your child?

1. Learn the material along with your child.
2. Team up with another homeschooling family and teach the subjects you're strong in.
3. Contact local support groups for team-teaching possibilities.

4. Hire a tutor to teach the subject, possibly a local college student.
5. Use a video course.
6. Use a computer course.
7. See if the local junior college offers this course to high school students.
8. Take the class at a local junior college along with your high school student.
9. Check into online schools and the possibility of taking just one course.
10. Solicit help from a friend who is strong in the subject.

Tip: Many times college and high school credit can be earned simultaneously by taking a course at a junior college.

What about college?

College may be a long way off for your little one, but your decision to homeschool may affect your child's future educational outcomes, so you have to start thinking about it now. More than nine hundred colleges nationwide, including many rated as "highly selective," regularly admit homeschooled students.

Homeschooled students apply for college the same way traditional students do. Contact the schools your child is interested in attending to find out if they have special admission requirements for homeschooled students. Some (Stanford, for example) have created guidelines to help homeschoolers with the application process (and Stanford has admitted numerous homeschoolers). Many have developed policies for evaluating such kids' records—for example, considering student portfolios, a transcript of coursework prepared by parents, and the student's SAT or ACT test scores. Homeschooling parents must maintain their child's portfolio diligently, as it will form the basis of your student's "transcript." And you should start communicating with the admissions office for your college of choice as early as eighth grade to ensure that you are meeting their requirements.

In some cases, the homeschooled student is very noticeable among the masses of applicants. Why? Many colleges are beginning to recognize that homeschooled kids tend to make fantastic college students—they know how to learn instead of how just to be taught, which can give homeschooled kids an advantage.

From Stephanie

Most of the homeschooling parents I've met are very happy with their decision. They love being with their kids. They find great value in siblings learning compassion for one another and socializing with each other rather than a classroom full of strangers. Most of the homeschoolers I've met have significant religious philosophies and beliefs that they want to pass on to their children more frequently than just Sunday mornings. And all of them tell me that finishing their daily lessons by lunchtime is an enormous benefit. Every parent who chooses to homeschool his or her children has my total admiration and respect.

But I must confess that homeschooling is not for me. As I've said, I don't have the patience or the discipline. Also, in my opinion, there is value in kids learning to survive and navigate life in the mainstream. Their futures will depend on that, and I believe that the more sheltered they are now, the harder it will be for them to function in the real world. The real world isn't segregated. You don't get to work with only Christians or only people from your socioeconomic level. Diversity is what America is all about, and companies have whole departments focusing on creating diversity within their ranks. So for that reason, I believe there are a lot of benefits to traditional schooling.

Only you can make the right choice for your child. And we hope this chapter has given you solid facts and good insight to help you make your decision.

Clutter-Busting Resources

"Public vs. Private: Which Is Right for Your Child?"
www.parentcenter.com

Council for American Private Education
www.capenet.org

Charter schools
www.uscharterschools.org

Homeschooling laws state by state
www.homeedmag.com/lawregs/lawregs.html
www.homeschool.com
www.homeschooldiscount.com
http://homeschooling.gomilpitas.com
http://homeschooling.about.com
This website offers anything and everything you need to know about homeschooling your children. It was developed by Beverly Hernandez, who is a veteran homeschooler of eighteen years, a mother of three, and a grandmother of four.
www.abeka.org

46

Starting School

Preparing for Kindergarten

From Stephanie

Okay, stop crying and listen. I know it's scary and sad and just plain wrong that another person is going to be spending the entire day with your child instead of you. Sara and I both were complete basket cases in the weeks before our little girls started kindergarten. We complained and cried and considered homeschooling. I was up all night before the first day of school, pouring my heart out on paper and crying my eyes out. But here's what we want you to know up front: you will get through this (probably with less pain and fewer tears than you think) and, believe it or not, in a week or two you're going to actually *like* it. (I promise.)

Yes, I realize you're giving up time with your little child. But a lot of great things are going to happen to your relationship with your child too, and it is enormously rewarding to watch her grow. You will be amazed at what your child can do. About a week after school began, I came to have lunch with my daughter and was amazed to see her following the class routine, punching her ID number into the keypad in the cafeteria, and interacting with her fellow students as if they had their own little community. I never would have guessed that she was capable of all that. I'm convinced that's the reason they take them away from us so early—we hold them back and baby them and seldom challenge them adequately.

And please realize too that you are not alone. I worked with my daughter's kindergarten teacher to help the class write a book for parents dealing with their children starting kindergarten. In the process, we sent home interview questions that asked parents what they were most worried about. So many of their answers came back the same, even though some of them sounded ridiculous! Several parents were worried about their child dropping his or her lunch tray in the cafeteria. Some were worried that their child would be a disciplinary problem, or that he wouldn't be able to do the work assigned. Many were concerned that their child wouldn't find the right bus at the end of the day. And of course, everyone was concerned about missing their child.

Once our children had been in school for a few months, we all laughed about how silly we were. Everyone boarded the correct bus; the teachers had discipline under control; everyone was able to do the work, or received special attention if they were struggling; and even if a lunch tray was dropped, there would be another one supplied immediately, and ladies with hairnets would swoop in for the cleanup faster than your child could shed a single tear. As for missing your child, yes, you'll miss him a little the first week. But you'll soon start to fill that time with other things, and before you know it, you'll be time-depleted once again. I filled my time by volunteering at the school, playing tennis, and trying to get all the housework done so that I could be with my daughter when she got home from school instead of trying to keep her occupied while I did chores. Trust me, and mothers with school-age children everywhere: you'll soon start to enjoy and appreciate those few hours a day when your child is away.

Starting school actually adds another layer to your relationship with your child. You will have common goals to achieve together, like homework. Our kindergarten teacher was a strong believer in giving kindergartners homework because it starts good study habits from the very beginning. It also forces busy moms to sit down and make one-on-one time with their kids. I really looked forward to finding out what the homework was each week and working with my daughter to accomplish it. You need to be prepared for this and make homework and school projects a time to connect and really focus on your child. Homework shouldn't be viewed as a negative, and it's important for you to send that message from the very beginning. You'll need to really dig deep into your creative side to keep it fun and interesting. When learning her sight words each week became a nuisance for my daughter, I decided to make Go Fish cards from her words. We'd play game after game of Go Fish. Turning study time into a game is an awesome way to get your child interested in learning. There are websites that provide bingo cards and crossword puzzles and word finds for learning sight words. The most important thing you can do for your kindergartner is to give her the love of learning. If you can do that, the rest of her school career will be much easier on both of you.

I encourage you to get involved and volunteer in the classroom or at the school as much as possible. Being there means you'll get the inside scoop. You'll get to know the personality of your school, who the best teachers are, and what plans the school has for the future. Parent involvement is what makes schools great. And there are personal rewards too. I learned how to teach my kids more efficiently by being in the classroom and listening to the teacher. I was better at communicating with my little student during homework because I knew some of the terms and tricks that her teacher used.

And don't be surprised about how serious kindergarten is nowadays. My daughter was reading within eight weeks! She came home with her first library book and I said,

"Oh! A library book! Want me to read it to you?" She replied, "No, Mommy. Let me read it to you." I gave her a smile and a sarcastic, "Oh . . . okay." And to my astonishment, she did! Every word! I couldn't take a bit of credit for it. I had no idea that her class was already working on blending words and reading sentences. And this is definitely another thing to look forward to because once your child starts reading, things progress quickly. Now we take turns reading books to each other at bedtime.

Once your child starts school, you have to be more careful than ever about what you say. For one thing, they can spell now, so you can no longer get away with spelling out inappropriate words about your mother-in-law to your spouse when your child is in the room. And *never* let your child hear you talk about your own shortcomings. I requested a meeting with our school principal before my daughter started kindergarten. During our meeting, she advised me never to say "I was terrible at math" in front of my daughter. It makes children think they can use that excuse and not be good at math also—just like Mommy. I took her advice to heart and never said that again when my daughter was around. And I believe her 100 percent, because my daughter *loves* math. She's great at it. She sits around during playtime doing math calculations in her notebook! I'm astonished because she's the first female in our family that has had an affinity for math. It makes me wonder if I would have struggled less in math if I hadn't heard my own mother denounce the subject. Your influence is more powerful than you realize, so be sure to send positive messages.

So what's the best way to prepare your child for kindergarten? Many parents make the mistake of cramming ABC's and 123's down their kids' throats. Pam Hayes, twenty-three-year veteran kindergarten and first-grade teacher, recommends giving your children experiences. Take them to the zoo, the carnival, and the library. Reading to them and taking them on adventures give them life experiences that will wake up their minds and make learning easier. Water, mud, sand, bugs, the backyard, the petting zoo, and even the grocery store can be opportunities for learning.

Master the Morning

One obstacle to prepare for is school mornings. Start their morning off right. Plenty of rest and a good breakfast are just the beginning. Be sure to keep them in good spirits and give them a good send-off. Instead of saying, "Have fun today," try sending messages like "Be a good listener today!" or "Learn something new today so you can teach me!" or "Do your best!" The words you leave your children with in the morning can affect their entire day.

The secret to a smooth morning is preparation the night before. If your child has issues with her school clothes, as many do, be sure to have her pick out and approve her outfits the night before. And pick out everything from head to toe (shoes, socks, barrettes, etc.), because sometimes the little things can cause a big scene. My daughter was fussy about everything: sleeves had to be a certain length, underwear had to have seams in exactly the right places, socks couldn't be too long, shoestrings had to be wrenched tight, and so on. Our morning battles got so bad I finally relinquished the job to my husband.

You see, he and I have very different opinions about how a morning should run. Everywhere I go I'm fifteen minutes early, and he's consistently fifteen minutes late. I wanted to teach her my habits, so I wanted her to be dressed, hair done, bed made, teeth brushed, and shoes on before she ate breakfast and watched her favorite A.M. cartoon. He, on the other hand, eased her out of bed with a waffle and a cartoon before getting dressed. Of course, they missed the bus a few times, and she left without her teeth brushed more than once, but she was a lot happier when she walked out the door. So I combined our techniques and found a compromise: whatever clothes she picked out the night before were the clothes that she had to wear the next morning, no matter what. Otherwise, she would change socks for fifteen minutes and end up late. My son, on the other hand, finds it impossible to accomplish any task while the TV is on. So he had to follow the "no TV until you are completely dressed" rule.

Be prepared to pick your battles. My daughter goes to school every day with her hair down. I would give anything to pull it back in pretty bows or braids, but she's perfectly happy just brushing it and going. That does not make me a bad mother, but just in case, I told her teacher not to think badly of me because it just wasn't worth the battle in the morning, and she fully agreed. It really doesn't matter if your child's clothes match or if her hair is perfect when she leaves in the morning. As long as her clothes are appropriate for the school dress code and the weather, you've done your job.

The First Day

Just one note about that first day of school. Much like my advice from the day care chapter, hanging around is only going to make it worse on your child. Hovering in the hallway and prolonged hugs are not the way to handle the first day of school. Put on your bravest happy face, be excited, and talk to your child about all the fun things he'll get to do, like eating lunch at a big table with all his new friends, playing on the playground, riding the bus, having his own special seat, etc. Notice the room when you enter. Look at how much fun it is, and think about how much your child will love being in this environment. Don't stick around. Your child needs to concentrate on his new job, not on leaving you. A quick hug and kiss is the best, and then sprint down the hallway so you can cry in your car. I've heard of moms who scheduled a "boo-hoo breakfast," meeting at someone's house or a local restaurant to console each other on the first day. Of course, some moms will be ready to celebrate the first day of school. This year, I orchestrated a party at the pool for my fellow moms. I called it "adult swim," and there were no kids allowed. We'd spent the summer at the pool with kids hanging on us and trying to solve sibling disputes and searching for lost pool toys. This party was a chance for moms to enjoy the pool in peace and sip a few mimosas in celebration. I'm always sad to see them go back to school at the end of summer; this was a nice diversion on the first day of school.

Whatever category you fall into, where your children are concerned it's important to never let them see you sweat. This is an exciting new adventure for them; it shouldn't be about you. And just so you know, it's not the kids who the teachers worry about on the first day of school (ask any of them).

A Note About Behavior

From Sara

One of the toughest things for me to get used to when my daughter started kindergarten was how awful she was when she got home in the afternoons. Anna is a well-behaved kid, and just generally easy to be with, but those first few months of school she came home in the foulest of foul moods and acted like she hated all of us (especially her little brother) for the first hour she was home. She didn't even like the dogs. It wasn't fun for anyone. After talking with some other moms, I've found this is pretty common. Kindergarten is a big adjustment, and sometimes it's even harder for rule followers like Anna. She would rather *die* than have her behavior card moved from green to yellow or (God forbid) red. She worked so hard all day making sure she was doing everything right that when she got home she unloaded all her frustrations on her family members. So don't be surprised if this happens with your child too.

Remember, they save their worst behavior for the safety of home and family, so it's not that your child has suddenly decided to hate you now that he is in kindergarten. And relax—this too shall pass. Eventually.

What Teachers Wish Parents Knew

From Stephanie

My daughter's kindergarten teacher gave me a book called *What America's Teachers Wish Parents Knew,* compiled by Judy and Tony Privett. A large group of teachers contributed, and it became a great little handbook full of humor, straight talk, and thought-provoking ideas for parents. Here are a few of my favorite quotes:

> "I wish that parents would realize the tragic irony in the fact that sixteen years of education was required of me before I was allowed to teach; yet their job as a parent, which requires no education at all, is so much more important than mine."
>
> —Seventh-grade language arts teacher

"I wish parents would allow their child to fail. Too many parents make excuses for any error a child makes. As adults, we make mistakes and think nothing of them. When children do something wrong, some parents find a reason or think it wasn't their fault. Making mistakes helps children learn."

—Kindergarten teacher

"I wish parents knew that if a child reads for 60 minutes a day, he could increase his standardized test scores by 90 percent. Reading for 30–40 minutes a day would improve scores considerably."

—Third- and fifth-grade teacher

"I wish parents realized that their last contact with their child tremendously affects that child's self-concept and desire to learn on that day. Whether it is the night prior or the morning before they leave, make it positive and loving. Don't underestimate love!"

—First-grade teacher

"I wish parents would believe only half of what their child tells them about the teacher! I only believe half of what their child tells me about them."

—First-grade teacher

"I wish parents would realize that when children are having problems at school, they already feel bad about it and don't need to feel worse when they get home."

—Seventh-grade teacher

How to Read to Your Kids

It's never too early to start reading to your kids daily. There are many books that infants can enjoy, with textures on pages or pictures of other babies' faces. Reading to your baby and toddler helps in their development. And as your child grows, reading becomes even more important. Here are just a few of the benefits:

- It gives you a reason to bond. Reading with your child is a great way to spend some quality time together.
- Reading helps to build your child's vocabulary.
- Listening to you read will help your child learn to read with voice inflection and tone. They will learn how to end sentences and ask questions and will become better readers themselves.
- Reading will help your child learn to follow a story from beginning to end, and help with comprehension skills.
- Reading to your child will make him a better writer.

- Your child will be a better student, make better grades, and have a better chance of attending college if you read to him each day.

Here are some tips for getting the most out of reading with your child.

It All Adds Up

According to the U.S. Department of Education, if you read to your child from infancy until age five for:

- Thirty minutes daily, you will have read to your child for 900 hours!
- Thirty minutes weekly, you will have read to your child for 130 hours!
- Less than thirty minutes weekly, you will have read to your child for 60 hours!

Before You Read

1. Take a "picture walk" through the book. Look at the pictures and talk about what might happen in the story. Talk about the characters that you see, where the story takes place, etc. Make some predictions about the book. Pictures help new readers make sense out of the words.

2. Help your child think out loud. Make connections from the book to your own life, other books you've read, or something you know about this topic. Successful readers rely on their prior knowledge to help them understand the story.

3. Help your child understand the parts of the book: the title page, the author, the illustrator, etc.

When You Are Reading

Remember that the goal is to read for enjoyment. After reading it the first time, try these:

1. Point to the words as you read them so beginning readers can get a feeling for the left-to-right motion.

2. Point out words that start the same, rhyming words, big/little words, words that start with the letters your child knows, little words that are "hiding" in big words, etc.

3. Stop at certain parts of the story to talk about and reflect on what happened, what might happen, etc. Talk about why a character did what he did, how it makes your child feel, etc.

4. If your child can't sound out a word, suggest skipping it, reading the rest of the sentence, and deciding what word would make sense.

When You Finish the Story

1. Ask your child if he liked or disliked the book and why. What was her favorite or least favorite part? Who was his favorite or least favorite character?

2. Have your child draw his favorite part of the story, or make puppets or masks and reenact it. Give the drawing to a friend to encourage that child to read the book.

3. Rewrite the ending. Let your child choose how the story ends. She can write it, draw it, or act it out.

4. Compare the book to others you've read. If your child really likes the book, look for others written by the same author or about the same topic.

Never Stop Reading Aloud to Your Child

Many of us think that once our child starts reading, we should let them always read to us for practice. That's not true. While it is important for your child to practice her skills, when you take a turn, you let her enjoy books that may be beyond her ability. This builds her vocabulary by exposing her to new words, and it's important for your child to learn to read smoothly and with expression—and listening to you is the best way to teach her those skills.

Even if you can only fit in a mere ten minutes at bedtime, reading is one of the most important things you can do for your kids each day. It needs to be a priority, just like brushing teeth and getting dressed.

Always choose a quiet, comfortable place to read or listen to your child read. Having a designated spot just makes it more special.

Getting Kids to Read

- Leave notes for your child in their lunch box, on the fridge, or on their bedroom door. They'll love reading a note from Mom or Dad.
- Take your new reader to the library and sign him up for his own library card. (It's a big deal.)
- Ask older children to read books to younger kids, cousins, or neighbors. Kids love to show off their skills, and they are an inspiration to younger siblings. I loved watching my kids bond when my daughter began reading to my son (plus they stopped fighting for a few precious moments).

Choosing the Right Book

There are millions of books to suit your child's interests and get her excited about reading, but sometimes when you're standing in the bookstore or library, it's hard to decide if a book is appropriate for your child's skill level. Use the "five-finger rule." Ask your child to open the book to any page in the middle and read that page. Ask him to hold up one finger each time he comes across a word he doesn't know. If he gets to five fingers before finishing the page, there's a good chance that the book is too hard. If he doesn't hold up any fingers, the book is probably too easy. Books that are too easy aren't necessarily a bad thing—they help build confidence and fluency. If your child holds up two or three fingers, the book is probably a good level to help improve his skills.

Clutter-Busting Resources

GREAT SITES TO HELP KINDERGARTNERS LEARN

www.starfall.com
www.bookadventure.com
www.enchantedlearning.com
www.funschool.com
www.scholastic.com
www.primarygames.com
www.uptoten.com
www.funbrain.com
www.Iknowthat.com
www.kidsreads.com
www.kinderstart.com

WEBSITES THAT CAN HELP YOU FIND THE MOST POPULAR BOOKS

Scholastic Books Parents Resources
www.scholastic.com

Kids Program from Random House
www.randomhouse.com/kids

Mother to Mother

47

Holiday Survival Tactics

The stress, the rush, the headaches, the kids screaming while we stand there sweating in those endless lines at the cash register . . . ah, the holidays. But the truth is, we do it to ourselves. Our own delusions of grandeur are our worst enemy during the holidays. And we all have them. Everything has to be perfect: the perfect tree, the perfect gifts, the perfect food. Just look around at all the magazines targeted toward women, with the beautiful photographs of gorgeous homemade gift wrap and glistening little trees made out of ten thousand pearl pushpins stuck into some kind of fruit.

And please notice, if you will, that men's magazines never persuade men to add to *their* to-do list. Their magazines encourage them to sit down with a cold one and watch the game. They don't rush to the craft store for glue gun refills. They don't fret about making sure that Aunt Ida's Christmas place mats are the perfect shade of green to match her newly painted kitchen. And they don't give a hoot about what Martha made out of toothpicks, candle wax, and dried apricots on her show that day. So why do we do it? This year, we challenge you to give yourself a break. When you reflect on what it was that you remember most about your holidays as a child, we can guarantee it had nothing to do with decorations, centerpieces, or dried fruit.

"Most women put off entertaining until the kids are grown."

—Erma Bombeck

We've learned in the school of hard knocks to forget perfection. You see, in spite of our best efforts, our own family gatherings tend to turn into something not quite suitable for Norman Rockwell: think too much alcohol, expletives, and phone calls to 911. What memories! The only embarrassment our holidays haven't included is bailing someone out of jail, but you never know if this could be the year.

What all this drama and debacle has taught both of us is to lower our expectations. After all, does the holiday table really need to be perfect if a child is going to vomit black olives all over it anyway? As far as we're concerned, if no one ends up in the emergency room, throws up repeatedly, gets obnoxiously drunk, or kicks everyone out of the house, then consider your holiday a resounding success.

Stephanie's Holiday from Hell

There's nothing like a holiday to stimulate a good family drama. No matter how much I prepare, plan, and dream, most family holidays turn into a scene from *The Twilight Zone*. A holiday with the Triplett family can pretty much guarantee one or more trips to the hospital (or at least disturbing an on-call nurse), somebody upchucking, a lot of crying, and sometimes even blood . . . but they *are* memorable.

One particular Thanksgiving was a holiday from hell that I will never forget. My son still has the scar to prove it, and we had to buy a new couch. My mother-in-law was coming to join us for the holiday, which I was fine with. She's great, and even better, she wanted to bring the turkey. She showed up with a twenty-three-pound bird! There were only a few adults and two very young children present for dinner, but she's really into turkey leftovers. I, however, hate turkey leftovers because they make your entire refrigerator smell like a dead turkey carcass for weeks, and personally I don't find that appetizing. Plus, I just worry a lot about how safe it is to eat turkey that's more than a couple of days old.

Well, common turkey knowledge is that you have to roast the turkey for something like twenty minutes for every pound of bird, so that meant I had to start cooking this massive turkey at around nine o'clock in the morning. Unfortunately, my sweet mother-in-law got a little confused about my double oven. You see, one oven is digital and the other is the regular dial oven, and she accidentally turned the oven off. (See, we tend to have this little power struggle going on in the kitchen—I cook everything on high to get it done really fast, and she cooks everything on low, so it takes her like two hours to make bacon.) Anyway, the oven with the turkey got turned off, and nobody realized it.

In the meantime, I'd bought a can of black olives, trying to respect some of my husband's family traditions—I'm not sure what black olives have to do with Pilgrims, but his family always serves them on Thanksgiving, so I put some out. Our daughter, who was three at the time, loved them. She ate a lot of them. At around 7:00 P.M., just as I was pulling the turkey out of the oven (hours later than planned), my daughter said, "Mommy, I feel sick." I told her it was okay, she was just really hungry, and then she proceeded to vomit black olives all over our white couch. Let me tell you, when mixed with stomach acid, black olives are pretty much permanent when poured over white fabric.

Also, you should know that my daughter has some weird sensitive gag reflex, and every time she has ever started vomiting, she's ended up in the hospital due to dehydration. So my husband began trying to mop the vomit off the couch, and I was on the phone trying to find a doctor who would call in a prescription for those super-cool suppositories that make you stop vomiting, and trying to find a pharmacy that was open on Thanksgiving night (thank God for Walgreens, by the way).

So there I was. My son's head was bleeding because he'd fallen in the basement earlier that day and hit his head on the weight bench (hence the aforementioned scar). My husband was out driving around Atlanta trying to find the one Walgreens location that was open on Thanksgiving night. My daughter was vomiting everywhere, and as if that wasn't bad enough, I had a family member who was so drunk, she actually did a forward roll off my couch! Needless to say, we all ate cold turkey that night, after spending an entire day cooking it. I'm strongly considering just serving a nice precooked ham this year, and I can pretty much guarantee that the black olive tradition ends here!

Christmas Is Canceled (or, Sara's Very Special Thanksgiving)

Lots of us still entertain the Norman Rockwell ideal of Thanksgiving, with the father proudly holding a turkey on a platter in front of a tableful of smiling family members. My holidays are rarely like that. Especially when you mix in too many relatives, a breakup, and a really bad hangover.

One Thanksgiving, one of my male relatives, who will of course remain nameless, was scheduled to host everyone at his house for the post-turkey football-watching marathon. The problem was that the night before, his girlfriend had unexpectedly dumped him. Being a mature and responsible adult, he handled the situation by staying out all night drinking. He didn't have a hangover when all the family arrived at his house, but that was because he was still drunk. I say that not to condemn him but in an effort to explain the behavior I am about to recount.

When we all showed up at his house ready to continue the family sharing and bonding that comes with watching eight hours of sports together, our host was in his basement playing pool with a couple of people who'd come home with him from the bar the night before. We came in and made ourselves at home, but after a while he'd apparently had enough of the family being at his house and the dirty looks his mother was giving him for not coming upstairs to join everyone, because he walked into the family room, looked at everyone assembled in front of the television, and unceremoniously said, "Get the ——— out." (I'm sure you can fill in the blank.)

Everyone looked at each other, wondering if he had just said what we thought he'd just said. Noticing the confusion, he decided to make himself perfectly clear by asking, "What part of 'Get the ——— out' do you not understand?"

What do you do when a relative makes a statement like this? You get out. Everyone left except for an uncle who had taken a walk and came back to find the house deserted. I'm sure that at that moment, he was really thankful that he'd traveled eight hundred miles to spend Thanksgiving with his relatives.

The whole debacle caused such a family uproar that for a while we considered just bypassing Christmas altogether. In the end we decided that we wouldn't cancel Christmas, but we did change the venue to someone else's house.

Stephanie and I tell you our horror stories not to embarrass our relatives (that's just a bonus) but to significantly lower the bar on your holiday expectations. Having low standards is really the formula for success. Concentrate on your family and what a special holiday would be for them. Ask them and you'll discover that it doesn't have to be as complicated as you've imagined it. We hope that hearing our holiday traumas will help convince you.

Here are some tips to help give you some perspective and help you to spend your time doing the things that really matter this holiday season.

Tips from Stephanie

Scale Back—It Will Be Okay

You're a mom now, and the number one thing you can do to make your family's holiday pleasant is to relax and concentrate on *them*. Don't get sucked into all the impressive projects and decorations that you did before you were a mother. All the extra cooking, shopping, and gift wrapping that go along with having children is already more than you used to have to do, and you don't want to spend the entire month of December ignoring your children. Think back to your own childhood and concentrate on doing the things that meant the most to you. It's so important to schedule family time during this hectic season. Your kids aren't going to remember the centerpiece you crafted, but they will remember sharing special time with you singing or reading or playing games together. You also don't want them to remember you as being grumpy, rushed, and frazzled. Mom sets the tone for the entire family, so scale back on the pressures you put on yourself and make sure you have time to feel the joy.

Smart Shopping

The Internet is a mom's best friend during the holiday season. Why drag the kids into store after store when it's all at your fingertips? Many online stores offer free shipping during this hectic season, so it actually costs less than driving to the stores (especially with the price of gas these days). Some even offer free gift wrapping! There are websites like www.clubmom.com that offer great gift ideas and even have a point-earning program so you can reward yourself. If you do have to visit the stores, avoid the crowds by shopping during the week or during your lunch break, when most of the other shoppers are at work.

Every year, my mother finishes her holiday shopping by October. She can't stand the crowds, the waiting, and the germs. And although I can't promise to be dedicated enough to finish in October, I do think about my gift list starting in August. Purchasing a little something here and there makes the budget a lot more comfortable in December and eliminates some of the rush.

The Indispensable List

How can any mother function without a list? I keep a list on my computer of all the people I have to buy for and what I plan to buy them. When the item has been purchased, or if I buy something that's not on the list, I update my list. If you use Excel, your list will even help you budget and plan your expenditures. The list helps me figure out what stores or websites I need to visit so I don't make wasted trips. It ensures that my son and daughter have an equal number of presents to open. And most of all, it prevents anxiety. If you're feeling overwhelmed or stressed out, take five minutes and jot down a list of all the things you have to do. When you see it on paper, it will seem a lot more manageable than when it was all floating around in your head. There is something very calming about a good list.

Delegate

Your survival requires assistance from your family, so get them involved. Kids are great with envelopes and stamps. Turn chores into family activities. Talk to your kids in advance and let them know that Mommy is going to need lots of extra help.

Food

This is one of the biggest challenges for moms. My children were three and four years old when we spent our first Christmas alone together in our house without any relatives. Even so, I was absolutely amazed at the amount of time I spent in the kitchen preparing breakfast, lunch, and then a nice holiday dinner. So make lists, shop ahead of schedule, and freeze as many foods as you can. When you cook, make double—many casseroles and foods can be frozen, so you can simply reheat them when you're in a rush. And we recommend a wonderful mommy cookbook called *The One-Armed Cook* by Cynthia Stevens Graubart and Catherine Fliegel. This book contains everything a mom needs to know about keeping her sanity while putting an impressive meal on the table. The authors provide recipes and information on cooking and freezing foods ahead of time so you can spend your holiday with your family instead of in the kitchen.

Leave Room on the Calendar

Remember that you have to get really good at saying no for the next couple of months. Leave some room on your calendar for unexpected events and some free time for yourself. Try to leave a few days completely unscheduled.

Get Your Beauty Sleep

Studies show that Americans report losing a tremendous amount of sleep between Thanksgiving and New Year's Day. Don't stay up late finishing projects; you need your rest. It boosts your immune system, gives you energy, and helps your overall mood and efficiency.

Lists from the Kids

My kids love making their own lists. Every year, I give them the toy catalogs and a pair of scissors. They love pasting their wishes into little notebooks or small photo albums. These lists are a great way for small children to communicate and remember their requests. It also keeps them from asking for everything they see and helps them set limits. When they were very young, they brought their list along when they visited Santa. It's quite a Kodak moment to see them showing their wishes to Santa.

Tips from Sara

You're Not Alone

According to a recent online survey, 71 percent of the mothers surveyed said they find the holidays very stressful. And if you haven't yet experienced your first Christmas as a mom, you're going to have a whole new appreciation for how hard *your* mom worked to give you those wonderful holiday memories. Planning, shopping, and preparing all the food alone was a bigger ordeal than I ever imagined. Not to mention assembling all the toys, keeping track to make sure everyone gets the right number of gifts, preparing the dining room, wrapping the presents, basting the turkey . . . I need a Xanax just thinking about it.

Simplify Your Menu

Use the KISS method: keep it simple, stupid. Last year my oven decided to go on the fritz before Christmas. Talk about being stressed. My in-laws were coming for Christmas dinner and I had no oven! But it turned out to be the best thing ever. It was a great excuse to keep things simple. Thankfully, we had a deep fryer, so my husband took care of the turkey and I made everything else on the stovetop and in my toaster oven. I didn't try to do anything elaborate, just the holiday standards, and it was great! It was the perfect way to lower my own expectations, even if I didn't realize it at the time!

Time for You

We moms have been known to go an entire day without even five minutes for ourselves. One of the most effective ways to ease tension is exercise. Try to schedule some time to exercise or do something relaxing that makes you happy . . . and do it *every day.* So go ahead and make yourself that cup of hot chocolate and read another chapter in your current book while the kids are napping, instead of getting another chore done. It will invigorate you, and you'll be able to accomplish even more—plus get it done with a happy heart and a lighter spirit.

Bag the Diet

Save the dieting for another time of the year. We're not saying go ahead and pig out, but do enjoy the delicious foods of the season without guilt. There are just too many temptations this time of year to be successful at dieting. That's what New Year's resolutions are for.

Sometimes It's Worth It to Drive to the Store

This is where I have to disagree with Stephanie. I do a fair share of shopping online, but I have found at Christmas that it does have its pitfalls. Such as when a package shows up at the door with "Toys R Us" on the shipping label. My seven-year-old is pretty savvy about figuring out what the box might contain. I've fumbled to explain what it was (it's something Daddy ordered) and then gotten caught in my lie (why didn't Daddy open the box when he got home?) in order to keep Santa alive in the minds of my children (something I hope to maintain until they are in their teens—ha). I've found it is easier to do covert shopping while the kids are in school and hide my purchases before they get home. And letting someone else wrap your Christmas gifts? The idea! I love wrapping Christmas gifts and shopping for paper and ribbon. I think it's much more personal and meaningful to get something that you know the giver has wrapped. Unless, of course, it's in one of those robin's-egg-blue boxes from Tiffany's. That's a different matter entirely.

Communicate with Your Spouse

Married couples are usually dealing with two sets of relatives during holiday functions. So be sure to talk to your husband ahead of time about what you envision and what really matters to you about the upcoming holiday. Make sure you are both on the same page so that you won't be thrown for any unnecessary surprises—like the fact that his brother is allergic to nuts and your stuffing recipe includes pecans. Discuss schedules and plans for the day and exactly who is coming so you won't be left high and dry when he announces that the men are going to play golf just when you were hoping for his help in the kitchen.

Avoid Touchy Subjects with Relatives

Around the Christmas table is not the time to bring up the presidential elections or the recently appointed openly gay bishop. Nor is it the time to mention Uncle Eddie's unfortunate stint in rehab or that little Jimmy was expelled from school again. Just don't go there. Focus on the positive and keep it light.

When You Can't Prevent Conflict

If you can't head off a conflict, avoid it! If you know Aunt Louise and your sister Joyce always bicker, try not to have them over at the same time. Or if you can't get around it, plan activities that keep them in different parts of the house. Decide in advance that if the arguing starts, you're going to head outside for a walk or suggest that everyone watch the video of your child's preschool Christmas sing-along. That'll teach 'em.

Delegating: Getting Husbands Involved

From Stephanie

I know my husband is as surprised as the kids are every Christmas morning because he has absolutely *no* idea what they're going to open, and that's because other than bringing home the paycheck that funds the whole event, he hasn't helped do anything to prepare for the big day. And most husbands I've met are the same way. In fact, if you ask any mom, she'll tell you that most of the time, all they do is sit back and complain about how much money we're spending—while we're out doing all the work.

Here are five ways to get your hubby involved. These came straight from my own useless husband's mouth, so they *should* work.

1. Communication is key. Stop being a Lone Ranger and talk things through with your spouse. Make a list of all the people you have to buy for, what gifts you have in mind, what stores those gifts will be found in, and an estimated price. It will help you both (and your budget) to see it all laid out in black and white.

2. Encourage your husband to go shopping with a friend. Daddies enjoy a night out too. They can grab a bite to eat and hit the stores with the list that you

both created. It will put him in the Christmas spirit and he'll have some fun helping out.

From Sara

That may work for Tim, but David would rather be stabbed in the eye repeatedly with an ice pick than go shopping. And he sure as hell wouldn't do it with another guy. If I did get him to bite on that idea, I can tell you exactly what would happen. He and his buddy would go to eat at a sports bar, and after they were done eating they'd mosey over to the bar to watch the rest of the football game that happened to be on, and never darken the door of a shopping mall.

3. Divide the kids' gift budget in half. If you don't want to deal with a list, then decide together how much you are going to spend on the kids and each go shopping with half the money. You might be pleasantly surprised at the choices he makes.

4. Ask for help without complaining. Tell him what you want him to do without insulting him. If there's a deadline required, then explain what it is and why.

5. Describe the rewards. Make him think about how much fun it is to watch them open the gift you've chosen for them. Paint a visual picture for him of the suspense and how excited their reactions are when you've chosen something they really like.

The bottom line is that to control holiday stress and capture that holiday magic you want to create for your children, you have to be a little selfish. Think of it this way: when you're on a plane, they say, "If oxygen masks come down, put one on yourself first before you help someone else." Busy moms have to remember the same rule. We have to keep breathing first before we can give breath to our kids. We have to be focused on that holiday spirit before we can pass it on to our families.

Clutter-Busting Resources

WEBSITES

Club Mom
www.clubmom.com

BOOKS

The One-Armed Cook: Quick and Easy Recipes, Smart Meal Plans, and Savvy Advice for New (and not-so-new Moms)
by Cynthia Stevens Graubart and Catherine Fliegel, R.N.

48

Flying Without Fear

From Sara

David and I often tell people that he had to almost die in a plane crash before we figured out we were ready to start a family. That's really not an exaggeration. About five years into our marriage, he was on a small commuter plane going to visit his grandfather when smoke filled the cabin. Then the right engine stopped (he found out later the pilots had actually turned it off). The plane was so small there were no flight attendants on board to tell the passengers what was going on. I'd just happened to call the airline to check on his flight and was put on hold after they told me the plane was having a mechanical problem and was trying to find a place to land. Let me tell you, those were five excruciating minutes on hold. When my husband finally returned home safely, we ditched the birth control and started a family immediately. (I'm not kidding. I was pregnant within a month.)

Now why am I telling you this story in a chapter that is supposed to ease your fears about flying? Because the point is, the plane landed safely. David said it was amazing how well it flew with one engine . . . it felt no different than with two. Every safety precaution was taken—a battery of fire trucks and rescue units was waiting for them when they landed at the airport. The pilots were in constant communication with the tower, and the oxygen masks dropped down from the ceiling in the plane just like they were supposed to.

I've had some pretty significant fear issues with flying after that incident, and even more after having children. When I do fly, I've found that the drug Xanax (used to treat panic disorders and anxiety) makes the flight much more tolerable. Finding that out, however, involved asking my doctor if I could take both Zoloft and Xanax. Hey, ya gotta do what ya gotta do.

I've also listened to some fear-of-flying podcasts called *Wings of Discovery* (see "Clutter-Busting Resources"), and Stephanie's husband, Tim, has hypnotized me to help with my fear. Both have worked to reduce the stress I feel when I am on a plane. And the podcasts taught me some very important things about airplane safety. The reality is, we put ourselves and our children in much greater danger every time we strap them into their car seats. Yet most of us don't give that a second thought. Flying is incredibly safe. For an average American, your risk of dying in a plane crash is about one in eleven million. Your risk of dying in a car crash is one in five thousand. Your risk of dying of heart disease is one in four hundred. So if you think of it that way, eating a Big Mac is actually riskier to your health than getting on a plane.

Safety is of utmost importance to airlines. The FAA imposes strict standards about the distance planes have to keep apart. Redundancies are built into airline operations. There are at least two pilots on every plane, and air traffic controllers monitor every flight. Try to remember that the next time you are sitting on a plane wiping your sweaty palms on your pants. And if that doesn't work, ask your doctor for a prescription for Xanax for your next flight.

From Stephanie

We wanted to talk to you about flying because for many of us, boarding an airplane became something entirely different once we became mothers. Suddenly, we realized we had a reason to live. As a mom, you're less worried about how much longer it's going to take for the beverage cart to arrive and more worried about whether the plane is going to flip upside down and spiral toward the ground, leaving your child motherless. Now, to some of you, this is going to sound absolutely crazy. But the majority of you are saying, "Thank God, it's not just me!" We've spoken to many mothers who have shared with us how they suddenly became afraid of air travel—some were even flight attendants.

Personally, I never loved flying; it always made me a little nervous. I found it exciting and felt somewhat privileged to have a job that allowed me to travel frequently and see our beautiful country (and eat at all the great restaurants). But I was just a few weeks pregnant when boarding an airplane brought on a whole new feeling . . . fear. That motherly instinct kicked in, and I didn't want anything to happen to my unborn baby—I didn't want to take any chances. Luckily, I was sitting next to a flight attendant that day, and when I confessed my newly acquired fear, she told me that it happens a lot. In fact, she was friends with another flight attendant who ended up quitting her job for exactly that reason. Sara has experienced the same thing, and so have countless other women we've talked to. So we decided to include this chapter to help women who feel that fear of flying to overcome it (although I must admit, I still feel more comfortable when my husband and I book different flights—just in case).

Okay, so let's talk a little about the fear of flying. When you're about to board an airplane, do you have heart palpitations, butterflies, or nausea? Do you sweat a lot? Or, like me, do you sit there gripping your armrests, white-knuckled, and trying to take deep breaths, hoping that no one will notice that you're a freak? One of my old bosses used to make fun of me because we traveled together a few times and I always had a death grip on his arm every time the plane turned. One day I was by myself and had a really terrifying flight (the kind that made grown men gasp and groan), and upon surviving, I was trying to tell everyone in my office about it. My boss said, "Triplett, I've flown with you—old ladies are sittin' there reading magazines and you're freaking out trying to drive the plane from your seat." So they didn't believe me. (I get no respect.)

Actually, one out of every six Americans is afraid to fly—that's slightly over fifty million people. The statistics tell us that it is an irrational fear, but there are plenty of us who have it, irrational or not. There are all sorts of reasons why people develop a fear of flying. Heredity is a factor—if your parents are afraid of flying, you probably have inherited the personality traits that make you afraid too. Some of us have personalities that just make us more susceptible to fears and phobias. If you have trouble trusting people, there's a good chance you'll be afraid to fly. (You have to trust the pilots and flight attendants because it's a situation where you have no control, right?)

Many of us (me included) have a hard time understanding why we are suddenly afraid to fly after becoming parents. Many people report having flown earlier in their lives with no trace of fear or discomfort. There are many factors that make us afraid to fly. Take, for example, the media. The media love a good airplane crash—the problem is that they usually add hype to the story by focusing on people's feelings and reactions instead of the actual facts. Studies have shown that you would have to fly once a day every day for over fifteen thousand years in order to statistically be involved in an aircraft accident! Yet stories of aircraft accidents are two hundred times more likely to receive front-page coverage than other, more common causes of death. As far as the media are concerned, dying on an airplane is much more glamorous and newsworthy than dying in a car accident. So people who are afraid to fly develop a negative bias toward flying. They will pay more attention to those events and experiences that support their fears. How many people would venture to drive if we had the same detailed, vivid, and intense coverage of the carnage that occurs in traffic accidents every day?

It's not just birth that can bring on these fears. Weddings, funerals, or even a promotion or graduation are all events that trigger us to think about our mortality. That explains why so many mothers are now afraid to fly. We start thinking about who would raise our children if something happened to us or how we don't want to miss seeing our children grow up. This kind of thinking produces a heightened concern about death and the kinds of events that might cause it. It's perfectly normal and quite common.

The funny thing is that statistics show that choosing an alternative form of transportation means we are actually exposing ourselves to a higher probability of accidental death! Airplanes are much, much safer than trains, cars, or buses. Statistically, you are at far greater risk driving to the airport than getting on an airplane. This is especially true for us moms who are reaching around the seat trying to recover that pacifier that landed on the floor. However, the *perception* is that you have more control over your fate when you are in your car than you do as an airplane passenger. Considering that over fifty thousand people are killed on the highways every year, that's obviously not the case.

The problem with those of us who are afraid to fly really has to do with the way we've trained ourselves to think. When we board the plane, we're looking to see how old the equipment is, and during the flight we watch the flight attendants' faces for signs of fear. When the plane turns, we lean the other way, as if we could balance it, and all those mysterious beeps and signals make us wonder if it's a secret code to the flight attendants that we've lost an engine. If the pilot asks the flight attendants to take their seats, we begin to panic. And let's not even talk about what happens when we hit turbulence.

To overcome our fear of flying, all we really have to do is train ourselves to think differently and have different thoughts. My husband, Tim, is a professional hypnotist. And while he prefers making people do hilarious things onstage, he has also helped a great number of people with their phobias (including Sara). Fear of flying is one that people ask for help with quite often. During the session, he asks his subjects to imagine in their mind the entire flight from beginning to end—boarding, flying, landing, getting off the plane, and getting to the destination—using as many mental pictures and details as possible. Then he has the subject replay the same events backward, over and over again. Before you know it, you've tricked your mind into concentrating on the landing and arrival and forgotten to worry about having trouble along the way. If you would like to order one of his CDs on curing phobias, please visit his website at www.timtriplett.com. (I know that was a shameless plug, but I've seen his methods help lots of people—so you'll cure your fear, maybe I can buy a new pair of shoes, and everybody's happy.)

So, let's briefly cover some of the things that scare us the most. The more educated you are, the safer you will feel. When we had a radio show on this topic, we asked my friend Jeff Sabol to join us. He is a very good friend and an experienced pilot. Jeff was a pilot with TWA and American Airlines for nine years, where he flew mostly international flights. He's had his pilot's license since he was eighteen years old and is currently working as a corporate pilot. But what makes him even more qualified for the purpose of grilling him about flying is that he is married to my girlfriend Cindy. I was so happy when she started

Flying Fact

Most fearful flyers are sure that the takeoff is the most dangerous part of the flight, but actually it's the landing. But it is not as dangerous as crossing the street, eating a hot dog, or climbing a ladder. Pilots perform safe landings thousands of times every day, all over the world. On any given day more than eighty-seven thousand flights are in the skies in the United States. In one year, air traffic controllers handle an average of sixty-four million takeoffs and landings.

dating a pilot because I've always been a little afraid of flying, and now I had a real pilot that I could talk to about all my insane phobias. I was like an obsessed gambler looking for tips from a bookie. And so, my friends, this poor man has had to cope with me cornering him at every party and asking him hundreds of stupid, irrational questions about flying. He's always been so patient and explained everything so well, even when he was probably thinking, *I sure wish the crazy I'm-going-to-die-on-an-airplane lady would get the hell out of my way so I could get back to the bar.*

Frequently Asked Questions

Some of the following questions and answers come straight from Jeff's experience as a pilot and research gleaned from our radio show.

Is Turbulence Dangerous?

No. Turbulence can never cause a plane to crash. Why? Airplanes are designed to ride over the currents of air, just like a boat is designed to ride over waves. Turbulence is not a threat; it is just converging currents that cause a ripple of air. The only way it can hurt you is if you fall down while on board the plane. It won't harm the airplane in any way. Jeff told us that most pilots don't enjoy turbulence either (probably because they don't want to spill their coffee) and they'll do their best to find a smoother path to make you more comfortable.

What Is the Most Dangerous Part of the Flight?

Jeff once told me that the length of time a pilot is concerned about a flight is about three seconds. So ever since then, I pick a time and count, "One one thousand, two one thousand, three one thousand," and then I say, "Okay, it's over."

Jeff finally confessed during our radio show that the moments when the wheels leave the ground during takeoff and just before they touch the ground during landing are probably the two times when pilots are most on their guard and prepared to handle any problem. The rest of the trip is like driving a car as far as pilots are concerned.

Where Is the Best Place to Sit on an Airplane?

This depends on your own fears. If your fear is based on a phobia of heights, then sit on an aisle or sit by a window where you can pull down the shade and control your visual space.

If turbulence is what frightens you, then know that you will feel less turbulence at the front of the plane. The tail of the plane moves around a lot more, and it is usually very loud because the engines are mounted there.

If your fear is based on claustrophobia, then choose a seat in first class or business class—if you can afford it, of course—or on an aisle so you have more space. The most stable place to sit is over the wings, but this is also one of the noisiest places to sit because the landing gear, flaps, and sometimes the engines are located under the wings.

And just so you know, no area on a plane is safer than any other.

Is It Safer to Fly During the Day or at Night?

It makes no difference—one is just as safe as the other. So once again, base it on what will make you feel the safest. Some people like to fly during the day so they can see the ground. My anxiety is worsened by my fear of heights, so I'm more comfortable flying at night when I can't see the ground.

How Dangerous Are Thunderstorms?

The FAA requires commercial aircraft to remain twenty miles from the core of a thunderstorm, where there are usually high winds, hail, and heavy rain. Pilots will steer clear just to give you a smooth ride. As for lightning: the fact is that lightning strikes planes all the time. It doesn't hurt the plane because the plane is not grounded. It can be frightening because it's usually accompanied by a loud clap of thunder. The radar onboard airplanes prevents pilots from flying through a storm.

What Is an Air Pocket?

We've all heard terrifying stories about planes falling hundreds of feet. But the fact is, there is no such thing as an air pocket. The term *air pocket* was coined during World War I by a journalist who was trying to describe turbulence. It is literally impossible for an airplane to fall hundreds of feet. Planes travel at an airspeed of 450 to 550 mph. When a plane hits turbulence, it's just like your car hitting a speed bump—there's a bump, but you keep moving forward. The largest drop reported was fifty feet, which occurred dur-

Flying Fact

Duane Brown's book *Flying Without Fear* says that if you really want to know how a plane functions in a thunderstorm, contact the U.S. Weather Bureau and ask for a copy of the videotapes made by planes known as "hurricane hunters." The U.S. Weather Bureau sends out daily reconnaissance planes into each hurricane to take readings of wind velocity and other facts that measure the intensity of the storm. These planes fly through embedded thunderstorms and high winds. The crew on those tapes look as if they're in a blender, but the planes survive quite easily. You should also know that these planes are not specially built for the purpose of flying into thunderstorms—they're just regular planes.

ing severe turbulence—and that's not very much considering that the plane was flying at twenty-five thousand feet.

Do Pilots Have Trouble Controlling the Plane During Turbulence?

The movies have given us all this image of the pilot fighting to keep the plane under control. The fact is, most times the plane is on autopilot when flying through turbulence.

Why Do Planes Fly So High?

The higher you fly, the fewer planes there are. Also, the higher a plane is, the more room it has to glide in the one-in-a-trillion chance that all engines fail. And jet engines also run more economically at higher altitudes.

Let's Talk Wind Shear

We've all heard that wind shear is one of the most deadly conditions in air travel. But what is it, and what measures are taken to help pilots avoid it?

Wind shear is the term often used when you have diverging winds at different speeds. When you are high in the sky, the turbulence you feel is usually wind shear, so it's not a threat. When wind shear is a threat is during takeoff and landing. But all commercial aircraft now have equipment on board to detect wind shear, as well as equipment at the airport that detects wind shear on the runway, so it is no longer a threat.

Do Pilots Use Autopilot a Lot and Is It Safe?

Yes, most pilots use autopilot 95 percent of the time on some planes. Certain airlines require their pilots to use autopilot the majority of the time. That is not the chance for pilots to read the sports page; it frees the pilot up to make better decisions.

Our Conversation with a Flight Attendant

Angie Thomas is a good friend of Sara's who is also a mom and a former flight attendant. We wanted to get her perspective too, so we asked her a few questions.

What's the number one no-no that parents do when traveling?

Some parents don't strap their child in during takeoff and landing. If a child is under two, the airlines don't require you to buy him his own seat. But flight attendants recommend buying a seat for your child and bringing your car seat to strap him in. Planes travel at airspeeds of up to 550 mph. Just as in the case of a car accident, you are not strong enough to hold a child in your lap during severe turbulence.

What makes flight attendants mad?

There are no microwaves on board an aircraft, so please don't ask flight attendants to warm a bottle because they can't. Also, there are no refrigerators on an airplane, so they can't store the milk for you either (you have to bring your own cooler). Flight attendants *can* fill bottles with warm water to make formula, or bring you hot water to warm a bottle.

Where is the best place to change a diaper on a plane?

Please don't ask the flight attendant to let you do it in the galley where the food is served. The bathroom is the only acceptable place for a diaper change. Most larger airplanes now have fold-down tables in the restroom. Or put the toilet seat down and then put your blanket or padding down. And above all, please don't pass a dirty diaper to the flight attendant. Put it in a bag and dispose of it in the trash can inside the lavatory.

What should parents do to prepare when flying with babies and children?

Bring everything you need for your children and plan for delays. Remember snacks, and bring a blanket (temperatures change dramatically, and blankets provided on airplanes are not washed after every flight). Bring extra everything! Airports don't sell baby supplies or formula, and sometimes flights can be delayed for several hours, so plan for the worst.

Clutter-Busting Resources

WEBSITES

Top ten tips for flying
www.airsafe.com/ten_tips.htm

CDC's tips for traveling with children
www.cdc.gov/travel/child_travel.htm

Flying Without Fear
www.flyingwithoutfear.com

Fear of Flying Help Course (*Wings of Discovery* podcasts)
www.fearofflyinghelp.com

Hypnosis for phobias
www.timtriplett.com

BOOKS

Flying Without Fear
by Duane Brown, Ph.D.

49

When a Parent Travels

From Stephanie

When one parent has to travel frequently, it can cause quite an array of issues. I should know. When my son was born, my daughter was only seventeen months old, and my husband traveled almost every week. There was one day in particular that sticks in my memory. I had been at home with a newborn and a sick twenty-month-old baby. Just getting a shower each day was a miraculous feat of juggling naptimes and *Wiggles* episodes. Plus I was healing from a C-section and still feeling the fatigue that plagues all new mothers. All I could think about was how my husband was having a nice dinner in a fancy restaurant and returning to a quiet hotel room, with the sheets turned back and a chocolate mint on his pillow. On the day he returned from a long trip, he went to throw something into the trash can. When he opened the cabinet door, some trash came spilling out because the bag was so full. This annoyed him and he actually had the audacity to complain to me about not taking out the trash. At the exact moment that this sentence left his mouth, I happened to be standing on the other side of the room with the TV remote control in my hand, and I snapped. I hurled the remote at him as hard as I could. Unfortunately, I missed (he ducked—he's very athletic), and it hit the floor dramatically and the batteries went flying out of it in every direction. He suggested I see my doctor for some kind of medication. I was more interested in a divorce attorney.

How Traveling Affects the Family

If you are the parent who is doing the traveling, there are a few things you need to keep in mind. Your spouse will probably be feeling overwhelmed and left to fend for himself.

He's left with the task of keeping the household going—paying bills, caring for children, shopping, and keeping up with all the household tasks. The kicker is that he's doing all of this without so much as a ten-minute break from the activity. He's probably envious of all the free time you have and the quiet hotel room that lets you get an uninterrupted night's sleep. If the spouse at home has a job on top of all this, he is going to feel even more overwhelmed. You must acknowledge and appreciate what your partner is doing to keep your home running smoothly while you're away. And if you don't show your appreciation, your spouse is going to end up resenting you and your absence and you can forget any kind of warm welcome when you return.

If you are the one keeping the home fires burning, don't forget that the traveling spouse is missing the kids and home, often missing out on milestones in their children's lives. Traveling parents may begin to feel unneeded or that they are merely wanted for their paycheck. And traveling is tiring. Navigating airports and transportation and schedules is exhausting and frustrating work. And usually the nature of their work when traveling is stressful due to presentations or being "on" for days at a time.

And let's not forget the kids. It's not easy for them either. I know that my children are always the happiest and most secure when both parents are home. So before you go, talk to your kids about where you are going and when you will return. Mark days on a calendar or give them something personal of yours so they can hold it when they miss you. And be sure to stay in touch when you're gone. Set a specific time to call each day and communicate with your family. The kids love talking to you on the phone, and it gives your spouse a chance to tell you what's going on and feel less alone.

When You Return

Spend some special time with the kids as soon as you get home. This gives the home-bound parent a much-needed break and gives you some time to reconnect with your kids.

If you travel frequently, respect the rules, schedules, and boundaries that your spouse has established. It takes a lot of organization to manage a household and family alone, and you need to acknowledge that and stick with the plan. And by all means—don't criticize! It's also a good idea to try to plan a date with your spouse so the two of you can reconnect as well.

Best Tips for Traveling Parents

Here are some great tips we liked from a book called *The Business Traveling Parent: How to Stay Close to Your Kids When You're Far Away.* Some of these have worked very well in our family.

- Before you leave, write a love note to your child telling him how much you'll miss him. Put it somewhere that your child will find it.
- Use a map or atlas to trace out your journey and destination.
- Your older child will love getting a copy of your flight itinerary or other materials that help him figure out where you are and what you're doing at any given time of day. (You can ask your child to give you his agenda too so you can take it with you.)
- Sometimes it's fun to have a special farewell dinner. This is a great way to establish a routine around your travel schedule. Order something special, light a few candles, even make a sign or two. Have fun with it.
- A fun way to leave your hotel phone number for your kids to dial is to use the magnetic numbers we all have sticking to the refrigerator door. Together, you and your child can spell out the numbers and set a time for him to call. (Just make sure you leave a number written on paper, in case the numbers get rearranged.)
- Purchase a map and bulletin board and use pushpins to mark the cities and towns that you've visited. This is a great way for kids to learn about the world.
- Before you leave for your trip, ask your child to name an activity that she would really like to do with you when you return. Use markers or your computer to make a coupon that can be redeemed for that activity when you return. It's a great reminder of time you'll soon be spending together. Kids love them.
- While you're away, send your kids a letter or postcard. Kids love getting mail. Even a quick note jotted on hotel stationery is fun for them.
- Have your child keep a journal of daily events while you're away. Small children can use construction paper and draw pictures, and older children can journal. This is the best way to make sure you don't miss anything (because so many little things get forgotten by the time you return).
- Make a big deal out of welcoming the traveling parent home. Make signs and have a special dinner.
- Plan a family outing that starts the minute your family picks you up from the airport. Dress so you're ready to go as soon as you leave the gate. You can even plan it with your spouse and surprise the kids.
- "Did you bring me something?" Haven't we all heard that before? I think coming home with a present in hand is a great way to let kids know that you thought of them while you were gone. It also builds great anticipation for your return. You can build even more anticipation by making them wait until after dinner or after you've had some time to talk or unpack.
- Sometimes traveling means that you miss major milestones. If that's the case, make the night you return a special event night. Recelebrate the birthday, or

watch videos or photos of the big game or the recital. Celebrate the little things too, like losing a tooth or learning to tie a shoe.

Please take the time to put some extra thought and effort into your family when a parent travels frequently. It is a strain on every member of the family, but a little thought and some quality time can make a huge difference in reestablishing the bond.

Clutter-Busting Resources

The Business Traveling Parent: How to Stay Close to Your Kids When You're Far Away
by Dan Verdick and Scott Pollack

Parent's Guide to Business Travel: Practical Advice and Wisdom for When You Have to Be Away
by Charlie Hudson

50

Grandparents

From Sara

The moment you become a mother, your relationship with your parents and in-laws changes significantly. The shift occurs on both sides. Having a child of your own, you are suddenly aware of the huge amount of love your parents have for you. You experience for yourself the sacrifices your parents made for your well-being. And you now truly understand why all those nights you missed curfew caused them so much anxiety.

While you may appreciate what your own parents did for you more than ever, you might not appreciate it so much when they try to impart their parental wisdom to you now. Don't get me wrong—they do mean well. It's just that times and parenting methods have changed since they parented you. Even though no one would dare put bourbon on a teething baby's pacifier nowadays, I can guarantee that someone—either your parents, your in-laws, or someone their age—will tell you to do just that. They'll be shocked when you don't put rice cereal in the baby's bottle because that's what they used to do. Some grandparents can be pretty forceful about challenging your parenting methods, which can create tension if you don't handle it head on. And let me tell you, these people are hands down the best, most affordable, and most willing babysitters you will ever meet. So it's in your best interest to handle these sticky situations carefully. Here's hoping you can learn from our own triumphs and tragedies in this area.

"These Are Not the People Who Raised Me"

Bill Cosby has the best line on grandparents we've ever heard: "These are not the people who raised me." He's absolutely right. We can promise you that your parents will seem like completely different people as grandparents. They will defend behavior in your children that would have earned you a beating when you were a kid. They'll shower your children with gifts. They'll let them stay up late and eat ice cream (and then tell *you* you're spoiling them). They'll sit on the floor and play with them for hours even if you never remember them playing with you like that.

The reality is that now they probably have more time and money at their disposal than they did when they were raising you. It was likely the same with your own grandparents. Try to relax and let them spoil their grandchildren a little. It's not a bad thing for your kids to know that the rules are more relaxed at Nana's house. That's why my daughter cries when she leaves my parents' house. Life is good at Grandma's. Really good. Be thankful they feel that way.

Grandparent Insanity

On the other hand, you'll also frequently think your parents have lost their minds. Somehow over the years they have managed to erase from their minds every less-than-stellar moment of your childhood and remember only the really good stuff. And if there wasn't something good to remember, they simply invent something. My mother-in-law swears all three of her kids slept through the night as soon as they came home from the hospital. Yeah, sure they did. And even though my husband says he remembers wetting the bed until he was in first grade, she refuses to admit that he ever did. My mother says she loved getting up in the middle of the night to feed us as babies. Right, Mom. Because everyone loves being woken up at 3:00 A.M. by a crying baby.

We've heard stories of kids who potty-trained themselves, rode a bike at eighteen months (without training wheels), walked at six months, and never ever cried, not once. Mmm-hmmm. Take this all with a very large grain of salt. Just smile and pretend to believe them, but know that what they are telling you is at best 50 percent truth. It's been a very long time since they were where you are right now, and they get nostalgic for those days because they've conveniently blocked out all the bad parts. Yes, raising you was the most blissful, stress-free experience of their entire lives. You were a brilliant, athletic, gorgeous, popular child with impeccable hygiene. In fact, you were almost as wonderful as their grandchild. Almost.

The Greater Role of Grandparents

All kidding aside, grandparents play a larger role than ever in children's lives. Studies show that children who are fortunate to have involved grandparents are more likely to have successful futures. Grandparents tend to crave close relationships with their grandchildren and stay connected by visiting, volunteering at school, attending performances and games, calling on the phone, and e-mailing. Actively involved grandparents make a child feel loved and special. They have time to do things for children that busy parents often don't. They can be positive role models, expanding our children's world and teaching them valuable life lessons.

Grandparents often help financially by purchasing baby gear and furniture. A night at Grandma and Grandpa's gives Mom and Dad a much-needed break from the rigors of parenthood. Many grandparents provide regular child care for their grandchildren. Don't underestimate the impact of your child's relationship with your parents or in-laws.

Practical Tips for Dealing with Grandparents

Here are some very practical ways you can make the most of this relationship, for both you and your child.

Safety First

Because kids nowadays do spend a great deal of time with their grandparents, it's important to keep Grandma and Grandpa up to date on the latest safety and health information. Don't assume they know about a recent toy recall or current product safety standards. For instance, if grandparents are watching your infant child, they should know that babies are put to sleep on their backs, not their tummies like years ago. They should put helmets on kids riding bicycles and keep hazardous household products out of reach of tiny hands. See "Clutter-Busting Resources" for a grandchild safety checklist.

Respecting Boundaries

A new baby means an adjustment period not only for the parents but for the grandparents too. For first-time grandparents, this is a new role—one they may not quite understand how to handle at first. Arthur Kornhaber, M.D., author of *The Grandparent Solution*, says the first reaction of grandparents is often to treat the parent as the older sibling of the new child. Give your parents time to adjust to being Grandma and Grandpa. After a while, if they still aren't treating you as the parents in charge, sit down and have a conversation with them. Keep it as light as possible and give them a chance to correct the situation. They may not even realize they're not respecting your new role.

What Happens at Grandma's Stays at Grandma's

Yes, it's important that grandparents understand and respect the rules established by Mom and Dad. But grandparents should also get some wiggle room. Grandparents are *supposed* to be a little less rigid than Mom and Dad. These are the people who changed your diapers, packed your lunches, and lay awake at night worrying about you. They've earned the right to some flexibility. Show them you trust them to do what's right by giving them some freedom to do things their own way. And realize that it's your child, not your mother, who will likely be the one informing you that Grandma let her have Mountain Dew with dinner or that she stayed up way past bedtime. As long as it's not something that endangers your child or is inappropriate, don't sweat it. Bendable rules are just one more thing that makes being at Grandma's really fun.

Dealing with Unsolicited Advice

It can be extremely tempting for grandparents to offer their unsolicited advice when they see you parenting differently than they did. Some just can't resist offering their opinions. Yes, grandparents may play a greater role than ever, but you are your child's parent and that fact must be respected. If you find yourself confronted with unsolicited advice, ask your parents if you can please discuss the issue at another time, in private. Explain that being challenged in front of your child undermines your authority as the parent. Do hear the grandparents out, keeping in mind that the parenting decisions are yours to make. If you still disagree, ask the grandparents to trust you and to respect your role. It's also important not to overreact.

New moms are often overly sensitive at first because we're unsure of ourselves. Sometimes a grandparent's comments—comments that are really intended to be harmless—get misconstrued. Try not to take these remarks too seriously. They may be no more than a grandparent reminiscing.

Jealousy

Because most grandparents crave time with the grandkids, the division of time between your parents and your spouse's can get tricky. Some grandparents are relaxed and enjoy their grandkids when they see them without worrying about how much time the "other" grandparents are getting. Yet, unfortunately, with many it becomes a real source of tension. Some seem to keep tally sheets in their heads, tracking the hours you spent at your husband's parents or how many vacations you've taken with *your* parents. You may find that neutral territory (your own home) may be the best place to gather for holidays and special occasions.

Jealousy over money can become a problem too—for instance, if one set of grandparents gives extravagant gifts or savings account contributions the others can't afford. Setting limits on gift giving is one way to avoid these conflicts. Explain to your parents that you want your children to truly appreciate what they are given, so you don't want them to overdo it, even if they can afford to. When it comes to grandparents contributing to a college fund or savings account, try to keep the gift private and ask the contributing grandparents to do so as well, especially if the other grandparents aren't able to give monetary gifts.

If, in spite of your best efforts, jealousy issues arise, ask the grandparents to talk to you about them at an appropriate time—not in the presence of the children. Help your parents understand that you are doing the best you can, and look for mutually workable ways they can be more involved with their grandchildren.

When You Need to Speak Up

You've told the grandparents you don't want your child playing with toy guns, but they show up with one anyway. Or they decide to buy your son his first bike without discussing it with you first. There will inevitably be times you'll need to speak up. Don't wait too long before talking to them, or the issue will fester and the conversation will get harder and harder to have. Be sure to first thank them for their interest in their grandchildren and everything they do for them. Ask them to let you take the lead on parenting. Explain that although you don't necessarily expect them to follow your rules to a T, you do expect them to generally respect your guidelines and not undermine the way you parent, or infringe on the special times and gifts you want to share with your child. Suggest that they recall the time in their own lives when they were new parents. What were those experiences like for them? If they can mentally put themselves in your shoes, your parents are much more likely to remember who's really Mom and Dad here.

Clutter-Busting Resources

WEBSITES

Grandchild Safety Checklist
www.cpsc.gov/cpscpub/pubs/grand/704.html

Grandparenting: The Joys and Challenges
Free booklet from the AARP
www.aarp.org

"8 Things Grandparents Wish You Knew"
www.parenting.com/article/mom/Relationships/things-grandparents-wish-you-knew

Diplomatic Guide for Grandparents
www.webmd.com/healthy-aging/guide/diplomatic-guide-for-grandparents

BOOKS

The Grandparent Guide: The Definitive Guide to Coping with the Challenges of Modern Grandparenting
by Arthur Kornhaber, M.D.

51

Comparing the Experts

So far, we've shared what has worked and hasn't worked for us. There are many choices and differing expert opinions for moms to sort through, and seldom do they agree. In this chapter, we've compared and contrasted some of the most popular baby gurus and their baffling advice. Ever notice they are all telling us to do something different?

From Stephanie

Sara and I spent a lot of time reading in those first few months of motherhood, and what we discovered is that it seemed every expert was telling us to do something different. We mothers have all these people telling us what to do all the time, but few are recommending the same thing. So how's a mother to know who's right and who's full of crap? There were times when something was working really well for us, and then we read in a book that it was bad.

Take the book *Babywise*, for example. I once became so enraged and frustrated with this book that I actually threw it across the room. My pediatrician reprimanded me for feeding my newborn with the strict schedule that this book recommends. My baby lost too much weight during her first week at home, and I was miserable listening to her cry and trying to stick to a stringent schedule. I hated this book. Sara, on the other hand, loved it.

In this chapter, we've proven our mantra that *there is no one right way to be a mom* by taking some of the most popular experts and looking at their stances on various parenting issues. And we're going to give you the skinny on what each expert has to say. But if you want to entirely skip this chapter, I've summed it up for you in the following paragraph.

Different things work for different families. If you search long enough, you can find an "expert" (and I use the term loosely) to agree with you on just about anything, as well as research to prove their point. And you'll find more research that disputes the findings and the accuracy of the first batch of studies. Plus, every so-called expert's opinion is usually based on their own lifetime experiences, background, religious beliefs, and parenting conundrums, just like your own parenting choices. This simply proves that you need to have the confidence to trust your own choices as a mother. No one knows your child as well as you do. Our advice is to get as much information as you can, from as many experts as you can, and then choose what feels right for you and your family. And don't judge other mothers if they don't make the same choices for their kids, because every family is unique and what works for you might not be the ideal solution for someone else. Now, if you want to know the details, and who's arguing with whom—then read on.

From Sara

A couple of months after my first child was born, a friend recommended *Babywise* to me. I was bleary-eyed, exhausted, and felt like this new ten-pound member of our family had taken control of every minute of my existence. *Babywise* helped me regain some control of my life by teaching me how to start implementing a schedule of feedings, awake time, and sleep and reminding me that I had to take some time for myself in order to be a good parent. David and I have never been rigid in our child rearing, so I went with a flexible version of the *Babywise* schedule. It worked great for me. And for the record, the *Babywise* book does say that if your baby is hungry, you should feed her, schedule or no schedule. Stephanie must have been really sleep-deprived when she read that chapter!

Children are complex little creatures, and they don't often fit into the formulas being promoted in books and television shows. Family dynamics are equally complicated and constantly changing as children grow and new members arrive. David and I got a real eye-opener when our son, Cade, was born. Anna was two and a half and we thought we had this baby/toddler thing pretty well mastered. Then along came Cade, who was a good baby but threw horrible temper tantrums as a toddler—something we had never seen the likes of with Anna. I remember sitting on the kitchen floor with him as he screamed and banged his little forehead on the hardwood. He would violently wrestle free if I tried to hold him, and go into sheer hysteria if I tried to walk away. So I just sat there until he stopped. It didn't take long for us to learn that the parenting strategies we used with Anna were not going to work with Cade. Children are individuals. Any seasoned parent knows they come into this world with distinct personalities that evolve and change as they grow. Savvy parents are constantly reassessing and adapting their tactics based on each child's needs. And I haven't found a book yet that can tell you how to parent any and every personality. Sure, there are facets of your parenting that are constant regardless of personality issues, particularly in matters of discipline—lying is not acceptable, and it doesn't matter who is doing it. But the majority of your parenting will be a lesson in adaptability and responding to ever-changing needs. At least it has been for me.

Experts, even though they're called experts, don't have all the answers. Some books have been extremely useful to me, others not at all. Some have been useful for one child but not the other. Then there are books that I've gleaned some great information from and pretty much discarded the rest. I recently read a book about getting a baby to sleep by twelve weeks that said rocking a baby to sleep is like constantly carrying around a two-year-old. I couldn't disagree more. I rocked my children to sleep and I wouldn't trade those times for the world. Most babies are so busy crawling and walking before they are even a year old that they give you a stiff arm to the chest if you try to cuddle them! The point is, it's all just information and opinion until it's meaningful to you. Remember that. Use what works for you, and don't worry about the rest. After all, you are the person who knows your children better than anyone else on the planet, and that makes you the true expert when it comes to your family.

Here's a brief look at how some parenting experts stack up on six key parenting issues.

The Experts on Crying It Out

"Crying it out" is a somewhat controversial tactic promoted by some sleep experts. Basically it means that parents, once they know their baby is fed and dry, can let their babies cry in order to fall asleep. Most experts recommend checking on (and often soothing) the baby every few minutes but not picking the baby up out of his crib. (Crying it out does *not* mean leaving baby to cry for hours in his crib!) Many new parents, desperate for sleep, have successfully used the "cry it out" method and say that it is not as harsh as it sounds and that in fact it helps babies learn how to self-soothe. However, crying it out does have quite a few critics.

For It

Solve Your Child's Sleep Problems by Richard Ferber, M.D.

"Crying it out" first became popular in the 1980s when pediatrician Richard Ferber wrote *Solve Your Child's Sleep Problems.* Although letting kids cry it out became known as "Ferberizing," Dr. Ferber actually never used the phrase. What he did say is that for some babies, crying is an unavoidable part of sleep training. Advocates of the "cry it out" method believe that if your baby gets used to you rocking him to sleep, you will always have to help him get to sleep. Letting your baby cry or fuss a little before sleeping helps him learn to self-soothe and get himself back to sleep should he wake up in the middle of the night. Proponents say the short-term pain of letting the baby cry is worth the long-term benefits of a child who consistently sleeps through the night.

***Sleeping Through the Night: How Infants, Toddlers, and Their Parents Can Get a Good Night's Sleep* by Jodi A. Mindell, Ph.D.**

Dr. Mindell says that a baby who has been rocked to sleep, nursed to sleep, or driven around the neighborhood to sleep is going to need all those things again when he wakes up at 3:00 A.M. She recommends leaving baby for increasingly longer periods of time so that he can learn to soothe himself and fall asleep.

***Twelve Hours' Sleep by Twelve Weeks Old* by Suzy Giordano**

Ms. Giordano is known as "The Baby Coach" to her clients in the Washington, D.C., area. She suggests that even as babies, children need an authoritative figure who will set limits and boundaries. She believes rocking a twelve-week-old baby over and over is the equivalent of carrying a two-year-old around in your arms all the time. She recommends starting "baby boot camp" between four and eight weeks old and when baby weighs at least nine pounds and is eating a minimum of twenty-four ounces of breast milk or formula per day. She says that babies need not cry a lot and that parents should pat and make reassuring noises to baby in the crib but not pick him up. She also suggests putting a toy that has the mother's scent on it in the crib, even though the American Academy of Pediatrics advises parents to put babies to sleep without any kind of toy or pillow.

Against It

***Healthy Sleep Habits, Happy Child* by Marc Weissbluth, M.D.**

Dr. Weissbluth doesn't endorse crying it out, but he does say that some crying may be necessary for the child to establish good sleep habits. He recommends sticking to a pretty strict nap and bedtime schedule. Babies should not be picked up or soothed when they make mild stirring noises in the crib; rather, parents should wait until baby is fussing loudly before going into the room.

***The Happiest Baby on the Block* by Harvey Karp, M.D.**

Dr. Karp is not a fan of letting babies cry it out. He says it makes about as much sense as listening to your screeching car alarm while you wait for the battery to die. Dr. Karp believes adding white noise in the nursery can help babies fall asleep. He says babies constantly hear noise in the womb—noise louder than a vacuum cleaner. He says it is your job as parents to adapt to your newborn, not the other way around. Dr. Karp recommends a system called the 5 S's to help settle your baby and stop her from crying. These include swaddling, holding baby on her side or stomach, shushing sounds, swinging movements, and sucking (which can be accomplished with bottle, breast, pacifier, or finger).

Dr. Karp's theory is based on the fact that some fussy babies just have trouble making the transition from womb to the world. He gives tools for re-creating a womblike atmosphere to help your baby make the transition. He says that most babies sleep through the night at four months (a much more realistic estimate, in our view).

***The Baby Book* by William Sears, M.D., and Martha Sears, R.N.**

These authors believe that letting a baby cry it out sends the signal to your baby that no one is there to meet his needs. They say, "A baby whose cries are not answered does not become a 'good' baby (though he may become a quiet baby); he does become a discouraged baby. He learns the one thing you don't want him to: that he can't communicate or trust that his needs will be met." They remind us that your baby's cries are *supposed* to annoy you—we mothers have hormones that cause us to react to the sound of a baby crying. They believe that meeting babies' needs in the early months will create solid trust and communication patterns between you and baby. And as baby grows, you can gradually delay your response to help your baby learn to accept waiting and develop self-help skills.

***Sleep: The Brazelton Way* by T. Berry Brazelton, M.D., and Joshua D. Sparrow, M.D.**

Drs. Brazelton and Sparrow are somewhere in the middle between the "cry it out" and "attachment parenting" extremes. Dr. Brazelton says not to rush in and pick up a baby who cries at night. He recommends crooning with a chant to help settle a baby and encourages offering a "lovey" (a toy, a blanket, even a thumb) so the child will learn to self-soothe.

What We Think

"Crying it out" works for some babies, but not for others. Stephanie tried the "cry it out" method with her daughter, and her baby daughter cried for so long, she ended up vomiting in her crib. After about an hour, and changing several crib sheets, Stephanie decided this wasn't for her. Not only was it hard for the baby, it was really hard for Stephanie. It was heart-wrenching to sit in the hallway and listen to the baby crying. Stephanie was crying, her baby was crying, and the whole scene just totally went against her parenting style.

Sara used the middle ground, letting her babies cry for just a little while and comforting them between crying spells. It worked just fine for her. Some parents love the "cry it out" technique; others think it's cruel. Once again, we empower you to make the decision based on your baby's personality and your family's needs.

The Experts on Feeding Your Baby on Demand (vs. Scheduled Feedings)

Every new mom grapples with the question of whether to feed her baby on demand or stick to a schedule. Feeding on demand simply means feeding baby whenever he gives you cues that he is hungry, such as crying or sucking his fists. During those first weeks and months it can be difficult when the baby seems to be constantly crying (and you want to soothe him) but others are continually advising you to "get the baby on a schedule." Then again, setting scheduled feedings looks like a really smart idea when you're exhausted from nursing what seems like every five minutes. Yet there are critics of both methods. What's a mom to do?

For Feeding on Demand

William Sears, M.D., author of *The Baby Book* (and over thirty other books on child care)

Dr. Sears is a proponent of "attachment parenting," which advocates breast-feeding, sleeping with or close to your baby, and wearing baby in a sling as a way to bond with your child. Dr. Sears is a strong supporter of breast-feeding and encourages mothers to nurse as often as baby demands, in order to bond with baby (he says that sometimes the baby may want to nurse for closeness and comfort) and to build the mother's milk supply. Even for mothers who are bottle-feeding, Dr. Sears says that smaller, more frequent feedings work best in the beginning because baby's stomach is tiny, about the size of her own fist. He says that babies often spit up after feeding because they are getting more than their little tummies can hold.

Your Baby's First Year by the American Academy of Pediatrics

The American Academy of Pediatrics says that whether you are breast-feeding or bottle-feeding, newborns should be fed on demand. As the baby gets a little older, feedings will become more regular and then you can implement a schedule. But it was surprising to read that they believe most babies don't need a middle-of-the-night feeding by two months! We've always heard that twelve is the magic number when it comes to baby sleeping through the night, but twelve stands for twelve pounds *and* twelve weeks. It's a matter of weight *and* time.

Touchpoints: Your Child's Emotional and Behavioral Development and *Feeding: The Brazelton Way,* both by T. Berry Brazelton, M.D.

Dr. Brazelton says that in the first three to four weeks, *baby* is in charge of the feedings. For breast-feeding mothers this is especially important, as they do not yet have enough milk to satisfy their babies for longer periods. Feeding on demand helps establish your milk supply, too. As the supply increases, baby will need to feed less frequently. After that, parents can begin stretching out the feedings, which he encourages to make life easier on the parents. He advises new mothers to at first feed the baby whenever she cries in order to learn which cries mean hunger and which ones mean other things. He says you should work toward a schedule by stretching out the times between feedings but that you really need to feed on demand in the first few weeks. He also suggests that if baby doesn't wake after four hours, you should wake her and feed her. Dr. Brazelton also reminds moms that baby should be eating at least six times per day.

Against Feeding on Demand

Babywise by Gary Ezzo and Robert Bucknam, M.D.

The authors of *Babywise* promote something called "parent directed feeding," which they describe as a concept with "enough structure to bring security and order to your baby's world, yet enough flexibility to give mom freedom to respond to any need at any time. It teaches parents how to lovingly guide their baby's day rather than be guided or enslaved to the infant's unknown needs." The authors of *Babywise* are critical of attachment parenting (feeding on demand, baby wearing, and co-sleeping), which Dr. William Sears promotes in his books. They use examples of "exhausted parents" and suggests that mothers who use attachment parenting deal with every cry or need with the breast, implying that they overlook baby's real needs. They also say that attachment parenting produces an emotionally stressed, high-need, insecure baby, which is a gross generalization (to say the least) and not backed up by research.

Babywise also recommends separating your baby's activities into three basic cycles: feedings, awake time, and sleeping. The book recommends feeding every two and a half to three hours but states that mothers using the *Babywise* method have the flexibility to feed their babies *whenever* they are hungry.

Babywise has drawn a lot of criticism from moms who had experiences similar to Stephanie's trying to implement the book's concepts. These mothers are not alone in their concern. Even the American Academy of Pediatrics has voiced apprehension about the feeding methods outlined in *Babywise.* On the other hand, many parents have found success in the parent-directed feeding method. The authors of *Babywise* have responded to the criticism on their website with direct quotes from the book:

- "With Parent Directed Feeding, a mother feeds her baby when he is hungry, but takes advantage of the first few weeks to guide the baby's hunger patterns by a basic routine."
- "If your baby is hungry, feed him or her. If the child routinely shows signs of hunger before the next scheduled feeding, then find out why, rather than letting the baby cry it out."
- "Hunger cues, not the clock, determine feedings."

We think it's important to note that although *Babywise* author Robert Bucknam is a pediatrician, Gary Ezzo is not a physician. If you plan on using the *Babywise* method, you should discuss it with your pediatrician first.

***Secrets of the Baby Whisperer* by Tracy Hogg with Melinda Blau**

The authors say that feeding on demand creates a demanding baby and forces parents to surrender their entire lives to the baby's needs. On the other hand, Hogg also dismisses rigid schedules and offers her own method that she names E.A.S.Y., which stands for "Eating, Activity, Sleep, and You Time." According to Hogg, eating should take twenty-five to forty minutes every two and a half to three hours, activity should last about forty-five minutes, and the baby should sleep for about an hour, during which time mom should enjoy some "you time" while the baby sleeps. (Any mother of a newborn knows that this "you time" will likely consist of cleaning the kitchen, taking a nap, or soaking your hemorrhoids—woo-hoo!) While she acknowledges that the exact amount of time will vary from baby to baby, she does advocate sticking to a schedule to avoid the household falling into chaos.

What We Think

From Stephanie

Once again, Sara and I differed greatly on our approach to feeding. As I shared earlier, feeding on a schedule turned out to be a very bad thing for my young baby. I believe that newborn babies should be fed on demand. It's very important those first few weeks that your baby gains weight, and as we all know, the best way to do that is to eat whenever you want to. As baby gets a little older, I understand the need to schedule his feedings; you have to put the Kitchen Is Closed sign out sometimes or you'd spend your entire life just feeding them. Even at ages six and seven, my children have flawless timing—as soon as I am finished putting the dishes away and cleaning off the last kitchen counter and about to sit down and relax for the evening, they're hungry again. Never fails. I've learned to give them a warning that the "kitchen will be open for another five minutes" so they can get their last-minute requests before Mom clocks out for the night. Older babies usually thrive on schedules and it will help you plan your day when you have a set time for naps and meals.

"Only the baby—not the doctor or a book—can tell you when you're on the right track."

—T. Berry Brazelton, M.D.

From Sara

I implemented a schedule with my babies when they were about a month old. I personally think it's just too early to schedule a baby before that. I think it was easier for me to use a schedule because my babies were bottle-fed and didn't get hungry as frequently as breast-fed babies do. I also knew how much I was feeding them every time (because it's right there on the bottle), so I didn't wonder if they were still hungry if they cried a half hour after being fed. I could pretty easily assume it was a wet diaper or gas (which proved to be the case most of the time!).

The Experts on Spanking

From Stephanie

Some parents defend spanking because their parents spanked them and they turned out "fine." I was spanked plenty as a child, sometimes even with a switch. My grandmother tells me stories about how her mother would require her to go out to the forsythia bushes and choose a switch for her whipping (I kinda wish she had decided not to pass that tradition on to me). Years ago, parents prided themselves on spanking their children. Nowadays, mothers are arrested and the videotape of them spanking their kid in Wal-Mart is all over the six o'clock news.

For It

The Holy Bible

We've all heard the phrase "spare the rod and spoil the child." But contrary to popular belief, this phrase is *not* found in the Christian Bible. It was first written in a poem by Samuel Butler in 1664. However, the Bible is definitely an advocate of spanking. Just look at these quotes from the King James Version of the Bible:

- "He that spareth his rod hateth his son: but he that loveth him chasteneth him betimes." (Proverbs 13:24)
- "Chasten thy son while there is hope, and let not thy soul spare for his crying." (Proverbs 19:18)
- "Foolishness is bound in the heart of a child; but the rod of correction shall drive it far from him." (Proverbs 22:15)
- "Thou shalt beat him with the rod, and shalt deliver his soul from hell." (Proverbs 23:14)

Sheesh! Harsh, right? Looking back on my own childhood, I can't help wondering if my parents, who were devout Christians, had read the Bible and attended church a little less, maybe I wouldn't have received so many of those "rods of correction." King Solomon is credited with writing the book of Proverbs, and apparently Solomon's son was quite the pill, since Solomon's parenting style was pretty hard-core. As an adult,

Solomon's son, Rehoboam, was portrayed as vicious, unfeeling, inconsiderate of others, and having very little regard for human life. In fact, he was widely hated and barely escaped assassination by his own people.

Some believe that if you read between the lines, you'd realize that the Bible's true message here is that perhaps you shouldn't follow Solomon's parenting style—but if you ask me, that's a bit of a stretch. "Thou shalt beat him with a rod and deliver his soul from hell" is a pretty clear message and a little difficult to defend or soften.

There are a plethora of websites (usually religious in nature) that give instructions for the "proper" ways to spank a child. Some even instruct parents not to use their hands to spank but to use an object like a wooden spoon! (C'mon, people . . . seriously?)

There are also many religion-based websites and experts who have decided that maybe modern parents shouldn't take the Bible's instructions on spanking quite so literally. Gordon B. Hinckley, president of the Church of Jesus Christ of Latter-day Saints, said: "I have never accepted the principle of 'spare the rod and spoil the child.' . . . I am persuaded that violent fathers produce violent sons. . . . Children don't need beating. They need love and encouragement. They need fathers to whom they can look with respect rather than fear. Above all, they need example."

Truthfully, it's hard to find any experts these days who condone spanking. It's just not an effective or smart way to discipline your child.

James Dobson, Focus on the Family

Parenting "expert" James Dobson (founder of the Christian organization Focus on the Family) says, "Spanking isn't the only discipline option, but it remains a valuable tool." He advises using a neutral object such as a paddle or a switch to administer spankings to children. His belief is that this preserves the image of a parent's hand as an object of love, not punishment. It is crucial, he emphasizes, that parents maintain control over their tempers and always balance firmness with love. (*From Sara: But isn't the parent's hand* holding *the spoon?*)

Against It

American Academy of Pediatrics

The American Academy of Pediatrics reports that 44 percent of parents admit that they spank because they "lose it." Even if a parent could deliver a spanking using calm, cool discipline (the "this is going to hurt me more than it hurts you" angle) 100 percent of the time, spanking is simply effective only for an instant. They'll stop what they're doing at that moment, but they'll probably do it again in the future.

Although most American parents say they are against spanking, an estimated 90 percent of parents have spanked. According to a study from the State University of New York at Buffalo, 85 percent of those who spank would rather not.

FamilyEducation.com

The popular website FamilyEducation.com states that another reason parents spank is "related to the education level of the parent (the more educated, the less likely they are to spank). Many parents occasionally hit their kids when they are frightened (the child has done something dangerous), or from sheer stress, frustration, or fear of having no other options. If, occasionally, you *lose* it and spank your child, you aren't going to damage him or your relationship forever. Although it's not an effective or positive approach to discipline, it's a more serious problem if you commonly spank your child, or if it's one of your dominant disciplinary methods."

- Spanking teaches your child that violence (hitting) is an acceptable way to handle conflict.
- It only works in the short term.
- After spanking your child, you will feel guilt and remorse and begin to doubt your parenting skills.
- Spanking is harmful to your child's emotional well-being. It makes your child feel like he is bad (rather than just having exhibited a bad behavior). It can cause poor body image and poor self-esteem.
- Spanking makes a child feel powerless. That feeling leads to other bad behavior in an effort to regain power or control.
- Spanking breaks the trust you have with your child and destroys your child's sense of security (that they should always feel when their parents are around).

Murray Straus, renowned expert on the effects of spanking

Murray Straus is a professor of sociology at the University of New Hampshire and after more than forty years of studying spanking is probably the world's expert on spanking research. Straus says spanking "leads to more antisocial behavior in childhood, as well as increased aggression, spousal abuse, and child abuse in adulthood."

What We Think

From Stephanie

Maybe it's just me, but hitting my child with a switch or paddle or wooden spoon just doesn't seem like someone who is "maintaining control." Why don't you just calmly lay them down in the driveway and back over them?

Study after study after study proves that children who are spanked suffer later in life with anxiety, depression, alcohol abuse, and general antisocial and/or criminal and abusive behavior. Our fear is that parents who choose to spank are doing so out of anger.

Spanking can easily turn to abuse, and all too often does. Parents who spank can easily cross the line. So we think it's better to have a policy of not hitting your child at all.

Most people who believe in spanking believe that children should "fear" their parents. That is a parenting style that has proven ineffective time and time again. These people believe that kids today are out of control. We believe that it's not that kids are out of control, it's that society has become evolved enough to realize that our expectations are often too high, that developmentally kids just can't do what we ask of them 100 percent of the time. We also think that those people who think kids are out of control are taking one instance of bad behavior and projecting that instance to represent a child's entire existence. Did these judgmental folks ever consider that maybe the child misbehaving in the store has already been to six other stores that day and his mother is asking too much? Or did you ever consider that the child who just threw her food on the floor of the restaurant is actually a straight-A student, Girl Scout, and well-mannered child who is tired from a sleepover and just having a bad day? We're not saying that you should let your children run wild. But we do believe that oftentimes the reason for the misbehavior can fall on the part of the parent who has unrealistic expectations. We also believe that there are many strategies for disciplining your child that are far more effective than hitting them. And, as a reformed spanker, I can assure you that spanking *is* hitting.

So if you do decide to spank your children, just go ahead and do us all a favor and admit that you're doing it because it makes you feel better. I speak from experience when I tell you that it may make you feel better for the moment, but remember that anger puts a barrier between you and your child. Your relationship with your child loses a little something after every spanking that is hard (if not impossible) to get back. Please don't be ignorant enough to think that it's actually helping or teaching your child anything. Spanking gets immediate results for the parents but produces long-term negative results for the child.

From Sara

I have never believed that spanking is an acceptable method of discipline. However, I have "popped" my children on their legs a few times with my hand. I'm not sure that counts as spanking, but I can tell you it immediately made me feel like an awful parent because I clearly acted out of frustration and anger. And I knew hitting my kids didn't help them or me. Yet, as I've already admitted, I've done this more than once. Being a mom is a tough, often aggravating job that can push just about anyone past her limits. Even with the absolute best intentions for our children, we sometimes screw up and revert to acting like a three-year-old ourselves. Personally, I've found the best thing for me to do when my children are tap dancing on my last nerve is to leave the room for a few minutes and regain my composure before dealing with the situation. And I am happy to say that as my kids have gotten a little older, there are fewer and fewer of these moments. So hang in there. It does get better.

The Experts on Pacifiers

One of the first questions parents often struggle with is whether or not to give their baby a pacifier. They worry the pacifier will become a crutch, cause their child to have crooked teeth, and that their baby will look like he has been "plugged up" by a lazy parent. Yet many experts cite a baby's need to suck and some studies even link pacifier use to a lower risk of SIDS (sudden infant death syndrome).

For It

Parenting for Dummies by Sandra Hardin Gookin and Dan Gookin

This book says sucking is not only natural for babies, but a high priority for them, and it recommends that pacifiers and a pacifier clip should be on your list of baby equipment.

Healthy Sleep Habits, Happy Child by Marc Weissbluth, M.D.

This book promotes pacifiers because he states that anything you can do to encourage your baby to suck will help soothe him. Sucking is a powerful way to calm a baby.

Touchpoints by T. Berry Brazelton, M.D.

Dr. Brazelton believes thumb sucking or pacifier sucking are just fine. He points out that babies suck their thumbs in utero and that a baby who uses a thumb or pacifier to soothe himself is showing healthy signs of competence. He also points out that studies have shown that there is little difference in the need for braces in children who sucked a thumb or pacifier and those who didn't. For parents who worry that they are perpetuating a bad habit, Dr. Brazelton reminds readers that "very few people go to college sucking their thumbs or pacifiers."

Your Baby's First Year Week by Week by Glade B. Curtis, M.D., and Judith Schuler, M.S.

This book says pacifiers are okay to use; many babies may need something to suck on to soothe themselves.

The American Academy of Pediatrics

Pacifiers do not cause psychological or medical problems. Some babies need to suck more than others and pacifiers help them meet this need.

Against It

The Baby Book by William Sears, M.D., and Martha Sears, R.N.

Well, they're sort of against it. They believe that the only thing a newborn baby should have in its mouth is its mother's nipple. So for the first few weeks, they recommend not using a pacifier. Babies suck differently on a pacifier than they do on mother's nipple, and they believe that this can confuse a newborn baby and cause poor latch-on techniques. They recommend that you avoid pacifiers until your baby has good latch-on techniques and you have a good milk supply. They also remind us (and some parents do need this reminder) that pacifiers are for the comfort of babies and not the convenience for the parents. Sometimes babies just need to be held.

The World Health Organization

The World Health Organization (WHO) is the directing and coordinating authority for health within the United Nations system. The WHO is against pacifier use, stating that pacifiers can lead to poor hygiene (by getting dirty), increase ear infections, cause babies to wake up during sleep should they lose their pacifier, and may signal to a child that crying is unacceptable, even though it is one of baby's few means of communication.

La Leche League

The La Leche League is generally against pacifier use but says pacifiers can have their place in the lives of breast-fed babies. But they caution that this use should be sparing. "Frequent use of pacifiers can create little 'addicts' who are rarely seen without a 'plug' in their mouth. Overuse of pacifiers will also create breastfeeding problems, and a mother with concerns about her milk supply or a baby who is reluctant to take the breast should reevaluate the choices she's made about pacifiers and bottles. However, mothers know their babies best. A well-informed approach to the decision about using a pacifier will help them make good decisions about what's best for their families."

What We Think

From Stephanie

Any of you who have read the chapter on finding the right day care know how I feel about pacifiers. Babies have an inherent need to suck. Period. They were doing it in the womb before birth, and they are born with this urge that is designed to help them sustain life. Why would anyone say that's bad? I don't agree with the whole nipple confusion theory—plenty of babies breast-feed and use a pacifier without any detriment to their latching-on skills. In my opinion, trying to keep a baby from a pacifier is just one more ridiculous event in what I call the "Baby Olympics"—that crowd of overachieving parents who try to be the first in getting their babies to sleep through the night, the first to get them started on solid foods, the first to potty-train, the first to read, and later, the first to realize that there are no trophies or recognition at the end of this stressful road of firsts.

What I will say is that children who are walking around aren't babies anymore and if they can run around and say a few words, they shouldn't have a pacifier in their mouth.

That is usually a sign of parents who are too lazy, too complacent, or too scared to take away the pacifier. And almost all of them are amazed that when they finally do take it away, those first few days and nights are never as bad as they imagined. I also agree with the theory that pacifiers keep toddlers from learning to talk—how can you talk when you have that big piece of rubber in your mouth? And toddlers desperately need to express themselves—it's a frustrating age when they're trying to gain more control and being able to talk is a huge help.

From Sara

I am a fan of pacifiers over fingers or thumbs for sucking because I watched my sister struggle with finger sucking until she was over ten years old. I wanted my babies to take a pacifier because I knew it would be a much easier habit to break because I could take the passie away. My pediatrician recommended stopping pacifier use at eighteen months, and as Stephanie said, getting rid of it wasn't nearly as big a deal as I feared. My kids both started using their pacifiers as teethers when their teeth started coming in. They chewed on the nipples of their passies so much they got holes in them. Once a passie nipple has a hole in it, most babies don't want it anymore because it constantly deflates (and you should take it away anyway because it is no longer safe). So at that point, it was just a natural progression to stop giving them a pacifier.

The Experts on Vaccines

This is yet another heated debate among parents. If you are a parent who chooses not to vaccinate your children, you probably think the rest of us are either too lazy to seek out the necessary information or just plain crazy to be willing to inject our kids with all those foreign substances. If you're a parent who *does* vaccinate your children, you are simply following the advice of the American Academy of Pediatrics, almost every other health organization, and your own doctor. And frankly, you're a little incensed at the fact that there are those granola-eating parents out there who are putting *your* child at risk by sending them to public school without their vaccines.

No matter what side you're on, you are passionate about your decision. Here's what we learned about both sides of the debate.

Against It

Dr. Joseph Mercola, who maintains a website at www.mercola.com

Dr. Mercola dramatically warns against traditional vaccines. His website states, "Anti-vaccination philosophies are sometimes difficult to find and anti-vaccinationists are called names in an attempt to discredit their reasoning. If vaccines were safe and effective there would be no issue here. Anti-vaccination literature only wants to support the truth and honestly tell the facts as they really are. Only by becoming educated in this very important issue can one make an informed decision. Few people realize that vaccines are grown on monkey kidneys, mice brains and chicken embryos. Few people realize the dire consequences of injecting foreign animal tissues (DNA/RNA) and the auto-immune reactions they can induce. Few people realize that vaccines are immune depressing and may cause cancers, leukemias and even have been linked to AIDS."

Here are some of the beliefs commonly cited by parents who choose not to vaccinate their children:

- Unvaccinated children have a level of health that is unsurpassed by "normal" children, because they have not had their immune systems depressed or tampered with by vaccines.
- Vaccines are unsafe, or in other words harmful, because they are made up of chemicals and other elements that are poisonous to the body.
- The foreign proteins found in vaccines can trigger numerous allergic and inflammatory reactions and can produce anaphylactic shock in susceptible infants.
- The dramatic rise in childhood cancer, autism, juvenile diabetes, asthma, and neurological disorders over the past fifty years has directly coincided with the era of drugs, vaccines, and chemical poisons in our food, water, and environment.
- Most believe that the recommendation of vaccines has to do with power and profit. "The vaccine business has continued to thrive in spite of its disastrous failure, for the mere reason that it nets millions of dollars for the promoters, and this buys power with governments and propaganda control over the masses who don't know how to think for themselves," writes Eleanor McBean, Ph.D., in *The Poisoned Needle.*

Dr. William Sears (author of over thirty parenting books)

Dr. William Sears estimates that about 20 percent of his patients in his San Clemente, California, practice do not vaccinate, and another 20 percent partially vaccinate. "I don't think it is such a critical public health issue that we should force parents into it," Dr. Sears told the *New York Times.* "I don't lecture the parents or try to change their mind; if they flat out tell me they understand the risks I feel that I should be very respectful of their decision."

For It

An article in the *New York Times* says, "While nationwide over 90 percent of children old enough to receive vaccines get them, the number of exemptions worries many health officials and experts. They say that vaccines have saved countless lives, and that personal-belief exemptions are potentially dangerous and bad public policy because they are not based on sound science." Worldwide, 242,000 children a year die from measles, but it used to be near one million. The deaths have dropped because of vaccination, a 68 percent decrease from 1999 to 2006, which is attributed to the United Nations' measles initiative.

Another problem with the growing group of parents who choose not to vaccinate is that (due to their overall belief in the evils of traditional medicine) they tend to avoid doctors as much as possible. That means that an unvaccinated child may not be diagnosed with a highly contagious disease in time to prevent serious outbreaks among their peers. No vaccine is 100 percent guaranteed—nothing in current medicine is. So they choose to put children other than their own at risk.

Learn More

To learn about the diseases that we currently immunize against in the United States, and the damage they cause, as well as what might happen if we choose to ignore vaccines, visit this website: www.cdc.gov/vaccines/vac-gen/whatifstop.htm.

So what could explain the increased rates of autism in recent years? First of all, the definition of "autism" has become much broader, meaning it is applied to more children who show varying degrees of the symptoms. There is also a greater awareness among doctors. Remember when we were young, kids with obvious learning and social differences were often called retarded. Most people were unaware of autism and dyslexia, and attentional dysfunction (what we currently call ADD and ADHD) was essentially unheard of.

Remember too that although autism is rising, the rates of MMR (mumps, measles, and rubella) vaccinations are not (some suspect a connection between this vaccine and autism). And the average diagnosis of autism has been found to be the same in both children who have and children who have not received the MMR vaccine. What has been discovered is that symptoms of autism are often present before a child's first birthday and are going unnoticed. (The first dose of MMR is given at twelve months of age.)

What We Think

From Stephanie

I think that the media scared parents into thinking that vaccines could be dangerous for our children, but the most current research has since proven that vaccines are not linked to autism. Most of the websites against vaccines cite mistakes that date back to the early 1900s, and most current research has disproved many of the dangers that were once associated with vaccines. The fact is, *no* study has *ever* been able to link vaccines *to* the rise of autism. To further prove the point, since the chemicals mercury and thimerosal (those thought to have caused autism) were taken out of vaccines, the diagnosis of autism has continued to rise anyway. And the confusion and controversy that the media scare caused ended up diverting attention and resources away from efforts to determine the true causes of autism.

Please don't forget that immunizations have protected millions of children from potentially deadly diseases and saved thousands of lives! And remember too that, although they are rare, most diseases that can be prevented by vaccines still exist in the world, even in the United States. Because international travel is so common, it's hard to know who your child will come in contact with—and viruses have been known to hop halfway around the world in a matter of days.

There are a few rare situations when an existing condition can cause a problem when a vaccine is introduced. Your pediatrician is the best person to decide when a child should not receive a vaccine or if a vaccine should be delayed.

Understand that the CDC, the American Academy of Pediatrics, and other institutions have put enormous amounts of research and decision making behind the vaccines that are recommended for our children. This isn't just about drug companies making a profit. There are thousands of experts involved in the decision to recommend vaccines—and they too are parents and grandparents who are giving the same vaccines to their children and grandchildren. The vaccines that we give our children prevent horrific diseases that are deadly or can cause brain damage, permanent physical disabilities, seizures, deafness, and other awful symptoms. And many of these diseases still exist in the world today!

Think about this: If you're considering skipping immunization (because all the other kids are already vaccinated), there's a good chance that another parent is too. And every child who isn't immunized gives contagious diseases a better chance of being spread. Consider what happened in 1989 and 1991 when an epidemic of measles broke out in the United States because immunizations were skipped by a large group of preschool-age children. This choice led to a sharp jump in the number of cases of measles, resulting in deaths and permanent brain damage in the children who were not immunized. Similar outbreaks of whooping cough (pertussis) struck Japan and the United Kingdom in the 1970s right after immunization rates declined. History tells us that skipping vaccines could be deadly for your children and the children they come in contact with. And since we're all more mobile than ever, there's no way of knowing if everyone your child comes in contact with has been immunized.

Bottom line? Based on the most current research and historical evidence, I think choosing to not vaccinate your kids is too risky.

From Sara

I can't completely agree with that. Several years ago I was invited to speak to a group of nurses about postpartum depression. During the conference I heard a pediatrician give a presentation on vaccines and autism and she firmly stated she believed there was a connection. I also have a dear friend whose son has a form of autism and she says she could see the difference in his behavior after getting a round of shots. My sister, who recently had a baby boy, is spreading out his vaccinations so that he is never getting three or four shots at once, which some experts say may overload the immune system. Boys are at

Statement from the CDC on Mercury and Vaccines (Thimerosal)

Thimerosal is a mercury-containing preservative used in some vaccines and other products since the 1930s. There is no convincing scientific evidence of harm caused by the low doses of thimerosal in vaccines, except for minor reactions like redness and swelling at the injection site. However, in July 1999, the Public Health Service agencies, the American Academy of Pediatrics, and vaccine manufacturers agreed that thimerosal should be reduced or eliminated in vaccines as a precautionary measure. Since 2001, with the exception of some influenza (flu) vaccines, thimerosal is not used as a preservative in routinely recommended childhood vaccines.

much greater risk of autism, so I think I would do the same if I currently had an infant son. Even though the Centers for Disease Control says that the "weight" of the evidence shows that vaccines are not related to autism (that means that some studies did show a link), they are continuing to research this important topic. So the jury is still out in my opinion. Although I am not a proponent of not vaccinating, I would give it a hard look and consider a more spaced-out schedule for a baby under a year old.

I know from watching what my friend has gone through with her son that autism is a serious disorder that is life-changing for the entire family. I don't blame concerned parents one bit for investigating the need for vaccines fully. Traditional medicine is great, and I have my own good health to thank for it, but I always remember that it took doctors *years* (back in the nineteenth century) to realize that they needed to wash their hands between patients to prevent the spread of disease. Unfortunately, the medical community can sometimes be slow to recognize issues and change long-established practices.

Clutter-Busting Resources:

General immunization questions can be answered by the CDC Contact Center at 1-800-CDC-INFO (800-232-4636) English and Español

WEBSITES

National Vaccine Information Center
www.909shot.com or www.nvic.org
www.revolutionhealth.com/healthy-living/parenting

Dr. Joseph Mercola
www.mercola.com

BOOKS

What Your Doctor May Not Tell You About Children's Vaccinations
by Stephanie Cave

The Experts on Television and Video Games

For It

The American Academy of Pediatrics

The AAP says preschoolers can actually benefit from watching educational shows like those you'll find on Playhouse Disney and PBS. Even nature programs and music concerts can be a good thing. They remind us that educational television is never a substitute for reading and playing with Mom and Dad.

However, the AAP also warns us that most programs are not suitable for young children and even cartoons can be full of violence and dangerous suggestions. The violence in cartoons teaches children that this is an acceptable way to deal with problems, and since the characters hit each other and even blow each other up, and no one ever gets hurt, your child doesn't see any harm in hitting or violent play.

The AAP recommends that your child should watch no more than one to two hours of television per day. Parents should always monitor their child's TV watching and choose what shows to watch.

Parents should also remember that studies reveal that kids who watch TV more than twenty hours per week have a greater chance of becoming obese. Young children are like little sponges, and all those ads for sugary cereals and sweets are not going to assist you in your mission to feed them healthy foods. And, it's not a good idea to let your child get into the habit of eating while watching TV. This may lead to "unconscious" eating in some children, meaning that they will get into the habit of eating well past the point of being full.

And maybe video games aren't so evil after all. The latest information proves that the theory that video games turn our kids' brains to mush is fast becoming a myth. "A good video game is challenging, entertaining, and complicated. It usually takes fifty to sixty minutes of intense concentration to finish one. Even kids who can't sit still in school can spend hours trying to solve a video or computer game," says James Gee, an education professor at the University of Wisconsin, Madison.

Some researchers believe that the violence in video games is linked to a higher rate of violence among teens. But what those studies left out is that the majority of the teens in the study also admitted that their parents did not impose a time limit on the number of hours they were allowed to play the games, and most of their parents were unaware of the content rating (by the Entertainment Software Rating Board) of the game. Which means that they played violent games for exceptionally long periods of time.

The facts reveal that kids who play computer games usually end up knowing more about computers than their parents do. And the latest research shows that as long as they're not abused (used as babysitters), video and computer games can inspire learning and help players improve their coordination and visual skills. Researchers at the University of Rochester recently found that video games improve kids' visual skills. Kids who regularly played video games were better at seeing what was happening around them. They could keep track of more objects at a time and they were faster when picking objects out of a cluttered environment. Video games teach your kids to make decisions and think about the future. Some studies even noted improvement among brain surgeons and fighter pilots after they were asked to regularly play video games.

Against It

Many studies claim that teens who play violent video games for extended periods of time tend to be more aggressive, are more prone to confrontation with their peers and teachers, and suffer a decline in grades and school functions.

Another negative about video games is that players are actually rewarded for violence. The more zombies they kill, the higher the level and the more points they achieve. Some worry that this sends a bad message.

The American Medical Association, American Academy of Pediatrics, American Psychological Association, American Academy of Family Physicians, and American Academy of Child and Adolescent Psychiatry all caution parents about violence in the media and its negative effect on children. They warn that exposure to violent media can elevate aggressive feelings and thoughts, especially in children. These effects on aggressive behavior can be long-term.

In a testimony on media violence given to the U.S. Senate Commerce Committee, AAP president Donald Cook, M.D., FAAP, warned, "Children learn the ways of the world by observing and imitating—they cannot help but be influenced by media. Exposure to media violence, particularly violence perpetrated by dramatic heroes or, in the case of video games, the children themselves, results in an increased acceptance of violence as an appropriate means of conflict resolution. Media exaggerate the prevalence of violence in the world and offer strong motivation to protect oneself by carrying a weapon and being more aggressive. Perhaps the most insidious and potent effect of media violence is that it desensitizes viewers to 'real life' violence and to the harm caused its victims."

What We Think

From Stephanie

I think that as long as they don't abuse the privilege, TV and video games aren't such a bad thing. It's the age-old rule . . . too much of a good thing could end up being a bad thing. I also encourage you to be aware of the content rating scales offered by the ESRB

(Entertainment Software Rating Board) to make sure that the games are appropriate for your child's age and/or developmental level and contain as little violence as possible.

Sara and I will both testify to the fact that neither of us would have been able to take a shower the entire first year of our daughters' lives if it wasn't for the brilliant videos that Julie Aigner-Clark filmed in her basement and nurtured into the Baby Einstein empire. And I have to admit that I am totally amazed at what my six-year-old son has mastered in the video game arena. The reasoning skills and memory that it takes to play some of his favorite games are baffling to me. And the other advantage is the bonding that's taken place between father and son. Since my husband is also a devout video gamer (to my utter disgust), I have to admit I've gotten a kick out of listening to their discussions. It's like they're speaking in their own language, and they spend time talking and comparing notes about characters and scenarios that I've never heard of. It's like they were abducted by aliens and then brought back to earth with all these experiences they shared that I'm not privy to. But it's very cute.

I think that as long as you set boundaries and time limits and interact with your child while they are enjoying this type of entertainment, that it's a good thing. The bottom line is, if your kids aren't fluent in computer and video games, it will be a detriment to them both socially and professionally.

From Sara

Well, I don't know if I'd go that far. Yes, it's true that kids need computer skills these days, but they can just as easily get those playing educational games on the computer. My children have both loved Webkinz, which are stuffed animals that come with a code so that kids can play in a virtual world online. Each Webkinz comes with its own room, and kids can play games and do jobs to earn Kinz Cash to buy food and items for their pet. Many of the games are educational and kids are encouraged to feed their pets healthy food and give them plenty of exercise.

We recently purchased a Nintendo Wii for our son for his birthday and I've been very happy with it. We only have sports games, so there is no violence to worry about, and everyone in our family can play—and we all enjoy it! I can't say I have had that experience with other games, however.

It's amazing to me what can pass for acceptable and get an "E for Everyone" rating. I once purchased a Spider-Man video game (one of those that comes with a joystick and plugs straight into the television) and I was appalled at the amount of violence in the game. There were hostages and masked men holding what looked like machine guns. And it was rated "E for Everyone"! Are you kidding me? And I am still amazed that any parent would let their child play a video game with the title *Grand Theft Auto.* I may be a fuddy-duddy, but I can't believe they even let that go to market.

Video games have their place, but I think riding a bike, climbing a tree, reading a book, or playing a board game should be first picks for entertainment.

You Are the Expert

We could go on and on with charts and graphs showing you the similarities and differences in opinions and methods of caring for your children. But as you can see from just these examples, the experts are all over the board. That's why the best thing you can do for yourself and your baby is to become as educated as you possibly can (from the best sources available) and then choose the things that work best and feel best for you personally.

Most of us moms want and need reassurance that we are doing things "right." That's probably why so many of these "expert" books are best sellers. When we adopt a method that has been endorsed by a famous pediatrician or baby guru, we feel justified in our methods and maybe a little off the hook if it doesn't work out so well.

Our advice to you is to pay attention to your child and trust your instincts. Your baby will teach you more about what she needs than any book can. And you know your family better than any expert who's never set foot in your house. Do your research, but be sure to consider the source. Is what you are reading fact or opinion? Can it be backed up with research? Does the "expert" have an agenda that conflicts with your beliefs? The American Academy of Pediatrics is a good benchmark to measure all others against. But just because experts don't agree with the AAP doesn't mean they are wrong. They may just not have the research to back up their opinion or they may be ahead of their time. Ultimately, you are the one who decides if the information is valid for your family.

It doesn't matter if other parents don't agree with you. If you feel you are doing the best for your baby, then you are. And how baby eats and sleeps is just the beginning. Parents will have differing opinions about all kinds of things as their children get older. Remember, what works for you may not work for the family next door. So give your fellow parents a little respect—even if they choose to do something differently than you do.

Clutter-Busting Resources

www.sciencenewsforkids.org

www.aap.org/advocacy

52

Mommy Myths

"If you go outside without a hat on, you'll catch a cold."

"If you sit too close to the television, you'll ruin your eyes!"

"Eating carrots improves your eyesight."

"Don't swallow that gum or it'll stay in your stomach for six years!"

"If you cross your eyes, they'll stay that way."

You've heard them all, right? If your own mother wasn't yelling these parenting slurs at you, you probably overheard these ridiculous old wives' tales aimed at another poor soul. If any of these sound familiar, I promise that you will get immense pleasure in reading this chapter. We are going to let you in on how many of these familiar parenting directives are actually real and how many are completely and totally insane. We included this chapter for two reasons: so that you can take a few minutes to laugh at your own parents (Lord knows they've been criticizing us since we first landed in the delivery room), and to prevent you from filling your own kids' heads with this ignorant crap. So read on—you'll be amazed.

"If you go outside with wet hair, you'll catch a cold."

This is false. Cold weather, wet hair, and chills don't cause colds. Viruses do. People catch colds more often in the winter because viruses are spread more easily indoors, because there is more contact with dry air and people who are sick. When people spend more time indoors, they get sick more often (even in the middle of summer). And even though we know this as a true, scientific fact, I still hear mothers arguing about this one. My dear mother-in-law is absolutely convinced that being cold gives you a cold—and, like 90 percent of mothers from her generation, you cannot change her mind. So we've arrived at a truce, which has something to do with the fact that if your body is fighting to stay warm, it can lower your immune system.

"Feed a cold, starve a fever."

False. Both high fevers and colds can cause you to lose precious fluid. Drinking plenty of liquids such as water, fruit juice, and vegetable juice can help prevent dehydration. And missing meals means missing nutrients. Your body needs nutrients to help you fight off the sickness, so missing a meal can actually make you sicker.

"Wait an hour after eating before swimming."

False. According to the American Red Cross, it's usually not necessary for you or your child to wait an hour before swimming after a meal. However, if you've had a big, fatty meal and you plan to swim strenuously, you should wait until digestion has begun. The Red Cross also advises that you never chew gum or eat while you're in the water due to the risk of choking.

"Coffee stunts your growth."

False. Coffee won't affect a child's growth, but too much caffeine shouldn't be in any child's diet. Excess caffeine can prevent the absorption of calcium and other nutrients. There have also been studies that caffeine interferes with normal brain development. Bottom line: it's just not necessary, so try to avoid it.

"Fish is brain food."

True. If you can actually get your kids to eat fish, it is a great source of omega-3 fatty acids, which have been found to be very important for brain function. Certain fish including swordfish, shark, and tuna have significant levels of mercury, and the Food and Drug Administration (FDA) suggests that pregnant women and women of childbearing age decrease their exposure to these fish.

"If you cross your eyes, they'll stay that way."

False. Only about 4 percent of the children in the United States have a disorder called strabismus. It means the eyes are not aligned correctly and gives the appearance that they're looking in different directions. Making faces and crossing your eyes cannot cause strabismus.

"Eating carrots will improve your eyesight."

False. Experts think this tale may have started during World War II, when British intelligence spread a rumor that their pilots had remarkable night vision because they ate lots of carrots. They started this propaganda because they didn't want the Germans to know they were using newly invented radar. Carrots do help maintain healthy eyesight, but so do many other vegetables high in vitamin A. Eating a truckload of carrots a month will not improve your vision.

"Chocolate causes acne."

True and false. Studies show that no specific food has been proven to cause acne. However, some people may notice their breakouts are worse after eating certain foods, and these foods are different depending on the person. For example, some people may notice breakouts after eating chocolate, while others are fine with chocolate but notice they get breakouts after eating too many fried foods. If you've noticed such a reaction, then try to avoid the foods that cause it.

"Spicy foods can cause ulcers."

False. Spicy foods may aggravate ulcer symptoms in some people, but they don't cause ulcers to form. A bacterial infection or overuse of pain medications such as aspirin or anti-inflammatory drugs are the most common causes.

"Reading in dim light will damage your eyes."

False. Reading without proper lighting can make your eyes feel more fatigued, but it will not harm your eyes.

"Too much TV is bad for your eyes."

False. Watching television won't hurt your eyes, no matter how close to the TV you sit. But watching too much TV can be bad for kids. Research shows that children who consistently spend more than ten hours a week watching TV are more likely to be overweight, aggressive, and slower to learn in school.

"Thumb sucking causes buck teeth."

True . . . and false. Thumb sucking often begins in the womb before birth and usually continues until around age five. You should stop your child from sucking his thumb before age four because this is when the gums, jaw, and permanent teeth make their most significant growth. Sucking a thumb, pacifier, finger, etc. may contribute to deformed teeth if it continues past age four or five.

"Too much loud noise can cause hearing loss."

True. Just fifteen minutes of listening to loud music, machinery, or other noises can cause temporary hearing loss and ringing in the ears. Although temporary hearing loss usually disappears within a day or two, continuous exposure to loud noise can result in permanent hearing loss. So if your child is wearing headphones and you can hear the music, the volume is too high.

"Cats can steal the air from a baby's mouth."

Not only is this false, it's also completely insane. This tale goes back hundreds of years to a time when cats were associated with witchcraft and evil spirits. It is impossible for a cat or any other animal to suffocate a baby by sealing the baby's mouth with its own. However, cats and other pets can suffocate a very young baby if they lie on the baby's face, so take measures to keep cats out of baby's crib. All pets should be supervised around small children and introduced to a baby gradually.

"If you swallow your gum, it takes six months to digest."

From Stephanie

This is false, and I'm embarrassed to admit that it was one I believed until I was well into my thirties (thanks a lot, Mom). Gum is definitely hard to digest, but it does not stay in your stomach. Gum comes out when your child poops and is passed at the same rate as other food. It does, however, come out relatively unchanged—sort of like corn!

"Cutting or shaving your child's hair makes it grow back thicker."

This is totally false. My daughter didn't get much hair until she was almost three and a half years old. I had all sorts of people trying to convince me to shave her head because it would cause the hair to grow back more quickly. Thank God I didn't listen. Cutting does not stimulate new growth. This belief probably comes from the perception that short hair seems to be tougher than longer hair. The part of the hair that we style is already dead—the living portion of your hair lies beneath the surface of your scalp. Cutting dead hair is not going to affect growth.

"Eat the crust of the bread if you want curly hair."

Both false and insane. When I was a kid, people told me this all the time. Parents came up with this one to get their kids to eat their bread crusts during a time when every little girl wanted hair like Shirley Temple's. According to today's fashions, there is absolutely no desire to have curly hair (if there was, I wouldn't have spent $100 on a straightening iron). My question is, what was the big deal about eating bread crusts? A child's stomach is too small to eat an entire sandwich anyway, so why were they so obsessed about us eating the crust in the first place? This has to be one of those weird practices left over from the Great Depression. It's the same reason our grandparents reuse aluminum foil and zip-top bags (they weren't doing it to save the planet).

Now that you know the real facts, you can spend your time yelling the other valuable things we've learned from our parents, like "Stop crying before I give you something to cry about!"—all those things you vowed you'd never scream at your kids that actually feel really good coming out of your mouth now that you're a parent. Now you understand why it's so annoying to have your car seat kicked from behind, or why the question "Are we almost there?" can cause your jaws to lock and bring a grown man to tears. My point is, we probably all need to give our parents a break. They were doing the best they could with the information they had at the time. And since you now know the facts, you can actually yell at your children a little less. So go ahead, little Johnny, sit with your nose touching the television screen—it's not a problem.

In Closing

From Sara

If you're reading this now, you already know how much fuller and richer your life is and will be with children. Yet at the same time, it's also frustrating and aggravating and perpetually messy. I recently went through a serious health crisis that gave me a lot of perspective on what being a mom means to me. In that instant when the doctor told me I had cancer, everything superfluous in my life fell away, exposing the very raw core of my heart. And that core is my family. In a flash I felt the real, true, immeasurable meaning of a mother's love and how nothing can take the place of it.

Watching my daughter start kindergarten last year, I mourned her growing up. Now I realize that being able to watch one's children become adults is the greatest gift a parent gets. I won't ever begrudge them growing up again, although I do wish I could slow down the passing of time a bit.

Since that moment on the phone with the doctor, my health has been restored and it looks as if it's going to stay that way. After six long months of treatment, life has again taken on the tempo it had before I got sick. And you know what? I find myself still getting exasperated with the kids arguing over who's singing too loudly or who's getting the favorite spot on the couch. I still try to get too much done in a day and still have to tell myself to drop the impossible motherhood standards.

The point is, I will always need reminding of what's important, even after a serious illness that put it so clearly in perspective by threatening to take it away. It's impossible not to get caught up in the busyness of life as a mom. That's why Stephanie and I wanted to write this book. Not to tell you how to be a mom, but, we hope, to make the job a little easier and give you more time to kiss their chubby cheeks and hold them tight while they are still small enough for you to hold.

From Stephanie

I love being a mom. I had no idea that it would be so intensely and deeply fulfilling. My sister got pregnant a couple of years before I did. Before I had children, I remember her telling me how being a mother was the most important and wonderful thing she had ever done. I remember thinking, *But I've done some pretty exciting things with my life. I think it's going to take more than a smelly little baby to top what I've accomplished.* I couldn't have been a bigger fool. Likewise, it's hard for me to explain to my friends who aren't mothers exactly what it is that's so fulfilling. It's a privilege to be a mother—to be responsible for molding and shaping a new person. It's challenging to try to look at your own life—your triumphs, your mistakes, the wisdom you've gained—and pass all that on to your children to try to elevate their life a step or two above your own. It's so much fun to recall your favorite childhood memories and re-create them for your own children. To live it again, but through their eyes and from your new perspective.

I love holidays and birthdays and any kind of celebration. Children get so excited over such simple things that it becomes very easy to make an ordinary afternoon something memorable and exciting. Often when I'm complaining to people, usually my mother-in-law, they remind me that these are very special times in my life. And you know, I honestly don't need reminding. I have been given two special gifts in life. One is that I have an uncanny ability to fit that last dish into the dishwasher, no matter how full it seems to the mere mortal. And second, I know. I know that while my children are young, these are the sweetest years of my life. I know that they are perfect. I know that I think every day about how wonderful life is when they're here with me, running around, making messes, crying about skinned knees, and complaining about taking their medicine. I know that my life would have been meaningless without them. I know that these two little people have erased all my past mistakes; nothing matters except the beauty and joy and laughter that they've brought with them. I know that they will grow up to be great people. I know they will have lots of friends and will find work that they love. I know they will make good choices in the people they take as spouses. And I know that my heart will be broken when it comes time for them to leave my home and start their own. I know that time will come much too soon. I know that I must cherish this time and make the most of every birthday, every autumn afternoon, every puzzle, every bike ride, every recital, every game, every holiday, every summer, every hug, every chance to soothe a boo-boo or help solve a homework equation. I know that my life is their life. And that their lives are the sweetest part of mine. I just know.

Sara and I are so excited to give you this book. Through our friendship and our differences, as well as our experiences as moms and authors and radio show hosts, we have learned so much about moms and their mothering. There are so many different kinds of mothers, and we're all trying so hard. This is all information that we needed and wanted to know—and it was hard to find. You'd see it on a magazine cover from time to time, or hear it on the radio, or spend hours searching for it on the Internet. We hope that by gathering this information all in one book, we have given you a one-stop reference tool that will help you in your search to find the information you need in your efforts to learn to be a good mom. And if it helps, please know that we think you're doing a great job, and we're rooting for you. Enjoy every moment and know that you have the most influential job in the world.

Please visit our website to keep in touch:
www.saraandstephanie.com
or
www.themusthavemommanual.com

Acknowledgments

From Sara and Stephanie

Special thanks to our wonderful agent, Marly Rusoff, and her team. Stephanie calls you our Fairy Godmother (except we all know you're much too young for that). We are so glad you joined our journey.

A big thank you to Susanna Porter at Ballantine for your careful and thoughtful editing of this book. Every time we read one of your comments we were grateful to have your skillful eyes looking at this manuscript. We both would like to thank all of the staff at Ballantine for your many hours of hard work in helping to bring this book to life.

We are especially grateful to David Huff of Back 40 Films for the opportunity to take our story to the big screen—and for believing motherhood is the most important job on earth. We're sure you've learned way more about having babies than you ever wanted to!

Huge thanks to our dynamic producer and fellow mom, Tiffany Hanssen. You make us sound like we really know what we're doing and we're so grateful for all the time and effort you've invested in us.

From Sara

I would like to thank my dear friends Veronica, Julie, Susan, Kristina, Betsy, Jan, Christi, Angie, Allison, and Jennifer for your support, help, and friendship through this long and enormous project. I am fortunate to call a long list of incredible women my girlfriends—they make the good times even better and they sustain me through the bad. Thank you all.

I am especially grateful to my sisters, Laura and Jennifer (whom I also consider my girlfriends), for always being there to listen, laugh, and understand. As a new mom, Jen's reviews and comments on this manuscript were particularly helpful.

Many thanks to my mother-in-law, Sharyn, who so gladly helped take care of her grandchildren whenever I needed her and never let me think for a minute that everything wasn't going to be just fine.

Through every high and low, my parents' unwavering support has been my rock. They have been my soft place to fall and they have told me when it was time to get up and keep going. Now more than ever, I realize how blessed I am to have them.

Most of all I am thankful for my husband, David, who is here with me through it all, good, bad, ugly, and sometimes hilarious. Without his support, this book would not have been possible. He has been a great father and husband, taking over the daily duties and giving me the space (and quiet!) I needed to write and edit. And although I'm sure he'll be surprised to read this, I am grateful for all the times he convinced me to stop working and go outside and enjoy the sunshine.

For my amazing daughter, Anna, I hope that I am somehow setting an example for you that it is okay to pursue your own dreams and be a mother. And I hope you someday know how grateful I am to have you as my child and that from the day you were born you have inspired me to be a better person.

And for my sweet and wonderful son, Cade, even though I will surely never be able to answer your many questions to your satisfaction, I hope that every day you feel the unconditional love I have for you. You bring light and laughter to our family life every day.

I am thankful to my children for being my best spiritual teachers. Because of you, my favorite pens only ever last a day on my desk, my stapler is always missing, my computer keys are coated with Capri Sun juice . . . the lessons in patience just keep coming.

Last but certainly not least, I am thankful to Stephanie Triplett for her unfailing laughter and friendship. There's absolutely no one else with whom I'd want to share this ride.

From Stephanie

To my network of amazing moms: my tennis team, neighbors, and friends. You are a powerful force and a tremendous blessing. Whatever the need, you're always there. Babysitting, a meal, a trip to the grocery store, a pat on the back, a hug for encouragement, a hug in celebration, a recipe, a laugh, a diagnosis, a counselor, a shoulder or an ear . . . you deliver consistently: Chrise, Kathryn, Erica, Maureen, Karen, Nancy, Kelly, Anne, Barb, Cindy I., Cindy S., Kim, Teresa, Tanya, Cynthia, Michelle, Stacia, Sheri, Robyn, Sandy, Michele, Melanie, Laura, Angie, and all of you who stand behind me. Please know that I feel you there and I am immensely thankful for you.

Thank you to my husband, Tim. Despite the annoying fact that you lose your keys at least twice a week, and you're never entirely sure where your shoes are, I'm still in love with you. Let's keep laughing.

To my daughter, Sara, and my son, Timmy, you are splendid. Everything found in this book you have either taught me, or inspired me to learn so I could be a better mother. I am not always perfect for you, but you are absolutely perfect to me. I adore you.

Thank you, Mom, Dad, Julie, and Grammy. Your generous love and support makes everything better. I could never say thank you enough.

Sara Ellington: I love you dearly, even when you're talking politics. (That's true love.) Where would I be today without you yelling at me about where the punctuation goes and boring me with the minute details of your dog's spleen? (I loved that dog too.) Thanks for putting up with my bad jokes, bad grammar, and bad attitude. Wanna go out to eat?

Index

About the Authors

Stephanie Triplett is co-author of *The Mommy Chronicles: Conversations Sharing the Comedy and Drama of Pregnancy and New Motherhood* with Sara Ellington. She worked with the Disney/ABC Family cable television network in Atlanta, leaving to take care of her children full-time. She has managed the marketing and promotion of everything from television shows and fitness professionals to gas pumps and dog vaccines. She also worked with Sara Ellington to develop *The Mommy Chronicles,* an hour-long weekly talk radio show for moms, which aired from 2005 through 2006 on Sirius Satellite Radio. Stephanie Triplett lives in Atlanta with her husband, Tim, and their two children.

Sara Ellington is co-author of *The Mommy Chronicles: Conversations Sharing the Comedy and Drama of Pregnancy and New Motherhood* with Stephanie Triplett. Before becoming a mother, she worked as a copywriter for advertising agencies in Virginia and North Carolina. Her award-winning advertising work has appeared in *The Wall Street Journal, Southern Living,* and *The Charlotte Observer.* As a freelance author, she has written articles for *Charlotte Ventures* magazine, Mothers & More's national newsletter, *Forum,* and a NASCAR television pilot. Along with co-hosting *The Mommy Chronicles,* a radio show, she and Stephanie Triplett were selected as "spokesmoms" by Johnson & Johnson for a national satellite media tour announcing the birth of the three hundred millionth American. Sara lives in Charlotte, North Carolina, with her husband, David Behnke, and their two children.